ESSAYS ON THE GREAT DEPRESSION

ESSAYS ON THE GREAT DEPRESSION

Ben S. Bernanke

PRINCETON UNIVERSITY PRESS   PRINCETON, NEW JERSEY

Second printing, and first paperback printing, 2004
Paperback ISBN-13: 978-0-691-11820-8
Paperback ISBN-10: 0-691-11820-5

The Library of Congress has cataloged the cloth edition of this book as follows

Bernanke, Ben.
Essays on the great depression / Ben S. Bernanke.
p.   cm.
Includes bibliographical references and index.
ISBN 0-691-01698-4 (cloth : alk. paper)
1. Depressions—1929—United States.   2. Depressions—1929.
I. Title.
HB3717   1929.B365
338.5'42—dc21   99-41738

British Library Cataloging-in-Publication Data is available

This book has been composed in Goudy

Printed on acid-free paper. ∞

pup.princeton.edu

Printed in the United States of America

10   9   8

Contents

Preface

MY PARTICULAR RESEARCH SPECIALTY is macroeconomics, not economic history. Nevertheless, throughout my academic career, I have returned many times to the study of the vertiginous economic decline of the 1930s, now known as the Great Depression. I guess I am a Great Depression buff, the way some people are Civil War buffs. I don't know why there aren't more Depression buffs. The Depression was an incredibly dramatic episode—an era of stock market crashes, bread lines, bank runs, and wild currency speculation, with the storm clouds of war gathering ominously in the background all the while. Fascinating, and often tragic, characters abound during this period, from hapless policymakers trying to make sense of events for which their experience had not prepared them to ordinary people coping heroically with the effects of the economic catastrophe. For my money, few periods are so replete with human interest.

I have enjoyed studying the Great Depression because it is a fascinating event at a pivotal time in modern history. How convenient for me, then, professionally speaking, that there is also so much to learn from the Depression about the workings of the economy. (Those who doubt that there is much connection between the economy of the 1930s and the supercharged, information-age economy of the twenty-first century are invited to look at the current economic headlines—about high unemployment, failing banks, volatile financial markets, currency crises, and even deflation. The issues raised by the Depression, and its lessons, are still relevant today.)

Fundamentally, the Depression is informative about the economy for two main reasons: it was a (very) big event, and it affected most of the world's countries. Because the Depression was so big and so deep, the basic facts to be explained stand out in sharp relief. Indeed, the sheer magnitude of interwar economic fluctuations is sufficient to render implausible (for the Depression, at least) some popular explanations of the business cycle, such as the hypothesis that recessions are the result of temporary slowdowns in the march of technological progress. And because the Depression's impact was felt by nearly all the countries of the world, but not to an equal degree, the period also provides a marvelous laboratory for studying the link between economic policies and institutions on the one hand and economic performance on the other. A striking example of what can be learned by international comparisons is the fact, emphasized by Barry Eichengreen and Jeffrey Sachs among others, that countries that abandoned the gold standard at an early stage recovered more quickly from the Depression. This robust empirical finding has proven to be the key to a greatly improved understanding of both the Depression itself and the effects of monetary policies and exchange rate systems in general, as I discuss extensively in this book.

This volume comprises nine essays I have written (with various coauthors) on the macroeconomics of the Great Depression. Although these articles were composed over a span of nearly two decades, I am pleased to find in rereading that they present a largely coherent view of the causes and propagation of the Depression.

Chapter 1 provides an effective introduction and overview. Because the Depression was characterized by sharp declines in both output and prices, the premise of this essay is that declines in aggregate demand were the dominant factor in the onset of the Depression. This starting point leads naturally to two questions: First, what caused the worldwide collapse in aggregate demand in the late 1920s and early 1930s (the "aggregate demand puzzle")? Second, why did the Depression last so long? In particular, why didn't the "normal" stabilizing mechanisms of the economy, such as the adjustment of wages and prices to changes in demand, limit the real economic impact of the fall in aggregate demand (the "aggregate supply puzzle")?

The two main sections of the book provide my answers to these questions. As elaborated in Chapter 2 through 4, I believe that there is now overwhelming evidence that the main factor depressing aggregate demand was a worldwide contraction in world money supplies. This monetary collapse was itself the result of a poorly managed and technically flawed international monetary system (the gold standard, as reconstituted after World War I). In this conclusion I agree very substantially with the thesis advanced most forcibly by Barry Eichengreen; the main contribution of my research on this point has been the provision of quantitative detail that helps to substantiate and flesh out the story.

However, I also have ascribed an important role to nonmonetary financial factors, such as banking panics and business failures, in choking off normal flows of credit and hence exacerbating the world economic collapse. My 1983 paper (Chapter 2) was among the first to explore the possible macroeconomic implications of financial crises, a connection that has now received considerable attention not only for the case of the Depression but in the context of recent events in East Asia and elsewhere. The three papers in Section Two provide empirical detail on both the monetary and financial determinants of the collapse of aggregate demand in the early stages of the Depression.

Section Three (Chapters 5–9), addresses issues of aggregate supply in the Depression, with particular emphasis on the functioning of labor markets. A central theme here is that the adjustment of nominal wages in response to declines in aggregate demand during the 1930s was surprisingly slow and incomplete. Instead of cutting wages, employers adjusted on other margins, including the length of the workweek and the intensity of labor utilization. Legislatures also resisted wage (and price) cuts, for example, by measures designed to limit competition. On the other hand, as discussed in Chapter 7, one need not hypothesize glacially slow wage adjustment to account for the persistence of unemployment in the Depression. Economies during this period received not one but a series of major negative shocks to aggregate demand, which drove them far away from full employment. The size and persistence of these shocks was sufficient to overwhelm the stabilizing properties of wage and price adjustments in many countries. When intense downward pressures on aggregate demand were removed (for example, through devaluation of the exchange rate or the abandonment of the gold standard), many countries experienced fairly rapid recoveries in output and employment.

I owe a particular debt of thanks to the coauthors of these essays, including my students Kevin Carey, Ilian Mihov, and Martin Parkinson, and my colleagues Harold James and James Powell. Special thanks are due to my editor at Princeton University Press, Peter Dougherty, for his help, and to the journals in which these essays first appeared for permitting them to be reprinted here. I dedicate this book to my wife Anna, in gratitude for her unwavering support.

ESSAYS ON THE GREAT DEPRESSION

Part One

OVERVIEW

One

The Macroeconomics of the Great Depression: A Comparative Approach

TO UNDERSTAND THE GREAT DEPRESSION is the Holy Grail of macroeconomics. Not only did the Depression give birth to macroeconomics as a distinct field of study, but also—to an extent that is not always fully appreciated—the experience of the 1930s continues to influence macroeconomists' beliefs, policy recommendations, and research agendas. And, practicalities aside, finding an explanation for the worldwide economic collapse of the 1930s remains a fascinating intellectual challenge.

We do not yet have our hands on the Grail by any means, but during the past fifteen years or so substantial progress toward the goal of understanding the Depression has been made. This progress has a number of sources, including improvements in our theoretical framework and painstaking historical analysis. To my mind, however, the most significant recent development has been a change in the focus of Depression research, from a traditional emphasis on events in the United States to a more comparative approach that examines the experiences of many countries simultaneously. This broadening of focus is important for two reasons: First, though in the end we may agree with Romer (1993) that shocks to the domestic U.S. economy were a primary cause of both the American and world depressions, no account of the Great Depression would be complete without an explanation of the worldwide nature of the event, and of the channels through which deflationary forces spread among countries. Second, by effectively expanding the data set from one observation to twenty, thirty, or more, the shift to a comparative perspective substantially improves out ability to identify—in the strict econometric sense—the forces responsible for the world depression. Because of its potential to bring the profession toward agreement on the causes of the Depression—and perhaps, in consequence, to greater consensus on the central issues of contemporary macroeconomics—I consider the improved identification provided by comparative analysis to be a particularly important benefit of that approach.

In this lecture I provide a selective survey of our current understanding of

Reprinted with permission from *Journal of Money, Credit, and Banking*, vol. 27, no. 1 (February 1995) Copyright 1995 by The Ohio State University Press.

The author thanks Barry Eichengreen for his comments and Ilian Mihov for excellent research assistance.

the Great Depression, with emphasis on insights drawn from comparative research (by both myself and others). For reasons of space, and because I am a macroeconomist rather than a historian, my focus will be on broad economic issues rather than historical details. For readers wishing to delve into those details, Eichengreen (1992) provides a recent, authoritative treatment of the monetary and economic history of the interwar period. I have drawn heavily on Eichengreen's book (and his earlier work) in preparing this lecture, particularly in section 1 below.

To review the state of knowledge about the Depression, it is convenient to make the textbook distinction between factors affecting aggregate demand and those affecting aggregate supply. I argue in section 1 that the factors that depressed aggregate demand around the world in the 1930s are now well understood, at least in broad terms. In particular, the evidence that monetary shocks played a major role in the Great Contraction, and that these shocks were transmitted around the world primarily through the working of the gold standard, is quite compelling.

Of course, the conclusion that monetary shocks were an important source of the Depression raises a central question in macroeconomics, which is why nominal shocks should have real effects. Section 2 of this lecture discusses what we know about the impacts of falling money supplies and price levels on interwar economies. I consider two principal channels of effect: (1) deflation-induced financial crisis and (2) increases in real wages above market-clearing levels, brought about by the incomplete adjustment of nominal wages to price changes. Empirical evidence drawn from a range of countries seems to provide support for both of these mechanisms. However, it seems that, of the two channels, slow nominal-wage adjustment (in the face of massive unemployment) is especially difficult to reconcile with the postulate of economic rationality. We cannot claim to understand the Depression until we can provide a rationale for this paradoxical behavior of wages. I conclude the paper with some thoughts on how the comparative approach may help us make progress on this important remaining issue.

1. Aggregate Demand: The Gold Standard and World Money Supplies

During the Depression years, changes in output and in the price level exhibited a strong positive correlation in almost every country, suggesting an important role for aggregate demand shocks. Although there is no doubt that many factors affected aggregate demand in various countries at various times, my focus here will be on the crucial role played by monetary shocks.

For many years, the principal debate about the causes of the Great Depression in the United States was over the importance to be ascribed to monetary factors. It was easily observed that the money supply, output, and prices all fell precipitously in the contraction and rose rapidly in the recovery; the difficulty lay in establishing the causal links among these variables. In their classic study of U.S. monetary history, Friedman and Schwartz (1963) presented a monetarist interpretation of these observations, arguing that the main lines of causation ran from monetary contraction—the result of poor policy-making and continuing crisis in the banking system—to declining prices and output. Opposing Friedman and Schwartz, Temin (1976) contended that much of the monetary contraction in fact reflected a passive response of money to output; and that the main sources of the Depression lay on the real side of the economy (for example, the famous autonomous drop in consumption in 1930).

To some extent the proponents of these two views argued past each other, with monetarists stressing the monetary sources of the latter stages of the Great Contraction (from late 1930 or early 1931 until 1933), and antimonetarists emphasizing the likely importance of nonmonetary factors in the initial downturn. A reasonable compromise position, adopted by many economists, was that both monetary and nonmonetary forces were operative at various stages (Gordon and Wilcox 1981). Nevertheless, conclusive resolution of the importance of money in the Depression was hampered by the heavy concentration of the disputants on the U.S. case—on one data point, as it were.[1]

Since the early 1980s, however, a new body of research on the Depression has emerged which focuses on the operation of the international gold standard during the interwar period (Choudhri and Kochin 1980; Eichengreen 1984; Eichengreen and Sachs 1985; Hamilton 1988; Temin 1989; Bernanke and James 1991; Eichengreen 1992). Methodologically, as a natural consequence of their concern with international factors, authors working in this area brought a strong comparative perspective into research on the Depression; as I suggested in the introduction, I consider this development to be a major contribution, with implications that extend beyond the question of the role of the gold standard. Substantively—in marked contrast to the inconclusive state of affairs that prevailed in the late 1970s—the new gold-standard research allows us to assert with considerable confidence that *monetary factors played an important causal role*, both in the worldwide decline in prices and output and in their eventual recovery. Two well-documented observations support this conclusion.[2]

---

[1] That both sides considered only the U.S. case is not strictly true; both Friedman and Schwartz (1963) and Temin (1976) made useful comparisons to Canada, for example. Nevertheless, the Depression experiences of countries other than the United States were not systematically considered.

[2] More detailed discussions of these points may be found in Eichengreen and Sachs (1985), Temin (1989), Bernanke and James (1991), and Eichengreen (1992). An important early precursor is Nurkse (1944).

First, exhaustive analysis of the operation of the interwar gold standard has shown that much of the worldwide monetary contraction of the early 1930s was not a passive response to declining output, but instead the largely unintended result of an interaction of poorly designed institutions, short-sighted policy-making, and unfavorable political and economic preconditions. Hence the correlation of money and price declines with output declines that was observed in almost every country is most reasonably interpreted as reflecting primarily the influence of money on the real economy, rather than vice versa.

Second, for reasons that were largely historical, political, and philosophical rather than purely economic, some governments responded to the crises of the early 1930s by quickly abandoning the gold standard, while others chose to remain on gold despite adverse conditions. Countries that left gold were able to reflate their money supplies and price levels, and did so after some delay; countries remaining on gold were forced into further deflation. To an overwhelming degree, the evidence shows that countries that left the gold standard recovered from the Depression more quickly than countries that remained on gold. Indeed, no country exhibited significant economic recovery while remaining on the gold standard. The strong dependence of the rate of recovery on the choice of exchange-rate regime is further, powerful evidence for the importance of monetary factors.

Section 1.1 briefly discusses the first of these two observations, and section 1.2 considers the second.

1.1. The Sources of Monetary Contraction: Multiple Monetary Equilibria?

Despite the focus of the earlier monetarist debate on the U.S. monetary contraction of the early 1930s, this country was hardly unique in that respect: The same phenomenon occurred in most market-oriented industrialized countries, and in many developing nations as well. As the recent research has emphasized, what most countries experiencing monetary contraction had in common was adherence to the international gold standard.

Suspended at the beginning of World War I, the gold standard had been laboriously reconstructed after the war: The United Kingdom returned to gold at the prewar parity in 1925, France completed its return by 1928, and by 1929 the gold standard was virtually universal among market economies. (The short list of exceptions included Spain, whose internal political turmoil prevented a return to gold, and some Latin American and Asian countries on the silver standard.) The reconstruction of the gold standard was hailed as a major diplomatic achievement, an essential step toward restoring monetary and financial conditions—which were turbulent during the 1920s—to the relative tranquility that characterized the classical (1870–

1913) gold-standard period. Unfortunately, the hoped-for benefits of gold did not materialize: Instead of a new era of stability, by 1931 financial panics and exchange-rate crises were rampant, and a majority of countries left gold in that year. A complete collapse of the system occurred in 1936, when France and the other remaining "Gold Bloc" countries devalued or otherwise abandoned the strict gold standard.

As noted, a striking aspect of the short-lived interwar gold standard was the tendency of the nations that adhered to it to suffer sharp declines in inside money stocks. To understand in general terms why these declines happened, it is useful to consider a simple identity that relates the inside money stock (say, M1) of a country on the gold standard to its reserves of monetary gold:

$$M1 = (M1/BASE) \times (BASE/RES) \times (RES/GOLD)$$
$$\times PGOLD \times QGOLD \tag{1}$$

where

M1 = M1 money supply (money and notes in circulation plus commercial bank deposits),

BASE = monetary base (money and notes in circulation plus reserves of commercial banks),

RES = international reserves of the central bank (foreign assets plus gold reserves), valued in domestic currency,

GOLD = gold reserves of the central bank, valued in domestic currency
     = PGOLD × QGOLD,

PGOLD = the official domestic-currency price of gold, and

QGOLD = the physical quantity (for example, in metric tons) of gold reserves.

Equation (1) makes the familiar points that, under the gold standard, a country's money supply is affected both by its physical quantity of gold reserves (QGOLD) and the price at which its central bank stands ready to buy and sell gold (PGOLD). In particular, ceteris paribus, an inflow of gold (an increase in QGOLD) or a devaluation (a rise in PGOLD) raises the money supply. However, equation (1) also indicates three additional determinants of the inside money supply under the gold standard:

(1) The "money multiplier," M1/BASE. In fractional-reserve banking systems, the total money supply (including bank deposits) is larger than the monetary base. As is familiar from textbook treatments, the so-called money multiplier, M1/BASE, is a decreasing function of the currency-deposit ratio chosen by the public and the reserve-deposit ratio chosen by commercial banks. At the beginning of the 1930s, M1/BASE was relatively low (not much above one) in countries in which banking was less developed, or in which people retained a preference for currency in transactions. In contrast,

in the financially well-developed United States this ratio was close to four in 1929.

(2) *The inverse of the gold backing ratio, BASE/RES.* Because central banks were typically allowed to hold domestic assets as well as international reserves, the ratio *BASE/RES*—the inverse of the gold backing ratio (also called the coverage ratio)—exceeded one. Statutory requirements usually set a minimum backing ratio (such as the Federal Reserve's 40 percent requirement), implying a maximum value for *BASE/RES* (for example, 2.5 in the United States). However, there was typically no statutory minimum for *BASE/RES*, an important asymmetry. In particular, sterilization of gold inflows by surplus countries reduced average values of *BASE/RES*.

(3) *The ratio of international reserves to gold, RES/GOLD.* Under the gold-exchange standard of the interwar period, foreign exchange convertible into gold could be counted as international reserves, on a one-to-one basis with gold itself.[3] Hence, except for a few "reserve currency" countries, the ratio *RES/GOLD* also usually exceeded one.

Because the ratio of inside money to monetary base, the ratio of base to reserves, and the ratio of reserves to monetary gold were all typically greater than one, the money supplies of gold-standard countries—far from equalling the value of monetary gold, as might be suggested by a naive view of the gold standard—were often large multiples of the value of gold reserves. Total stocks of monetary gold continued to grow through the 1930s; hence, the observed sharp declines in inside money supplies must be attributed entirely to contractions in the average money-gold ratio.

Why did the world money-gold ratio decline? In the early part of the Depression period, prior to 1931, the consciously chosen policies of some major central banks played an important role (see, for example, Hamilton 1987). For example, it is now rather widely accepted that Federal Reserve policy turned contractionary in 1928, in an attempt to curb stock market speculation. In terms of quantities defined in equation (1), the ratio of the U.S. monetary base to U.S. reserves (*BASE/RES*) fell from 1.871 in June 1928, to 1.759 in June 1929, to 1.626 in June 1930, reflecting both conscious monetary tightening and sterilization of induced gold inflows.[4] Because of this decline, the U.S. monetary base fell about 6 percent between June 1928 and June 1930, despite a more-than-10 percent increase in U.S. gold reserves during the same period. This flow of gold into the United

---

[3] The gold-exchange standard was proposed by participants at the Genoa Conference of 1922, as a means of averting a feared shortage of monetary gold. Although the Genoa recommendations were not formally adopted, as the gold standard was reconstructed the reliance on foreign exchange reserves increased significantly relative to the prewar practice.

[4] U.S. monetary data in this paragraph are from Friedman and Schwartz (1963). Sumner (1991) suggests the use of the coverage ratio as an indicator of the stance of monetary policy under a gold standard.

States, like a similarly large inflow into France following the Poincare' stabilization, drained the reserves of other gold-standard countries and forced them into parallel tight-money policies.[5]

However, in 1931 and subsequently, the large declines in the money-gold ratio that occurred around the world did not reflect anyone's consciously chosen policy. The proximate causes of these declines were the waves of banking panics and exchange-rate crises that followed the failure of the Kreditanstalt, the largest bank in Austria, in May 1931. These developments affected each of the components of the money-gold ratio: First, by leading to rises in aggregate currency-deposit and bank reserve-deposit ratios, banking panics typically led to sharp declines in the money multiplier, M1/BASE (Friedman and Schwartz 1963; Bernanke and James 1991). Second, exchange-rate crises and the associated fears of devaluation led central banks to substitute gold for foreign exchange reserves; this flight from foreign-exchange reserves reduced the ratio of total reserves to gold, RES/GOLD. Finally, in the wake of these crises, central banks attempted to increase gold reserves and coverage ratios as security against future attacks on their currencies; in many countries, the resulting "scramble for gold" induced continuing declines in the ratio BASE/RES.[6]

A particularly destabilizing aspect of this process was the tendency of fears about the soundness of banks and expectations of exchange-rate devaluation to reinforce each other (Bernanke and James 1991; Temin 1993). An element that the two types of crises had in common was the so-called "hot money," short-term deposits held by foreigners in domestic banks. On one hand, expectations of devaluation induced outflows of the hot-money deposits (as well as flight by domestic depositors), which threatened to trigger general bank runs. On the other hand, a fall in confidence in a domestic banking system (arising, for example, from the failure of a major bank) often led to a flight of short-term capital from the country, draining international reserves and threatening convertibility. Other than abandoning the parity altogether, central banks could do little in the face of combined banking and exchange-rate crises, as the former seemed to demand easy money policies while the latter required monetary tightening.

From a theoretical perspective, the sharp declines in the money-gold ratio during the early 1930s have an interesting implication: namely, that under the gold standard as it operated during this period, *there appeared to be multiple potential equilibrium values of the money supply*.[7] Broadly speaking, when

---

[5] The gold flow into France was exacerbated by a 1928 law that induced a systematic conversion of foreign exchange reserves into gold by the Bank of France; see Nurkse (1944).

[6] Declines in BASE/RES also reflected sterilization of gold inflows by gold-surplus countries concerned about inflation; and, more benignly, the revaluation of gold reserves following currency devaluations.

[7] I am investigating this possibility more formally in ongoing work with Ilian Mihov.

financial investors and other members of the public were "optimistic," be-
lieving that the banking system would remain stable and gold parities would
be defended, the money-gold ratio and hence the money stock itself remained "high." More precisely, confidence in the banks allowed the ratio of
inside money to base to remain high, while confidence in the exchange rate
made central banks willing to hold foreign exchange reserves and to keep
relatively low coverage ratios. In contrast, when investors and the general
public became "pessimistic," anticipating bank runs and devaluation, these
expectations were to some degree self-confirming and resulted in "low"
values of the money-gold ratio and the money stock. In its vulnerability to
self-confirming expectations, the gold standard appears to have borne a
strong analogy to a fractional-reserve banking system in the absence of deposit insurance: For example, Diamond and Dybvig (1983) have shown that
in such a system there may be two Nash equilibria, one in which depositor
confidence ensures that there will be no run on the bank, the other in
which the fears of a run (and the resulting liquidation of the bank) are self-
confirming.

An interpretation of the monetary collapse of the interwar period as a
jump from one expectational equilibrium to another one fits neatly with
Eichengreen's (1992) comparison of the classical and interwar gold-standard
periods [see also Eichengreen (forthcoming)]. According to Eichengreen, in
the classical period, high levels of central bank credibility and international
cooperation generated stabilizing expectations, for example, speculators' activities tended to reverse rather than exacerbate movements of currency
values away from official exchange rates. In contrast, Eichengreen argues, in
the interwar period central banks' credibility was significantly reduced by
the lack of effective international cooperation (the result of lingering ani-
mosities and the lack of effective leadership) and by changing domestic
political equilibria—notably, the growing power of the labor movement,
which reduced the perceived likelihood that the exchange rate would be
defended at the cost of higher unemployment. Banking conditions also
changed significantly between the earlier and later periods, as war, reconstruction, and the financial and economic problems of the 1920s left the
banks of many countries in a much weaker financial condition, and thus
more crisis-prone. For these reasons, destabilizing expectations and a resulting low-level equilibrium for the money supply seemed much more likely in
the interwar environment.

Table 1 illustrates equation (1) with data from six representative countries. The first three countries in the table were members of the Gold Bloc,
who remained on the gold standard until relatively late in the Depression
(France and Poland left gold in 1936, Belgium in 1935). The remaining
three countries in the table abandoned gold earlier: the United Kingdom
and Sweden in 1931, the United States in 1933. [Throughout this lecture I
follow Bernanke and James (1991) in treating any major departure from

Table 1
Determinants or the Money Supply in Six Countries 1929–1936

France (devalued October 1936)

	M1	M1/BASE	BASE/RES	RES/GOLD	PGOLD	QGOLD
1929	101562	1.354	1.109	1.623	16.96	2456.3
1930	111720	1.325	1.106	1.489	16.96	3158.4
1931	122748	1.239	1.101	1.307	16.96	4059.4
1932	121519	1.263	1.010	1.054	16.96	4893.9
1933	114386	1.264	1.156	1.015	16.96	4544.9
1934	113451	1.244	1.098	1.012	16.96	4841.2
1935	108009	1.230	1.298	1.020	16.96	3908.1
1936	117297	1.218	1.557	1.024	22.68	2661.8

Poland (imposed exchange control April 1936, devalued October 1936)

	M1					
1929	2284	1.339	1.390	1.750	5.92	118.3
1930	2212	1.328	1.709	1.735	5.92	94.9
1931	1945	1.267	1.888	1.355	5.92	101.3
1932	1773	1.275	2.177	1.273	5.92	84.7
1933	1802	1.280	2.496	1.185	5.92	80.3
1934	1861	1.301	2.693	1.056	5.92	84.9
1935	1897	1.277	3.155	1.061	5.92	74.9
1936	2059	1.340	3.634	1.076	5.92	66.3

Belgium (devalued March 1935)

	M1					
1929	42788	2.504	1.949	1.492	23.90	245.9
1930	46420	2.336	1.697	1.707	23.90	287.1
1931	44863	2.047	1.266	1.358	23.90	533.4
1932	41349	1.805	1.395	1.265	23.90	543.1
1933	40382	1.754	1.314	1.282	23.90	571.9
1934	NA	NA	1.113	1.266	23.90	524.0
1935	39956	1.579	1.063	1.378	33.19	520.8
1936	43314	1.617	1.098	1.293	33.19	561.6

United Kingdom (suspended gold standard September 1931)

	M1					
1929	1328	1.560	5.825	1.0	0.1366	1069.8
1930	1361	1.618	5.699	1.0	0.1366	1080.8
1931	1229	1.579	6.452	1.0	0.1366	883.8
1932	1362	1.667	6.823	1.0	0.1366	877.2
1933	1408	1.680	4.395	1.0	0.1366	1396.4
1934	1449	1.642	4.590	1.0	0.1366	1408.1
1935	1565	1.694	4.615	1.0	0.1366	1465.2
1936	1755	1.700	3.291	1.0	0.1366	2297.0

Sweden (suspended gold standard September 1931)

	M1					
1929	988	1.498	1.280	2 092	2.48	98.8
1930	1030	1.508	1.082	2.618	2.48	97.2

Table 1 (*cont.*)

	M1	M1/BASE	BASE/RES	RES/GOLD	PGOLD	QGOLD
1931	1021	1.522	2.631	1.238	2.48	83.1
1932	1004	1.373	1.740	2.039	2.48	83.1
1933	1085	1.106	1.202	2.205	2.48	149.2
1934	1205	1.211	1.101	2.575	2.48	141.5
1935	1353	1.268	1.029	2.542	2.48	164.5
1936	1557	1.211	1.032	2.355	2.48	213.3

United States (suspended gold standard March 1933)

1929	26434	3.788	1.746	1.0	0.6646	6014.0
1930	24922	3.498	1.655	1.0	0.6646	6478.9
1931	21894	2.831	1.854	1.0	0.6646	6278.8
1932	20341	2.534	1.900	1.0	0.6646	6358.6
1933	19759	2.380	2.057	1.0	0.6646	6072.7
1934	22774	2.396	1.154	1.0	1.1253	7320.9
1935	27032	2.335	1.144	1.0	1.1253	8997.8
1936	30852	2.327	1.178	1.0	1.1253	10004.7

Notes: The table illustrates the identity, equation (1), for six countries. Where possible, values are end-of-year. Data sources are given in the Appendix.

Definitions are as follows: M1 = Money and notes in circulation plus commercial bank deposits; in local currency (millions). BASE = Money and notes in circulation plus commercial bank reserves; in local currency. RES = International reserves (gold plus foreign assets); valued in local currency. GOLD = Gold reserves, valued in local currency at the official gold price = PGOLD × QGOLD. PGOLD = Official gold price (units of local currency per gram); for countries not on the gold standard, a legal fiction rather than a market price. QGOLD = Physical quantity of gold reserves; in metric tons.

gold-standard rules, including devaluation or the imposition of exchange controls, as "leaving gold."] Of course, the gold leavers gained autonomy for their domestic monetary policies; but as these countries continued to hold gold reserves and set an official gold price, the components of equation (1) could still be calculated for those countries.

Several useful points may be gleaned from Table 1: First, observe the strong correspondence between gold-standard membership and falling M1 money supplies (a minor exception is Poland, which managed a small growth in nominal M1 between 1932 and 1936). Second, note the sharp declines in M1/BASE and RES/GOLD, reflecting (respectively) the banking crises and exchange crises (both of which peaked in 1931). Third, the table shows the tendency of gold-surplus countries to sterilize (that is, BASE/RES tends to fall in countries experiencing increases in gold stocks, QGOLD).

A striking case shown in Table 1 is that of Belgium: Although that country was the beneficiary of large gold inflows early in the Depression, the

combination of declines in M1/*BASE* (reflecting banking panics), *RES*/
GOLD (reflecting liquidation of foreign-exchange reserves), and *BASE/RES*
(the result of conscious sterilization early in the period, and of attempts to
defend the exchange rate against speculative attack later in the period)
induced sharp declines in the Belgian money stock. Similarly, because of
falls in M1/*BASE* and *RES/GOLD*, France experienced almost no nominal
growth in M1 between 1930 and 1934, despite a more than 50 percent
increase in gold reserves. The other Gold Bloc country in the table, Poland,
experienced monetary contraction principally because of loss of gold
reserves.

Another interesting phenomenon shown in Table 1 is the tendency of
countries devaluing or leaving the gold standard to attract gold away from
countries still on the gold standard. In the table, the United Kingdom,
Sweden, and the United States all experienced significant gold inflows
starting in 1933. This seemingly perverse result reflected the greater confidence of speculators in already depreciated currencies, relative to the
clearly overvalued currencies of the Gold Bloc. This flow of gold away
from some important Gold Bloc countries was the final nail in the gold
standard's coffin.

1.2. The Macroeconomic Implications of the Choice
of Exchange-rate Regime

We have seen that countries adhering to the international gold standard
suffered largely unintended and unanticipated declines in their inside
money stocks in the late 1920s and early 1930s. These declines in inside
money stocks, particularly in 1931 and later, were naturally influenced by
macroeconomic conditions; but they were hardly continuous, passive responses to changes in output. Instead, money supplies evolved discon-
tinuously in response to financial and exchange-rate crises, crises whose
roots in turn lay primarily in the political and economic conditions of the
1920s and in the institutional structure as rebuilt after the war. Thus, to a
first approximation, it seems reasonable to characterize these monetary
shocks as exogenous with respect to contemporaneous output, suggesting a
significant causal role for monetary forces in the world depression.

However, even stronger evidence for the role of nominal factors in the
Depression is provided by a comparison of the experiences of countries that
continued to adhere to the gold standard with those that did not. Although,
as has been mentioned, the great majority of countries had returned to gold
by the late 1920s, there was considerable variation in the strength of national allegiances to gold during the 1930s: Many countries left gold following the crises of 1931, notably the "sterling bloc" (the United Kingdom and
its trading partners). Other countries held out a few years more before capit-

ulating (for example, the United States in 1933, Italy in 1934). Finally, the diehard Gold Bloc nations, led by France, remained on gold until the final collapse of the system in late 1936. Because countries leaving gold effectively removed the external constraint on monetary reflation, to the extent that they took advantage of this freedom we should observe these countries enjoying earlier and stronger recoveries than the countries remaining on the gold standard.

That a clear divergence between the two groups of countries did occur was first noticed in a pathbreaking paper by Choudhri and Kochin (1980), who considered the relative performances of Spain (which as mentioned never joined the gold standard club), three Scandinavian countries (which left gold following the sterling crisis in September 1931), and four countries that remained part of the Gold Bloc (the Netherlands, Belgium, Italy, and Poland). Choudhri and Kochin found that the gold-standard countries suffered substantially more severe contractions in output and prices than did Spain and the three Scandinavian nations. In another important paper, Eichengreen and Sachs (1985) examined a number of macro variables in a sample of ten major countries over the period 1929–1935; they found that by 1935 countries that had left gold relatively early had largely recovered from the Depression, while the Gold Bloc countries remained at low levels of output and employment. Bernanke and James (1991) confirmed the general findings of the earlier authors for a broader sample of twenty-four (mostly industrialized) countries, and Campa (1990) did the same for a sample of Latin American countries.

If choices of exchange-rate regime were random, these results would leave little doubt as to the importance of nominal factors in determining real outcomes in the Depression. Of course, in practice the decision about whether to leave the gold standard was endogenous to a degree, and so we must be concerned with the possibility that the results of the literature are spurious, that is, that some underlying factor accounted for both the choice of exchange-rate regime and the subsequent differences in economic performance. In fact, these results are very unlikely to be spurious, for two general reasons:

First, as has been documented in detail by Eichengreen (1992) and others, for most countries the decision to remain on or leave the gold standard was strongly influenced by internal and external political factors and by prevailing economic and philosophical beliefs. For example, the French decision to stay with gold reflected, among other things, a desire to preserve at any cost the benefits of the Poincaré stabilization and the associated distributional bargains among domestic groups; an overwhelmingly dominant economic view (shared even by the Communists) that sound money and fiscal austerity were the best long-run antidotes to the Depression; and what can only be described as a strong association of national pride with maintenance of the gold standard.[8] Indeed, as Bernanke and James (1991) point out, economic conditions in 1929 and 1930 were on average quite similar in those countries that were to leave gold in 1931 and those that would not; thus it is difficult to view this choice as being simply a reflection of cross-sectional differences in macro-economic performance.

Second, and perhaps even more compelling, is that any bias created by endogeneity of the decision to leave gold would appear to go the wrong way, as it were, to explain the facts: The presumption is that economically weaker countries, or those suffering the deepest depressions, would be the first to devalue or abandon gold. Yet the evidence is that countries leaving gold recovered substantially more rapidly and vigorously than those who did not. Hence, any correction for endogeneity bias in the choice of exchange-rate regime should tend to strengthen the association of economic expansion and the abandonment of gold.

Tables 2 and 3 below extend the results of Bernanke and James (1991) on the links between exchange-rate regime and macroeconomic performance, using a data set similar to theirs. Both tables employ annual data on thirteen macroeconomic variables for up to twenty-six countries, depending on availability (see the Appendix for a list of countries, data sources, and data availabilities). Following similar tables in Bernanke and James, Table 2 shows average values of the log-changes of each variable (except for nominal and real interest rates, which are measured in percentage points) for all countries in the sample, and for the subsets of countries on and off the gold standard in each year.[9] Averages for the whole sample are reported for each year from 1930 to 1936; because almost all countries were on gold in 1930 and almost all had left gold by 1936, averages for the subsamples are shown for 1931–1935 only.

The statistical significance of the divergences between gold and nongold countries is assessed in Table 3. Lines marked "a" in Table 3 present the

---

[8] The differences in world views were most apparent at the ill-fated 1933 London Economic Conference, in which Gold Bloc delegates decried lack of sound money as the root of all evil, while representatives of the sterling bloc stressed the imperatives of reflation and economic expansion (Eichengreen and Uzan 1993). The persistence of these attitudes across decades is fascinating; note the attachment of the French to the *franc fort* in the recent troubles of the EMS, and the contrasting willingness of the British (as in September 1931) to abandon the fixed exchange rate in the pursuit of domestic macroeconomic objectives.

[9] As noted earlier, we treat a country as leaving gold if it deviates seriously from gold-standard rules, for example, by imposing comprehensive controls or devaluing, as well as if it formally renounces the gold standard. Dates of changes in gold-standard policies for twenty-four of our countries are given by Bernanke and James, Table 2.1. In addition, we take Argentina and Switzerland as leaving gold on their official devaluation dates (December 1929 and October 1936, respectively). Reported values are simple within-group averages of the data; however, weighting the results by gold reserves held or relative to 1929 production levels (available in League of Nations 1945) did not qualitatively change the results.

Table 2

Average Behavior of Selected Macro Variables for Countries on and off the Gold Standard, 1930–1936

	1930	1931	1932	1931	1934	1935	1936
1. Manufacturing production (log-change)							
Average	−.066	−.116	−.090	.076	.100	.074	.072
ON		−.117	−.173	.068	.025	−.001	
OFF		−.113	−.057	.078	.120	.008	
2. Wholesale prices (log-change)							
Average	−.116	−.122	−.045	−.017	.018	.024	.048
ON		−.140	−.133	−.065	−.037	−.038	
OFF		−.084	−.011	−.002	.033	.036	
3. M1 money supply (log-change)							
Average	.016	−.088	−.068	−.006	.019	.027	.074
ON		−.094	−.088	−.045	−.013	−.067	
OFF		−.076	−.060	.007	.028	.046	
4. M1-currency ratio (log-change)							
Average	.030	−.129	−.006	−.024	−.002	−.011	−.011
ON		−.142	−.052	−.009	−.016	−.037	
OFF		−.102	.014	−.030	.002	−.006	
5. Nominal wages (log-change)							
Average	.004	−.030	−.053	−.030	−.002	−.001	.031
ON		−.027	−.070	−.033	−.031	−.022	
OFF		−.039	−.045	−.029	.007	.004	
6. Real wages (log-change)							
Average	.122	.094	.007	−.009	−.023	−.022	−.018
ON		.110	.064	.032	.005	.016	
OFF		.059	−.020	−.025	−.032	−.031	
7. Employment (log-change)							
Average	−.066	−.117	−.074	.050	.096	.064	.068
ON		−.113	−.137	.006	.028	−.016	
OFF		−.127	−.047	.065	.113	.083	
8. Nominal interest rate (percentage points)							
Average	5.31	5.43	5.29	4.37	3.97	3.89	3.79
ON		5.22	4.20	3.69	3.26	4.05	
OFF		5.90	5.68	4.56	4.13	3.86	

Table 2 (*cont.*)

	1930	1931	1932	1931	1934	1935	1936
9. Ex-post real interest rate (percentage points)							
Average	16.89	9.39	6.51	2.78	1.11	−1.19	−8.93
ON		10.38	9.41	6.94	3.35	−4.92	
OFF		7.16	5.47	1.64	0.61	−0.62	
10. Relative price of exports (log-change)							
Average	−.033	−.011	−.047	.076	.084	−.067	.039
ON		.003	−.019	.134	.140	−.112	
OFF		−.040	−.058	.058	.070	−.058	
11. Real exports (log-change)							
Average	−.073	−.179	−.222	.014	.056	.021	.072
ON		−.193	−.292	−.008	.015	−.024	
OFF		−.146	−.192	.021	.067	.030	
12. Real imports (log-change)							
Average	−.071	−.211	−.264	.004	.038	−.020	.049
ON		−.159	−.250	−.006	−.067	−.012	
OFF		−.315	−.271	.008	.070	.027	
13. Real share prices (log-change)							
Average	−.107	−.186	−.214	.133	.060	.091	.115
ON		−.181	−.219	.139	−.028	.062	
OFF		−.198	−.211	.130	.092	.098	

Notes: For each variable and year, the table presents the overall average value of the variable, and the average for countries on and off the gold standard in that year (see Bernanke and James 1991). As most countries were on the gold standard in 1930 and off the gold standard in 1936, disaggregated data for those years are not presented. Data are annual and for up to twenty-six countries, depending on data availability (see the Appendix). Real wages, real share prices, and the ex post real rate of interest are computed using the wholesale price index. If a country is on the gold standard for a fraction f of a particular year, the values of its variables for the whole year are counted with the gold standard countries with weight f and with non-gold-standard countries with weight $1-f$ for that year. The proportion of country-months "on gold" in each year are as follows: 0.676 (1931), 0.282 (1932), 0.237 (1933), 0.205 (1934), 0.160 (1935).

Table 3
Regressions of Selected Macro Variables against Gold Standard and Banking Panic Dummies, 1931–1935

Dependent Variable		ONGOLD	PANIC	Adjusted R^2
Manufacturing production	(1a)	−.0704		0.601
		(4.04)		
	(1b)	−.0496	−.0926	0.634
		(2.80)	(3.50)	
Wholesale prices	(2a)	−.0914		0.622
		(8.20)		
	(2b)	−.0885	−.0129	0.620
		(7.47)	(0.73)	
Money supply (M1)	(3a)	−.0534		0.297
		(3.26)		
	(3b)	−.0344	−.0846	0.352
		(2.06)	(3.40)	
M1-currency ratio	(4a)	−.0329		0.263
		(1.91)		
	(4b)	−.0176	−.0680	0.294
		(0.99)	(2.55)	
Nominal wages	(5a)	−.0204		0.196
		(2.62)		
	(5b)	−.0145	−.0262	0.219
		(1.78)	(2.16)	
Real wages	(6a)	.0605		0.466
		(5.84)		
	(6b)	.0656	−.0230	0.470
		(5.99)	(1.41)	
Employment	(7a)	−.0610		0.557
		(4.38)		
	(7b)	−.0507	−.0458	0.569
		(3.48)	(2.10)	
Nominal interest rate	(8a)	−1.22		0.109
		(2.83)		
	(8b)	−1.00	−0.97	0.116
		(2.20)	(1.43)	
Ex-post real interest rate	(9a)	2.70		0.264
		(2.07)		
	(9b)	2.16	2.39	0.266
		(1.56)	(1.16)	
Relative price of exports	(10a)	.0464		0.198
		(1.70)		
	(10b)	.0288	.0783	0.213
		(1.00)	(1.83)	
Real exports	(11a)	−.0745		0.323
		(2.08)		

Table 3 (*cont.*)

Dependent Variable		*ONGOLD*	*PANIC*	Adjusted R^2
	(11b)	−.0523	−.0990	0.334
		(1.39)	(1.76)	
Real imports	(12a)	−.0000		0.416
		(0.00)		
	(12b)	.0232	−.1036	0.435
		(0.75)	(2.25)	
Real share prices	(13a)	−.0299		0.354
		(1.12)		
	(13b)	−.0206	−0.413	0.354
		(0.72)	(0.97)	

Notes: Entries are estimated coefficients from regressions of the dependent variables against dummies for adherence to the gold standard (*ONGOLD*) and for the presence of a banking panic (*PANIC*). Absolute values of *t*-statistics are in parentheses. Dependent variables are measures in log-changes, except for the nominal and ex post real interest rates, which are in percentage points (levels). Data are annual, 1931 to 1935 inclusive, and for up to twenty-six countries, depending on data availability (see the Appendix). Each regression includes a complete set of year dummies *ONGOLD* and *PANIC* are measured as the number of months during the year in which the country was on gold or experiencing a banking panic (see text), divided by twelve.

results of panel-data regressions of each of the macroeconomic variables in Table 2 against a constant, yearly time dummies, and a dummy variable for gold-standard membership (*ONGOLD*). (Lines in Table 3 marked "b" should be ignored for now.) For each country-year observation, the variable *ONGOLD* indicates the fraction of the year that the country was on the gold standard (the number of months on the gold standard divided by twelve). The regressions use data for 1931–1935 inclusive, but the results are not sensitive to adding data from 1930 or 1936 or to dropping 1931. Because each regression contains a full set of annual time dummies, the estimated coefficients of *ONGOLD* in each regression may be interpreted as reflecting purely cross-sectional differences between countries on and off gold, holding constant average macroeconomic conditions. Absolute values of *t*-statistics, given under each estimated coefficient, indicate the significance of the between-group differences.

Tables 2 and 3 are generally quite consistent with the conclusions that (1) monetary contraction was an important source of the Depression in all countries; (2) subsequent to 1931 or 1932, there was a sharp divergence between countries which remained on the gold standard and those that left it; and (3) this divergence arose because countries leaving the gold standard had greater freedom to initiate expansionary monetary policies.

Turning first to the behavior of money supplies, we can see from Table 2 (line 3) that the inside money stocks of all countries contracted sharply in 1931 and 1932. In an arithmetic sense, much of this contraction can be attributed to declines in the ratio of M1 to currency (line 4), which in turn primarily reflected the effects of banking crises (note the concentration of this effect in 1931).[10] During the period 1933–1935, however, Table 2 shows that the money supplies of gold-standard countries continued to contract, while those of countries not on the gold standard expanded. Table 3 (line 3a) indicates that, over the 1931–1935 period, the growth rate of M1 (line 3a) in countries on gold average about 5 percentage points per year less than in countries off gold, with an absolute t-value of 3.26.

The behavior of price levels corresponded closely to the behavior of money stocks. Table 2 (line 2) shows that, although a sharp deflation occurred in all countries through 1931, in countries leaving gold wholesale prices stabilized in 1932–1933 and began, on average, to rise in 1934.[11] Countries remaining on gold experienced continuing deflation through 1935, leading to a cumulative difference in log price levels over 1932–1935 of .329. According to Table 3 (line 2a), over the 1931–1935 period wholesale price inflation was about 9 percentage points per year lower (absolute t-value = 8.20) in countries on gold.

Declines in output and employment were strongly correlated with money and price declines: Manufacturing production (Table 2, line 1) and employment (Table 2, line 7) fell in all countries in 1930–1931 but afterward began to diverge between the two groups. Over the period 1932–1935, the cumulative difference in log output levels was .310, and the cumulative difference in log employment levels was .301, in favor of countries not on gold. The corresponding absolute t-values (Table 3, lines 1a and 7a, for the 1931–1935 sample) were 4.04 and 4.38 for output and employment, respectively. These are highly significant differences, both economically and statistically.

The behavior of other macro variables shown in Tables 2 and 3 are also generally consistent with the monetary-shocks story. For example, a standard Mundell-Fleming analysis of a small gold-standard economy (Eichengreen and Sachs 1986) would predict that monetary contraction abroad

---

[10] The preferred measure, M1/BASE, is not used owing to lack of data on commercial bank reserves for many countries in the sample. Note from Table 3, line 4a, that the fall in the M1-currency ratio is greater on average in gold-standard countries (and the difference is statistically significant at approximately the 5 percent level), consistent with our earlier observation that banking problems were more severe in gold-standard countries.

[11] Thus price-level stabilization preceded monetary stabilization in the typical country leaving gold. A possible explanation is that devaluation raised expectations of future inflation, lowering money demand and raising current prices.

would depress domestic aggregate demand by raising the domestic real interest rate. It also would predict an increase in the domestic real exchange rate (price of exports), relative to countries not on gold, and an accompanying decline in real exports. Table 2 (line 9) shows that ex post real interest rates were universally high in 1930, coming down gradually in both gold and nongold countries, but being consistently lower in countries not on gold.[12] Table 3 (line 9a) confirms that, on average, ex post real interest rates were 2.7 percentage points higher in gold-standard countries ($t = 2.07$). The real exchange rate in gold-standard countries (line 10a of Table 3, measured relative to the United States) grew on average close to 5 percentage points per year relative to that of nongold countries (but with a t-value of only 1.70), and correspondingly real exports (Table 3, line 11a) of gold-standard countries fell between 7 and 8 percentage points per year more quickly (absolute t-value = 2.08). There was no difference in the growth rates of imports between gold and nongold countries (Table 3, line 12a), presumably reflecting the offsetting effects in Gold Bloc countries of lower domestic income and improved terms of trade.

Interestingly, real share prices (a nominal share-price index deflated by the wholesale price index) did not fare that much worse in gold-standard countries, falling about 3 percentage points a year faster (absolute t-value = 1.12). There are significant differences between gold and nongold countries in the behavior of nominal and real wages, but as these variables are most closely linked to issues of aggregate supply, we defer discussion of them until the next section.

2. Aggregate Supply: The Failure of Nominal Adjustment

Although the consensus view of the causes of the Great Depression has long included a role for monetary shocks, we have seen in section 1 that recent

---

[12] A finding that ex post real interest rates were higher in gold-standard countries of course does not settle whether ex ante real interest rates were higher; that depends on whether deflation was anticipated. For the U.S. case, Cecchetti (1992) finds evidence for, and Hamilton (1992) find evidence against, the proposition that people anticipated the declines in the price level. (I do not know of any studies of this issue for countries other than the United States.) This debate bears less on the question of whether the initiating shocks were monetary than it does on the particular channel of transmission: If deflation was anticipated, so that the ex ante real interest rate was high, then the channel of monetary transmission was through conventional IS curve effects. If deflation was unanticipated, as both Cecchetti and Hamilton note, then one must rely more on a debt-deflation mechanism (see section 2). The behavior of nominal interest rates, which remained well above zero in most countries and were not substantially lower in gold-standard than in non-gold-standard countries (Table 2, line 8), suggests to me that much of the deflation was not expected, at least at the medium-term horizon. Evans and Wachtel (1993) draw a similar conclusion based on U.S. nominal interest rate behavior.

research taking a comparative perspective has greatly strengthened the empirical case for money as a major driving force. Further, the effects of monetary contraction on real economic variables appeared to be persistent as well as large. Explaining this persistent non-neutrality is particularly challenging to contemporary macroeconomists, since current theories of non-neutrality (such as those based on menu costs or the confusion of relative and absolute price levels) typically predict that the real effects of monetary shocks will be transitory.

On the aggregate supply side, then, we still have a puzzle: Why did the process of adjustment to nominal shocks appear to take so long in interwar economies? In this section I will discuss the evidence for two leading explanations of how monetary shocks may have had long-lived effects: induced financial crisis and sticky nominal wages.

2.1. Deflation and the Financial System

If one thinks about important sets of contracts in the economy that are set in nominal terms, and which are unlikely to be implicitly insured or indexed against unanticipated price-level changes, financial contracts (such as debt instruments) come immediately to mind. In my 1983 paper I argued that nonindexation of financial contracts may have provided a mechanism through which declining money stocks and price levels could have had real effects on the U.S. economy of the 1930s. I discussed two related channels, one operating through "debt-deflation" and the other through bank capital and stability.

The idea of debt-deflation goes back to Irving Fisher (1933). Fisher envisioned a dynamic process in which falling asset and commodity prices created pressure on nominal debtors, forcing them into distress sales of assets, which in turn led to further price declines and financial difficulties.[13] His diagnosis led him to urge President Roosevelt to subordinate exchange-rate considerations to the need for reflation, advice that (ultimately) FDR followed. Fisher's idea was less influential in academic circles, though, because of the counterargument that debt-deflation represented no more than a redistribution from one group (debtors) to another (creditors). Absent implausibly large differences in marginal spending propensities among the groups, it was suggested, pure redistributions should have no significant macroeconomic effects.

However, the debt-deflation idea has recently experienced a revival, which has drawn its inspiration from the burgeoning literature on imperfect

---

[13] Kiyotaki and Moore (1993) provide a formal analysis that captures some of Fisher's intuition.

information and agency costs in capital markets.[14] According to the agency approach, which has come to dominate modern corporate finance, the structure of balance sheets provides an important mechanism for aligning the incentives of the borrower (the agent) and the lender (the principal). One central feature of the balance sheet is the *borrower's net worth*, defined to be the borrower's own ("internal") funds plus the collateral value of his illiquid assets. Many simple principal-agent models imply that a decline in the borrower's net worth increases the deadweight agency costs of lending, and thus the net cost of financing the borrower's proposed investments. Intuitively, if a borrower can contribute relatively little to his or her own project and hence must rely primarily on external finance, then the borrower's incentives to take actions that are not in the lender's interest may be relatively high; the result is both deadweight losses (for example, inefficiently high risk-taking or low effort) and the necessity of costly information provision and monitoring. If the borrower's net worth falls below a threshold level, he or she may not be able to obtain funds at all.

From the agency perspective, a debt-deflation that unexpectedly redistributes wealth away from borrowers is not a macroeconomically neutral event: To the extent that potential borrowers have unique or lower-cost access to particular investment projects or spending opportunities, the loss of borrower net worth effectively cuts off these opportunities from the economy. Thus, for example, a financially distressed firm may not be able to obtain working capital necessary to expand production, or to fund a project that would be viable under better financial conditions. Similarly, a household whose current nominal income has fallen relative to its debts may be barred from purchasing a new home, even though purchase is justified in a permanent-income sense. By inducing financial distress in borrower firms and households, debt-deflation can have real effects on the economy.

If the extent of debt-deflation is sufficiently severe, it can also threaten the health of banks and other financial intermediaries (the second channel). Banks typically have both nominal assets and nominal liabilities and so over a certain range are hedged against deflation. However, as the distress of banks' borrowers increases, the banks' nominal claims are replaced by claims on real assets (for example, collateral); from that point, deflation squeezes the banks as well.[15] Actual and potential loan losses arising from debt-deflation impair bank capital and hurt banks' economic efficiency in several

---

[14] An important early paper that applied this approach to consumer spending in the Depression is Mishkin (1978). Bernanke and Gertler (1990) provide a theoretical analysis of debt-deflation. See Calomiris (1993) for a survey of the role of financial factors in the Depression.

[15] Banks in universal banking systems, such as those of central Europe, held a mixture of real and nominal assets (for example, they held equity as well as debt). Universal banks were thus subject to pressure even earlier in the deflationary process.

ways: First, particularly in a system without deposit insurance, depositor runs and withdrawals deprive banks of funds for lending; to the extent that bank lending is specialized or information-intensive, these loans are not easily replaced by nonbank forms of credit. Second, the threat of runs also induces banks to increase the liquidity and safety of their assets, further reducing normal lending activity. (The most severely decapitalized banks, however, may have incentives to make very risky loans, in a gambling strategy.) Finally, bank and branch closures may destroy local information capital and reduce the provision of financial services.

How macroeconomically significant were financial effects in the interwar period? My 1983 paper, which considered only the U.S. case, showed that measures of the liabilities of failing commercial firms and the deposits of failing banks helped predict monthly changes in industrial production, in an equation that also included lagged values of money and prices. However, this evidence is not really conclusive: For example, as Green and Whiteman (1992) pointed out, the spikes in commercial and banking failures in 1931 and 1932 could well be functioning as a dummy variable, picking up whatever forces—financial or otherwise—caused the U.S. Depression to take a sharp second dip during that period. As with the debate on the role of money, the problem is the reliance on what amounts to one data point.

However, in the comparative spirit of the new gold standard research, Bernanke and James (1991) studied the macroeconomic effects of financial crises in a panel of twenty-four countries. The expansion of the sample brought with it data limitations: Bernanke and James used annual rather than monthly data, and lack of data on indebtedness and financial distress forced them to confine their analysis to the effects of banking panics. Further, not having a consistent quantitative measure of banking instability, they chose to use dummy variables to indicate periods of banking crisis (as suggested by their reading of historical sources). Offsetting these disadvantages, expanding the sample made it possible to compare the U.S. case with both countries that also suffered severe banking problems and countries in which banking remained stable despite the Depression. In particular, Bernanke and James argued that cross-national differences in vulnerability to banking crises had more to do with institutional and policy differences than macroeconomic conditions, strengthening the case that banking panics had an independent macroeconomic effect (as opposed to being a purely passive response to the general economic downturn).[16]

As a measure of banking instability, Bernanke and James constructed a

[16] Factors cited by Bernanke and James as contributing to banking panics included banking structure ("universal" banking systems and systems with many small banks were more vulnerable); reliance on short-term foreign liabilities; and the country's financial and economic experiences and banking policies during the 1920s. See Grossman (1993) for a more detailed and generally complementary analysis of the causes of interwar banking panics.

dummy variable called *PANIC*, which they defined as the number of months during each year that countries in their sample suffered banking crisis.[17] In regressions controlling for a variety of factors, including the rate of change of prices, wages, and money stocks, the growth rate of exports, and discount rate policy, Bernanke and James found an economically large and highly stastistically significant effect of banking panics on industrial production.

A reduced-form summary of the effects of *PANIC* on our list of macro variables is given in the rows of Table 3 marked "b," which reports estimated coefficients from regressions of each macro variable against *PANIC*, the dummy for gold standard membership (*ONGOLD*), and time dummies for each year. For these estimates we have divided the Bernanke-James *PANIC* variable by twelve, so that its estimated coefficients may be interpreted as annualized effects.

The results suggest important macroeconomic effects of bank panics that are both independent of gold-standard effects and consistent with theoretical predictions: On the real side of the economy, *PANIC* is found to have economically large and statistically significant effects on manufacturing production (line 1b) and employment (line 7b). In particular, with gold-standard membership controlled for, the effect of a year of banking panic on the log-change of manufacturing production is estimated to be $-.0926$ with an absolute t-value of 3.50; and the effect on the log-change of employment is $-.0456$, with a t-value of 2.10. Banking panics are also found to reduce both real and nominal wages (lines 6b and 5b), hurt competitiveness and exports (lines 10b and 11b), raise the ex post real interest rate (line 9b), and reduce real share prices (line 13b), although estimated coefficients are not always statistically significant.

On the nominal side of the economy, banking prices significantly lower the money multiplier (proxied in line 4b of Table 3 by the ratio of M1 to currency), as expected. We also find (line 3b) that banking panics in a country significantly reduce the M1 money stock. This effect on the money supply is actually inconsistent with a simple Mundell-Fleming model of a small open economy on the gold standard: With worldwide conditions held

[17] Bernanke and James dated periods of crisis as starting from the first severe banking problems, as determined from a reading of primary and secondary sources. If there was some clear demarcation point, such as the U.S. banking holiday of March 1933, that point was used as the ending data of the crisis; otherwise, they arbitrarily assumed that the effects of the crisis would last for one year after its most intense point. Countries with nonzero values of *PANIC* included Austria, Belgium, Estonia, France, Germany, Hungary, Italy, Latvia, Poland, Rumania, and the United States. Results presented here add data for Argentina and Switzerland to the Bernanke-James sample; consistent with the Bernanke-James banking crisis chronology, we treat Switzerland (July 1931–November 1933) as a crisis country. Grossman (1993) includes all of these countries as "crisis" countries to his study but differs in counting Norway as a crisis country as well.

constant (by the time dummies), a small country's money stock is determined by domestic money demand, so that any declines in the money multiplier should be offset by endogenous inflows of gold reserves. Possible reconciliations of the empirical result with the model are that banking panics lowered domestic M1 money demand or raised the probability of exchange-rate devaluation (either would induce an outflow of reserves); our finding above that panics raised the real interest rate fit with the latter possibility. A finding that *is* consistent with the Mundell-Fleming model is that, once gold-standard membership is controlled for, banking panics had no effect on wholesale prices (line 2b). This last result is impotant, because it suggests that the observed effects of panics on output and other real variables are operating largely through nonmonetary channels, for example, the disruption of credit flows.

As with the earlier debate about the role of monetary shocks, moving from a focus on the U.S. case to a comparative international perspective provides much stronger evidence on the potential role of banking crisis in the Depression. Ideally, we should like to extend this evidence to the broader debt-deflation story as well. Indeed, the strong presumption is that debt-deflation effects were much more pervasive than banking crises, which were relatively more localized in space and time. Unfortunately, consistent international data on types and amounts of inside debt, and on various indicators of financial distress, are not generally available.[18]

2.2. Deflation and Nominal Wages

Induced financial crisis is a relatively novel proposal for solving the aggregate supply puzzle of the Depression. The more traditional explanation of monetary nonneutrality in the 1930s, as in macroeconomics more generally, is that nominal wages and/or prices were slow to adjust in the face of monetary shocks. In fact, widely available price indexes, such as wholesale and consumer price indexes, show relatively little nominal inertia during this period (admittedly, the same is not true for many individual prices, such as industrial prices). Hence—in contradistinction to contemporary macroeconomics, which has come to emphasize price over wage rigidity—research on the interwar period has focused on the slow adjustment of nominal wages as a source of nonneutrality. Following that lead, in this subsection I discuss the comparative empirical evidence for sticky wages in the Depression. I defer for the moment the deeper question of how wages could have failed to adjust, given the extreme labor-market conditions of the Depression era.

The link between nominal wage adjustment and aggregate supply is

[18] Eichengreen and Grossman (1994) attempt to measure debt-deflation by an indirect indicator, the spread between the central bank discount rate and the interest rate on commercial paper. As they note, this indicator is not wholly satisfactory and they obtain mixed results.

straightforward: If nominal wages adjust imperfectly, then falling price levels raise real wages; employers respond by cutting their workforces.[19] Similarly, in a country experiencing monetary reflation, real wages should fall, permitting reemployment. Although the cyclicality of real wages has been much debated in the postwar context, these two implications of the sticky-wage hypothesis are clearly borne out by the comparative interwar data, as can be seen in Tables 2 and 3:

First, during the worldwide deflation of 1930 and 1931, nominal wages worldwide fell much less slowly than (wholesale) prices, leading to significant increases in the ratio of nominal wages to prices (Table 2, lines 2, 5, and 6). Associated with this sharp increase in real wages were declines in employment and output (Table 2, lines 7 and 1).[20]

Second, from about 1932 on, there was a marked divergence in real-wage behavior between countries on and off the gold standard (Table 2, line 6): In countries leaving gold, prices rose more quickly than nominal wages (indeed, the latter continued to fall for a while), so that real wages fell; simultaneously, employment rose sharply. In countries remaining on gold, real wages rose or stabilized and employment remained stagnant. Table 3 (line 6a) indicates a difference in real wage growth between countries on and off the gold standard equivalent to about 6 percentage points per year, with a t-value of 5.84.

This latter result, that real-wage behavior varied widely between countries in and out of the Gold Bloc, was first pointed out in the previously cited article by Eichengreen and Sachs (1985). Using data from ten European countries for 1935, Eichengreen and Sachs showed that Gold Bloc countries systematically had high real wages and low levels of industrial output, while countries not on gold had much lower real wages and higher levels of production (all variables were measured relative to 1929).

In a recent paper, Bernanke and Carey (1994) extended the Eichengreen-Sachs analysis in a number of ways: First, they expanded the sample from ten to twenty-two countries, and they employed annual data for 1931–1936 rather than for 1935 only. Second, to avoid the spurious attribution to real

[19] In the standard analysis, increases in the real wage lead to declines in employment because employers move northwest along their neoclassical labor demand curves. An alternative possible channel is that higher wage payments deplete firms' liquidity, leading to reduced output and investment for the types of financial reasons discussed above (my thanks to Mark Gertler and Bruce Greenwald for independently making this suggestion). This latter channel might be tested by observing whether smaller or less liquid firms responded to real-wage increases by cutting employment more severely than did large, financially more robust firms.

[20] The wholesale price index is not the ideal deflator for nominal wages; to find the product wage, which is relevant to labor demand decisions, one should deflate by an index of output prices. The very limited international data on product wages are less supportive of the sticky-wage hypothesis than the evidence given here, see Eichengreen and Hatton (1988) or Bernanke and James (1991) for further discussion.

wages of price effects operating through nonwage channels,[21] in regressions they separated the real wage into its nominal-wage and price-level components. Third, they controlled for factors other than wages affecting aggregate supply and used instrumental variables techniques to correct for simultaneity bias in output and wage determination.[22] With these modifications, Bernanke and Carey's "preferred" equation describing output supply in their sample was (their Table 4, line 9):

$$q = -.600 \, w + .673 \, p + .540 \, q_{-1} - .144 \, PANIC - .69\text{-}05 \, STRIKE \quad (2)$$
$$\quad\;\; (3.84) \quad\;\; (5.10) \quad\; (7.66) \qquad\;\; (5.79) \qquad\qquad (3.60)$$

where

q, q_{-1} = current and lagged manufacturing production (in logs),
w = nominal wage index (in logs),
p = wholesale price index (in logs),
$PANIC$ = number of months in each year of banking panic [see the text or Bernanke-James (1991)], divided by 12, and
$STRIKE$ = working days lost to labor disputes (per thousand employees).

Absolute values of t-statistics are shown in parentheses. The regression pooled cross-sectional data for 1931–1936 and included time dummies and fixed country effects. A consistent estimate of within-country first-order serial correlation of $-.066$ was obtained by application of nonlinear least squares.

The equation indicates that banking panics ($PANIC$) and work stoppages ($STRIKE$) had large and statistically significant effects on the supply of output,[23] and the coefficient on lagged output indicates that output adjusted about half-way to its "target" level in any given year. Most importantly, the coefficient on nominal wages is highly significant and approximately equal and opposite in magnitude to the coefficient on the price level, as suggested by the sticky-wage hypothesis.[24] In particular, equation (2) indicates that

[21] Suppose that deflation affects output through a nonwage channel, such as induced financial crisis, and that nominal-wage data are relatively noisy (for example, they reflect official wage rates rather than rates actually paid). Then we might well observe an inverse relationship between measured real wages and output, even though wages are not part of the transmission channel.

[22] Instruments used in the equation to follow included, as aggregate demand shifters, a trade-weighted import price index and the discount rate for Gold Bloc countries, and M1 for countries off gold. Additionally, the banking panic and strike variables, and lagged values of the nominal wage and output, were treated as predetermined.

[23] The coefficient on $PANIC$ implies that one year of banking crisis reduced output by approximately 14 percent. The coefficient on $STRIKE$ is about what one would expect if output losses due to strikes are proportional to hours of work lost. See Bernanke and Carey (1994) for further discussion.

[24] That the coefficients on wages and prices are equal and opposite is easily accepted at standard significance levels ($p = .573$).

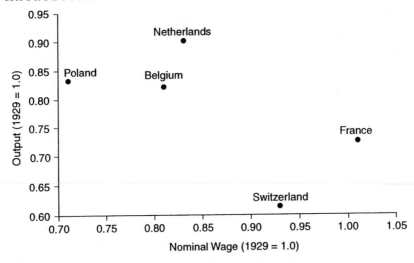

Figure 1. Output and Wages in the Gold Bloc, 1935

countries in which nominal wages adjusted relatively slowly toward changing price levels experienced the sharpest declines in manufacturing output.

To illustrate this last point in a very simple way, Figure 1 shows 1935 outputs and nominal wages for five Gold Bloc countries (Belgium, France, the Netherlands, Poland, and Switzerland). As they shared a common monetary standard throughout the period, these countries had similar wholesale price levels in 1935, but nominal wages differed among the countries. As Figure 1 indicates, France and Switzerland had significantly higher nominal wages than the other three countries (indeed, those countries had shown almost no nominal wage adjustment since 1929); these two countries also had significantly lower output levels. A regression for just these five data points of the log of output on a constant and the log of the nominal wage yields a coefficient on the nominal wage of $-.628$ with a t-statistic of -1.49.

Although Bernanke and Carey (1994) found cross-sectional evidence for the sticky-wage hypothesis, they emphasized that the time-series evidence is much weaker (recall that their regression included yearly time dummies, so that the results are based entirely on cross-country comparisons). Broadly, the problem with sticky wages as an explanation of the time-series behavior of output in the Depression is as follows: Although real wages rose sharply around the world during the 1929–1931 downturn, in most countries real wages didn't decline much during the recovery phase of the Depression; indeed, some countries (such as the United States) enjoyed strong recoveries despite rising real wages. Bernanke and Carey report that, for the twenty-two countries in their sample, average output in 1936 was nearly 10 percent above 1929 levels, even though real wages in 1936 remained nearly

20 percent higher than in 1929.[25] One possible reconciliation of the cross-section and time-series results is that actual wages paid fell relative to reported or official wage rates as the Depression wore on; and that the ratio of actual to reported wages was similar among the countries in the sample.

2.3. Can Failures of Nominal Adjustment in the Depression Be Explained?

I have discussed two general reasons for the failure of interwar economies to adjust to the large nominal shocks that hit them in the early 1930s: (1) nonindexed debt contracts, through which deflation induced redistribution and financial crisis; and (2) slow adjustment of nominal wages (and presumably other elements of the cost structure as well). From an economic theorist's point of view, there is an important distinction between these two sources of nonneutrality, which is that—following an unanticipated deflation—there are incentives for the parties to renegotiate nominal wage (or price) agreements, but not nominal debt contracts. In particular, if the nominal wage is "too high" relative to labor market equilibrium both the employer and the worker (who otherwise would be unemployed) should be willing to accept a lower wage, or to take other measures to achieve an efficient level of employment (Barro 1977). In contrast, there is no presumption that the distributive effects of unanticipated deflation operating through debt contracts will be undone by some sort of implicit indexing or renegotiation ex post, since large net creditors do gain from deflation and have no incentive to give up those gains.[26] Hence the failure of nominal wages (and, similarly, prices) to adjust seems inconsistent with the postulate of economic rationality, while deflation-induced financial crisis does not (given that nonindexed financial contracts exist in the first place[27]).

One interesting possibility for reconciling wage-price stickiness with economic rationality is that the nonindexation of financial contracts, and the associated debt-deflation, might in some way have been a *source* of the slow

---

[25] In principle this result could be explained by secular increases in capacity at a given real wage. However, Bernanke and Carey estimate that trend capacity growth of 5.6 percent per year on average would be needed to reconcile the behavior of output and real wages.

[26] Formal models in the literature, such as Bernanke-Gertler (1990), typically predict that debt-deflation lowers aggregate output and investment but does not lead to a situation that is Pareto-inefficient (given the information constraints). Thus there is no incentive for renegotiation between creditors and debtors. If the Bernanke-Gertler model were enhanced by assuming production or aggregate demand externalities, then debt-deflation could imply Pareto-inefficiency, but not of the sort that can easily be remedied by bilateral renegotiation.

[27] Nonindexation of financial contracts might be rationalized as an attempt to minimize transactions costs ex ante. This strategy is reasonable if the monetary authority is expected to keep inflation stable—an understandable assumption given the restoration of the gold standard.

adjustment of wages and other prices. Such a link would most likely arise for political reasons: As deflation proceeded, both the growing threat of financial crisis and the complaints of debtors increased pressure on governments to intervene in the economy in ways that inhibit adjustment. In the case of France, for example (which, note from Figure 1, seemed a particularly slow adjuster), a historian reported:

> as prices broke and incomes declined, as farmers, shopkeepers, merchants, and industrialists faced bankruptcy, the state began, on an empirical basis, to build up a complex and inchoate array of interventionist measures which interfered with the free operation of market forces in order to preserve certain *situations acquises.* (Kemp 1972, p. 101)

Examples of interventionist measures by the French government included tough agricultural import restrictions and minimum grain prices, intended to support the nominal incomes of farmers (a politically powerful group of debtors); government-supported cartelization of industry, as well as import protection, with the goal of increasing prices and profits; and measures to reduce labor supply, including repatriation of foreign workers and the shortening of workweeks.[28] These measures (comparable to New Deal-era actions in the United States) tended to block the downward adjustment of wages and prices.

Other links from debt-deflation to wage-price behavior operated through more strictly economic channels. For example, in France, heavy industries such as iron and steel expanded extensively during the 1920s, which left them with heavy debt burdens. In response to the financial distress caused by deflation, firms acted singly and in combination to try to restrict output, raise prices, and maintain profit margins (Kemp 1972, pp. 89ff.) Such behavior is predicted by modern industrial organization theory and evidence (see, for example, Chevalier and Scharfstein 1994).

A variety of other factors no doubt contributed to incomplete nominal adjustment. In some countries, many wages and prices were either directly controlled by the government (so that change involved administrative or legislative action, with the usual lags), or were highly politicized. Legislatively set taxes, fees, and tariffs were an additional source of nominal rigidity [see Crucini (1994) on tariffs]. Complex, decentralized economies also no doubt faced serious problems of coordination, both internally and with other economies, an issue that has been the subject of recent theoretical work (see, for example, Cooper 1990).

---

[28] Of course, the most obvious interventions would have been to stop the deflation by devaluing or to mandate a writedown of all nominal claims. As we have seen, however, in France devaluation was widely considered as heralding a plunge into chaos; while the writedown of debts and other claims, besides being administratively complex, would have been considered a politically unacceptable violation of the sanctity of contracts.

I believe that, as with other issues relating to the Depression, the comparative international approach holds the most promise for improving our understanding of the sources of incomplete nominal adjustment. In this case, though, the comparative analysis will need to include political and institutional variables, such as the proportion of workers covered by unions; the extent of representation of workers, farmers, industrialists, etc., in the legislature; the share of the workforce employed by the government; and so on. More qualitatively, historical and case-study comparisons of the political response to deflation in different countries may help explain the differing degrees of economic damage inflicted by falling prices.

3. Conclusion

Methodologically, the main contribution of recent research on the Depression has been to expand the sample to include many countries other than the United States. Comparative studies of a large set of countries have greatly improved our ability to identify the forces that drove the world into depression in the 1930s. In particular, the evidence for monetary contraction as an important cause of the Depression, and for monetary reflation as a leading component of recovery, has been greatly strengthened.

On the aggregate supply side of the economy, we have learned and will continue to learn a great deal from the interwar period. One key result is that wealth redistributions may have aggregate effects, if they are of the form to induce systematic financial distress. Empirical evidence has also been found for incomplete adjustment of nominal wages as a factor leading to monetary nonneutrality. Understanding this latter phenomenon will probably require a broad perspective that takes into account political as well as economic factors.

Appendix: Data Sources

Manufacturing production data are from League of Nations (1945). Wages and employment data are from International Labour Organization, *Year Book of Labor Statistics*, various issues. Data on commercial bank reserves, used in constructing monetary base measures, are taken from League of Nations, II.A Economic and Financial Series: *Money and Banking*, various issues. Monetary data for the United State are from Friedman and Schwartz (1963) and Board of Governors (1943). Other data are from League of Nations, *Statistical Year Book* and *Monthly Bulletin of Statistics,* various issues.

All data are annual and were collected for as many of the following twenty-six countries as possible: Australia, Argentina, Austria, Belgium,

Canada, Czechoslovakia, Denmark, Estonia, Finland, France, Germany, Greece, Hungary, Italy, Japan, Latvia, the Netherlands, Norway, New Zealand, Poland, Rumania, Sweden, Spain, Switzerland, the United Kingdom, and the United States.

Data availability by variable is described below. Inclusion of countries in the data set was based on the availability of data for key variables, particularly output and prices.

Data Availability

Manufacturing production: All countries, except Spain for 1936. Industrial production used for Argentina, from Thorp (1984).

Wholesale prices: All countries.

Money and notes in circulation: All countries.

Commercial bank deposits: All countries, except Greece and Spain for 1936.

Nominal wages: All countries, except Finland, Greece, Rumania, Spain.

Employment: All countries, except Austria, Belgium, Czechoslovakia, Greece, Spain, and Denmark for 1930.

Discount rate: All countries, except Argentina and Switzerland.

Exchange rates (relative to French francs): All countries.

Exports: All countries, except Argentina and Spain for 1936.

Imports: All countries, except Estonia, Finland, Greece, and Spain for 1936.

Share price index: Available for Austria, Belgium, Canada, Czechoslovakia, Denmark, France, Germany, Hungary, Italy, the Netherlands, Norway, Sweden, Spain, Switzerland, the United Kingdom, and the United States.

Literature Cited

Barro, Robert J. "Long-term Contracting, Sticky Prices, and Monetary Policy." *Journal of Monetary Economics* 3 (1977), 305–16.

Bernanke, Ben. "Nonmonetary Effects of the Financial Crisis in the Propagation of the Great Depression." *American Economic Review* 73 (June 1983), 257–76.

Bernanke, Ben, and Kevin Carey. "Nominal Wage Stickiness and Aggregate Supply in the Great Depression." Unpublished, Princeton University, January 1994.

Bernanke, Ben, and Mark Gertler. "Financial Fragility and Economic Performance." *Quarterly Journal of Economics* 105 (February 1990), 87–114.

Bernanke, Ben, and Harold James. "The Gold Standard, Deflation, and Financial Crisis in the Great Depression: An International Comparison." In R. G. Hubbard, ed., *Financial Markets and Financial Crises*, Chicago: University of Chicago Press, 1991.

Board of Governors of the Federal Reserve System. *Banking and Monetary Statistics*. Washington: National Capital Press, 1943.

Calomiris, Charles W. "Financial Factors in the Depression." *Journal of Economic Perspectives* 7 (Spring 1993), 61–86.

Campa, Jose Manuel. "Exchange Rates and Economic Recovery in the 1930s: An Extension to Latin America." *Journal of Economic History* 50 (September 1990), 677–82.

Cecchetti, Stephen G. "Prices during the Great Depression: Was the Deflation of 1930–1932 Really Unanticipated?" *American Economic Review* 82 (March 1992), 141–56.

Chevalier, Judith A., and David S. Scharfstein. "Capital Market Imperfections and Countercyclical Markups: Theory and Evidence." National Bureau of Economic Research working paper no. 4614. January 1994.

Choudhri, Ehsan U., and Levis A. Kochin. "The Exchange Rate and the International Transmission of Business Cycle Disturbances: Some Evidence from the Great Depression." *Journal of Money, Credit, and Banking* 12 (1980), 565–74.

Cooper, Russell. "Predetermined Wages and Prices and the Impact of Expansionary Government Policy." *Review of Economic Studies* 57 (1990), 205–14.

Crucini, Mario. "Sources of Variation in Real Tariff Rates: The United States, 1900–1940." *American Economic Review* 84 (June 1994), 732–43.

Diamond, Douglas W., and Philip H. Dybvig. "Bank Runs, Deposit Insurance, and Liquidity." *Journal of Political Economy* 91 (June 1983), 401–19.

Eichengreen, Barry. "Central Bank Cooperation under the Interwar Gold Standard." *Explorations in Economic History* 21 (1984), 64–87.

———. *Golden Fetters: The Gold Standard and the Great Depression, 1919–1939*. New York: Oxford University Press, 1992.

———. "Central Bank Cooperation and Exchange Rate Commitments: The Classical and Interwar Gold Standards Compared." *Financial History Review* (forthcoming).

Eichengreen, Barry, and Richard Grossman. "Debt Deflation and Financial Instability: Two Historical Explorations." Unpublished, University of California at Berkeley, June 1994.

Eichengreen, Barry, and Timothy J. Hatton. "Interwar Unemployment in International Perspective: An Overview." In Eichengreen, B. and Hatton, T., eds., *Interwar Unemployment in International Perspective*. London: Kluwer Academic Publishers, 1988.

Eichengreen, Barry, and Jeffrey Sachs. "Exchange Rates and Economic Recovery in the 1930s." *Journal of Economic History* 45 (1985), 925–46.

———. "Competitive Devaluation and the Great Depression: A Theoretical Reassessment." *Economics Letters* 22 (1986), 67–71.

Eichengreen, Barry, and Marc Uzan. "The 1933 World Economic Conference as an Instance of Failed International Cooperations." In Peter B. Evans et al., eds., *Double-Edged Diplomacy*, Berkeley, Calif.: University of California Press, 1993.

Evans, Martin, and Paul Wachtel. "Were Price Changes during the Great Depression Anticipated? Evidence from Nominal Interest Rates." *Journal of Monetary Economics* 32 (August 1993), 3–34.

Fisher, Irving. "The Debt-Deflation Theory of Great Depressions." *Econometrica* 1 (October 1933), 337–57.

Friedman, Milton, and Anna J. Schwartz. *A Monetary History of the United States, 1867–1960.* Princeton: Princeton University Press, 1963.

Gordon, Robert J., and James Wilcox. "Monetarist Interpretations of the Great Depression: Evaluation and Critique." In Karl Brunner, ed., *The Great Depression Revisited.* Boston: Martinus Nijhoff, 1981, 49–107.

Green, Susan J., and Charles H. Whiteman. "A New Look at Old Evidence On 'Nonmonetary Effects of the Financial Crisis in the Propagation of the Great Depression'." University of Iowa, April 1992.

Grossman, Richard S. "The Shoe That Didn't Drop: Explaining Banking Stability during the Great Depression." Wesleyan University, March 1993.

Hamilton, James D. "Monetary Factors in the Great Depression." *Journal of Monetary Economics* 19 (1987), 145–69.

———. "The Role of the International Gold Standard in Propagating the Great Depression." *Contemporary Policy Issues* 6 (1988), 67–89.

———. "Was the Deflation during the Great Depression Anticipated? Evidence from the Commodity Futures Market." *American Economic Review* 82 (March 1992), 157–78.

Kemp, Tom. *The French Economy, 1913–39: The History of a Decline.* London: Longman Group, 1972.

Kiyotaki, Nobu, and John H. Moore. "Credit Cycles." Unpublished, University of Minnesota and LSE, March 1993.

League of Nations. *Industrialization and Foreign Trade.* Geneva, 1945.

Mishkin, Frederic S. "The Household Balance Sheet and the Great Depression." *Journal of Economic History* 38 (December 1978), 918–37.

Nurkse, Ragnar (with W. A. Brown, Jr.). *International Currency Experience: Lessons of the Inter-War Period.* Princeton, N.J.: Princeton University Press for the League of Nations, 1944.

Romer, Christina. "The Nation in Depression." *Journal of Economic Perspectives* 7 (Spring 1993), 19–40.

Sumner, Scott. "The Equilibrium Approach to Discretionary Monetary Policy under an International Gold Standard: 1926–1932." *The Manchester School of Economic Studies* (December 1991), 378–94.

Temin, Peter. *Did Monetary Forces Cause the Great Depression?* New York: W. W. Norton, 1976.

———. *Lessons from the Great Depression.* Cambridge, Mass.: MIT Press, 1989.

———. "Transmission of the Great Depression." *Journal of Economic Perspectives* 7 (Spring 1993), 87–102.

Thorp, Rosemary, ed. *Latin America in the 1930s: The Role of the Periphery in the World Crisis.* New York: St. Martin's Press, 1984.

Part Two

MONEY AND FINANCIAL MARKETS

Two

Nonmonetary Effects of the Financial Crisis in the Propagation of the Great Depression

DURING 1930–33, THE U.S. FINANCIAL SYSTEM experienced conditions that were among the most difficult and chaotic in its history. Waves of bank failures culminated in the shutdown of the banking system (and of a number of other intermediaries and markets) in March 1933. On the other side of the ledger, exceptionally high rates of default and bankruptcy affected every class of borrower except the federal government.

An interesting aspect of the general financial crises—most clearly, of the bank failures—was their coincidence in timing with adverse developments in the macroeconomy.[1] Notably, an apparent attempt at recovery from the 1929–30 recession[2] was stalled at the time of the first banking crisis (November–December 1930); the incipient recovery degenerated into a new slump during the mid-1931 panics; and the economy and the financial system both reached their respective low points at the time of the bank "holiday" of March 1933. Only with the New Deal's rehabilitation of the financial system in 1933–35 did the economy begin its slow emergence from the Great Depression.

A possible explanation of these synchronous movements is that the financial system simply responded, without feedback, to the declines in aggregate output. This is contradicted by the facts that problems of the financial system tended to lead output declines, and that sources of financial panics unconnected with the fall in U.S. output have been documented by many writers. (See Section IV below.)

Among explanations that emphasize the opposite direction of causality, the most prominent is the one due to Friedman and Schwartz. Concentrating on the difficulties of the banks, they pointed out two ways in which these worsened the general economic contraction: first, by reducing the

Reprinted with permission from *American Economic Review*, vol. 73 (June 1983).

I received useful comments from too many people to list here by name, but I am grateful to each of them. The National Science Foundation provided partial research support.

[1] This is documented more carefully in Sections I.C and IV below.

[2] This paper does not address the causes of the initial 1929–30 downturn. Milton Friedman and Anna Schwartz (1963) have stressed the importance of the Federal Reserve's "anti-speculative" monetary tightening. Others, such as Peter Temin (1976), have pointed out autonomous expenditure effects.

wealth of bank shareholders; second, and much more important, by leading to a rapid fall in the supply of money. There is much support for the monetary view. However, it is not a complete explanation of the link between the financial sector and aggregate output in the 1930's. One problem is that there is no theory of monetary effects on the real economy that can explain *protracted* nonneutrality. Another is that the reductions of the money supply in this period seems quantitatively insufficient to explain the subsequent falls in output. (Again, see Section IV.)

The present paper builds on the Friedman-Schwartz work by considering a third way in which the financial crises (in which we include debtor bankruptcies as well as the failures of banks and other lenders) may have affected output. The basic premise is that, because markets for financial claims are incomplete, intermediation between some classes of borrowers and lenders requires nontrivial market-making and information-gathering services. The disruptions of 1930–33 (as I shall try to show) reduced the effectiveness of the financial sector as a whole in performing these services. As the real costs of intermediation increased, some borrowers (especially households, farmers, and small firms) found credit to be expensive and difficult to obtain. The effects of this credit squeeze on aggregate demand helped convert the severe but not unprecedented downturn of 1929–30 into a protracted depression.

It should be stated at the outset that my theory does not offer a complete explanation of the Great Depression (for example, nothing is said about 1929–30). Nor is it necessarily inconsistent with some existing explanations.[3] However, it does have the virtues that, first, it seems capable (in a way in which existing theories are not) of explaining the unusual length and depth of the depression; and, second, it can do this without assuming markedly irrational behavior by private economic agents. Since the reconciliation of the obvious inefficiency of the depression with the postulate of rational private behavior remains a leading unsolved puzzle of macroeconomics, these two virtues alone provide motivation for serious consideration of this theory.

There do not seem to be any exact antecedents of the present paper in the formal economics literature.[4] The work of Lester Chandler (1970, 1971) provides the best historical discussions of the general financial crisis extant; however, he does not develop very far the link to macroeconomic performance. Beginning with Irving Fisher (1933) and A. G. Hart (1938), there is a literature on the macroeconomic role of inside debt; an interesting recent example is the paper by Frederic Mishkin (1978), which stresses household

[3] See Karl Brunner (1981) for a useful overview of contemporary theories of the depression. Also, see Robert Lucas and Leonard Rapping's article in Lucas (1981).

[4] This is especially true of the more recent work, which tends to ignore the nonmonetary effects of the financial crisis. Older writers often seemed to take the disruptive impact of the financial breakdown for granted.

balance sheets and liquidity. Benjamin Friedman (1981) has written on the relationship of credit and aggregate activity. Hyman Minsky (1977) and Charles Kindleberger (1978) have in several places argued for the inherent instability of the financial system, but in doing so have had to depart from the assumption of rational economic behavior.[5] None of the above authors has emphasized the effects of financial crisis on the real costs of credit intermediation, the focus of the present work.

The paper is organized as follows: Section I presents some background on the 1930–33 financial crisis, its sources, and its correspondence with aggregate output movements. Section II begins the principal argument of the paper. I explain how the runs on banks and the extensive defaults could have reduced the efficiency of the financial sector in performing its intermediary functions. Some evidence of these effects is introduced.

Possible channels by which reduced financial efficiency might have affected output are discussed in Section III. Reduced-form estimation results, reported in Section IV, suggest that augmenting a purely monetary approach by my theory significantly improves the explanation of the financial sector-output connection in the short run. Section V looks at the persistence of these effects.

Some international aspects of the financial sector-aggregate output link are briefly discussed in Section VI and Section VII concludes.

I. The Financial Collapse: Some Background

The problems faced by the U.S. financial system between October 1930 and March 1933 have been described in detail by earlier authors,[6] but it will be useful to recapitulate some principal facts here. Given this background, attention will be turned to the more central issues of the paper.

The two major components of the financial collapse were the loss of confidence in financial institutions, primarily commercial banks, and the widespread insolvency of debtors. I give short discussions of each of these components and of their joint relation to aggregate fluctuations.

A. The Failure of Financial Institutions

Most financial institutions (even semipublic ones, like the Joint Stock Land Banks) came under pressure in the 1930's. Some, such as the insurance companies and the mutual savings banks, managed to maintain something close to normal operations. Others, like the building-and-loans (which, de-

[5] I do not deny the possible importance of irrationality in economic life; however, it seems that the best research strategy is to push the rationality postulate as far as it will go.

[6] See especially Chandler (1970, 1971) and Friedman and Schwartz.

spite their ability to restrict withdrawals by depositors, failed in significant numbers) were greatly hampered in their attempts to carry on their business.[7] Of most importance, however, were the problems of the commercial banks. The significance of the banking difficulties derived both from their magnitude and from the central role commercial banks played in the financial system.[8]

The great severity of the banking crises in the Great Depression is well known to students of the period. The percentages of operating banks which failed in each year from 1930 to 1933 inclusive were 5.6, 10.5, 7.8, and 12.9; because of failures and mergers, the number of banks operating at the end of 1933 was only just above half the number that existed in 1929.[9] Banks that survived experienced heavy losses.

The sources of the banking collapse are best understood in the historical context. The first point to be made is that bank failures were hardly a novelty at the time of the depression. The U.S. system, made up as it was primarily of small, independent banks, had always been particularly vulnerable. (Countries with only a few large banks, such as Britain, France, and Canada, never had banking difficulties on the American scale.) The dominance of small banks in the United States was due in large part to a regulatory environment which reflected popular fears of large banks and "trusts"; for example, there were numerous laws restricting branch banking at both the state and national level. Competition between the state and national banking systems for member banks also tended to keep the legal barriers to entry in banking very low.[10] In this sort of environment, a significant number of failures was to be expected and probably was even desirable. Failures due to "natural causes" (such as the agricultural depression of the 1920's upon which many small, rural banks foundered) were common.[11]

Besides the simple lack of economic viability of some marginal banks, however, the U.S. system historically suffered also from a more malign source of bank failures; namely, financial panics. The fact that liabilities of banks were principally in the form of fixed-price, callable debt (i.e., demand deposits), while many assets were highly illiquid, created the possibility of the perverse expectational equilibrium known as a "run" on the banks. In a

[7] Hart describes the problems of the building-and-loans. An interesting sidelight here is the additional strain on housing lenders caused by the existence of the Postal Savings System; see Maureen O'Hara and David Easley (1979).

[8] According to Raymond Goldsmith (1958), commercial banks held 39.6 percent of the assets of all financial intermediaries, broadly defined, in 1929. See his Table 11.

[9] Cyril Upham and Edwin Lamke (1934, p. 247). Since smaller banks were more likely to fail, the fraction of deposits represented by suspended banks was somewhat less. Eventual recovery by depositors was about 75 percent; see Friedman and Schwartz, p. 438.

[10] Benjamin Klebaner (1974) gives a good brief history of U.S. commercial banking.

[11] Upham and Lamke, p. 247, report that approximately 2–3 percent of all banks in operation failed in each year of the 1920's.

run, fear that a bank may fail induces depositors to withdraw their money, which in turn forces liquidation of the bank's assets. The need to liquidate hastily, or to dump assets on the market when other banks are also liquidating, may generate losses that actually do cause the bank to fail. Thus the expectation of failure, by the mechanism of the run, tends to become self-confirming.[12]

An interesting question is why banks at this time relied on fixed-price demand deposits, when alternative instruments might have reduced or prevented the problem of runs.[13] An answer is provided by Friedman and Schwartz: They pointed out that, before the establishment of the Federal Reserve in 1913, panics were usually contained by the practice of suspending convertibility of bank deposits into currency. This practice, typically initiated by loose organizations of urban banks called clearinghouses, moderated the dangers of runs by making hasty liquidation unnecessary. In conjunction with the suspension of convertibility practice, the use of demand deposits created relatively little instability.[14]

However, with the advent of the Federal Reserve (according to Friedman-Schwartz), this roughly stable institutional arrangement was upset. Although the Federal Reserve introduced no specific injunctions against the suspension of convertibility, the clearinghouses apparently felt that the existence of the new institution relieved them of the responsibility of fighting runs. Unfortunately, the Federal Reserve turned out to be unable or unwilling to assume this responsibility.

No serious runs occurred between World War I and 1930; but the many pieces of bad financial news that came in from around the world in 1930–32 were like sparks around tinder. Runs were clearly an important part of the banking problems of this period. Some evidence emerges from contemporary accounts, including descriptions of specific events precipitating runs. Also notable is the fact that bank failures tended to occur in short spasms, rather than in a steady stream (see Table 1, col. 2, for monthly data on the deposits of failing banks). The problem was not arrested until government intervention became important in late 1932 and early 1933.

We see, then, that the banking crises of the early 1930's differed from earlier recorded experience both in magnitude and in the degree of danger posed by the phenomenon of runs. The result of this was that the behavior of almost the entire system was adversely affected, not just that of marginal banks. The bankers' fear of runs, as I shall argue below, had important macroeconomic effects.

[12] Douglas Diamond and Philip Dybvig (1981) formalize this argument. For an alternative analysis of the phenomenon of runs, see Robert Flood and Peter Garber (1981).

[13] For example, equity-like instruments, such as those used by modern money-market mutual funds, could have been used as the transactions medium. See Kenneth Cone (1982).

[14] Diamond and Dybvig derive this point formally, with some caveats.

B. *Defaults and Bankruptcies*

The second major aspect of the financial crisis (one that is currently neglected by historians) was the pervasiveness of debtor insolvency. Given
that debt contracts were written in nominal terms,[15] the protracted fall in
prices and money incomes greatly increased debt burdens. According to
Evans Clark (1933), the ratio of debt service to national income went from
9 percent in 1929 to 19.8 percent in 1932–33. The resulting high rates of
default caused problems for both borrowers and lenders.

The "debt crisis" touched all sectors. For example, about half of all residential properties were mortgaged at the beginning of the Great Depression;
according to the *Financial Survey of Urban Housing* (reported in Hart), as of
January 1, 1934,

> The proportion of mortgaged owner-occupied houses with some interest of princi-
> pal in default was in none of the twenty-two cities [surveyed] less than 21 percent
> (the figure for Richmond, Virginia); in half it was above 38 percent; in two (Indi-
> anapolis and Birmingham, Alabama) between 50 percent and 60 percent; and in
> one (Cleveland), 62 percent. For rented properties, percentages in default ran
> slightly higher. (p. 164)

Because of the long spell of low food prices, farmers were in more difficulty than homeowners. At the beginning of 1933, owners of 45 percent of
all U.S. farms, holding 52 percent of the value of farm mortgage debt, were
delinquent in payments (Hart, p. 138). State and local governments—many
of whom tried to provide relief for the unemployed—also had problems
paying their debts: As of March 1934, the governments of 37 of the 310
cities with populations over 30,000 and of three states had defaulted on
obligations (Hart, p. 225).

In the business sector, the incidence of financial distress was very uneven.
Aggregate corporate profits before tax were negative in 1931 and 1932, and
after-tax retained earnings were negative in each year from 1930 to 1933
(Chandler, 1971, p. 102). But the subset of corporations holding more than
$50 million in assets maintained positive profits throughout this period,
leaving the brunt to be borne by smaller companies. Solomon Fabricant
(1935) reported that, in 1932 alone, the losses of corporations with assets of
$50,000 or less equalled 33 percent of total capitalization; for corporations
with assets in the $50,000–$100,000 range, the comparable figure was 14
percent. This led to high rates of failure among small firms.

Although the deflation of the 1930's was unusually protracted, there had
been a similar episode as recently as 1921–22 which had not led to mass

---

[15] The lack of indexed debt during the deflationary 1930's—as in the inflationary 1970's—
remains a puzzle.

insolvency. The seriousness of the problem in the Great Depression was due not only to the extent of the deflation, but also to the large and broad-based expansion of inside debt in the 1920's. Charles Persons surveyed the credit expansion of the predepression decade in a 1930 article: He reported that outstanding corporate bonds and notes increased from $26.1 billion in 1920 to $47.1 billion in 1928, and that non-federal public securities grew from $11.8 billion to $33.6 billion over the same period. (This may be compared with a 1929 national income of $86.8 billion.) Perhaps more significantly, during the 1920's, small borrowers, such as households and unincorporated businesses, greatly increased their debts. For example, the value of urban real estate mortgages outstanding increased from $11 billion in 1920 to $27 billion in 1929, while the growth of consumer installment debt reflected the introduction of major consumer durables to the mass market.

Like the banking crises, then, the debt crisis of the 1930's was not qualitatively a new phenomenon; but it represented a break with the past in terms of its severity and pervasiveness.

C. Correlation of the Financial Crisis with Macroeconomic Activity

The close connection of the stages of the financial crisis (especially the bank failures) with changes in real output has been noted by Friedman and Schwartz and by others. An informal review of this connection is facilitated by the monthly data in Table 1. Column 1 is an index of real industrial production. Columns 2 and 3 are the (nominal) liabilities of failing banks and nonbank commercial businesses, respectively.

The industrial production series reveals that a recession began in the United States during 1929. By late 1930, the downturn, although serious, was still comparable in magnitude to the recession of 1920–22; as the decline slowed, it would have been reasonable to expect a brisk recovery, just as in 1922.

With the first banking crisis, however, there came what Friedman and Schwartz called a "change in the character of the contraction" (p. 311). The economy first flattened out, then went into a new tailspin just as the banks began to fail again in June 1931.

A lengthy slide of both the general economy and the financial system followed. The banking situation calmed in early 1932, and nonbank failures peaked shortly thereafter. A new recovery attempt began in August, but failed within a few months.[16] In March 1933, the bottom was reached for

---

[16] Judging by Table 1, the failure of this recovery seems to be unrelated to financial sector difficulties. However, accounts from the time suggest that the banking crisis of late 1932 and early 1933 (which ended in the banking holiday) was in fact quite severe; see Susan Kennedy (1973). The relatively low reported rate of bank failures at this time may be an artifact of state moratoria, restrictions on withdrawals, and other interventions.

Table 1
Selected Macroeconomic Data, July 1929–March 1933

Month	IP	Banks	Fails	ΔL/PI	L/DEP	DIF
1929 J	114	60.8	32.4	.163	.851	2.31
A	114	6.7	33.7	.007	.855	2.33
S	112	9.7	34.1	.079	.860	2.33
O	110	12.5	31.3	.177	.865	2.50
N	105	22.3	52.0	.121	.854	2.68
D	100	15.5	62.5	−.214	.851	2.59
1930 J	100	26.5	61.2	−.228	.837	2.49
F	100	32.4	51.3	−.102	.834	2.48
M	98	23.2	56.8	.076	.835	2.44
A	98	31.9	49.1	.058	.826	2.33
M	96	19.4	55.5	−.028	.820	2.41
J	93	57.9	63.1	.085	.818	2.53
J	89	29.8	29.8	−.055	.802	2.52
A	86	22.8	49.2	−.027	.800	2.47
S	85	21.6	46.7	.008	.799	2.41
O	83	19.7	56.3	−.010	.791	2.73
N	81	179.9	55.3	−.067	.777	3.06
D	79	372.1	83.7	−.144	.775	3.49
1931 J	78	75.7	94.6	−.187	.763	3.21
F	79	34.2	59.6	−.144	.747	3.08
M	80	34.3	60.4	−.043	.738	3.17
A	80	41.7	50.9	−.104	.722	3.45
M	80	43.2	53.4	−.133	.706	3.99
J	77	190.5	51.7	−.120	.707	4.23
J	76	40.7	61.0	−.013	.704	3.93
A	73	180.0	53.0	−.103	.706	4.29
S	70	233.5	47.3	−.050	.713	4.82
O	68	471.4	70.7	−.310	.716	5.41
N	67	67.9	60.7	−.101	.726	5.30
D	66	277.1	73.2	−.120	.732	6.49
1932 J	64	218.9	96.9	−.117	.745	4.87
F	63	51.7	84.9	−.138	.757	4.76
M	62	10.9	93.8	−.183	.744	4.91
A	58	31.6	101.1	−.225	.718	6.78
M	56	34.4	83.8	−.154	.696	7.87
J	54	132.7	76.9	−.170	.689	7.93
J	53	48.7	87.2	−.219	.677	7.21
A	54	29.5	77.0	−.130	.662	4.77
S	58	13.5	56.1	−.091	.641	4.19
O	60	20.1	52.9	−.095	.623	4.44
N	59	43.3	53.6	−.133	.602	4.79
D	58	70.9	64.2	−.039	.596	5.07

Table 1 (*cont.*)

Month	IP	Banks	Fails	$\Delta L/PI$	L/DEP	DIF
1933 J	58	133.1	79.1	−.139	.576	4.79
F	57	62.2	65.6	−.059	.583	4.09
M	54	3276.3[a]	48.5	−.767[a]	.607[a]	4.03

Notes: IP = seasonally adjusted index of industrial production, 1935–39 = 100; *Federal Reserve Bulletin*. Banks = deposits of failing banks, $millions; *Federal Reserve Bulletin*. Fails = liabilities of failing commercial businesses, $millions; *Survey of Current Business*. $\Delta L/PI$ = ratio of net extensions of commercial bank loans to (monthly) personal income; from *Banking and Monetary Statistics* and *National Income*. L/D = ratio of loans outstanding to the sum of demand and time deposits, weekly reporting banks; *Banking and Monetary Statistics*. DIF = difference (in percentage points) between yields on Baa corporate bonds and long-term U.S. government bonds; *Banking and Monetary Statistics*.

[a] A national bank holiday was declared in March 1933.

both the financial system and the economy as a whole. Measures taken after the banking holiday ended the bank runs and greatly reduced the burden of debt. Simultaneously aggregate output began a recovery that was sustained until 1937.

The leading explanation of the correlation between the conditions of the financial sector and of the general economy is that of Friedman and Schwartz, who stressed the effects of the banking crises on the supply of money. I agree that money was an important factor in 1930–33, but, because of reservations cited in the introduction, I doubt that it completely explains the financial sector-aggregate output connection. This motivates my study of a nonmonetary channel through which an additional impact of the financial crisis may have been felt.

II. The Effect of the Crisis on the Cost of Credit Intermediation

This paper posits that, in addition to its effects via the money supply, the financial crisis of 1930–33 affected the macroeconomy by reducing the quality of certain financial services, primarily credit intermediation. The basic argument is to be made in two steps. First, it must be shown that the disruption of the financial sector by the banking and debt crises raised the real cost of intermediation between lenders and certain classes of borrowers. Second, the link between higher intermediation costs and the decline in aggregate output must be established. I present here the first step of the argument, leaving the second to be developed in Sections III–V.

In order to discuss the quality of performance of the financial sector, I must first describe the real services that the sector is supposed to provide.

The specification of these services depends on the model of the economy one has in mind. We shall clearly not be interested in economies of the sort described by Eugene Fama (1980), in which financial markets are complete and information/transactions costs can be neglected. In such a world, banks and other intermediaries are merely passive holders of portfolios. Banks' choice of portfolios or the scale of the banking system can never make any difference in this case, since depositors can offset any action taken by banks through private portfolio decisions.[17]

As an alternative to the Fama complete-markets world, consider the following stylized description of the economy. Let us suppose that savers have many ways of transferring resources from present to future, such as holding real assets or buying the liabilities of governments or corporations on well-organized exchanges. One of the options savers have is to lend resources to a banking system. The banks also have a menu of different assets to choose from. Assume, however, that banks specialize in making loans to small, idiosyncratic borrowers whose liabilities are too few in number to be publicly traded. (Here is where the complete-markets assumption is dropped.)

The small borrowers to whom the banks lend will be taken, for simplicity, to be of two extreme types, "good" and "bad." Good borrowers desire loans in order to undertake individual-specific investment projects. These projects generate a random return from a distribution whose mean will be assumed always to exceed the social opportunity cost of investment. If this risk is nonsystematic, lending to good borrowers is socially desirable. Bad borrowers try to look like good borrowers, but in fact they have no "project." Bad borrowers are assumed to squander any loan received in profligate consumption, then to default. Loans to bad borrowers are socially undesirable.

In this model, the real service performed by the banking system is the differentiation between good and bad borrowers.[18] For a competitive banking system, I define the *cost of credit intermediation (CCI)* as being the cost of channeling funds from the ultimate savers/lenders into the hands of good borrowers. The CCI includes screening, monitoring, and accounting costs, as well as the expected losses inflicted by bad borrowers. Banks presumably choose operating procedures that minimize the CCI. This is done by developing expertise at evaluating potential borrowers; establishing long-term relationships with customers; and offering loan conditions that encourage potential borrowers to self-select in a favorable way.[19]

---

[17] It should be noted that the phenomena emphasized by Friedman and Schwartz—the effects of the contraction of the banking system on the quantity of the transactions medium and on real output—are also impossible in a complete-markets world.

[18] To concentrate on credit intermediation, I neglect the transactions and other services performed by banks.

[19] See Dwight Jaffee and Thomas Russell (1976) and Joseph Stiglitz and Andrew Weiss (1981) on the way banks induce favorable borrower self-selection.

Given this simple paradigm, I can describe the effects of the two main components of the financial crisis on the efficiency of the credit allocation process (i.e., on the CCI).

A. Effect of the Banking Crises on the CCI

The banking problems of 1930–33 disrupted the credit allocation process by creating large, unplanned changes in the channels of credit flow. Fear of runs led to large withdrawals of deposits, precautionary increases in reserve-deposit ratios, and an increased desire by banks for very liquid or rediscount-able assets. These factors, plus the actual failures, forced a contraction of the banking system's role in the intermediation of credit.[20] Some of the slack was taken up by the growing importance of alternative channels of credit (see below). However, the rapid switch away from the banks (given the banks' accumulated expertise, information, and customer relationships) no doubt impaired financial efficiency and raised the CCI.[21]

It would be useful to have a direct measure of the CCI; unfortunately, no really satisfactory empirical representation of this concept is available. Reported commercial loan rates reflect loans that are actually made, not the shadow cost of bank funds to a representative potential borrower; since banks in a period of retrenchment make only the safest and highest-quality loans, measured loan rates may well move inversely to the CCI. I obtained a number of interesting results using the yield differential between Baa corporate bonds and U.S. government bonds as a proxy for the CCI; however, the use of the Baa rate is not consistent with my story that bank borrowers are those whose liabilities are too few to be publicly traded.

While we cannot observe directly the effects of the banking troubles on the CCI, we can see their impact on the extension of bank credit: Table 1 gives some illustrative data. Column 4 gives, as a measure of the flow of bank credit, the monthly change in bank loans outstanding, normalized by monthly personal income.[22] One might have expected the loan-change-to-income ratio to be driven primarily by loan demand and thus by the rate of production. Comparison with the first two columns of Table 1 shows, however, that the banking crises were as important a determinant of this vari-

[20] For an interesting contemporary account of this process, see the article by Eugene H. Burris in the American Banker, October 15, 1931.

[21] Since intermediation resources could have been shifted out of the beleaguered banking sector (given enough time), mine is basically a costs-of-adjustment argument.

[22] In the construction of the bank loans series, data from weekly reporting member banks (which held about 40 percent of all bank loans) were used to interpolate between less frequent aggregate observations. Note that, for our purposes, looking at the change in loans is preferable to considering the stock of real loans outstanding: In a regime of nominally contracted debt and sharp unanticipated deflation, stability of the stock of real debt does *not* signal a comfort-able situation for borrowers.

able as output. For example, except for a brief period of liquidation of speculation loans after the stock market crash, credit outstanding declined very
little before October 1930—this despite a 25 percent fall in industrial production that had occurred by that time. With the first banking crisis of
November 1930, however, a long period of credit contraction was initiated.
The shrinkage of credit shared the rhythm of the banking crises; for example, in October 1931, the worst month for bank failure before the bank
holiday, net credit reduction was a record 31 percent of personal income.[23]

The fall in bank loans after November 1930 was not simply a balance
sheet reflection of the decline in deposits. Column 5 in Table 1 gives the
monthly ratio of outstanding bank loans to the sum of demand and time
deposits. This ratio declined sharply as banks switched out of loans and into
more liquid investments.

The perception that the banking crises and the associated scrambles for
liquidity exerted a deflationary force on bank credit was shared by writers of
the time. A 1932 National Industrial Conference Board survey of credit
conditions reported that "During 1930, the shrinkage of commercial loans
no more than reflected business recession. During 1931 and the first half of
1932 (the period studied), it unquestionably represented pressure by banks
on customers for repayment of loans and refusal by banks to grant new
loans" (p. 28). Other contemporary sources tended to agree (see, for example, Chandler, 1971, pp. 233–39, for references).

Two other observations about the contraction of bank credit can be
made. First, the class of borrowers most affected by credit reductions were
households, farmers, unincorporated businesses, and small corporations; this
group had the highest direct or indirect reliance on bank credit. Second, the
contraction of bank credit was twice as large as that of other major countries, even those which experienced comparable output declines (Klebaner,
p. 145).

The fall in bank loans outstanding was partly offset by the relative expansion of alternative forms of credit. In the area of consumer finance, retail
merchants, service creditors, and nonbank lending agencies improved their
position relative to banks and primarily bank-supported installment finance
companies (Rolf Nugent, 1939, pp. 114–16). Small firms during this period
significantly reduced their traditional reliance on banks in favor of trade
credit (Charles Merwin, 1942, pp. 5 and 75). But, as argued above, in a
world with transactions costs and the need to discriminate among borrowers, these shifts in the loci of credit intermediation must have at least

---

[23] The effect of bank failures on credit outstanding is somewhat exaggerated by the fact that
the credit contraction measure includes the loans of suspending banks that were not transferred
to other banks; however, I estimate that this accounting convention is responsible for less than
one-eighth of the total (measured) credit contraction between October 1930 and February
1933.

temporarily reduced the efficiency of the credit allocation process, thereby raising the effective cost of credit to potential borrowers.

B. The Effect of Bankruptcies on the CCI

I turn now to a brief discussion of the impact of the increase in defaults and bankruptcies during this period on the cost of credit intermediation.

The very existence of bankruptcy proceedings, rather than being an obvious or natural phenomenon, raises deep questions of economic theory. Why, for example, do the creditor and defaulted debtor make the payments to third parties (lawyers, administrators) that these proceedings entail, instead of somehow agreeing to divide those payments between themselves? In a complete-markets world, bankruptcy would never be observed; this is because complete state-contingent loan agreements would uniquely define each party's obligations in all possible circumstances, rendering third-party arbitration unnecessary. That we do observe bankruptcies, in our incomplete-markets world, suggests that creditors and debtors have found the combination of simple loan arrangements and *ex post* adjudication by bankruptcy (when necessary) to be cheaper than attempting to write and enforce complete state-contingent contracts.

To be more concrete, let us use the "good borrower-bad borrower" example. In writing a loan contract with a potential borrower, the bank has two polar options. First, it might try to approximate the complete state-contingent contract by making the borrower's actions part of the agreement and by allowing repayment to depend on the outcome of the borrower's project. This contract, if properly written and enforced, would completely eliminate the possibility of either side not being able to meet its obligations; its obvious drawback is the cost of monitoring which it involves. The bank's other option is to write a very simple agreement ("payment of such-amount to be made on such-date"), then to make the loan only if it believes that the borrower is likely to repay. The second approach usually dominates the first, of course, especially for small borrowers.

A device which makes the cost advantage of the simpler approach even greater is the use of collateral. If the borrower has wealth that can be attached by the bank in the event of nonpayment, the bank's risk is low. Moreover, the threat of loss of collateral provides the right incentives for borrowers to use loans only for profitable projects. Thus, the combination of collateral and simple loan contracts helps to create a low effective CCI.

A useful way to think of the 1930–33 debt crisis is as the progressive erosion of borrowers' collateral relative to debt burdens. As the representative borrower became more and more insolvent, banks (and other lenders as well) faced a dilemma. Simple, noncontingent loans faced increasingly higher risks of default; yet a return to the more complex type of contract involved many other costs. Either way, debtor insolvency necessarily raised the CCI for banks.

One way for banks to adjust to a higher CCI is to increase the rate that they charge borrowers. This may be counterproductive, however, if higher interest charges increase the risk of default. The more usual response is for banks just not to make loans to some people that they might have lent to in better times. This was certainly the pattern in the 1930's. For example, it was reported that the extraordinary rate of default on residential mortgages forced banks and life insurance companies to "practically stop making mortgage loans, except for renewals" (Hart, p. 163). This situation precluded many borrowers, even with good projects, from getting funds, while lenders rushed to compete for existing high-grade assets. As one writer of the time, D. M. Frederiksen, put it:

> We see money accumulating at the centers, with difficulty of finding safe investment for it; interest rates dropping down lower than ever before; money available in great plenty for things that are obviously safe, but not available at all for things that are in fact safe, and which under normal conditions would be entirely safe (and there are a great many such), but which are now viewed with suspicion by lenders. (1931, p. 139)

As this quote suggests, the idea that the low yields on Treasury or blue-chip corporation liabilities during this time signalled a general state of "easy money" is mistaken; money was easy for a few safe borrowers, but difficult for everyone else.

An indicator of the strength of lender preferences for safe, liquid assets (and hence of the difficulty of risky borrowers in obtaining funds) is the yield differential between Baa corporate bonds and Treasury bonds (Table 1, column 6). Because this variable contains no adjustment for the reclassification of firms into higher risk categories, it tends to understate the true difference in yields between representative risky and safe assets. Nevertheless, this indicator showed some impressive shifts, going from 2.5 percent during 1929–30 to nearly 8 percent in mid-1932. (The differential never exceeded 3.5 percent in the sharp 1920–22 recession.) The yield differential reflected changing perceptions of default risk, of course; but note also the close relationship of the differential and the banking crises (a fact first pointed out by Friedman and Schwartz). Bank crises depressed the prices of lower-quality investments as the fear of runs drove banks into assets that could be used as reserves or for rediscounting. This effect of bank portfolio choices on an asset price could not happen in a Fama-type, complete-markets world.

Finally, it is instructive to consider the experience of a country that had a debt crisis without a banking crisis. Canada entered the Great Depression with a large external debt, much of it payable in foreign currencies. The combination of deflation and the devaluation of the Canadian dollar led to many defaults. Internally, debt problems in agriculture and in mortgage markets were as severe as in the United States, while major industries (notably pulp and paper) experienced many bankruptcies (A. E. Safarian, 1959, ch. 7). Although Canadian bankers did not face serious danger of runs, they shifted away from loans to safer assets. This shift toward safety and liquidity, though less pronounced than in the U.S. case, drew criticism from all facets of Canadian society. The *American Banker* of December 6, 1932, reported the following complaint from a non-populist Canadian politician:

> The chief criticism of our present system appears to be that in good times credit is expanded to great extremes . . . but, when the pinch of hard times is first being felt, credit is suddenly and drastically restricted by the banks . . . At the present time, loans are only being made when the banks have a very wide margin of security and every effort is being made to collect outstanding loans. All our banks are reaching out in an endeavor to liquefy their assets. . . . (p. 1)

Canadian lenders other than banks also tried to retrench: According to the *Financial Post*, May 14, 1932, "Insurance, trust, and loan companies were increasingly unwilling to lend funds with real estate and rental values falling, a growing number of defaults of interest and principal, the increasing burden of property taxes, and legislation which adversely affected creditors" (quoted in Safarian, p. 130).

More careful study of the Canadian experience in the Great Depression would be useful. However, on first appraisal, that experience does not seem to be inconsistent with the point that even good borrowers may find it more difficult or costly to obtain credit when there is extensive insolvency. The debt crisis should be added to the banking crises as a potential source of disruption of the credit system.

III. Credit Markets and Macroeconomic Performance

If it is taken as given that the financial crises during the depression did interfere with the normal flows of credit, it still must be shown how this might have had an effect on the course of the aggregate economy.

There are many ways in which problems in credit markets might potentially affect the macroeconomy. Several of these could be grouped under the heading of "effects on aggregate supply." For example, if credit flows are dammed up, potential borrowers in the economy may not be able to secure funds to undertake worthwhile activities or investments; at the same time, savers may have to devote their funds to inferior uses. Other possible problems resulting from poorly functioning credit markets include a reduced feasibility of effective risk sharing and greater difficulties in funding large, indivisible projects. Each of these might limit the economy's productive capacity.

These arguments are reminiscent of some ideas advanced by John Gurley and E. S. Shaw (1955), Ronald McKinnon (1973), and others in an economic development context. The claim of this literature is that immature or repressed financial sectors cause the "fragmentation" of less developed economies, reducing the effective set of production possibilities available to the society.

Did the financial crisis of the 1930's turn the United States into a "temporarily underdeveloped economy" (to use Bob Hall's felicitous phrase)? Although this possibility is intriguing, the answer to the question is probably no. While many businesses did suffer drains of working capital and investment funds, most larger corporations entered the decade with sufficient cash and liquid reserves to finance operations and any desired expansion (see, for example, Friedrich Lutz, 1945). Unless it is believed that the outputs of large and of small businesses are not potentially substitutes, the aggregate supply effect must be regarded as not of great quantitative importance.

The reluctance of even cash-rich corporations to expand production during the depression suggests that consideration of the aggregate demand channel for credit market effects on output may be more fruitful. The aggregate demand argument is in fact easy to make: A higher cost of credit intermediation for some borrowers (for example, households and smaller firms) implies that, for a given *safe* interest rate, these borrowers must face a higher effective cost of credit. (Indeed, they may not be able to borrow at all.) If this higher rate applies to household and small firm borrowing but not to their saving (they may only earn the safe rate on their savings), then the effect of higher borrowing costs is unambiguously to reduce their demands for current-period goods and services. This pure substitution effect (of future for present consumption) is easily derived from the classical two-period model of savings.[24]

Assume that the behavior of borrowers unaffected by credit market problems is unchanged. Then the paragraph above implies that, for a given safe rate, an increase in the cost of credit intermediation reduces the total quantity of goods and services currently demanded. That is, the aggregate demand curve, drawn as a function of the safe rate, is shifted downward by a financial crisis. In any macroeconomic model one cares to use, this implies lower output and lower safe interest rates. Both of these outcomes characterized 1930–33, of course.

Some evidence on the magnitude of the effect of the financial market problems on aggregate output is now presented.

IV. Short-Run Macroeconomic Impacts of the Financial Crisis

This section studies the short-run or "impact" effects of the financial crisis. For this purpose, I use only monthly data on the relevant variables. In addition, rather than consider the 1929–33 episode outside of its context, I have

---

[24] The classical model may be augmented, if the reader desires, by considerations of liquidity constraints, bankruptcy costs, or risk aversion; see my 1981 paper.

widened the sample to include the entire period (January 1919–December 1941).

Section I.C above has already given some evidence of the relationship between the troubles of the financial sector and those of the economy as a whole. However, support for the thesis of this paper requires that nonmonetary effects of the financial crisis on output be distinguished from the monetary effects studied by Friedman and Schwartz. My approach will be to fit output equations using monetary variables, then to show that adding proxies for the financial crisis substantially improves the performance of these equations. Comparison of financial to totally nonfinancial sources of the Great Depression, such as those suggested by Temin, is left to future research.

To isolate the purely monetary influences on the economy, one needs a structural explanation of the money-income relationship. Lucas (1972) has presented a formal model in which monetary shocks affect production decisions by causing confusion about the price level. Influenced by this work, most recent empirical studies of the role of money have related national income to measures of "unanticipated" changes in money or prices.[25]

The most familiar way of constructing a proxy for unanticipated components of a variable is the two-step method of Robert Barro (1978), in which the residuals from a first-stage prediction equation for (say) money are employed as the independent variables in a second-stage regression. I experimented with both the Barro approach and some alternatives.[26] Since my conclusions were unaffected by choice of technique, I report here only the Barro-type results.

In the spirit of the Lucas-Barro analysis, I considered the effects of both "money shocks" and "price shocks" on output. Money shocks $(M - M^e)$ were defined as the residuals from a regression of the rate of growth of M1 on four lags of the growth rates of industrial production, wholesale prices, and M1 itself; price shocks $(P - P^e)$ were defined symmetrically.[27] I used ordinary least squares to estimate the effects of money and price shocks on the rate of growth of industrial production, relative to trend.

The basic regression results for the interwar sample period are given as equations (1) and (2) in Table 2. These two equations are of interest, independently of the other results of this paper. The estimated "Lucas supply curve," equation (2), shows an effect of price shocks on output that is statistically and economically significant. As such, it complements the results of Thomas Sargent (1976), who found a similar relationship for the postwar. The relationship of output to money surprises, equation (1), is a bit weaker. The fact that we discover a smaller role for money in the monthly data than

[25] A notable exception is Mishkin (1982).

[26] Principal alternatives tried were 1) the use of anticipated as well as unanticipated quantities as explanatory variables; and 2) reestimation of some equations by the more efficient but computationally more complex method of Andrew Abel and Mishkin (1981).

[27] The first-stage regressions were unsurprising and, for the sake of space, are not reported.

Table 2
Estimated Output Equations

---

(1) $Y_t = .623\ Y_{t-1} - .144\ Y_{t-2} + .407\ (M - M^e)_t + .141\ (M - M^e)_{t-1}$
  $\quad(10.21)\quad\quad(-2.37)\quad\quad(3.42)\quad\quad\quad\quad(1.16)$
  $\quad+ .051\ (M - M^e)_{t-2} + .144\ (M - M^e)_{t-3}$
  $\quad(0.42)\quad\quad\quad\quad(1.19)$

$\qquad\qquad s.e. = .0272\qquad D.W. = 2.02\qquad \text{Sample: } 1/19–12/41$

(2) $Y_t = .582\ Y_{t-1} - .118\ Y_{t-2} + .533\ (P - P^e)_t + .350\ (P - P^e)_{t-1}$
  $\quad(9.50)\quad\quad(-1.76)\quad\quad(5.33)\quad\quad\quad\quad(3.33)$
  $\quad+ .036\ (P - P^e)_{t-2} + .069\ (P - P^e)_{t-3}$
  $\quad(0.34)\quad\quad\quad\quad(0.66)$

$\qquad\qquad s.e. = .0260\qquad D.W. = 2.01\qquad \text{Sample: } 1/19–12/41$

(3) $Y_t = .613\ Y_{t-1} - .159\ Y_{t-2} + .332\ (M - M^e)_t + .113\ (M - M^e)_{t-1} + .110\ (M - M^e)_{t-2}$
  $\quad(9.86)\quad\quad(-2.63)\quad\quad(2.92)\quad\quad\quad\quad(0.99)\quad\quad\quad\quad(0.96)$
  $\quad+ 1.56\ (M - M^e)_{t-3} - .869E - 04\ DBANKS_t - .406E - 04\ DBANKS_{t-1}$
  $\quad(1.38)\quad\quad\quad\quad(-4.24)\quad\quad\quad\quad(-1.93)$
  $\quad- .258E - 03\ DFAILS_t - .325E - 03\ DFAILS_{t-1}$
  $\quad(-1.95)\quad\quad\quad\quad(-2.47)$

$\qquad\qquad s.e. = .0249\qquad D.W. = 1.99\qquad \text{Sample: } 1/21–12/41$

(4) $Y_t = .615\ Y_{t-1} - .131\ Y_{t-2} + .455\ (P - P^e)_t + .231\ (P - P^e)_{t-1} - .004\ (P - P^e)_{t-2}$
  $\quad(9.76)\quad\quad(-2.13)\quad\quad(3.99)\quad\quad\quad\quad(1.97)\quad\quad\quad\quad(-0.03)$
  $\quad+ .024\ (P - P^e)_{t-3} - .799E - 04\ DBANKS_t - .337E - 04\ DBANKS_{t-1}$
  $\quad(0.22)\quad\quad\quad\quad(-4.03)\quad\quad\quad\quad(-1.66)$
  $\quad- .202\ E - 03\ DFAILS_t - .242\ E - 03\ DFAILS_{t-1}$
  $\quad(-1.52)\quad\quad\quad\quad(-1.83)$

$\qquad\qquad s.e. = .0246\qquad D.W. = 1.98\qquad \text{Sample: } 1/21–2/41$

Notes: Y_t = rate of growth of industrial production (*Federal Reserve Bulletin*), relative to exponential trend. $(M - M^e)_t$ = rate of growth of M1, nominal and seasonally adjusted (Friedman and Schwartz, Table 4-1), less predicted rate of growth. $(P - P^e)_t$ = rate of growth of wholesale price index (*Federal Reserve Bulletin*), less predicted rate of growth. $DBANKS_t$ = first difference of deposits of failing banks (deflated by wholesale price index). $DFAILS_t$ = first difference of liabilities of failing businesses (deflated by wholesale price index). Data are monthly; t-statistics are shown in parentheses.

does Paul Evans (1981) is primarily the result of our inclusion of lagged values of production on the right-hand side. This inclusion seems justified both on statistical grounds and for the economic reason that costs of adjusting production can be presumed to create a serial dependence in output. Like Evans, I was not able to find effects of money (or prices) lagged more than three months.

While these regression results exhibit statistical significance and the expected signs for coefficients, they are disappointing in the following sense: When equations (1) and (2) are used to perform dynamic simulations of the path of output between mid-1930 and the bank holiday of March 1933, they capture no more than half of the total decline of output during the period. This is the basis of the comment in the introduction that the declines in money seem "quantitatively insufficient" to explain what happened to output in 1930–33.

Given the basic regressions (1) and (2), the next step was to examine the effects of including proxies for the nonmonetary financial impact as explanators of output. Based on the earlier analysis of this paper, the most obvious such proxies are the deposits of failing banks and the liabilities of failing businesses.

A preliminary problem with the bank deposits series that needs to be discussed is the value for March 1933, the month of the bank holiday. As can be seen in Table 1, the deposits of banks suspended in March 1933 is seven times that of the next worse month. The question arises if any adjustment should be made to that figure before running the regressions.

We believe that it would be a mistake to eliminate totally the bank holiday episode from the sample. According to contemporary accounts, rather than being an orderly and planned-in-advance policy, the imposition of the holiday was a forced response to the most panicky and chaotic financial conditions of the period. The deposits of suspended banks figure for March, as large as it is, reflects not all closed banks but only those not licensed to reopen by June 30, 1933. Of these banks, most were liquidated or placed in receivership; less than 25 percent had been licensed to reopen as of December 31, 1936.[28] Qualitatively, then, the March 1933 episode resembled the earlier crises; it would be throwing away information not to include in some way the effects of this crisis and of its resolution on the economy.

On the other hand, the mass closing of banks by government action probably created less confusion and fear of future crises than would have a similar number of suspensions occurring without government intervention. As a conservative compromise, I assumed that the "supervised" bank closings of March 1933 had the same effect as an "unsupervised" bank crisis involving 15 percent as much in frozen deposits. This scales down the March 1933 episode to about the size of the events of October 1931. The sensitivity of the results to this assumption is as follows: increasing the amount of importance attributed to the March 1933 crisis raises the magnitude and statistical significance of the measured effects of the financial crises on output. (It is in this sense that the 15 percent figure is conservative.) However, the bank failure coefficients in the regressions retained high significance even when less weight was given to March 1933.

I turn now to the results of adding (real) deposits of failing banks and

[28] *Federal Reserve Bulletin*, 1937, pp. 866–67.

liabilities of failing businesses to the output equations (see equations (3) and (4) in Table 2). The sample period begins in 1921 because of the un-availability of data on monthly bank failures before then. In both regressions, current and lagged first differences of the added variables enter the explanation of the growth rate of industrial production (relative to trend) with the expected sign and, taken jointly, with a high level of statistical significance. The magnitudes and significance of the coefficients of money and price shocks are not much changed. This provides at least a tentative confirmation that nonmonetary effects of the financial crisis augmented monetary effects in the short-run determination of output.

Some alternative proxies for the nonmonetary component of the financial crisis were also tried. For the sake of space, only a summary of these results is given. 1) To examine the direct effects of the contraction of bank credit on the economy, I began by regressing the rate of growth of bank loans on current and lagged values of suspended bank deposits and of failing business liabilities. (This regression indicated a powerful negative effect of financial crisis on bank loans.) The fitted series from this regression was used as a proxy for the portion of the credit contraction induced by the financial crisis. In the presence of money or price shocks, the effect of a decline in this variable on output was found to be negative for two months, positive for the next two months, then strongly negative for the fifth and sixth months after the decline. For the period from 1921 until the bank holiday, and with monetary variables included, the total effect of credit contraction on output (as measured by the sum of lag coefficients in a polynomial distributed lag) was large (comparable to the monetary effect), negative, and significant at the 95 percent level. For the entire interwar sample, however, the statistical significance of this variable was much reduced. This last result is due to the fact that the recovery of 1933–41 was financed by nonbank sources, with bank loans remaining at a low level.

2) Another proxy for the financial crisis that was tried was the differential between Baa corporate bond yields and the yields on U.S. bonds. As described in Section I.C, this variable responded strongly to both bank crises and the problems of debtors, and as such was a sensitive indicator of financial market conditions. The yield differential variable turned out to enter very strongly as an explanator of current and future output growth, overall and in every subsample. As much of this predictive power was no doubt due to pure financial market anticipations of future output declines, I also put the differential variable through a first-stage regression on the liabilities of bank and business failures. Assuming that these latter variables themselves were not determined by anticipations of future output declines (see below), the use of the fitted series from this regression "purged" the differential variable of its pure anticipatory component. The fitted series entered the output equations less strongly than the raw series, but it retained the right sign and statistical significance at the 95 percent confidence level.

In almost every case, then, the addition of proxies for the general financial crisis improved the purely monetary explanation of short-run (monthly) output movements. This finding was robust to the obvious experiments. For example, with the above-noted exception of the credit variable in 1933–41, coefficients remained roughly stable over subsamples. Another experiment was to include free dummy variables for each quarter from 1931:I to 1932:IV in the above regressions. The purpose of this was to test the suggestion that our results are only a reflection of the fact that both the output and financial crisis variables "moved a lot" during 1930–33. The rather surprising discovery was that the inclusion of the dummies *increased* the magnitude and statistical significance of the coefficients on bank and business failures. Finally, the economic significance of the results was tested by using the various estimated equations to run dynamic simulations of monthly levels of industrial production (relative to trend) for mid-1930 to March 1933. Relative to the pure money-shock and price-shock simulations described above, the equations including financial crisis proxies did well. Equations (3) and (4) reduced the mean squared simulation error over (1) and (2) by about 50 percent. The other (nonreported) equations did better; for example, those using the yield differential variable reduced the MSE of simulation from 90 to 95 percent.

These results are promising. However, a caveat must be added: To conclude that the observed correlations support the theory outlined in this paper requires an additional assumption, that failures of banks and commercial firms are not caused by anticipations of (future) changes in output. To the extent that, say, bank runs are caused by the receipt of bad news about next month's industrial production, the fact that bank failures tend to lead production declines does not prove that the bank problems are helping to cause the declines.[29]

While it may not be possible to convince the determined skeptic that bank and business failures are not purely anticipatory phenomena, a good case can be made against that position. For example, while in some cases a bad sales forecast may induce a firm to declare bankruptcy, more often that option is forced by insolvency (a result of past business conditions). For banks, it might well be argued that not only are failures relatively independent of anticipations about output, but that they are not simply the product of current and past output performance either: First, banking crises had never previous to this time been a necessary result of declines in output.[30] Second, Friedman and Schwartz, as well as other writers, have identified specific events that were important sources of bank runs during 1930–33. These include the revelation of scandal at the Bank of the United States (a

[29] Actually, a similar criticism might be made of Barro's work and my own money and price regressions.

[30] Philip Cagan (1965) makes this point; see pp. 216, 227–28. The 1920–22 recession, for example, did not generate any banking problems.

private bank, which in December 1930 became the largest bank to fail up to that time); the collapse of the Kreditanstalt in Austria and the ensuing financial panics in central Europe; Britain's going off gold; the exposure of huge pyramiding schemes in the United States and Europe; and others, all connected very indirectly (if at all) with the path of industrial production in the United States.

If it is accepted that bank suspensions and business bankruptcies were the product of factors beyond pure anticipations of output decline, then the evidence of this section supports the view that nonmonetary aspects of the financial crisis were at least part of the propagatory mechanism of the Great Depression. If it is further accepted that the financial crisis contained large exogenous components (there is evidence for this in the case of the banking panics), then there are elements of causality in the story as well.

V. Persistence of the Financial Crisis

The claim was made in the introduction that my theory seems capable, unlike the major alternatives, of explaining the unusual length and depth of the Great Depression. In the previous section, I attempted to deal with the issue of depth; simulations of the estimated regressions suggested that the combined monetary and nonmonetary effects of the financial crisis can explain much of the severity of the decline in output. In this section, the question of the length of the Great Depression is addressed.

As a matter of theory, the duration of the credit effects described in Section II above depends on the amount of time it takes to 1) establish new or revive old channels of credit flow after a major disruption, and 2) rehabilitate insolvent debtors. Since these processes may be difficult and slow, the persistence of nonmonetary effects of financial crisis has a plausible basis. (In contrast, persistence of purely monetary effects relies on the slow diffusion of information or unexplained stickiness of wages and prices.) Of course, plausibility is not enough; some evidence on the speed of financial recovery should be adduced.

After struggling through 1931 and 1932, the financial system hit its low point in March 1933, when the newly elected President Roosevelt's "bank holiday" closed down most financial intermediaries and markets. March 1933 was a watershed month in several ways: It marked not only the beginning of economic and financial recovery but also the introduction of truly extensive government involvement in all aspects of the financial system.[31] It might be argued that the federally directed financial rehabilitation—which took strong measures against the problems of both creditors and debtors—

---

[31] See Chandler (1970), ch. 15, and Friedman and Schwartz, ch. 8.

was the only major New Deal program that successfully promoted economic recovery.[32] In any case, the large government intervention is prima facie evidence that by this time the public had lost confidence in the self-correcting powers of the financial structure.

Although the government's actions set the financial system on its way back to health, recovery was neither rapid nor complete. Many banks did not reopen after the holiday, and many that did open did so on a restricted basis or with marginally solvent balance sheets. Deposits did not flow back into the banks in great quantities until 1934, and the government (through the Reconstruction Finance Corporation and other agencies) had to continue to pump large sums into banks and other intermediaries. Most important, however, was a noticeable change in attitude among lenders; they emerged from the 1930–33 episode chastened and conservative. Friedman and Schwartz (pp. 449–62) have documented the shift of banks during this time away from making loans toward holding safe and liquid investments. The growing level of bank liquidity created an illusion (as Friedman and Schwartz pointed out) of easy money; however, the combination of lender reluctance and continued debtor insolvency interfered with credit flows for several years after 1933.

Evidence of postholiday credit problems is not hard to find. For example, small businesses, which (as I have noted) suffered disporportionately during the Contraction, had continuing difficulties with credit during recovery. Lewis Kimmel (1939) carried out a survey of credit availability during 1933–38 as a companion to the National Industrial Conference Board's 1932 survey. His conclusions are generally sanguine (this may reflect the fact that the work was commissioned by the American Bankers Association). However, his survey results (p. 65) show that, of responding manufacturing firms normally dependent on banks, refusal or restriction of bank credit was reported by 30.2 percent of very small firms (capitalization less than $50,000); 14.3 percent of small firms ($50,001–$500,000); 10.3 percent of medium firms ($500,001–$1,000,000); and 3.2 percent of the largest companies (capital over $1 million). (The corresponding results from the 1932 NICB survey were 41.3, 22.2, 12.5, and 9.7 percent.)

Two well-known economists, Hardy and Viner, conducted a credit survey in the Seventh Federal Reserve District in 1934–35. Based on "intensive coverage of 2600 individual cases," they found "a genuine unsatisfied demand for credit by solvent borrowers, many of whom could make economically sound use of working capital. . . . The total amount of this unsatisfied demand for credit is a significant factor, among many others, in retarding

---

[32] E. Cary Brown (1956) has argued that New Deal fiscal policy was not very constructive. A paper by Michael Weinstein in Brunner (1981) points out counterproductive aspects of the N.R.A.

business recovery." They added, "So far as small business is concerned, the difficulty in getting bank credit has increased more, as compared with a few years ago, than has the difficulty of getting trade credit." (These passages are quoted in W. L. Stoddard, 1940.)

Finally, another credit survey for the 1933–38 period was done by the Small Business Review Committee for the U.S. Department of Commerce. This study surveyed 6,000 firms with between 21 and 150 employees. From these they chose a special sample of 600 companies "selected because of their high ratings by a standard commercial rating agency." Even within the elite sample, 45 percent of the firms reported difficulty in securing funds for working capital purposes during this period; and 75 percent could not obtain capital or long-term loan requirements through regular markets. (See Stoddard.)

The reader may wish to view the American Bankers Association and Small Business Review Committee surveys as lower and upper bounds, with the Hardy-Viner study in the middle. In any case, the consensus from surveys, as well as the opinion of careful students such as Chandler, is that credit difficulties for small business persisted for at least two years after the bank holiday.[33]

Home mortgage lending was another important area of credit activity. In this sphere, private lenders were even more cautious after 1933 than in business lending. They had a reason for conservatism; while business failures fell quite a bit during the recovery, real estate defaults and foreclosures continued high through 1935.[34] As has been noted, some traditional mortgage lenders nearly left the market: life insurance companies, which made $525 million in mortgage loans in 1929, made $10 million in new loans in 1933 and $16 million in 1934.[35] During this period, mortgage loans that were made by private institutions went only to the very best potential borrowers. Evidence for this is the sharp drop in default rates of loans made in the early 1930's as compared to loans made in earlier years (see Carl Behrens, 1952, p. 11); this decline was too large to be explained by the improvement in business conditions alone.

To the extent that the home mortgage market did function in the years immediately following 1933, it was largely due to the direct involvement of the federal government. Besides establishing some important new institutions (such as the FSLIC and the system of federally chartered savings and loans), the government "readjusted" existing debts, made investments in the shares of thrift institutions, and substituted for recalcitrant private institutions in the provision of direct credit. In 1934, the government-sponsored

[33] See Chandler (1970), pp. 150–51.
[34] U.S. Department of Commerce (1975), series N301.
[35] U.S. Department of Commerce (1975), N282.

Home Owners' Loan Corporation made 71 percent of all mortgage loans extended.[36]

Similar conditions obtained for farm credit and in other markets, but space does not permit this to be pursued here. Summarizing the reading of all of the evidence by economists and by other students of the period, it seems safe to say that the return of the private financial system to normal conditions after March 1933 was not rapid; and that the financial recovery would have been more difficult without extensive government intervention and assistance. A moderate estimate is that the U.S. financial system operated under handicap for above five years (from the beginning of 1931 to the end of 1935), a period which covers most of the time between the recessions of 1929–30 and 1937–38. This is consistent with the claim that the effects of financial crisis can help explain the persistence of the depression.

VI. International Aspects

The Great Depression was a worldwide phenomenon; banking crises, though occurring in a number of important countries besides the United States, were not so ubiquitous. A number of large countries had no serious domestic banking problems, yet experienced severe drops in real income in the early 1930's. Can this be made consistent with the important role we have ascribed to the financial crisis in the United States? A complete answer would require another paper; but I offer some observations:

1) The experience of different countries and the mix of depressive forces each faced varied significantly. For example, Britain, suffering from an overvalued pound, had high unemployment throughout the 1920's; after leaving gold in 1931, it was one of the first countries to recover. The biggest problems of food and raw materials exporters were falling prices and the drying up of overseas markets. Thus we need not look to the domestic financial system as an important cause in every case.

2) The countries in which banking crises occurred (the United States, Germany, Austria, Hungary, and others) were among the worst hit by the depression. Moreover, these countries held a large share of world trade and output. The United States alone accounted for almost half of world industrial output in 1925–29, and its imports of basic raw materials and foodstuffs in 1927–28 made up almost 40 percent of the trade in these commodities.[37] The reduction of imports as these economies weakened exerted downward pressure on trading partners.

3) There were interesting parallels between the troubles of the domestic financial system and those of the international system. One of the Federal

[36] U.S. Department of Commerce (1975), N278 and N283.
[37] U.S. Department of Commerce (1947), pp. 29–31.

Reserve's proudest accomplishments had been the establishment, during the 1920's, of an international gold-exchange standard. Unfortunately, like domestic banking, the gold-exchange standard had the instability of a fractional-reserve system. International reserves included not only gold but also foreign currencies, notably the dollar and the pound; for countries other than the United States and the United Kingdom, foreign exchange was 35 percent of total reserves.

In 1931, the expectations that the international financial system would collapse became self-fulfilling. A general attempt to convert currencies into gold drove one currency after another off the gold-exchange standard. Restrictions on the movement of capital or gold were widely imposed. By 1932, only the United States and a small number of other countries remained on gold.

As the fall of the gold standard parallelled domestic bank failures, the domestic insolvency problem had an international analogue as well. Largely due to fixed exchange rates, the deflation of prices was worldwide. Countries with large nominal debts, notably agricultural exporters (the case of Canada has been mentioned), became unable to pay. Foreign bond values in the United States were extremely depressed.

As in the domestic economy, these problems disrupted the worldwide mechanism of credit. International capital flows were reduced to a trickle. This represented a serious problem for many countries.

To summarize these observations: the fact that the Great Depression hit countries which did not have banking crises does not preclude the possibility that banking and debt problems were important in the United States (or, for that matter, that countries with strong banks had problems with debtor insolvency). Moreover, my analysis of the domestic financial system may be able to shed light on some of the international financial difficulties of the period.

VII. Conclusion

Did the financial collapse of the early 1930's have real effects on the macroeconomy, other than through monetary channels? The evidence is at least not inconsistent with this proposition. However, a stronger reason for giving this view consideration is the one stated in the introduction: this theory has hope of achieving a reconciliation of the obvious suboptimality of this period with the postulate of reasonably rational, market-constrained agents. The solution to this paradox lies in recognizing that economic institutions, rather than being a "veil," can affect costs of transactions and thus market opportunities and allocations. Institutions which evolve and perform well in normal times may become counterproductive during periods when exogenous shocks or policy mistakes drive the economy off course. The malfunctioning of financial institutions during the early 1930's exemplifies this point.

References

Abel, Andrew and Mishkin, Frederic, "An Integrated View of Tests of Rationality, Market Efficiency, and the Short-Run Neutrality of Monetary Policy," Working Paper 726, National Bureau of Economic Research, 1981.

Barro, Robert, "Unanticipated Money, Output, and the Price Level in the United States," *Journal of Political Economy*, August 1978, 86, 549–80.

Behrens, Carl, *Commercial Bank Activities in Urban Mortgage Financing*, New York: National Bureau of Economic Research, 1952.

Bernanke, Ben, "Bankruptcy, Liquidity, and Recession," *American Economic Review Proceedings*, May 1981, 71, 155–59.

Brown, E. Carey, "Fiscal Policy in the 'Thirties: A Reappraisal," *American Economic Review*, December 1956, 46, 857–79.

Brunner, Karl, *The Great Depression Revisited*, Boston: Martinus Nijhoff, 1981.

Cagan, Philip, *Determinants and Effects of Changes in the Stock of Money, 1875–1960*, New York: National Bureau of Economic Research, 1965.

Chandler, Lester, *America's Greatest Depression*, New York: Harper & Row, 1970.

——, *American Monetary Policy, 1928–1941*, New York: Harper & Row, 1971.

Clark, Evans, *The Internal Debts of the United States*, New York: Macmillan Co., 1933.

Cone, Kenneth, "Regulation of Depository Financial Intermediaries," unpublished doctoral dissertation, Stanford University, 1982.

Diamond, Douglas and Dybvig, Philip, "Bank Runs, Deposit Insurance, and Liquidity," mimeo., University of Chicago, 1981.

Evans, Paul, "An Econometric Analysis of the Causes of the Great Depression in the U.S.," mimeo., Stanford University, 1981.

Fabricant, Solomon, *Profits, Losses, and Business Assets, 1929–1934*, Bulletin 55, National Bureau of Economic Research, 1935.

Fama, Eugene, "Banking in the Theory of Finance," *Journal of Monetary Economics*, January 1980, 6, 39–57.

Fisher, Irving, "The Debt-Deflation Theory of Great Depressions," *Econometrica*, October 1933, 1, 337–57.

Flood, Robert and Garber, Peter, "A Systematic Banking Collapse in a Perfect Foresight World," Working Paper No. 691, National Bureau of Economic Research, 1981.

Frederiksen, D. M., "Two Financial Roads Leading Out of Depression," *Harvard Business Review*, October 1931, 10, 131–48.

Friedman, Benjamin, "Debt and Economic Activity in the United States," Working Paper No. 704, National Bureau of Economic Research, 1981.

Friedman, Milton, and Schwartz, Anna J., *A Monetary History of the United States, 1867–1960*, Princeton: Princeton University Press, 1963.

Goldsmith, Raymond, *Financial Institutions in the American Economy Since 1900*, Princeton: Princeton University Press, 1958.

Gurley, John G. and Shaw, E. S., "Financial Aspects of Economic Development," *American Economic Review*, September 1955, 45, 515–38.

Hart, A. G., *Debts and Recovery, 1929–1937*, New York: Twentieth Century Fund, 1938.

Jaffee, Dwight, and Russell, Thomas, "Imperfect Information and Credit Rationing," *Quarterly Journal of Economics*, November 1976, 90, 651–66.

Kennedy, Susan E., *The Banking Crisis of 1933*, Lexington: University Press of Kentucky, 1973.

Kimmel, Lewis H., *The Availability of Bank Credit, 1933–1938*, New York: National Industrial Conference Board, 1939.

Kindleberger, Charles P., *Manias, Panics, and Crashes*, New York: Basic Books, 1978.

Klebaner, Benjamin, *Commercial Banking in the United States: A History*, Hinsdale: Dryden Press, 1974.

Lucas, Robert E., Jr., "Expectations and the Neutrality of Money," *Journal of Economic Theory*, April 1972, 4, 103–24.

―――, *Studies in Business Cycle Theory*, Cambridge: Massachusetts Institute of Technology Press, 1981.

Lutz, Friedrich, *Corporate Cash Balances, 1914–43*, New York: National Bureau of Economic Research, 1945.

McKinnon, Ronald J., *Money and Capital in Economic Development*, Washington: The Brookings Institution, 1973.

Merwin, Charles L., *Financing Small Corporations*, New York: National Bureau of Economic Research, 1942.

Minsky, Hyman P., "A Theory of Systematic Fragility," in E. I. Altman and A. W. Sametz, eds., *Financial Crises*, New York: Wiley-Interscience, 1977.

Mishkin, Frederic, "The Household Balance Sheet and the Great Depression," *Journal of Economic History*, December 1978, 38, 918–37.

―――, "Does Anticipated Money Matter? An Econometric Investigation," *Journal of Political Economy*, February 1982, 90, 22–51.

Nugent, Rolf, *Consumer Credit and Economic Stability*, New York: Russell Sage Foundation, 1939.

O'Hara, Maureen and Easley, David, "The Postal Savings System in Depression," *Journal of Economic History*, September 1979, 39, 741–53.

Persons, Charles E., "Credit Expansion, 1920 to 1929 and Its Lessons," *Quarterly Journal of Economics*, November 1930, 45, 94–130.

Safarian, A. E., *The Canadian Economy in the Great Depression*, Toronto: University of Toronto Press, 1959.

Sargent, Thomas J., "A Classical Macroeconometric Model for the United States," *Journal of Political Economy*, April 1976, 84, 207–38.

Stiglitz, Joseph E. and Weiss, Andrew, "Credit Rationing in Markets with Imperfect Information," *American Economic Review*, June 1981, 71, 393–410.

Stoddard, W. L., "Small Business Wants Capital," *Harvard Business Review*, Spring 1940, 18, 265–74.

Temin, Peter, *Did Monetary Forces Cause the Great Depression?*, New York: W. W. Norton, 1976.

Upham, Cyril B. and Lamke, Edwin, *Closed and Distressed Banks: A Study in Public Administration*, Washington: The Brookings Institution, 1934.

Board of Governors of the Federal Reserve System, *Banking and Monetary Statistics*, 1943.

Federal Reserve Bulletin, various issues.

National Industrial Conference Board, *The Availability of Bank Credit*, New York, 1932.

Survey of Current Business, various issues.

U.S. Department of Commerce, *Historical Statistics of the United States*, Washington: USGPO, 1975.

——, *National Income*, Washington: USGPO, 1954.

——, *The United States in the World Economy*, Washington: USGPO, 1947.

Three

The Gold Standard, Deflation, and Financial Crisis in the Great Depression: An International Comparison

WITH HAROLD JAMES

1. Introduction

Recent research on the causes of the Great Depression has laid much of the blame for that catastrophe on the doorstep of the international gold standard. In his new book, Temin (1989) argues that structural flaws of the interwar gold standard, in conjunction with policy responses dictated by the gold standard's "rules of the game," made an international monetary contraction and deflation almost inevitable. Eichengreen and Sachs (1985) have presented evidence that countries which abandoned the gold standard and the associated contractionary monetary policies recovered from the Depression more quickly than countries that remained on gold. Research by Hamilton (1987, 1988) supports the propositions that contractionary monetary policies in France and the United States initiated the Great Slide, and that the defense of gold standard parities added to the deflationary pressure.[1]

The gold standard-based explanation of the Depression (which we will elaborate in section 2) is in most respects compelling. The length and depth of the deflation during the late 1920s and early 1930s strongly suggest a monetary origin, and the close correspondence (across both space and time) between deflation and nations' adherence to the gold standard shows the power of that system to transmit contractionary monetary shocks. There is also a high correlation in the data between deflation (falling prices) and

Reprinted with permission from R. Glenn Hubbard, ed., *Financial Markets and Financial Crises*, (Chicago: University of Chicago Press, 1991). Copyright © 1991 by the National Bureau of Economic Research. All rights reserved.

The authors thank David Fernandez, Mark Griffiths, and Holger Wolf for invaluable research assistance. Support was provided by the National Bureau of Economic Research and the National Science Foundation.

[1] The original diagnosis of the Depression as a monetary phenomenon was of course made in Friedman and Schwartz (1963). We find the more recent work, though focusing to a greater degree on international aspects of the problem, to be essentially complementary to the Friedman-Schwartz analysis.

depression (falling output), as the previous authors have noted and as we will demonstrate again below.

If the argument as it has been made so far has a weak link, however, it is probably the explanation of how the deflation induced by the malfunctioning gold standard caused depression; that is, what was the source of this massive monetary non-neutrality?[2] The goal of our paper is to try to understand better the mechanisms by which deflation may have induced depression in the 1930s. We consider several channels suggested by earlier work, in particular effects operating through real wages and through interest rates. Our focus, however, is on a channel of transmission that has been largely ignored by the recent gold standard literature; namely, the disruptive effect of deflation on the financial system.

Deflation (and the constraints on central bank policy imposed by the gold standard) was an important cause of banking panics, which occurred in a number of countries in the early 1930s. As discussed for the case of the United States by Bernanke (1983), to the extent that bank panics interfere with normal flows of credit, they may affect the performance of the real economy; indeed, it is possible that economic performance may be affected even without major panics, if the banking system is sufficiently weakened. Because severe banking panics are the form of financial crisis most easily identified empirically, we will focus on their effects in this paper. However, we do not want to lose sight of a second potential effect of falling prices on the financial sector, which is "debt deflation" (Fisher 1933; Bernanke 1983; Bernanke and Gertler 1990). By increasing the real value of nominal debts and promoting insolvency of borrowers, deflation creates an environment of financial distress in which the incentives of borrowers are distorted and in which it is difficult to extend new credit. Again, this provides a means by which falling prices can have real effects.

To examine these links between deflation and depression, we take a comparative approach (as did Eichengreen and Sachs). Using an annual data set covering twenty-four countries, we try to measure (for example) the differences between countries on and off the gold standard, or between countries experiencing banking panics and those that did not. A weakness of our approach is that, lacking objective indicators of the seriousness of financial problems, we are forced to rely on dummy variables to indicate periods of crisis. Despite this problem, we generally do find an important role for financial crises—particularly banking panics—in explaining the link between falling prices and falling output. Countries in which, for institutional or historical reasons, deflation led to panics or other severe banking problems

---

[2] Eichengreen and Sachs (1985) discuss several mechanisms and provide some cross-country evidence, but their approach is somewhat informal and they do not consider the relative importance of the different effects.

had significantly worse depressions than countries in which banking was more stable. In addition, there may have been a feedback loop through which banking panics, particularly those in the United States, intensified the severity of the worldwide deflation. Because of data problems, we do not provide direct evidence of the debt-deflation mechanism; however, we do find that much of the apparent impact of deflation on output is unaccounted for by the mechanisms we explicitly consider, leaving open the possibility that debt deflation was important.

The rest of the paper is organized as follows. Section 2 briefly recapitulates the basic case against the interwar gold standard, showing it to have been a source of deflation and depression, and provides some new evidence consistent with this view. Section 3 takes a preliminary look at some mechanisms by which deflation may have been transmitted to depression. In section 4, we provide an overview of the financial crises that occurred during the interwar period. Section 5 presents and discusses our main empirical results on the effects of financial crisis in the 1930s, and section 6 concludes.

2. The Gold Standard and Deflation

In this section we discuss, and provide some new evidence for, the claim that a mismanaged interwar gold standard was responsible for the worldwide deflation of the late 1920s and early 1930s.

The gold standard—generally viewed at the time as an essential source of the relative prosperity of the late nineteenth and early twentieth centuries—was suspended at the outbreak of World War I. Wartime suspension of the gold standard was not in itself unusual; indeed, Bordo and Kydland (1990) have argued that wartime suspension, followed by a return to gold at prewar parities as soon as possible, should be considered part of the gold standard's normal operation. Bordo and Kydland pointed out that a reputation for returning to gold at the prewar parity, and thus at something close to the prewar price level, would have made it easier for a government to sell nominal bonds and would have increased attainable seignorage. A credible commitment to the gold standard thus would have had the effect of allowing war spending to be financed at a lower total cost.

Possibly for these reputational reasons, and certainly because of widespread unhappiness with the chaotic monetary and financial conditions that followed the war (there were hyperinflations in central Europe and more moderate but still serious inflations elsewhere), the desire to return to gold in the early 1920s was strong. Of much concern however was the perception that there was not enough gold available to satisfy world money demands without deflation. The 1922 Economic and Monetary Conference at Genoa addressed this issue by recommending the adoption of a gold exchange standard, in which convertible foreign exchange reserves (principally dollars and pounds) as well as gold would be used to back national money supplies, thus "economizing" on gold. Although "key currencies" had been used as reserves before the war, the Genoa recommendations led to a more widespread and officially sanctioned use of this practice (Lindert 1969; Eichengreen 1987).

During the 1920s the vast majority of the major countries succeeded in returning to gold. (The first column of table 1 gives the dates of return for the countries in our data set.) Britain returned at the prewar parity in 1925, despite Keynes's argument that at the old parity the pound would be overvalued. By the end of 1925, out of a list of 48 currencies given by the League of Nations (1926), 28 had been pegged to gold. France returned to gold gradually, following the Poincaré stabilization, although at a new parity widely believed to undervalue the franc. By the end of 1928, except for China and a few small countries on the silver standard, only Spain, Portugal, Rumania, and Japan had not been brought back into the gold standard system. Rumania went back on gold in 1929, Portugal did so in practice also in 1929 (although not officially until 1931), and Japan in December 1930. In the same month the Bank for International Settlements gave Spain a stabilization loan, but the operation was frustrated by a revolution in April 1931, carried out by republicans who, as one of the most attractive features of their program, opposed the foreign stabilization credits. Spain thus did not join the otherwise nearly universal membership of the gold standard club.

The classical gold standard of the prewar period functioned reasonably smoothly and without a major convertibility crisis for more than thirty years. In contrast, the interwar gold standard, established between 1925 and 1928, had substantially broken down by 1931 and disappeared by 1936. An extensive literature has analyzed the differences between the classical and interwar gold standards. This literature has focused, with varying degrees of emphasis, both on fundamental economic problems that complicated trade and monetary adjustment in the interwar period and on technical problems of the interwar gold standard itself.

In terms of "fundamentals," Temin (1989) has emphasized the effects of the Great War, arguing that, ultimately, the war itself was the shock that initiated the Depression. The legacy of the war included—besides physical destruction, which was relatively quickly repaired—new political borders drawn apparently without economic rationale; substantial overcapacity in some sectors (such as agriculture and heavy industry) and undercapacity in others, relative to long-run equilibrium; and reparations claims and international war debts that generated fiscal burdens and fiscal uncertainty. Some writers (notably Charles Kindleberger) have also pointed to the fact that the prewar gold standards was a hegemonic system, with Great Britain the unquestioned center. In contrast, in the interwar period the relative decline

Table 1
Dates of Changes in Gold Standard Policies

Country	Return to Gold	Suspension of Gold Standard	Foreign Exchange Control	Devaluation
Australia	April 1925	December 1929	—	March 1930
Austria	April 1925	April 1933	October 1931	September 1931
Belgium	October 1926	—	—	March 1935
Canada	July 1926	October 1931	—	September 1931
Czechoslovakia	April 1926	—	September 1931	February 1934
Denmark	January 1927	September 1931	November 1931	September 1931
Estonia	January 1928	June 1933	November 1931	June 1933
Finland	January 1926	October 1931	—	October 1931
France	August 1926– June 1928	—	—	October 1936
Germany	September 1924	—	July 1931	—
Greece	May 1928	April 1932	September 1931	April 1932
Hungary	April 1925	—	July 1931	—
Italy	December 1927	—	May 1934	October 1936
Japan	December 1930	December 1931	July 1932	December 1931
Latvia	August 1922	—	October 1931	—
Netherlands	April 1925	—	—	October 1936
Norway	May 1928	September 1931	—	September 1931
New Zealand	April 1925	September 1931	—	April 1930
Poland	October 1927	—	April 1936	October 1936
Rumania	March 1927– February 1929	—	May 1932	—
Sweden	April 1924	September 1931	—	September 1931
Spain	—	—	May 1931	—
United Kingdom	May 1925	September 1931	—	September 1931
United States	June 1919	March 1933	March 1933	April 1933

Source: League of Nations, *Yearbook*, various dates; and miscellaneous supplementary sources.

of Britain, the inexperience and insularity of the new potential hegemon (the United States), and ineffective cooperation among central banks left no one able to take responsibility for the system as a whole.

The technical problems of the interwar gold standard included the following three:

1. *The asymmetry between surplus and deficit countries in the required monetary response to gold flows.* Temin suggests, correctly we believe, that this was the most important structural flaw of the gold standard. In theory, under the "rules of the game," central banks of countries experiencing gold inflows were supposed to assist the price-specie flow mechanism by expanding domestic money supplies and inflating, while deficit countries were supposed to reduce money supplies and deflate. In practice, the need to avoid a complete loss of reserves and an end to convertibility forced deficit countries to comply with this rule; but, in contrast, no sanction prevented surplus countries from sterilizing gold inflows and accumulating reserves indefinitely, if domestic objectives made that desirable. Thus there was a potential deflationary bias in the gold standard's operation.

This asymmetry between surplus and deficit countries also existed in the prewar period, but with the important difference that the prewar gold standard centered around the operations of the Bank of England. The Bank of England of course had to hold enough gold to ensure convertibility, but as a profit-making institution it also had a strong incentive not to hold large stocks of barren gold (as opposed to interest-paying assets). Thus the Bank managed the gold standard (with the assistance of other central banks) so as to avoid both sustained inflows and sustained outflows of gold; and, indeed, it helped ensure continuous convertibility with a surprisingly low level of gold reserves. In contrast, the two major gold surplus countries of the interwar period, the United States and France, had central banks with little or no incentive to avoid accumulation of gold.

The deflationary bias of the asymmetry in required adjustments was magnified by statutory fractional reserve requirements imposed on many central banks, especially the new central banks, after the war. While Britain, Norway, Finland, and Sweden had a fiduciary issue—a fixed note supply backed only by domestic government securities, above which 100% gold backing was required—most countries required instead that minimum gold holdings equal a fixed fraction (usually close to the Federal Reserve's 40%) of central bank liabilities. These rules had two potentially harmful effects.

First, just as required "reserves" for modern commercial banks are not really available for use as true reserves, a large portion of central bank gold holdings were immobilized by the reserve requirements and could not be used to settle temporary payments imbalances. For example, in 1929, according to the League of Nations, for 41 countries with a total gold reserve of $9,378 million, only $2,178 million were "surplus" reserves, with the rest required as cover (League of Nations 1944, 12). In fact, this overstates the quantity of truly free reserves, because markets and central banks became very worried when reserves fell within 10% of the minimum. The upshot of this is that deficit countries could lose very little gold before being forced to reduce their domestic money supplies; while, as we have noted, the absence of any maximum reserve limit allowed surplus countries to accept gold inflows without inflating.

The second and related effect of the fractional reserve requirement has to do with the relationship between gold outflows and domestic monetary contraction. With fractional reserves, the relationship between gold outflow and the reduction in the money supply was not one for one; with a 40% reserve requirement, for example, the impact on the money supply of a gold outflow was 2.5 times the external loss. So again, loss of gold could lead to an immediate and sharp deflationary impact, not balanced by inflation elsewhere.

2. *The pyramiding of reserves.* As we have noted, under the interwar gold-exchange standard, countries other than those with reserve currencies were encouraged to hold convertible foreign exchange reserves as a partial (or in some cases, as a nearly complete) substitute for gold. But these convertible

reserves were in turn usually only fractionally backed by gold. Thus, just as a shift by the public from fractionally backed deposits to currency would lower the total domestic money supply, the gold-exchange system opened up the possibility that a shift of central banks from foreign exchange reserves to gold might lower the world money supply, adding another deflationary bias to the system. Central banks did abandon foreign exchange reserves en masse in the early 1930s, when the threat of devaluation made foreign exchange assets quite risky. According to Eichengreen (1987), however, the statistical evidence is not very clear on whether central banks after selling their foreign exchange simply lowered their cover ratios, which would have had no direct effect on money supplies, or shifted into gold, which would have been contractionary. Even if the central banks responded only by lowering cover ratios, however, this would have increased the sensitivity of their money supplies to any subsequent outflow of reserves.

3. *Insufficient powers of central banks.* An important institutional feature of the interwar gold standard is that, for a majority of the important continental European central banks, open market operations were not permitted or were severely restricted. This limitation on central bank powers was usually the result of the stabilization programs of the early and mid 1920s. By prohibiting central banks from holding or dealing in significant quantities of government securities, and thus making monetization of deficits more difficult, the architects of the stabilizations hoped to prevent future inflation. This forced the central banks to rely on discount policy (the terms at which they would make loans to commercial banks) as the principal means of affecting the domestic money supply. However, in a number of countries the major commercial banks borrowed very infrequently from the central banks, implying that except in crisis periods the central bank's control over the money supply might be quite weak.

The loosening of the link between the domestic money supply and central bank reserves may have been beneficial in some cases during the 1930s, if it moderated the monetary effect of reserve outflows. However, in at least one very important case the inability of a central bank to conduct open market operations may have been quite destabilizing. As discussed by Eichengreen (1986), the Bank of France, which was the recipient of massive gold inflows until 1932, was one of the banks that was prohibited from conducting open market operations. This severely limited the ability of the Bank to translate its gold inflows into monetary expansion, as should have been done in obedience to the rules of the game. The failure of France to inflate meant that it continued to attract reserves, thus imposing deflation on the rest of the world.[3]

___

[3] To be clear, gold inflows to France did not increase the French monetary base directly, one for one; however, in the absence of supplementary open market purchases, this implied a rising

Given both the fundamental economic problems of the international economy and the structural flaws of the gold standard system, even a relatively minor deflationary impulse might have had significant repercussions. As it happened, both of the two major gold surplus countries—France and the United States, who at the time together held close to 60% of the world's monetary gold—took deflationary paths in 1928–29 (Hamilton 1987).

In the French case, as we have already noted, the deflationary shock took the form of a largely sterilized gold inflow. For several reasons—including a successful stabilization with attendant high real interest rates, a possibly undervalued franc, the lifting of exchange controls, and the perception that France was a "safe haven" for capital—beginning in early 1928 gold flooded into that country, an inflow that was to last until 1932. In 1928, France controlled about 15% of the total monetary gold held by the twenty-four countries in our data set (Board of Governors 1943); this share, already disproportionate to France's economic importance, increased to 18% in 1929, 22% in 1930, 28% in 1931, and 32% in 1932. Since the U.S. share of monetary gold remained stable at something greater than 40% of the total, the inflow to France implied significant losses of gold by countries such as Germany, Japan, and the United Kingdom.

With its accumulation of gold, France should have been expected to inflate; but in part because of the restrictions on open market operations discussed above and in part because of deliberate policy choices, the impact of the gold inflow on French prices was minimal. The French monetary base did increase with the inflow of reserves, but because economic growth led the demand for francs to expand even more quickly, the country actually experienced a wholesale price *deflation* of almost 11% between January 1929 and January 1930.

Hamilton (1987) also documents the monetary tightening in the United States in 1928, a contraction motivated in part by the desire to avoid losing gold to the French but perhaps even more by the Federal Reserve's determination to slow down stock market speculation. The U.S. price level fell about 4% over the course of 1929. A business cycle peak was reached in the United States in August 1929, and the stock market crashed in October.

The initial contractions in the United States and France were largely self-inflicted wounds; no binding external constraint forced the United States to deflate in 1929, and it would certainly have been possible for the French government to grant the Bank of France the power to conduct expansionary open market operations. However, Temin (1989) argues that, once these destabilizing policy measures had been taken, little could be done to avert

ratio of French gold reserves to monetary base. Together with the very low value of the French money multiplier, this rising cover ratio meant that the monetary expansion induced by gold flowing into France was far less significant than the monetary contractions that this inflow induced elsewhere.

deflation and depression, given the commitment of central banks to maintenance of the gold standard. Once the deflationary process had begun, central banks engaged in competitive deflation and a scramble for gold, hoping
by raising cover ratios to protect their currencies against speculative attack.
Attempts by any individual central bank to reflate were met by immediate
gold outflows, which forced the central bank to raise its discount rate and
deflate once again. According to Temin, even the United States, with its
large gold reserves, faced this constraint. Thus Temin disagrees with the
suggestion of Friedman and Schwartz (1963) that the Federal Reserve's failure to protect the U.S. money supply was due to misunderstanding of the
problem or a lack of leadership; instead, he claims, given the commitment
to the gold standard (and, presumably, the absence of effective central bank
cooperation), the Fed had little choice but to let the banks fail and the
money supply fall.

For out purposes here it does not matter much to what extent central
bank choices could have been other than what they were. For the positive
question of what caused the Depression, we need only note that a monetary
contraction began in the United States and France, and was propagated
throughout the world by the international monetary standard.[4]

If monetary contraction propagated by the gold standard was the source
of the worldwide deflation and depression, then countries abandoning the
gold standard (or never adopting it) should have avoided much of the deflationary pressure. This seems to have been the case. In an important paper,
Choudhri and Kochin (1980) documented that Spain, which never restored
the gold standard and allowed its exchange rate to float, avoided the declines in prices and output that affected other European countries. Choudhri
and Kochin also showed that the Scandinavian countries, which left gold
along with the United Kingdom in 1931, recovered from the Depression
much more quickly than other small European countries that remained
longer on the gold standard. Much of this had been anticipated in an in-
sightful essay by Haberler (1976).

Eichengreen and Sachs (1985) similarly focused on the beneficial effects
of currency depreciation (i.e., abandonment of the gold standard or devaluation). For a sample of ten European countries, they showed that depreciating countries enjoyed faster growth of exports and industrial production
than countries which did not depreciate. Depreciating countries also experienced lower real wages and greater profitability, which presumably helped to
increase production. Eichengreen and Sachs argued that depreciation, in
this context, should not necessarily be thought of as a "beggar thy neighbor"
policy; because depreciations reduced constraints on the growth of world

---

[4] Temin (1989) suggests that German monetary policy provided yet another contractionary
impetus.

money supplies, they may have conferred benefits abroad as well as at home (although a coordinated depreciation presumably would have been better than the uncoordinated sequence of depreciations that in fact took place).[5]

Some additional evidence of the effects of maintaining or leaving the gold standard, much in the spirit of Eichengreen and Sachs but using data from a larger set of countries, is given in our tables 2 through 4. These tables summarize the relationships between the decision to adhere to the gold standard and some key macroeconomic variables, including wholesale price inflation (table 2), some indicators of national monetary policies (table 3), and industrial production growth (table 4). To construct these tables, we divided our sample of twenty-four countries into four categories:[6] 1) countries not on the gold standard at all (Spain) or leaving prior to 1931 (Australia and New Zealand); 2) countries abandoning the full gold standard in 1931 (14 countries); 3) countries abandoning the gold standard between 1932 and 1935 (Rumania in 1932, the Untied States in 1933, Italy in 1934, and Belgium in 1935); and 4) countries still on the full gold standard as of 1936 (France, Netherlands, Poland).[7] Tables 2 and 4 give the data for each country, as well as averages for the large cohort of countries abandoning gold in 1931, for the remnant of the gold bloc still on gold in 1936, and (for 1932–35, when there were a significant number of countries in each category) for all gold standard and non-gold standard countries. Since table 3 reports data on four different variables, in order to save space only the averages are shown.[8]

---

[5] There remains the issue of whether the differences in timing of nations' departure from the gold standard can be treated as exogenous. Eichengreen and Sachs (1985) argue that exogeneity is a reasonable assumption, given the importance of individual national experiences, institutions, and fortuitous events in the timing of each country's decision to go off gold. Strong national differences in attitudes toward the gold standard (e.g., between the Gold Bloc and the Sterling Bloc) were remarkably persistent in their influence on policy.

[6] The countries in our sample are listed in table 1. We included countries for which the League of Nations collected reasonably complete data on industrial production, price levels, and money supplies (League of Nations' *Monthly Bulletin of Statistics and Yearbooks*, various issues; see also League of Nations, *Industrialization and Foreign Trade*, 1945). Latin America, however, was excluded because of concerns about the data and our expectation that factors such as commodity prices would play a more important role for these countries. However, see Campa (forthcoming) for evidence that the gold standard transmitted deflation and depression to Latin America in a manner very similar to that observed elsewhere.

[7] We define abandonment of the gold standard broadly as occurring at the first date in which a country imposes exchange controls, devalues, or suspends gold payments; see table 1 for a list of dates. An objection to this definition is that some countries continued to try to target their exchange rates at levels prescribed by the gold standard even after "leaving" the gold standard by our criteria; Canada and Germany are two examples. We made no attempt to account for this, on the grounds that defining adherence to the gold standard by looking at variables such as exchange rates, money growth, or prices risks assuming the propositions to be shown.

[8] In constructing the grand averages taken over gold and non-gold countries, if a country abandoned the gold standard in the middle of a year, it is included in both the gold and non-

The link between deflation and adherence to the gold standard, shown in table 2, seems quite clear. As noted by Choudhri and Kochin (1980), Spain's abstention from the gold standard insulated that country from the general deflation; New Zealand and Australia, presumably because they retained links to sterling despite early abandonment of the strict gold standard, did however experience some deflation. Among countries on the gold standard as of 1931, there is a rather uniform experience of about a 13% deflation in both 1930 and 1931. But after 1931 there is a sharp divergence between those countries on and those off the gold standard. Price levels in countries off the gold standard have stabilized by 1933 (with one or two exceptions), and these countries experience mild inflations in 1934–36. In contrast, the gold standard countries continue to deflate, although at a slower rate, until the gold standard's dissolution in 1936.

With such clearly divergent price behavior between countries on and off gold, one would expect to see similarly divergent behavior in monetary policy. Table 3 compares the average behavior of the growth rates of three monetary aggregates, called for short M0, M1, and M2, and of changes in the central bank discount rate. M0 corresponds to money and notes in circulation, M1 is the sum of M0 and commercial bank deposits, and M2 is the sum of M1 and savings bank deposits.[9] The expected differences in the monetary policies of the gold and non-gold countries seem to be in the data, although somewhat less clearly than we had anticipated. In particular, despite the twelve percentage point difference in rates of deflation between gold and non-gold countries in 1932, the differences in average money growth in that year between the two classes of countries are minor; possibly, higher inflation expectations in the countries abandoning gold reduced money demand and thus became self-confirming. From 1933 through 1935, however, the various monetary indicators are more consistent with the conclusion stressed by Eichengreen and Sachs (1985), that leaving the gold

---

gold categories with weights equal to the fraction of the year spent in each category. We use simple rather than weighted averages in the tables, and similarly give all countries equal weight in regression results presented below. This was done because, for the purpose of testing hypotheses (e.g., about the relationship between deflation and depression) it seems most reasonable to treat each country (with its own currency, legal system, financial system, etc.) as the basic unit of observation and to afford each observation equal weight. If we were instead trying to measure the overall economic significance of, for example, an individual country's policy decisions, weighted averages would be more appropriate.

[9] The use of the terms M1 and M2 should not be taken too literally here, as the transactions characteristics of the assets included in each category vary considerably among countries. The key distinction between the two aggregates is that commercial banks, which were heavily involved in commercial lending, were much more vulnerable to banking panics. Savings banks, in contrast, held mostly government securities, and thus often gained deposits during panic periods.

Table 2
Log-Differences of the Wholesale Price Index

	1930	1931	1932	1933	1934	1935	1936
1. Countries not on gold standard or leaving prior to 1931							
Spain	−.00	.01	−.01	−.05	.03	.01	.02
Australia (1929)	−.12	−.11	−.01	−.00	.04	−.00	.05
New Zealand (1930)	−.03	−.07	−.03	.03	.01	.03	.01
2. Countries abandoning full gold standard in 1931							
Austria	−.11	−.07	.03	−.04	.02	−.00	−.01
Canada	−.10	−.18	−.08	.01	.06	.01	.03
Czechoslovakia	−.12	−.10	−.08	−.03	.02	.04	.00
Denmark	−.15	−.13	.02	.07	.09	.02	.05
Estonia	−.14	−.11	−.09	.02	.00	−.01	.08
Finland	−.09	−.07	.07	−.01	.01	.00	.02
Germany	−.10	−.12	−.14	−.03	.05	.03	.02
Greece	−.10	−.11	.18	.12	−.01	.02	.02
Hungary	−.14	−.05	−.01	−.14	.00	.08	.03
Japan	−.19	−.17	.05	.11	−.01	.04	.06
Latvia	−.16	−.18	.00	−.02	−.01	.05	.04
Norway	−.08	−.12	.00	−.00	.02	.03	.05
Sweden	−.14	−.09	−.02	−.02	.06	.02	.03
United Kingdom	−.17	−.18	−.04	.01	.04	.04	.06
Average	−.13	−.12	−.01	.00	.02	.03	.04
3. Countries abandoning gold standard between 1932 and 1935							
Rumania (1932)	−.24	−.26	−.11	−.03	.00	.14	.13
United States (1933)	−.10	−.17	−.12	.02	.13	.07	.01
Italy (1934)	−.11	−.14	−.07	−.09	−.02	.10	.11
Belgium (1935)	−.13	−.17	−.16	−.06	−.06	.13	.09
4. Countries still on full gold standard as of 1936							
France	−.12	−.10	−.16	−.07	−.06	−.11	.19
Netherlands	−.11	−.16	−.17	−.03	.00	−.02	.04
Poland	−.12	−.14	−.13	−.10	−.06	−.05	.02
Average	−.12	−.13	−.15	−.07	−.04	−.06	.08
5. Grand averages							
Gold standard countries			−.13	−.07	−.04	−.05	
Non-gold countries			−.01	.00	.03	.04	

Note: Data on wholesale prices are from League of Nations, *Monthly Bulletin of Statistics* and *Yearbook*, various issues. Dates in parentheses are years in which countries abandoned gold, with "abandonment" defined to include the imposition of foreign exchange controls or devaluation as well as suspension; see table 1.

Table 3
Monetary Indicators

	1930	1931	1932	1933	1934	1935	1936
1. Countries abandoning full gold standard in 1931							
M0 growth	−.04	−.02	−.07	.06	.05	.05	.08
M1 growth	.01	−.11	−.07	.02	.05	.04	.08
M2 growth	.03	−.08	−.04	.03	.05	.05	.06
Discount rate change	−0.8	0.4	−0.2	−1.2	−0.4	−0.1	−0.1
2. Countries still on full gold standard as of 1936							
M0 growth	.03	.07	−.06	−.02	.01	−.03	.03
M1 growth	.05	−.06	−.07	−.05	.01	−.06	.08
M2 growth	.08	−.00	−.02	−.02	.02	−.03	.05
Discount rate change	−1.4	−0.4	0.1	−0.4	−0.4	0.8	−0.3
3. Grand averages: Countries on gold							
M0 growth			−.04	−.03	.01	−.02	
M1 growth			−.09	−.04	−.01	−.06	
M2 growth			−.05	−.01	.01	−.02	
Discount rate change			0.2	−0.5	−0.4	0.7	
4. Grand averages: Countries off gold							
M0 growth			−.07	.05	.03	.06	
M1 growth			−.06	.01	.04	.05	
M2 growth			−.03	.02	.04	.05	
Discount rate change			−0.3	−1.0	−0.4	−0.2	

Note: M0 is money and notes in circulation. M1 is base money plus commercial bank deposits. M2 is M1 plus savings deposits. Growth rates of monetary aggregates are calculated as log-differences. The discount rate change is in percentage points. The data are from League of Nations, *Monthly Bulletin of Statistics* and *Yearbook*, various issues.

standard afforded countries more latitude to expand their money supplies and thus to escape deflation.

The basic proposition of the gold standard-based explanation of the Depression is that, because of its deflationary impact, adherence to the gold standard had very adverse consequences for real activity. The validity of this proposition is shown rather clearly by table 4, which gives growth rates of industrial production for the countries in our sample. While the countries which were to abandon the gold standard in 1931 did slightly worse in 1930 and 1931 than the nations of the Gold Bloc, subsequent to leaving gold these countries performed much better. Between 1932 and 1935, growth of industrial production in countries not on gold averaged about seven per-

Table 4
Log-Differences of the Industrial Production Index

	1930	1931	1932	1933	1934	1935	1936
1. Countries not on gold standard or leaving prior to 1931							
Spain	−.01	−.06	−.05	−.05	.01	.02	NA
Australia (1929)	−.11	−.07	.07	.10	.09	.09	.07
New Zealand (1930)	−.25	−.14	.05	.02	.13	.09	.14
2. Countries abandoning full gold standard in 1931							
Austria	−.16	−.19	−.14	.03	.11	.13	.07
Canada	−.16	−.18	−.20	.04	.20	.10	.10
Czechoslovakia	−.11	−.10	−.24	−.05	.10	.05	.14
Denmark	.08	−.08	−.09	.14	.11	.07	.04
Estonia	−.02	−.09	−.17	.05	.17	.10	.10
Finland	−.10	−.13	.19	.02	.03	.10	.09
Germany	−.15	−.24	−.24	.13	.27	.16	.12
Greece	.01	.02	−.08	.10	.12	.12	−.03
Hungary	−.06	−.08	−.06	.07	.12	.07	.10
Japan	−.05	−.03	.07	.15	.13	.10	.06
Latvia	.08	−.20	−.08	.31	.15	.05	.04
Norway	.01	−.25	.17	.01	.04	.10	.09
Sweden	.03	−.07	−.08	.02	.19	.11	.09
United Kingdom	−.08	−.10	−.00	.05	.11	.07	.09
Average	−.05	−.12	−.07	.08	.13	.10	.08
3. Countries abandoning gold standard between 1932 and 1935							
Rumania (1932)	−.03	.05	−.14	.15	.19	−.01	.06
United States (1933)	−.21	−.17	−.24	.17	.04	.13	.15
Italy (1934)	−.08	−.17	−.15	.10	.08	.16	−.07
Belgium (1935)	−.12	−.09	−.16	.04	.01	.12	.05
4. Countries still on full gold standard as of 1936							
France	−.01	−.14	−.19	.12	−.07	−.04	.07
Netherlands	.02	−.06	−.13	.07	.02	−.03	.01
Poland	−.13	−.14	−.20	.09	.12	.07	.10
Average	−.04	−.11	−.17	.10	.02	.00	.06
5. Grand averages							
Gold standard countries			−.18	.09	.03	.01	
Non-gold countries			−.06	.08	.12	.09	

Note: Data on industrial production are from League of Nations, *Monthly Bulletin of Statistics* and *Yearbook*, various issues, supplemented by League of Nations, *Industrialization and Foreign Trade*, 1945.

centage points a year better than countries remaining on gold, a very substantial effect.

In summary, data from our sample of twenty-four countries support the
view that there was a strong link between adherence to the gold standard
and the severity of both deflation and depression. The data are also consistent with the hypothesis that increased freedom to engage in monetary expansion was a reason for the better performance of countries leaving the
gold standard early in the 1930s, although the evidence in this case is a bit
less clear-cut.

3. The Link between Deflation and Depression

Given the above discussion and evidence, it seems reasonable to accept the
idea that the worldwide deflation of the early 1930s was the result of a
monetary contraction transmitted through the international gold standard.
But this raises the more difficult question of what precisely were the channels linking deflation (falling prices) and depression (falling output). This
section takes a preliminary look at some suggested mechanisms. We first
introduce here two principal channels emphasized in recent research, then
discuss the alternative of induced financial crises.

1. *Real wages.* If wages possess some degree of nominal rigidity, then falling output prices will raise real wages and lower labor demand. Downward
stickiness of wages (or of other input costs) will also lower profitability,
potentially reducing investment. This channel is stressed by Eichengreen
and Sachs (see in particular their 1986 paper) and has also been emphasized
by Newell and Symons (1988).

Some evidence on the behavior of real wages during the Depression is
presented in table 5, which is similar in format to tables 2–4. Note that
table 5 uses the wholesale price index (the most widely available price index) as the wage deflator. According to this table, there were indeed large
real wage increases in most countries in 1930 and 1931. After 1931, countries leaving the gold standard experienced a mild decline in real wages,
while real wages in gold standard countries exhibited a mild increase. These
findings are similar to those of Eichengreen and Sachs (1985).

The reliance on nominal wage stickiness to explain the real effects of the
deflation is consistent with the Keynesian tradition, but is nevertheless
somewhat troubling in this context. Given (i) the severity of the unemployment that was experienced during that time; (ii) the relative absence of
long-term contracts and the weakness of unions; and (iii) the presumption
that the general public was aware that prices, and hence the cost of living,
were falling, it is hard to understand how nominal wages could have been so
unresponsive. Wages had fallen quickly in many countries in the contrac-

Table 5
Log-Differences of the Real Wage

	1930	1931	1932	1933	1934	1935	1936
1. Countries not on gold standard or leaving prior to 1931							
Spain			not available				
Australia (1929)	.10	.01	−.05	−.04	−.03	.01	−.03
New Zealand (1930)	.03	.00	−.00	−.05	−.01	−.01	.10
2. Countries abandoning full gold standard in 1931							
Austria	.14	.05	−.04	−.00	−.05	−.03	.06
Canada	.11	.15	.00	−.06	−.05	.02	−.01
Czechoslovakia	.14	.11	.08	.02	−.04	−.05	−.00
Denmark	.17	.11	−.03	−.07	−.09	−.01	−.04
Estonia	.16	.07	.02	−.06	−.01	.06	−.03
Finland			not available				
Germany	.12	.06	−.03	−.00	−.07	−.03	−.02
Greece			not available				
Hungary	.14	−.00	−.07	.09	−.06	−.11	−.00
Japan	.05	.21	−.04	−.12	.02	−.05	−.05
Latvia	.20	.18	−.15	−.05	.01	−.05	−.02
Norway	.08	.08	.02	−.02	−.01	−.03	−.02
Sweden	.17	.09	.01	−.02	−.06	−.01	−.02
United Kingdom	.17	.16	.02	−.02	−.03	−.03	−.03
Average	.14	.11	−.02	−.03	−.04	−.03	−.02
3. Countries abandoning gold standard between 1932 and 1935							
Rumania (1932)	.20	.14	−.10	−.05	−.02	−.15	−.12
United States (1933)	.10	.13	−.01	−.03	.04	−.03	.02
Italy (1934)	.10	.07	.05	.07	−.01	−.11	−.06
Belgium (1935)	.19	.10	.07	.04	.01	−.16	−.02
4. Countries still on full gold standard as of 1936							
France	.21	.09	.12	.07	.06	.09	−.06
Netherlands	.12	.14	.09	−.02	−.04	−.01	−.06
Poland	.11	.06	.05	.00	.01	.02	−.03
Average	.15	.10	.09	.02	.01	.03	−.05
5. Grand averages							
Gold standard countries			.05	.03	.01	.02	
Non-gold countries			−.02	−.03	−.03	−.04	

Note: The real wage is the nominal hourly wage for males (skilled, if available) divided by the wholesale price index. Wage data are from the International Labour Office, *Year Book of Labor Statistics*, various issues.

tion of 1921–22. In the United States, nominal wages were maintained until the fall of 1931 (possibly by an agreement among large corporations; see O'Brien 1989), but fell sharply after that; in Germany, the government actually tried to depress wages early in the Depression. Why then do we see these large real wage increases in the data?

One possibility is measurement problems. There are a number of issues, such as changes in skill and industrial composition, that make measuring the cyclical movement in real wages difficult even today. Bernanke (1986) has argued, in the U.S. context, that because of sharp reductions in work-weeks and the presence of hoarded labor, the measure real wage may have been a poor measure of the marginal cost of labor.

Also in the category of measurement issues, Eichengreen and Hatton (1987) correctly point out that nominal wages should be deflated by the relevant product prices, not a general price index. Their table of product wage indices (nominal wages relative to manufacturing prices) is reproduced for 1929–38 and for the five countries for which data are available as our table 6. Like table 5, this table also shows real wages increasing in the early 1930s, but overall the correlation of real wage increases and depression does not appear particularly good. Note that Germany, which had probably the worst unemployment problem of any major country, has almost no increase in real wages;[10] the United Kingdom, which began to recover in 1932, has real wages increasing on a fairly steady trend during its recovery period; and the United States has only a small dip in real wages at the beginning of its recovery, followed by more real wage growth. The case for nominal wage stickiness as a transmission mechanism thus seems, at this point, somewhat mixed.

2. *Real interest rates.* In a standard IS-LM macro model, a monetary contraction depresses output by shifting the LM curve leftwards, raising real interest rates, and thus reducing spending. However, as Temin (1976) pointed out in his original critique of Friedman and Schwartz, it is real rather than nominal money balances that affect the LM curve; and since prices were falling sharply, real money balances fell little or even rose during the contraction.

Even if real money balances are essentially unchanged, however, there is another means by which deflation can raise ex ante real interest rates: Since cash pays zero nominal interest, in equilibrium no asset can bear a nominal interest rate that is lower than its liquidity and risk premia relative to cash. Thus an expected deflation of 10% will impose a real rate of at least 10% on the economy, even with perfectly flexible prices and wages. In an IS-LM

[10] However, it must be mentioned that recent exponents of the real wage explanation of German unemployment invoke it to account for high levels of unemployment throughout the mid and late 1920s, and not just for the period after 1929 (Borchardt 1979).

Table 6
Indices of Product Wages

Year	United Kingdom	United States	Germany	Japan	Sweden
1929	100.0	100.0	100.0	100.0	100.0
1930	103.0	106.1	100.4	115.6	116.6
1931	106.4	113.0	102.2	121.6	129.1
1932	108.3	109.6	96.8	102.9	130.0
1933	109.3	107.9	99.3	101.8	127.9
1934	111.4	115.8	103.0	102.3	119.6
1935	111.3	114.3	105.3	101.6	119.2
1936	110.4	115.9	107.7	99.2	116.0
1937	107.8	121.9	106.5	87.1	101.9
1938	108.6	130.0	107.7	86.3	115.1

Source: Eichengreen and Hatton (1987, 15).

diagram drawn with the nominal interest rate on the vertical axis, an increase in expected deflation amounts to a leftward shift of the IS curve.

Whether the deflation of the early 1930s was anticipated has been extensively debated (although almost entirely in the United States context). We will add here two points in favor of the view that the extent of the worldwide deflation was less than fully anticipated.

First, there is the question of whether the nominal interest rate floor was in fact binding in the deflating countries (as it should have been if this mechanism was to operate). Although interest rates on government debt in the United States often approximated zero in the 1930s, it is less clear that this was true for other countries. The yield on French treasury bills, for example, rose from a low of 0.75% in 1932 to 2.06% in 1933, 2.25% in 1934, and 3.38% in 1935; during 1933–35 the nominal yield on French treasury bills exceeded that of British treasury bills by several hundred basis points on average.[11]

Second, the view that deflation was largely anticipated must contend with the fact that nominal returns on safe assets were very similar whether countries abandoned or stayed on gold. If continuing deflation was anticipated in the gold standard countries, while inflation was expected in countries leaving gold, the similarity of nominal returns would have implied large expected differences in real returns. Such differences are possible in equilibrium, if they are counterbalanced by expected real exchange rate changes; nevertheless, differences in expected real returns between countries on and

[11] In the French case, however, there may have been some fear of government default, given the large deficits that were being run; conceivably, this could explain the higher rate on French bills.

off gold on the order of 11–12% (the realized difference in returns between the two blocs in 1932) seem unlikely.[12]

3. *Financial crisis*. A third mechanism by which deflation can induce depression, not considered in the recent literature, works through deflation's effect on the operation of the financial system. The source of the non-neutrality is simply that debt instruments (including deposits) are typically set in money terms. Deflation thus weakens the financial positions of borrowers, both nonfinancial firms and financial intermediaries.

Consider first the case of intermediaries (banks).[13] Bank liabilities (primarily deposits) are fixed almost entirely in nominal terms. On the asset side, depending on the type of banking system (see below), banks hold either primarily debt instruments or combinations of debt and equity. Ownership of debt and equity is essentially equivalent to direct ownership of capital; in this case, therefore, the bank's liabilities are nominal and its assets are real, so that an unanticipated deflation begins to squeeze the bank's capital position immediately. When only debt is held as an asset, the effect of deflation is for a while neutral or mildly beneficial to the bank. However, when borrowers' equity cushions are exhausted, the bank becomes the owner of its borrowers' real assets, so eventually this type of bank will also be squeezed by deflation.

As pressure on the bank's capital grows, according to this argument, its normal functioning will be impeded; for example, it may have to call in loans or refuse new ones. Eventually, impending exhaustion of bank capital leads to a depositors' run, which eliminates the bank or drastically curtails its operation. The final result is usually a government takeover of the intermediation process. For example, a common scenario during the Depression was for the government to finance an acquisition of a failing bank by issuing its own debt; this debt was held (directly or indirectly) by consumers, in lieu of (vanishing) commercial bank deposits. Thus, effectively, government agencies became part of the intermediation chain.[14]

Although the problems of the banks were perhaps the more dramatic in the Depression, the same type of non-neutrality potentially affects nonfinancial firms and other borrowers. The process of "debt deflation," that is, the

---

[12] A possible response to this point is that fear of devaluation added a risk premium to assets in gold standard countries. This point can be checked by looking at forward rates for foreign exchange, available in Einzig (1937). The forward premia on gold standard currencies are generally small, except immediately before devaluations. In particular, the three-month premium on dollars versus the pound in 1932 had a maximum value of about 4.5% (at an annual rate) during the first week of June, but for most of the year was considerably less than that.

[13] The effect of deflation on banks, and the relationship between deflation and bank runs, has been analyzed in a theoretical model by Flood and Garber (1981).

[14] An important issue, which we cannot resolve here, is whether government takeovers of banks resulted in some restoration of intermediary services, or if, instead, the government functioned primarily as a liquidation agent.

increase in the real value of nominal debt obligations brought about by falling prices, erodes the net worth position of borrowers. A weakening financial position affects the borrower's actions (e.g., the firm may try to conserve financial capital by laying off workers or cutting back on investment) and also, by worsening the agency problems in the borrower-lender relationship, impairs access to new credit. Thus, as discussed in detail in Bernanke and Gertler (1990), "financial distress" (such as that induced by debt deflation) can in principle impose deadweight losses on an economy, even if firms do not undergo liquidation.

Before trying to assess the quantitative impact of these and other channels on output, we briefly discuss the international incidence of financial crisis during the Depression.

4. Interwar Banking and Financial Crises

Financial crises were of course a prominent feature of the interwar period. We focus in this section on the problems of the banking sector and, to a lesser extent, on the problems of domestic debtors in general, as suggested by the discussion above. Stock market crashes and defaults on external debt were also important, of course, but for the sake of space will take a subsidiary role here.

Table 7 gives a chronology of some important interwar banking crises. The episodes listed actually cover a considerable range in terms of severity, as the capsule descriptions should make clear. However the chronology should also show that (i) quite a few different countries experienced significant banking problems during the interwar period; and (ii) these problems reached a very sharp peak between the spring and fall of 1931, following the Creditanstalt crisis in May 1931 as well as the intensification of banking problems in Germany.

A statistical indicator of banking problems, emphasized by Friedman and Schwartz (1963), is the deposit-currency ratio. Data on the changes in the commercial bank deposit-currency ratio for our panel of countries are presented in table 8. It is interesting to compare this table with the chronology in table 7. Most but not all of the major banking crises were associated with sharp drops in the deposit-currency ratio; the most important exception is in 1931 in Italy, where the government was able to keep secret much of the banking system's problems until a government takeover was affected. On the other hand, there were also significant drops in the deposit-currency ratio that were not associated with panics; restructurings of the banking system and exchange rate difficulties account for some of these episodes.

What caused the banking panic? At one level, the panics were an endogenous response to deflation and the operation of the gold standard regime.

Table 7
A Chronology of Interwar Banking Crises, 1921–36

Date	Country	Crises
June 1921	Sweden	Beginning of deposit contraction of 1921–22, leading to bank restructurings. Government assistance administered through Credit Bank of 1922.
1921–22	Netherlands	Bank failures (notably Marx & Co.) and amalgamations.
1922	Denmark	Heavy losses of one of the largest banks, Danske Landmandsbank, and liquidation of smaller banks. Landmandsbank continues to operate until a restructing in April 1928 under a government guarantee.
April 1923	Norway	Failure of Centralbanken for Norge.
May 1923	Austria	Difficulties of a major bank, Allgemeine Depositenbank; liquidation in July.
September 1923	Japan	In wake of the Tokyo earthquake, bad debts threaten Bank of Taiwan and Bank of Chosen, which are restructured with government help.
September 1925	Spain	Failure of Banco de la Union Mineira and Banco Vasca.
July–September 1926	Poland	Bank runs cause three large banks to stop payments. The shakeout of banks continues through 1927.
1927	Norway, Italy	Numerous smaller banks in difficulties, but no major failures.
April 1927	Japan	Thirty-two banks unable to make payments. Restructuring of 15th Bank and Bank of Taiwan.
August 1929	Germany	Collapse of Frankfurter Allgemeine Versicherungs AG, followed by failures of smaller banks, and runs on Berlin and Frankfurt savings banks.
November 1929	Austria	Bodencreditanstalt, second largest bank, fails and is merged with Creditanstalt.
November 1930	France	Failure of Banque Adam, Boulogne-sur-Mer, and Oustric Group. Runs on provincial banks.

Table 7 (*cont.*)

Date	Country	Crises
	Estonia	Failure of two medium-sized banks, Estonia Government Bank Tallin and Reval Credit Bank; crisis lasts until January.
December 1930	U.S.	Failure of Bank of the United States.
	Italy	Withdrawals from three largest banks begin. A panic ensues in April 1931, followed by a government reorganization and takeover of frozen industrial assets.
April 1931	Argentina	Government deals with banking panic by allowing Banco de Nacion to rediscount commercial paper from other banks at government-owned Caja de Conversión.
May 1931	Austria	Failure of Creditanstalt and run of foreign depositors.
	Belgium	Rumors about imminent failure of Banque de Bruxelles, the country's second largest bank, induce withdrawals from all banks. Later in the year, expectations of devaluation lead to withdrawals of foreign deposits.
June 1931	Poland	Run on banks, especially on Warsaw Discount Bank, associated with Creditanstalt; a spread of the Austrian crisis.
April–July 1931	Germany	Bank runs, extending difficulties plaguing the banking system since the summer of 1930. After large loss of deposits in June and increasing strain on foreign exchanges, many banks are unable to make payments and Darmstädter Bank closes. Bank holiday.
July 1931	Hungary	Run on Budapest banks (especially General Credit Bank). Foreign withdrawals followed by a foreign creditors' standstill agreement. Bank holiday.
	Latvia	Run on banks with German connections. Bank of Libau and International Bank of Riga particularly hard hit.
	Austria	Failure of Vienna Mercur-Bank.

Table 7 (*cont.*)

Date	Country	Crises
	Czechoslovakia	Withdrawal of foreign deposits sparks domestic withdrawals but no general banking panic.
	Turkey	Run on branches of Deutsche Bank and collapse of Banque Turque pour le Commerce et l'Industrie, in wake of German crisis.
	Egypt	Run on Cairo and Alexandria branches of Deutsche Orientbank.
	Switzerland	Union Financière de Genève rescued by takeover by Comptoir d'Escompte de Geneve.
	Rumania	Collapse of German-controlled Banca Generala a Tarii Românesti. Run on Banca de Credit Romand and Banca Romaneasca.
	Mexico	Suspension of payments after run on Credito Espanol de Mexico. Run on Banco Nacional de Mexico.
August 1931	U.S.	Series of banking panics, with October 1931 the worst month. Between August 1931 and January 1932, 1,860 banks fail.
September 1931	U.K.	External drain, combined with rumors of threat to London merchant banks with heavy European (particularly Hungarian and German) involvements.
	Estonia	General bank run following sterling crisis; second wave of runs in November.
October 1931	Rumania	Failure of Banca Marmerosch, Blank & Co. Heavy bank runs.
	France	Collapse of major deposit bank Banque Nationale de Crédit (restructured as Banque Nationale pour le Commerce et l'Industrie). Other bank failures and bank runs.
March 1932	Sweden	Weakness of one large bank (Skandinaviska Kreditaktiebolaget) as result of collapse of Krueger industrial and financial empire, but no general panic.

Table 7 (*cont.*)

Date	Country	Crises
May 1932	France	Losses of large investment bank Banque de l'Union Parisienne forces merger with Crédit Mobilier Français.
June 1932	U.S.	Series of bank failures in Chicago.
October 1932	U.S.	New wave of bank failures, especially in the Midwest and Far West.
February 1933	U.S.	General banking panic, leading to state holidays and a nationwide bank holiday in March.
November 1933	Switzerland	Restructuring of large bank (Banque Populaire Suisse) after heavy losses.
March 1934	Belgium	Failure of Banque Belge de Travail develops into general banking and exchange crisis.
September 1934	Argentina	Bank problems throughout the fall induce government-sponsored merger of four weak banks (Banco Espanol del Rio de la Plata, Banco el Hogar Argentina, Banco Argentina-Uruguayo, Ernesto Tornquist & Co.).
October 1935	Italy	Deposits fall after Italian invasion of Abyssinia.
January 1936	Norway	After years of deposit stability, legislation introducing a tax on bank deposits leads to withdrawals (until fall).
October 1936	Czechoslovakia	Anticipation of second devaluation of the crown leads to deposit withdrawals.

When the peak of the world banking crisis came in 1931, there had already been almost two years of deflation and accompanying depression. Consistent with the analysis at the end of the last section, falling prices lowered the nominal value of bank assets but not the nominal value of bank liabilities. In addition, the rules of the gold standard severely limited the ability of central banks to ameliorate panics by acting as a lender of last resort; indeed, since banking panics often coincided with exchange crises (as we discuss further below), in order to maintain convertibility central banks typically *tightened* monetary policy in the face of panics. Supporting the

Table 8
Log-Differences of Commercial Bank Deposit-Currency Ratio

Country	1930	1931	1932	1933	1934	1935	1936
Australia	−.05	−.12*	.05	.01	.05	−.03	−.01
Austria	.17	−.40*	−.06	−.20*	−.07	−.01	−.02
Belgium	−.13*	−.22*	−.10*	.07	−.13*	−.27*	−.02
Canada	.07	−.01	.03	−.05	.00	.01	−.06
Czechoslovakia	−.11	−.08	.07	.02	.07	−.03	−.11*
Denmark	.08	−.03	.00	−.07	.02	.02	−.00
Estonia	.16	−.29*	−.02	−.05	.10	.05	.13
Finland	.09	−.05	.14	−.04	−.06	−.04	−.09
France	−.07	−.12*	−.01	−.10*	−.07	−.10	−.03
Germany	−.11*	−.40*	.05	−.09	−.01	−.08	−.02
Greece	.17	.07	−.27*	−.03	.06	−.04	.02
Hungary	.07	−.07	.10	−.03	−.08	−.05	−.03
Italy	.04	−.01	.05	.06	.01	−.20*	.08
Japan	.09	.03	−.12*	−.04	.03	−.00	.09
Latvia	.03	−.57*	.11	−.06	.12	.10	.45
Netherlands	.10	−.36*	−.05	−.06	−.05	−.08	.24
Norway	.04	−.15*	−.06	−.09	−.01	.03	−.23*
New Zealand	.04	−.11*	.03	.07	.15	−.08	−.32*
Poland	.07	−.29*	−.02	−.08	.10	−.06	.10
Rumania	.11	−.76*	−.05	−.11*	−.28*	.10	−.16*
Sweden	−.00	−.00	−.02	−.06	−.11*	−.08	−.07
Spain	.00	−.24*	.08	.03	.01	.06	N.A.
United Kingdom	.03	−.07	.10	−.07	−.02	.01	−.03
United States	.00	−.15*	−.26*	−.15*	.14	.05	.02

Note: Entries are the log-differences of the ratio of commercial bank deposits to money and notes in circulation. Data are from League of Nations, *Monthly Bulletin of Statistics* and *Yearbook*, various issues.

*Decline exceeds .10.

connection of banking problems with deflation and "rules of the game" constraints is the observation that there were virtually no serious banking panics in any country after abandonment of the gold standard—although it is also true that by time the gold standard was abandoned, strong financial reform measures had been taken in most countries.

However, while deflation and adherence to the gold standard were necessary conditions for panics, they were not sufficient; a number of countries made it through the interwar period without significant bank runs or failures, despite being subject to deflationary shocks similar to those experienced by the countries with banking problems.[15] Several factors help to explain which countries were the ones to suffer panics.

[15] In the next section we divide our sample into two groups: eleven countries with serious banking problems and thirteen countries without these problems. In 1930, the year before the peak of the banking crises, the countries that were to avoid banking problems suffered on average a 12% deflation and a 6% fall in industrial production; the comparable numbers for the group that was to experience panics were 13% and 8%. Thus, there was no large difference between the two groups early in the Depression. In contrast, in 1932 (the year following the

1. *Banking structure.* The organization of the banking system was an important factor in determining vulnerability to panics. First, countries with "unit banking," that is, with a large number of small and relatively undiversified banks, suffered more severe banking panics. The leading example is of course the United States, where concentration in banking was very low, but a high incidence of failures among small banks was also seen in other countries (e.g., France). Canada, with branch banking, suffered no bank failures during the Depression (although many branches were closed). Sweden and the United Kingdom also benefited from a greater dispersion of risk through branch systems.[16]

Second, where "universal" or "mixed" banking on the German or Belgian model was the norm, it appears that vulnerability to deflation was greater. In contrast to the Anglo-Saxon model of banking, where at least in theory lending was short term and the relationship between banks and corporations had an arm's length character, universal banks took long-term and sometimes dominant ownership positions in client firms. Universal bank assets included both long-term securities and equity participations; the former tended to become illiquid during a crisis, while the latter exposed universal banks (unlike Anglo-Saxon banks, which held mainly debt instruments) to the effects of stock market crashes. The most extreme case was probably Austria. By 1931, after a series of mergers, the infamous Creditanstalt was better thought of as a vast holding company rather than a bank; at the time of its failure in May 1931, the Creditanstalt owned sixty-four companies, amounting to 65% of Austria's nominal capital (Kindleberger 1984).

2. *Reliance of banks on short-term foreign liabilities.* Some of the most serious banking problems were experienced in countries in which a substantial fraction of deposits were foreign-owned. The so-called hot money was more sensitive to adverse financial developments than were domestic deposits. Runs by foreign depositors represented not only a loss to the banking system but also, typically, a loss of reserves; as we have noted, this additional external threat restricted the ability of the central bank to respond to the banking situation. Thus, banking crises and exchange rate crises became intertwined.[17] The resolution of a number of the central European banking crises required "standstill agreements," under which withdrawals by foreign creditors were blocked pending future negotiation.

---

most intense banking crisis), industrial production growth in countries without banking crises averaged -2%; in the group that experienced crises the comparable number was -16%.

[16] Although this correlation seems to hold during the Depression, we do not want to conclude unconditionally that branch banking is more stable; branching facilitates diversification but also increases the risk that problems in a few large banks may bring down the entire network.

[17] Causality could run in both directions. For example, Wigmore (1987) argues that the U.S. banking panic in 1933 was in part created by a run on the dollar.

International linkages were important on the asset side of bank balance sheets as well. Many continental banks were severely affected by the crises in Austria and Germany, in particular.

3. *Financial and economic experience of the 1920s.* It should not be particularly surprising that countries which emerged from the 1920s in relatively weaker condition were more vulnerable to panics. Austria, Germany, Hungary, and Poland all suffered hyperinflation and economic dislocation in the 1930s, and all suffered severe banking panics in 1931. While space constraints do not permit a full discussion of the point here, it does seem clear that the origins of the European financial crisis were at least partly independent of American developments—which argues against a purely American-centered explanation of the origins of the Depression.

It should also be emphasized, though, that not just the existence of financial difficulties during the 1920s but also the policy response to those difficulties was important. Austria is probably the most extreme case of nagging banking problems being repeatedly "papered over." That country had banking problems throughout the 1920s, which were handled principally by merging failing banks into still-solvent banks. An enforced merger of the Austrian Bodencreditanstalt with two failing banks in 1927 weakened that institution, which was part of the reason that the Bodencreditanstalt in turn had to be forceably merged with the Creditanstalt in 1929. The insolvency of the Creditanstalt, finally revealed when a director refused to sign an "optimistic" financial statement in May 1931, sparked the most intense phase of the European crisis.

In contrast, when banking troubles during the earlier part of the 1920s were met with fundamental reform, performance of the banking sector during the Depression was better. Examples were Sweden, Japan, and the Netherlands, all of which had significant banking problems during the 1920s but responded by fundamental restructurings and assistance to place banks on a sound footing (and to close the weakest banks). Possibly because of these earlier events, these three countries had limited problems in the 1930s. A large Swedish bank (Skandinaviska Kreditaktiebolaget) suffered heavy losses after the collapse of the Kreuger financial empire, and a medium-sized Dutch bank (Amstelbank) failed because of its connection to the Creditanstalt; but there were no widespread panics, only isolated failures.

A particularly interesting comparison in this regard is between the Netherlands and neighboring Belgium, where banking problems persisted from 1931 to 1935 and where the ultimate devaluation of the Belgian franc was the result of an attempt to protect banks from further drains. Both countries were heavily dependent on foreign trade and both remained on gold, yet the Netherlands did much better than Belgium in the early part of the Depression (see table 4). This is a bit of evidence for the relevance of banking difficulties to output.

Overall, while banking crises were surely an endogenous response to depression, the incidence of crisis across countries reflected a variety of institutional factors and other preconditions. Thus it will be of interest to compare the real effects of deflation between countries with and without severe banking difficulties.

On "debt deflation," that is, the problems of nonfinancial borrowers, much less has been written than on the banking crises. Only for the United States has the debt problem in the 1930s been fairly well documented (see the summary in Bernanke 1983 and the references therein). In that country, large corporations avoided serious difficulties, but most other sectors—small businesses, farmers, mortgage borrowers, state and local governments—were severely affected, with usually something close to half of outstanding debts being in default. A substantial portion of New Deal reforms consisted of various forms of debt adjustment and relief.

For other countries, there are plenty of anecdotes but not much systematic data. Aggregate data on bankruptcies and defaults are difficult to interpret because increasing financial distress forced changes in bankruptcy practices and procedures; when the League of Nations' *Monthly Bulletin of Statistics* dropped its table on bankruptcies in its December 1932 issue, for example, the reason given therein was that "the numerous forms of agreement by which open bankruptcies are now avoided have seriously diminished the value of the table" (p. 529). Perhaps the most extreme case of a change in rules was Rumania's April 1932 Law on Conversion of Debts, which essentially eliminated the right of creditors to force bankruptcy. Changes in the treatment of bankruptcy no doubt ameliorated the effects of debt default, but the fact that these changes occurred indicates that the perceived problem must have been severe. More detailed country-by-country study of the effects of deflation on firm balance sheets and the relation of financial condition to firm investment, production, and employment decisions—where the data permit—would be extremely valuable. A similar comment applies to external debt problems, although here interesting recent work by Eichengreen and Portes (1986) and others gives us a much better base of knowledge to build on than is available for the case of domestic debts.

5. Regression Results

In this section we present empirical results based on our panel data set. The principal question of interest is the relative importance of various transmission mechanisms of deflation to output. We also address the question, so far not discussed, of whether banking crises could have intensified the deflation process itself.

Table 9
Determinants of the Log-Differences of Industrial Production
(dependent variable: ΔlnIP)

	Independent Variables					
Equation	ΔlnPW	ΔlnEX	ΔlnW	DISC	PANIC	ΔlnM0
(1)	.855					
	(.098)					
(2)	.531				−.0191	
	(.095)				(.0026)	
(3)	.406	.231				
	(.121)	(.043)				
(4)	.300	.148			−.0157	
	(.111)	(.041)			(.0027)	
(5)	.364	.231	.272			
	(.141)	(.046)	(.206)			
(6)	.351	.150	−.072		−.0156	
	(.128)	(.044)	(.197)		(.0029)	
(7)	.296	.103	−.119	−.0358	−.0138	
	(.123)	(.044)	(.189)	(.0102)	(.0028)	
(8)		.217*	−.015		−.0126	.405
		(.048)	(.189)		(.0031)	(.098)

Note: For variable definitions, see text. The sample period is 1930–36. The panel consists of twenty-four countries except that, due to missing wage data, Finland, Greece, and Spain are excluded from equations (5)–(8). Estimates of country-specific dummies are not reported. Standard errors are in parentheses.

*Export growth is measured in real terms in equation (8).

The basic set of results is contained in table 9, which relates the log-differences in industrial production for our set of countries to various combinations of explanatory variables. The definitions of the right-hand-side variables are as follows:

ΔlnPW: log-difference of the wholesale price index;

ΔlnEX: log-difference of nominal exports;

ΔlnW: log-difference of nominal wage;

DISC: central bank discount rate, measured relative to its 1929 value (a government bond rate is used for Canada; since no 1929 interest rate could be found for New Zealand, that country is excluded in regressions including DISC);

PANIC: a dummy variable, set equal to the number of months during the year that the country experienced serious banking problems (see below);

ΔlnM0: log-difference of money and notes in circulation.

Exports are included to control for trade effects on growth, including the benefits of competitive devaluation discussed by Eichengreen and Sachs (1986); and the wage is included to test for the real wage channel of transmission from deflation to depression. Of course, theory says that both of these variables should enter in real rather than in nominal terms; unfortunately, in practice the theoretically suggested deflator is not always available (as we noted in our discussion of the real wage above). We resolve this problem by supposing that the true equation is, for example,

$$\Delta \ln IP = \beta_e (\Delta \ln EX - \Delta \ln P_e) + \beta_w (\Delta \ln W - \Delta \ln P_w) + \text{error} \qquad (1)$$

where P_e and P_w, the optimal deflators, are not available. Let the projections of log-changes in the unobserved deflators on the log-change in the wholesale price deflator be given by

$$\Delta \ln P_i = \psi_i \Delta \ln PW + u_i \quad i = e, w \qquad (2)$$

where the u_i are uncorrelated with $\Delta \ln PW$ and presumably the ψ_i are positive. Then (1) becomes

$$\Delta \ln IP = -(\beta_e \psi_e + \beta_w \psi_w)\Delta \ln PW + \beta_e \Delta \ln EX + \beta_w \Delta \ln W + \text{new error} \qquad (3)$$

This suggests allowing $\Delta \ln PW$ and the nominal growth rates of exports and wages to enter the equation separately, which is how we proceed.[18] Putting $\Delta \ln PW$ in the equation separately has the added advantage of allowing us to account for any additional effect of deflation (such as debt deflation) not explicitly captured by the other independent variables.

The discount rate $DISC$ is included to allow for the interest rate channel and as an additional proxy for monetary policy. Since $\Delta \ln PW$ is included in every equation, inclusion of the nominal interest rate $DISC$ is equivalent to including the actual ex post real interest rate, that is, we are effectively assuming that deflation was fully anticipated; this should give the real interest rate hypothesis its best chance.

In an attempt to control for fiscal policy, we also included measures of central government expenditure in our first estimated equations. Since the estimated coefficients were always negative (the wrong sign), small, and statistically insignificant, the government expenditure variable is excluded from the results reported here.

Construction of the dummy variable $PANIC$ required us to make a judgment about which countries' banking crises were most serious, which we did

---

[18] It has been pointed out to us that if nominal wages were literally rigid, then this approach would find no effect for wages even though changes in the real wage might be an important channel for the effects of deflation. The reply to this is that, if nominal wages are completely rigid, the hypothesis that real wages are important can never be distinguished from an alternative which proposes that deflation has its effects in some other way.

from our reading of primary and secondary sources. We dated periods of crisis as starting from the first severe banking problems; if there was some clear demarcation point (such as the U.S. bank holiday of 1933), we used that as the ending date of the crisis; otherwise we arbitrarily assumed that the effects of the crisis would last for one year after its most intense point. The banking crisis included in the dummy are as follows (see also table 7):

1. Austria (May 1931–January 1933): from the Creditanstalt crisis to the date of official settlement of the Creditanstalt's foreign debt.
2. Belgium (May 1931–April 1932; March 1934–February 1935): for one year after the initial Belgian crisis, following Creditanstalt, and for one year after the failure of the Banque Belge de Travail led to a general crisis.
3. Estonia (September 1931–August 1932): for one year after the general banking crisis.
4. France (November 1930–October 1932): for one year following each of the two peaks of the French banking crisis, in November 1930 and October 1931 (see Bouvier 1984).
5. Germany (May 1931–December 1932): from the beginning of the major German banking crisis until the creation of state institutes for the liquidation of bad bank debts.
6. Hungary (July 1931–June 1932): for one year following the runs in Budapest and the bank holiday.
7. Italy (April 1931–December 1932): from the onset of the banking panic until the takeover of bank assets by a massive new state holding company, the Istituto por le Riconstruzione Industriale (IRI).
8. Latvia (July 1931–June 1932): for one year following the onset of the banking crisis.
9. Poland (June 1931–May 1932): for one year following the onset of the banking crisis.
10. Rumania (July 1931–September 1932): from the onset of the crisis until one year after its peak in October 1931.
11. United States (December 1930–March 1933): from the failure of the Bank of the United States until the bank holiday.

The inclusion of Austria, Belgium, Estonia, Germany, Hungary, Latvia, Poland, Rumania, or the United States in the above list cannot be controversial; each of these countries suffered serious panics. (One might quibble on the margin about the exact dating given—for example, Temin [1989] and others have argued that the U.S. banking crisis did not really begin until mid 1931—but we doubt very much that changes of a few months on these dates would affect the results.) The inclusion of France and Italy is more controversial. For example, Bouvier (1984) argues that the French banking crisis was not as serious as some others, since although there were runs and many banks failed, the very biggest banks survived; also, according to Bouvier, French banks were not as closely tied to industry as other banking systems on the Continent. For Italy, as we have noted, early and massive government intervention reduced the incidence of panic (see Ciocca and Toniolo 1984); however, the banks were in very poor condition and (as noted above) eventually signed over most of their industrial assets to the IRI.

To check the sensitivity of our results, we reestimated the key equations omitting first the French crisis from the PANIC variable, then the French and Italian crises. Leaving out France had a minor effect (lowering the coefficient on PANIC and its t-statistic about 5% in a typical equation); the additional exclusion of the Italian crisis has essentially no effect.[19]

As a further check, we also reestimated our key equations omitting, in separate runs, (i) the United States; (ii) Germany and Austria; and (iii) all eastern European countries. In none of these equations were our basic results substantially weakened, which indicates that no single country or small group of countries is driving our findings.

The first seven equations in table 9 are not derived from any single model, but instead attempt to nest various suggested explanations of the link between deflation and depression. Estimation was by OLS, which opens up the possibility of simultaneity bias; however, given our maintained view that the deflation was imposed by exogenous monetary forces, a case can be made for treating the right-hand-side variables as exogenous or predetermined.

The principal inferences to be drawn from the first seven rows of table 9 are as follows:[20]

1. Export growth consistently enters the equation for output growth strongly, with a plausible coefficient and a high level of statistical significance.

2. When wage growth is included in the output equation along with only wholesale price and export growth (row 5), it enters with the wrong sign. Only when the PANIC variable is included does nominal wage growth have

[19] In another sensitivity check, we also tried multiplying PANIC times the change in the deposit-currency ratio, to allow for differential severity of panics. The results exhibited an outlier problem. When Rumania (which had a change in the deposit-currency ratio of $-.76$ in 1931) was excluded, the results were similar to those obtained using the PANIC variable alone. However, inclusion of Rumania weakened both the magnitude and statistical significance of the effect of panics on output. The "reason" for this is that, despite its massive deposit contraction, Rumania experienced a 5% growth of industrial production in 1931. Whether this is a strong contradiction of the view that panics affect real output is not clear, however, since according to the League of Nations the peak of the Rumania crisis did not occur until September or October, and industrial production in the subsequent year fell by 14%. Another reason to downplay these results is that the change in the deposit-currency ratio may not be a good indicator of the severity of the banking crisis, as the Italian case indicates.

[20] Results were unchanged when lagged industrial production growth was added to the equations. The coefficient on lagged production was typically small and statistically insignificant.

the correct (negative) sign (rows 6 and 7). In the equation encompassing all the various channels (row 7), the estimated coefficient on wage growth is of the right sign and a reasonable magnitude, but it is not statistically significant.

3. The discount rate enters the encompassing equation (row 7) with the right sign and a high significance level. A 100-basis-point increase in the discount rate is estimated to reduce the growth rate of industrial production by 3.6 percentage points.

4. The effect of banking panics on output is large (a year of panic is estimated in equation (7) to reduce output growth by 12 $\times$ .0138, or more than 16 percentage points) and highly statistically significant (t-statistics of 4.0 or better). The measured effect of the PANIC variable does not seem to depend much on what other variables are included in the equation.

5. There may be some residual effect of deflation on output not accounted for by any of these effects. To see this, note that in principle the coefficient on $\Delta \ln PW$ in equation (7) of table 9 should be equal to and opposite the weighted sum of the coefficients on $\Delta \ln EX$, $\Delta \ln W$, and DISC (where the weights are the projection coefficients of the respective "true" deflators on $\Delta \ln PW$). Suppose for the sake of illustration that each of the projection coefficients equals one (that is, the wholesale price index is the correct deflator). Then the expected value of the coefficient on $\Delta \ln PW$ should be approximately .052; the actual value is .296, with a standard error of .123. Thus there may be channels relating deflation to depression other than the ones explicitly accounted for here. One possibility is that we are simply picking up the effects of a simultaneity bias (a reverse causation from output to prices). Alternatively, it is possible that an additional factor, such as debt deflation, should be considered.

As an alternative to the procedure of nesting alternative channels in a single equation, in equation (8) of table 9 we report the results of estimating the reduced form of a simple aggregate demand-aggregate supply (AD-AS) system. Under conventional assumptions, in an AD-AS model output growth should depend on money growth and autonomous spending growth (represented here by growth in *real* exports[21]), which shift the AD curve; and on nominal wage growth, which shifts the AS curve. In addition, we allow PANIC to enter the system, since banking panics could in principle affect both aggregate demand and aggregate supply. The results indicate large and statistically significant effects on output growth for real export growth, money growth, and banking panics. Nominal wage growth enters with the correct sign, but the coefficient is very small and statistically insignificant.

---

[21] Deflation is by the wholesale price index.

We have so far focused on the effects of banking panics (and other variables) on output. There is an additional issue that warrants some discussion here; namely, the possibility that banking panics might have themselves worsened the deflationary process.

Some care must be taken with this argument. Banking panics undoubtedly had large effects on the composition of national money supplies, money multipliers, and money demand. Nevertheless, as has been stressed by Temin (1989), under a gold standard, small country price levels are determined by international monetary conditions, to which domestic money supplies and demands must ultimately adjust. Thus banking panics cannot intensify deflation in a small country.[22] Indeed, a regression (not reported) of changes in wholesale prices against the *PANIC* variable and time dummies (in order to isolate purely cross-sectional effects) confirms that there is very little relationship between the two variables.

The proposition that bank panics should not affect the price level does not necessarily hold for a large country, however. In econometric language, under a gold standard the price level of a large country must be cointegrated with world prices; but while this means that domestic prices must eventually adjust to shocks emanating from abroad, it also allows for the possibility that domestic shocks will influence the world price level. Notice that if banking panics led to deflationary shocks in a large country and these shocks were transmitted around the world by the gold standard, a cross-sectional comparison would find no link between panics and the price level.

The discussion of the gold standard and deflation in section 2 cited Hamilton's (1987) view that the initial deflationary impulses in 1928–29 came from France and the United States—both "big" countries, in terms of economic importance and because of their large gold reserves. This early deflation obviously cannot be blamed on banking panics, since these did not begin until at least the end of 1930. But it would not be in any way inconsistent with the theory of the gold standard to hypothesize that banking

[22] A possible exception to this proposition for a small country might be a situation in which there are fears that the country will devalue or abandon gold; in this case the country's price level might drop below the world level without causing inflows of reserves. An example may be Poland in 1932. A member of the Gold Bloc, Poland's wholesale price level closely tracked that of France until mid 1931, when Poland experienced severe banking problems and withdrawals of foreign deposits, which threatened convertibility. From that point on, even though both countries remained on the gold standard, money supplies and prices in Poland and France began to diverge. From the time of the Polish crisis in June 1931 until the end of 1932, money and notes and circulation dropped by 9.1% in Poland (compared to a gain of 10.5% in France); Polish commercial bank deposits fell 24.5% (compared to a 4.1% decline in France); and Polish wholesale prices declined 35.2% (compared to a decline of 18.3% in France). Despite its greater deflation, Poland lost about a sixth of its gold reserves in 1932, while France gained gold.

Table 10
Error-Correction Equations for U.S. and French Wholesale Prices

	Dependent Variable	
	ΔlnUSAWPI	ΔlnFRAWPI
Constant	.044	−.006
	($t = 3.81$)	($t = 1.57$)
Log USAWPI − log FRAWPI (lagged once)	−.166	.071
	($t = 2.77$)	($t = 1.10$)
Four lags of own WPI growth	−.530	.320
	($F = 1.57; p = .202$)	($F = 2.48; p = .057$)
Current and four lags of base money growth	1.412	.519
	($F = 5.62; p = .005$)	($F = 0.78; p = .569$)
Current and four lags of deposits of failing U.S. banks, in logs	−.020	
	($F = 5.61; p = .0005$)	
R^2	.531	.307
D-W	1.62	1.87

Note: Deposits of failing banks are from the *Federal Reserve Bulletin*. USAWPI and FRAWPI are wholesale price indexes for the United States and France, respectively. Monthly data from 1928 to 1932 are used.

panics in France and the United States contributed to world deflation during 1931–32.[23]

Empirical evidence bearing on this question is presented in table 10. We estimated equations for wholesale price inflation in the United States and France, using monthly data for the five-year period 1928–32. We included an error-correction term in both equations to allow for cointegration between the U.S. and French price levels, as would be implied by the gold standard. This error-correction term is the difference between the log-*levels* of U.S. and French wholesale prices in period $t − 1$; if U.S. and French prices are in fact cointegrated, then the growth rate of U.S prices should respond negatively to the difference between the U.S price and the French price, and the French growth rate of prices should respond positively. Also included in the equations are lagged inflation rates (to capture transitory price dynamics), current and lagged base money growth, and current and

---

[23] This hypothesis does not bear on Temin's claim that there was little that central banks could do about banking crises under the gold standard; rather, the argument is that if, fortuitously, French and U.S. banking panics had not occurred, world deflation in 1931–32 would have been less severe.

lagged values of the deposits of failing banks (for the United States only, due to data availability).

The results are interesting. First, there is evidence for cointegration: The error-correction terms have the right signs and reasonable magnitudes, although only the U.S. term is statistically significant. Thus we may infer that shocks hitting either French or U.S. prices ultimately affected both price levels. Second, both U.S. base money growth and bank failures are important determinants of the U.S. (and by extension, the French) deflation rates; these two variables enter the U.S. price equation with the right sign and marginal significance levels of .0005.

With respect to the effect of banking panics on the price level, then, the appropriate conclusion appears to be that countries with banking panics did not suffer worse deflation than those without panics;[24] however, it is possible that U.S. banking panics in particular were an important source of *world* deflation during 1931–32, and thus, by extension, of world depression.

6. Conclusion

Monetary and financial arrangements in the interwar period were badly flawed and were a major source of the fall in real output. Banking panics were one mechanism through which deflation had its effects on real output, and panics in the United States may have contributed to the severity of the world deflation.

In this empirical study, we have focused on the effects of severe banking panics. We believe it likely, however, that the effects of deflation on the financial system were not confined to these more extreme episodes. Even in countries without panics, banks were financially weakened and contracted their operations. Domestic debt deflation was probably a factor, to a greater or lesser degree, in every country. And we have not addressed at all the effect of deflation on the burden of external debt, which was important for a number of countries. As we have already suggested, more careful study of these issues is clearly desirable.

References

Bernanke, Ben. 1983. Non-monetary effects of the financial crisis in the propagation of the Great Depression. *American Economic Review* 73: 257–76.

———. 1986. Employment, hours, and earnings in the Depression: An analysis of eight manufacturing industries. *American Economic Review* 76: 82–109.

[24] Indeed, if banking panics induced countries to abandon gold, they may have indirectly contributed to an eventual rise in price levels.

Bernanke, Ben, and Mark Gertler. 1990. Financial fragility and economic performance. *Quarterly Journal of Economics* 105: 87–114.

Board of Governors of the Federal Reserve System. 1943. *Banking and monetary statistics, 1919–41.* Washington, DC: Government Printing Office.

Borchardt, Knut. 1979. Zwangslagen und Handlungsspielraume in der grossen Wirtschaftskrise der fruhen dreissiger Jahren: Zur Revision des uberlieferten Geschichtesbildes. *Jahrbuch der Bayerische Akademie der Wissenschaften*, 87–132. Munich.

Bordo, Michael, and Finn Kydland. 1990. The gold standard as a rule. Typescript, Rutgers University and Carnegie-Mellon University.

Bouvier, Jean. 1984. The French banks, inflation and the economic crisis, 1919–1939. *Journal of European Economic History* 13: 29–80.

Campa, Jose Manuel. Forthcoming. Exchange rates and economic recovery in the 1930s: An extension to Latin America. *Journal of Economic History*.

Choudhri, Ehsan U., and Levis A. Kochin. 1980. The exchange rate and the international transmission of business cycle disturbances: Some evidence from the Great Depression. *Journal of Money, Credit, and Banking* 12: 565–74.

Ciocca, Pierluigi, and Gianni Toniolo. 1984. Industry and finance in Italy, 1918–40. *Journal of European Economic History* 13: 113–36.

Eichengreen, Barry. 1986. The Bank of France and the sterilization of gold, 1926–1932. *Explorations in Economic History* 23: 56–84.

———. 1987. The gold-exchange standard and the Great Depression. Working Paper no. 2198 (March). Cambridge, Mass.: National Bureau of Economic Research.

Eichengreen, Barry, and T. J. Hatton. 1987. Interwar unemployment in international perspective: An overview. In *Interwar unemployment in international perspective*, ed. B. Eichengreen and T. J. Hatton, 1–59. Boston: Kluwer Academic Publishers.

Eichengreen, Barry, and Richard Portes. 1986. Debt and default in the 1930s: Causes and consequences. *European Economic Review* 30: 599–640.

Eichengreen, Barry, and Jeffrey Sachs. 1985. Exchange rates and economic recovery in the 1930s. *Journal of Economic History* 45: 925–46.

———. 1986. Competitive devaluation in the Great Depression: A theoretical reassessment. *Economic Letters* 21: 67–71.

Einzig, Paul. 1937. *The theory of forward exchange.* London: Macmillan.

Fisher, Irving. 1933. The debt-deflation theory of great depressions. *Econometrica* 1: 337–57.

Flood, Robert P., Jr., and Peter M. Garber. 1981. A systematic banking collapse in a perfect foresight world. NBER Working Paper no. 691 (June). Cambridge, Mass.: National Bureau of Economic Research.

Friedman, Milton, and Anna J. Schwartz. 1963. *A monetary history of the United States, 1867–1960.* Princeton: Princeton University Press.

Haberler, Gottfried. 1976. The world economy, money, and the Great Depression. Washington, DC: American Enterprise Institute.

Hamilton, James. 1987. Monetary factors in the Great Depression. *Journal of Monetary Economics* 19: 145–69.

———. 1988. The role of the international gold standard in propagating the Great Depression. *Contemporary Policy Issues* 6: 67–89.

Kindleberger, Charles P. 1984. Banking and industry between the two wars: An international comparison. *Journal of European Economic History* 13: 7–28.

League of Nations. 1926. *Memorandum on Currency and Central Banks, 1913–1925.* Geneva.

———. 1935. *Commercial banks, 1929–1934.* Geneva.

———. 1944. *International currency experience: Lessons of the inter-war period.* Geneva.

Lindert, Peter. 1969. Key currencies and gold, 1900–1913. *Princeton Studies in International Finance,* no. 24

Newell, Andrew, and J. S. V. Symons. 1988. The macroeconomics of the interwar years: International comparisons. In *Interwar unemployment in international perspective,* ed. B. Eichengreen and T. J. Hatton, 61–96. Boston: Kluwer Academic Publishers.

O'Brien, Anthony. 1989. A behavioral explanation for nominal wage rigidity during the Great Depression. *Quarterly Journal of Economics* 104: 719–35.

Temin, Peter. 1976. *Did monetary forces cause the Great Depression?* New York: W. W. Norton.

———. 1989. *Lessons from the Great Depression.* Cambridge, Mass.: MIT Press.

Wigmore, Barrie. 1987. Was the Bank Holiday of 1933 a run on the dollar rather than the banks? *Journal of Economic History* 47: 739–56.

Four

Deflation and Monetary Contraction in the Great Depression: An Analysis by Simple Ratios

WITH ILIAN MIHOV

RECENT RESEARCH INTO THE CAUSES of the Great Depression has ascribed a central role to the worldwide collapse in national money supplies, which led to sharp contractions in aggregate demand and falling prices during the late 1920s and early 1930s. The bulk of the worldwide monetary contraction, in turn, has been attributed by most recent authors to the technical flaws and poor management of the international gold standard, which a majority of the world's countries adopted (or returned to) during the latter part of the 1920s.[1]

The evidence for the culpability of monetary factors in general, and the gold standard in particular, is on the whole quite compelling. Perhaps the most persuasive element of the brief for the prosecution is the finding that countries that abandoned the gold standard early (thereby allowing for reflation of domestic money and prices) were the first to recover from the Depression (Choudhri and Kochin, 1980; Eichengreen and Sachs, 1985, 1986; Bernanke and James, 1991). It is also noteworthy that the phenomena of monetary contraction, deflation of prices, and severe declines in output and employment began almost simultaneously in virtually every country that had "returned to gold." The global nature of these events argues strongly against explanations specific to individual countries, such as (for example) the once-popular notions that "overproduction" of consumer durables or housing during the 1920s in the United States was a cause of the crash.

Although the view that monetary factors were dominant in the Depression now commands wide assent, the relative importance of specific sources of the declines in national price levels and money stocks is still being debated. In particular, within the overall context of the gold standard story, a number of possible deflationary factors have been noted. As explained in

The authors would like to thank the National Science Foundation for research support and Refet Gurkaynak for excellent research assistance.

[1] See Eichengreen (1992) for a detailed historical analysis. The gold standard of the interwar period is more precisely referred to as the "gold exchange" standard, reflecting the fact that convertible foreign exchange was used by many countries to supplement gold reserves. We discuss the implications of this practice below.

more detail below, possible mechanisms include the effects of banking crises on the money multiplier; the international "maldistribution" of gold (in particular, the large share of world monetary gold held by the United States and France); asymmetries in adjustment to gold flows between deficit and surplus countries; the liquidation of foreign exchange reserves by central banks; monetary policies that were excessively tight, even given the constraints of the gold standard; and a global shortage of monetary gold.

All of these factors bear on the *supply* of money under the gold standard. Changes in the *demand* for money have also been cited as sources of deflation in the Depression era. For example, it has often been suggested that the demand for real money balances in France rose significantly following the 1926–1928 Poincaré stabilization, and Friedman and Schwartz (1963) have noted the sharp declines in velocity that occurred in the United States and Canada between 1929 and 1933. Under the international gold standard, an increase in money demand will exert downward pressure on prices and output, in the home country and possibly also abroad, as gold flows in the direction of increased money demand.[2]

Another, related debate concerns the role of monetary factors at different stages of the Depression. In particular, while the importance of monetary factors beginning in 1931 is not seriously questioned, there is a divergence of views about the role of money in the initial phase of the Depression, say, from 1928 to 1931. For example, Kindleberger (1973) stressed the oversupply of commodities and the resulting declines in their prices as an important initiating factor in the Depression, and Temin (1976) argued for declines in aggregate demand result from nonmonetary causes (notably, an autonomous decline in consumption spending). In contrast, Hamilton (1987) suggested that contractionary monetary policies played an important role in depressing production and employment from as early as 1928.

The purpose of this chapter is to provide some quantitative evidence on both the timing and relative importance of the deflationary factors that gripped the world economy during the Depression era. A full analysis of this issue, we readily acknowledge, would require an accurate macroeconometric model of the world economy of the 1930s, an extensive data set, and a considerable amount of detailed historical and institutional information. While such an analysis would certainly be worth undertaking, in this chapter, we confine ourselves to a much simpler approach, consisting primarily of the examination of some basic identities relating money and prices to their determinants, the both a national and the multinational level. Our method is in the spirit of Friedman and Schwartz (1963), who examined the behav-

---

[2] Increased money demand can also affect money stocks under the gold standard, depending on the form that the added demand takes. An increased demand for currency relative to deposits, for example, by reducing the money multiplier, will lead to a smaller stock of money, all else being equal.

ior of the currency-deposit ratio, the reserve-deposit ratio, and the "money multiplier" to demonstrate the links between these determinants of the money stock and economic developments (see, for example, their Chart 31). Although our approach is not a substitute for a full structural analysis, we believe that it yields some useful insights into price level and monetary developments of the Depression era and perhaps helps to identify the issues that a more complete structural analysis should address.

Our analysis leads to the following conclusions, among others. First, in discussing the sources of interwar deflation it is important to specify which price index one is using. Wholesale prices fell much more sharply than consumer prices in the early stages of the Depression, reflecting the world-wide plunge in the prices of internationally traded commodities. Although further research is needed, it seems likely that there were important non-monetary factors behind the fall in wholesale prices, possibly consistent with the aforementioned views of Kindleberger (1973). Wholesale prices also seem to be good predictors of other macroeconomic variables during the early phase of the Depression.

The behavior of consumer prices, in contrast, seems reasonably well explained by the behavior of national money stocks, combined with normal changes in real money demand. There is little evidence that unusual changes in the demand for money (as alleged to have occurred in the United States and France, for example) had a major deflationary impact. There is, however, some indication that a disequilibrium adjustment process, set in train by poor choices of initial parities, can help to explain the behavior of consumer prices in the early part of the Depression.

Second, consistent with the views of Hamilton (1987), contraction or slow growth of nominal money stocks was an important source of deflation in the earlier phase of the Depression (prior to the banking and exchange rate crises of 1931), as well as after 1931. Although monetary factors played an important role throughout the Depression, the sources of monetary tightness varied substantially by period. Through 1930, the main reason for slow or negative money growth was unnecessarily contractionary policies by central banks, notably the sterilization of gold inflows by surplus countries, such as the United States. "Maldistribution" of gold among the major economies also had a contractionary influence during this period, but this adverse effect was more than outweighed by increases in the world supply of monetary gold.

After the crises of 1931, however, the sources of monetary contraction shifted radically, with serious deflation continuing through 1933. Banking panics, which lowered the money multiplier, and the "maldistribution" problem became the main sources of declines in the world money supply. On average, the discretionary component of monetary policy became more expansionary during this period, but not by enough to offset the contractionary effects of banking panics and the "maldistribution" of gold. The substitution of gold for foreign exchange reserves, sometimes cited as a deflationary factor, does not seem to have been important for the world price level, although it was relevant for some individual countries (notably France). A metaphorical summary of the causes of world monetary contraction might be that damage resulted from "self-inflicted wounds" prior to the financial crises of 1931, and "forces beyond our control" between 1931 and 1933.

Finally, our method sheds some light on the experiences of individual countries, the policies that were adopted by their central banks, and the effects of those policies on the world as a whole. The policies of the Bank of France seem most coherent, conditional on their adherence to the gold standard; for example, France is the only country that seemed to adhere to any degree to the gold standard's "rules of the game." However, the large gold inflows to France (reflecting in part the substitution of gold reserves for foreign exchange) and the relatively muted effect of gold inflows on the French money supply were significant causes of the world monetary contraction.

Our analysis of Germany rehabilitates to some extent the policies of Heinrich Brüning, who has been blamed for the sharp contraction in the German money supply during the year prior to Germany's banking crisis. We find instead that Brüning's policies tended to moderate the effects of Germany's gold losses and a declining money multiplier. The most misguided phase of German monetary policy, our analysis suggests, was instead the eighteen months following the 1931 panic, during which the Reichsbank actually reinforced a disastrous decline in the money stock.

Perhaps not too surprisingly, in light of the work of Friedman and Schwartz (1963), Hamilton (1987), and others, our analysis provides the clearest indictment of the Federal Reserve and U.S. monetary policy. Between mid-1928 and the financial crises that began in the spring of 1931, the Fed not only refused to monetize the substantial gold inflows to the United States but actually managed to convert positive reserve inflows into negative growth in the M1 money stock. Thus Fed policy was actively destabilizing in the pre-1931 period. Largely because of the size of the U.S. economy (its real output accounted for about half of the total of the eight major industrial countries we consider), our methods attribute a substantial portion of the worldwide deflation prior to 1931 to these policy decisions by the Federal Reserve.

The rest of the chapter is organized as follows. Section I provides an overview of the behavior of output, prices, and money in the eight industrial countries in our sample, and in an aggregate of these countries. Section II introduces our basic method, which is to decompose changes in price levels and money stocks into a series of economically interpretable ratios.

Using these ratios and monthly data from eight industrial countries, Section III analyzes the behavior of national and aggregate price levels, and Section IV considers the determinants of money stocks. Section V summarizes the method and findings.

I. The Behavior of Output, Prices, and Money: An Overview

The main purpose of this chapter is to develop and apply a simple method of analyzing price and money stock movements under the international gold standard. As background, however, we begin with an overview of the behavior of output, prices, and money stocks in the countries in our sample during the 1928–1936 period.

To begin, Figure 1 displays the behavior of industrial production and prices (both the consumer price index, or CPI, and the wholesale price index, or WPI) for the eight industrial countries we studied (Canada, France, Germany, Japan, Poland, Sweden, the United Kingdom, and the United States). Our selection of countries was dictated primarily by the availability of monthly data for the key monetary variables. Industrial production, probably the best available measure of economic activity for the interwar period, is shown in the left panels of Figure 1, and the two price indexes are shown in the right panels. For consistency with the aggregation scheme that we will use later, all variables in Figure 1 are measured as cumulative log changes from June 1928. However, in our discussion of Figure 1 we will refer to the data in the more familiar index-number form, with June 1928 = 100 unless otherwise noted. Visually, of course, the two measures are qualitatively similar.

Examination of Figure 1 shows that, among the countries in our sample, the most precipitous declines in output and prices occurred in Canada, the United States, and Germany. On an index of June 1928 = 100, Canadian industrial production rose to 119 by January 1929 but declined to 51 in February 1933. Output did not return to mid-1928 levels in Canada until September 1936. Canadian wholesale prices also hit bottom in February 1933, at an index value of 66, and consumer prices reached their troughs in April 1933, at 78. Prices (especially consumer prices) remained essentially flat in Canada after 1933.

The United States exhibited similar patterns. U.S. industrial production, which reached 115 in June 1929, fell to 55 in June 1932 and reached that level again in March 1933. Output did not return to the June 1928 level in the United States until November 1936. U.S. wholesale prices reached their trough in February 1933 at 61, and consumer prices reached their trough in April 1933 at 73, the same months as in Canada.

In Germany, output rose from 100 in June 1928 to 110 a year later, before

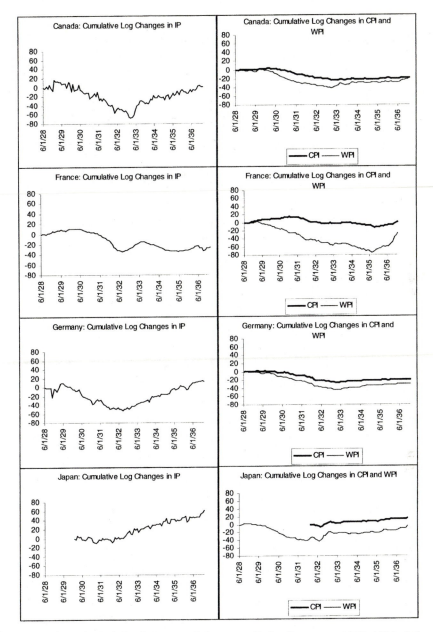

Figure 1. Industrial Production and Prices in Eight Countries, 1928–1936. *Left panels*, cumulative log differences for industrial production; *right panels*, cumulative log differences for consumer price index and wholesale price index.

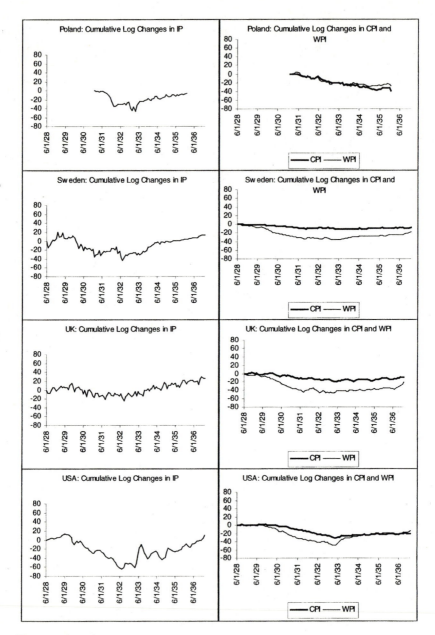

Figure 1. (*cont.*)

beginning a decline to 59 in August 1932. Wholesale prices bottomed out in Germany in April 1933, shortly after the troughs in the United States and Canada. German consumer prices hit 77 in March 1933, and then stabilized.

As documented in more detail by Eichengreen and Sachs (1985, 1986) and Bernanke and James (1991), among others, the behavior of output and prices in the major industrial countries was closely related to national exchange rate regimes and monetary policies. Notably, the troughs in both the United States and Canada corresponded almost exactly to the Roosevelt devaluation and bank holiday of March 1933, which were followed in turn by rapid monetary expansions in both countries. Although Germany effectively departed from the gold standard by imposing capital controls in mid-1931, it attempted to maintain a relationship between its money supply and its international reserves for several years after that. Thus the collapse of the German money supply was not ended until after Hitler's accession to power in 1933.

While Canada, the United States, and Germany maintained restrictive policies into 1933, the so-called Sterling Bloc, represented in our sample by the United Kingdom, Sweden, and Japan, suspended the gold standard and reversed the associated tightness of their monetary policies relatively early in the decade. Most famously, the United Kingdom abandoned gold in September 1931 and, after a brief delay, took advantage of its newfound flexibility to engage in modestly expansionary policies. Presumably as a result of these policies, British industrial production, which had reached a level of 117 in October 1929, fell to 81 as of August 1931, but then began to rise. Wholesale prices in Britain also bottomed out in August 1931, at 65. Consumer prices declined gradually for a bit longer, reaching 82 in March 1933.

Sweden left gold at the same time as Britain, in September 1931. At the time of the devaluation, Sweden was already in a severe depression, its index of industrial production having fallen all the way to 70 from a high of 129 in January 1929. After leaving gold, Sweden embarked on its well-known price level stabilization policy (see, e.g., Jonung, 1979). Significantly, however, the Swedish government did not take the step of reflating before stabilizing prices: the Swedish wholesale price index, which had declined to 71 in September 1931, was still at 70 in June 1933. Industrial production reached a low of 64 in July 1932. Beginning in June 1933, wholesale prices began to rise gradually, and Swedish output regained June 1928 levels by April 1935.

Japan also left gold relatively early, in December 1931. We do not have pre-1931 output data for Japan. Figure 1 shows, though, that subsequent to leaving gold, the Japanese economy grew relatively well, and prices rose modestly.

A third group of countries, the so-called Gold Bloc, remained stubbornly tied to the gold standard until 1935 or 1936. In our sample, the Gold Bloc is represented by France and Poland. As Figure 1 shows, France did not have as deep an overall decline in output as some other countries, possibly reflecting its strong gold inflows early in the decade, but its economic depression was significantly more persistent. After hovering at 112 from December 1929 to March 1930, French industrial production fell to 71 in July 1932. In May 1935 industrial production in France was still only at 71; in contrast, as we have noted, countries that had left the gold standard earlier had all enjoyed substantial recoveries by that point. The French wholesale price index bottomed out at 48 in July 1935, also a much later trough than in most other countries.

As in the case of Japan, our output data for Poland are incomplete. However, Poland, like other Gold Bloc countries, suffered severely in the Depression. Even with January 1931 taken as the base month (January 1931 = 100), Polish industrial production was down to 63 in March 1933. Again relative to January 1931, the Polish WPI hovered at 76 from August to December 1933, hitting its minimum at 75 in December 1934; the CPI declined until April 1935, reaching 69 in that month. The Polish economy recovered somewhat near the end of the period; output in December 1935 was at 93, and wholesale prices were at 77, again relative to January 1931 = 100.

An overall picture of output and price behavior is displayed in the top two panels of Figure 2, which show weighted ("world") averages of the data in Figure 1 for Canada, France, Germany, Sweden, the United Kingdom, and the United States.[3] Japan and Poland are omitted from the aggregates shown in Figure 2 because of missing data. The broad patterns in Figure 2 are clear enough, and familiar. "World" output, which had expanded by 10.0 log points between June 1928 and June 1929, began to decline in the autumn of 1929. By July 1932, the lowest point for the world aggregate, industrial production was 47.4 log points below the June 1928 level. Output sputtered until the spring of 1933, when, in large part because of the recovery in the United States, it began to rebound.

Average world price levels followed a pattern very similar to that of output. Wholesale prices, for example, began to fall in the summer of 1929 (ahead of movements in output and the CPI) and bottomed out in March 1933, 45.7 log points below the level of June 1928. The trough in aggregate consumer prices occurred in April 1933, 24.7 log points below the level of June 1928. As is evident from both Figures 1 and 2, recovery in prices was noticeably slower than that of output: Whereas aggregate output had

---

[3] The weights are based on relative 1928 real GDPs, calculated from Maddison (1982). See the Data Appendix for weights and all data sources. Note that the weight for the United States is close to one-half, reflecting the dominance of the U.S. economy in the period after World War I.

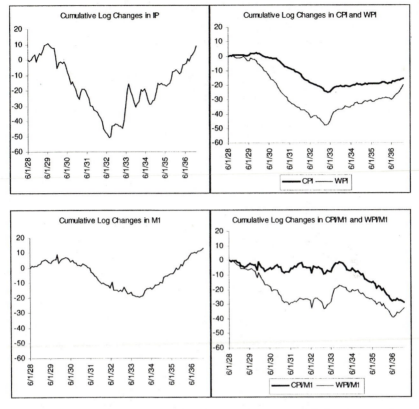

Figure 2. World Industrial Production, Prices, and Money Stock, Six-Country Averages, 1928–1936. Values are cumulative changes in the weighted averages of log industrial production, log CPI and WPI price levels, log M1 money stock, and the log ratios of prices to money stock. Japan and Poland are omitted due to insufficient data. See Data Appendix for the weights used.

reached its June 1928 level by September 1936, at the end of 1936 wholesale prices were 18.6 log points below their June 1928 level, and consumer prices remained 15.8 log points below the June 1928 level. The "world" M1 money stock, shown in the bottom left panel of Figure 2, displayed the same U-shape as industrial production and the price indexes, although it is interesting that the trough in M1 occurred a bit later (in October 1933) than the trough in world output and prices.

To look more carefully at lead-lag relations among output, prices, and money, we performed a series of Granger-causality tests for each country and for the world aggregate. Table 1 show results for the full sample (June 1928–December 1936), based on a variety of estimated vector autoregressions

Table 1
Granger-Causality Tests, 1928:6–1936:12

a. Dependent variable: IP

Variable	Specification	Country						
		U.S.	UK	Canada	France	Germany	Sweden	World
CPI	CPI	0.027	0.000	0.000			0.000	0.005
	CPI, M1	0.079	0.024	0.000			0.000	0.000
	CPI, WPI					0.045		
	CPI, M1, WPI					0.013		
M1	M1	0.075	0.003	0.001				
	M1, CPI		0.000	0.001	0.073			
	M1, WPI	0.053	0.000	0.008		0.058		0.064
	M1, CPI, WPI		0.000	0.001			0.039	0.015
WPI	WPI	0.043	0.014	0.010	0.020		0.005	0.049
	WPI, CPI	0.002		0.000	0.073		0.000	0.001
	WPI, M1	0.031	0.009		0.034		0.003	0.008
	WPI, M1, CPI	0.003		0.001			0.000	0.000

Table 1 (*cont.*)

b. Dependent variable: M1

Variable	Specification	Country						
		U.S.	UK	Canada	France	Germany	Sweden	World
CPI	CPI	0.059			0.036	0.001		0.016
	CPI, IP	0.016			0.015	0.027		0.004
	CPI, WPI	0.000		0.045		0.095		0.000
	CPI, IP, WPI	0.000			0.003			0.002
IP	IP	0.037		0.032	0.021	0.000	0.052	0.009
	IP, CPI			0.020	0.009	0.003	0.019	0.002
	IP, WPI			0.017		0.034	0.016	0.056
	IP, CPI, WPI			0.076	0.002		0.006	
WPI	WPI	0.000			0.021	0.000		0.040
	WPI, CPI	0.000				0.005		0.000
	WPI, IP					0.014		
	WPI, IP, CPI	0.000			0.037		0.083	0.015

Table 1 (*cont.*)

c. Dependent variable: CPI

Variable	Specification	Country						
		U.S.	UK	Canada	France	Germany	Sweden	World
IP	IP	0.000	0.000	0.000	0.047	0.000	0.001	0.000
	IP, M1	0.000		0.004	0.081	0.002	0.000	0.000
	IP, WPI	0.003	0.005					0.039
	IP, M1, WPI	0.001						0.000
M1	M1			0.001	0.075			
	M1, IP	0.092						0.041
	M1, WPI							
	M1, IP, WPI							0.000
WPI	WPI	0.000	0.001	0.000	0.000	0.000	0.000	0.000
	WPI, IP	0.002	0.005	0.000	0.000	0.001	0.005	0.000
	WPI, M1	0.000	0.004	0.000	0.000		0.000	0.000
	WPI, M1, IP	0.004	0.005	0.000	0.001	0.003	0.013	

Table 1 (*cont.*)

d. Dependent variable: WPI

Variable	Specification	Country						
		U.S.	UK	Canada	France	Germany	Sweden	World
CPI	CPI	**0.012**		**0.000**	**0.020**	0.067	**0.000**	**0.003**
	CPI, M1	**0.004**		**0.000**			**0.000**	**0.002**
	CPI, IP	**0.014**		**0.000**	**0.042**	0.070	**0.000**	0.089
	CPI, M1, IP	**0.001**		**0.000**			**0.000**	**0.002**
M1	M1		**0.000**	0.055	0.061	**0.040**	**0.005**	**0.005**
	M1, CPI		**0.000**					
	M1, IP		**0.038**			**0.011**	0.058	
	M1, CPI, IP	**0.033**	**0.030**			0.077		
IP	IP	**0.022**				**0.006**	**0.011**	**0.013**
	IP, CPI	**0.025**				**0.008**		
	IP, M1	**0.015**				**0.001**		**0.007**
	IP, M1, CPI	**0.003**				**0.004**		**0.002**

Notes: In each part of the table, the first column gives the variable that is being checked for Granger-causality with respect to the dependent variable. For example, part a tests whether the CPI, M1, and WPI, respectively, Granger-cause IP over the full sample, for each country and for the world aggregate. The second column lists the variables included in the particular VAR specification (in all cases, lags of the dependent variable are included). The last seven columns give the resulting significance level. Values indicating rejection of the null hypothesis of no Granger-causality at a 5 percent level of significance or better are shown in bold. Other values shown indicate Granger-causality at the 10 percent level but not the 5 percent level. Values that are not significant at at least the 10 percent level are omitted. Regressions are run with optimal lag length as determined by the BIC.

(VARs). For each country and the world aggregate, we estimated VARs including all possible combinations of industrial production, the wholesale price index, the consumer price index, and the M1 money stock (see the notes to the table for details). Boldface entries in the table indicate estimated Granger-causality relationships at the 5 percent level of significance or better.

The results shown in Table 1 are indicative of complex, multidirectional timing relationships among the variables. We find many statistically significant Granger-causality relationships, but no strong patterns stand out. For example, wholesale prices are the strongest predictors of output in the United States, France, Sweden, and the world aggregate, but M1 seems a somewhat more reliable predictor of output in the United Kingdom and Canada. The CPI also has predictive power for output in Canada, Sweden, and the world aggregate, even in the presence of both the WPI and M1. None of the variables reliably forecasts output in Germany.

Wholesale prices are strong predictors of consumer prices as well as output, but the effects are not one way, as there is also evidence of feedback from output and consumer prices to wholesale prices. The M1 money stock is forecast by output, prices, or both in all countries except for the United Kingdom. It is interesting that M1 does not have consistent predictive power for prices, except for wholesale prices in the United Kingdom and to a lesser extent in Germany. M1 has almost no predictive power for consumer prices.

Several aspects of the VARs underlying Table 1 may be responsible for the absence of sharp results. First, the use of the entire 1928–1936 sample risks conflating what may be rather different dynamics from the collapse and recovery stages of the Depression. Second, the inclusion of two measures of the price level may induce multicollinearity and thus obscure the relationships between prices and other variables. To address these issues, we also estimated VARs over the first part of the sample period (1928:6—1933:12) only, for IP, WPI, and M1 (that is, with the CPI excluded). With only three variables included, the possible alternative VAR specifications are restricted to trivariate or bivariate form. The results of conducting Granger-causality tests in these more restricted systems are shown in Table 2.

Perhaps the most consistent feature of the results in Table 2 is the leading-indicator property of wholesale prices. At the aggregate level, the WPI Granger-causes both M1 and IP at better than 1 percent significance in both trivariate and bivariate specifications. The WPI also Granger-causes IP at high significance levels in every country (except Germany) in all specifications. However, the lead of WPI over M1 at the level of individual countries is less consistent; it appears that the tendency of WPI to Granger-cause M1 at the aggregate level is being driven primarily by the U.S. data.

It is quite interesting that M1 does not consistently Granger-cause IP in

Table 2
Granger-Causality Tests, 1928:6–1933:12

a. Trivariate VARs

Forecasting Relationship	Country						
	U.S.	UK	Canada	France	Germany	Sweden	World
IP → M1					0.081		
M1 → IP		0.080					
IP → WPI	0.020						
WPI → IP	**0.016**	**0.000**	0.052	0.033	**0.010**	**0.010**	**0.006**
WPI → M1	**0.006**					0.092	**0.006**
M1 → WPI	0.060		0.054	0.083		**0.014**	**0.042**

b. Bivariate VARs

Forecasting Relationship	Country						
	U.S.	UK	Canada	France	Germany	Sweden	World
IP → M1				0.081	**0.000**		0.055
M1 → IP			**0.028**			**0.045**	
IP → WPI	0.071				**0.004**		
WPI → IP	**0.009**	**0.003**	**0.004**	**0.021**		**0.001**	**0.004**
WPI → M1	**0.002**			**0.037**	**0.001**		**0.001**
M1 → WPI			0.063	0.068		**0.018**	

Notes: Part a shows Granger-causality results from a trivariate VAR on IP, M1, and WPI. Part b is based on the indicated bivariate VAR. In each part of the table, the first column indicates the direction of Granger-causality being tested. The last seven columns give the resulting significance level. Values indicating rejection of the null hypothesis of no Granger-causality at a 5 percent level of significance or better are shown in bold. Other values shown indicate Granger-causality at the 10 percent level but not the 5 percent level. Values that are not significant at at least the 10 percent level are omitted. All samples end in 1933:12, and all VARs are estimated with two lags.

these data. There is modest evidence of Granger-causality from M1 to wholesale prices. Industrial production does not consistently Granger-cause money or prices in the three-variable system over the 1928–1933 sample period. These and other results reported Table 2 are not much changed when the sample is truncated in December 1932 instead of December 1933.

What are we to make of these findings? One might argue that the tendency of wholesale prices to lead other variables during the decline phase of the Depression, together with the relatively weak predictive power of the M1 money stock, is most consistent with nonmonetarist interpretations of the Depression. For example, these results seem to fit well with Kindleberger's (1973) thesis that falling commodity prices were an important driving force in the early stages of the Depression. There are other interpretations, however. One possibility is that commodity prices share some characteristics of asset prices, so that their early decline occurred to some extent in anticipation of subsequent declines in output and increases in interest rates (we know that commodity prices generally tend to be highly procyclical and leading variables). We return to these themes shortly, after a more general discussion of our methodology.

II. An Approach to Decomposing Price and Money Stock Movements

Our principal objective in this chapter is to interpret the behavior of prices and money in major industrial countries during the 1928–1936 period. To reiterate, our tack will be to examine the behavior of some economically interpretable ratios, in the spirit of Friedman and Schwartz's (1963) decomposition of U.S. money stock changes into changes in the monetary base and the components of the money multiplier.

The starting point for our analysis is the following tautological expression for the price level in country i at time t:

$$P_{it} = (P_{it} / M_{it})(M_{it} / BASE_{it})(BASE_{it} / RES_{it})(RES_{it} / GOLD_{it})$$
$$(QGOLD_{it} * PGOLD_{it}) \tag{1}$$

where

$P_{it} =$ *the price level (the WPI or CPI)*
$M_{it} =$ the nominal money supply (here, M1)
$BASE_{it} =$ the monetary base (notes in circulation plus bank reserves)
$RES_{it} =$ international reserves of the central bank (foreign assets plus gold reserves), valued in domestic currency
$GOLD_{it} =$ gold reserves of the central bank, valued in domestic currency $= QGOLD_{it} * PGOLD_{it}$
$QGOLD_{it} =$ gold reserves of the central bank, in ounces
$PGOLD_{it} =$ the official domestic-currency price of gold

Equation (1) may be viewed as a decomposition of the price level at a given time into an exhaustive set of determinants, as follows.

1. *The inverse of real money balances*, P_{it} / M_{it}. As we will see, in our sample, there is often considerable variability in the ratio of prices to money. Changes in this ratio are usually interpreted as reflecting changes in the quantity of real money balances that the public desires to hold. Implicitly, this interpretation relies on the assumption that prices adjust rapidly to equate the real money stock and real money demand. Changes in real money demand can arise from a variety of sources, including changes in real output, changes in expected inflation (as embodied in nominal interest rates), and changes in the payments technology. Also, during the Depression era, the public's distrust of banks and the riskiness of financial assets, such as stocks and corporate bonds, no doubt generated a motive for hoarding currency: Changes in the extent of hoarding may have affected overall money demand, although in principle the effect on total money demand could be either positive or negative, depending on whether desired increases in currency holdings exceed desired reductions in bank deposits.

An alternative interpretation of variations in the ratio of prices to money is that they reflect the workings of a disequilibrium adjustment process. When the world returned to gold in the late 1920s, many observers voiced concern about whether the absolute and relative values of the official parities were consistent with long-run equilibrium. Notably, Keynes argued that the pound was overvalued at the official parities, and it was widely believed that the franc was undervalued. The adjustment process for (say) an overvalued currency would involve reductions in both the money supply (through gold losses) and in prices, which would continue until both domestic real money balances and the real exchange rate reached long-run equilibrium levels. If domestic prices are sticky to some degree, this adjustment process could entail changes over time in the ratio of prices to money, independent of the notional demand for real balances. The precise dynamics of the ratio of prices to money would depend in a complicated way on the relative adjustment speeds of prices and gold stocks. To foreshadow our results, we find evidence below that this disequilibrium adjustment process may indeed have been at work in the early stages of the Depression.

The other four factors contributing to changes in the price level (as represented by equation (1)) are determinants of the nominal supply of money:

2. *The money multiplier*, $M_{it} / BASE_{it}$. In fractional-reserve banking systems, the quantity of inside money (M1) is a multiple of the quantity of outside money (the monetary base). As is familiar from Friedman and Schwartz (1963) and many subsequent textbook treatments, the money multiplier depends on the public's preferred ratio of currency to deposits and the ratio of bank reserves to deposits. The money multiplier varies among countries, in ways that depend on the degree of financial development and

the particular financial institutions in each country, and it may also change within a country as financial institutions change. However, sharp variations in the money multiplier—which must be associated with large changes in the ratios of currency and bank reserves to deposits—were typically associated with banking panics, or at least problems in the banking system, during the Depression era. For example, the money multiplier in the United States began to decline precipitously following the "first banking crisis" identified by Friedman and Schwartz, in December 1930, and fell more or less continuously until the final banking crisis in March 1933, when it stabilized. Therefore, below we interpret changes in national money stocks arising from changes in the money multiplier as being caused primarily by problems in the domestic banking system.

3. *The inverse of the cover ratio*, $BASE_{it} / RES_{it}$. The rules of the gold standard did not require the monetary base to be fully backed by gold or other international reserves; in other words, the ratio of international reserves to the monetary base (called the cover ratio, or the gold-backing ratio) could be and typically was less than one. Most countries did impose statutory minima on the cover ratio; for example, in the United States, the minimum legal value for the cover ratio was 40 percent during this period, implying a legal maximum of 2.5 for the inverse cover ratio, $BASE_{it} / RES_{it}$. Although the cover ratio was bounded from below, there were no constraints in the upward direction, which effectively allowed central banks on the gold standard some discretion in their domestic monetary policies (Sumner, 1991). For example, by sterilizing gold inflows, countries could raise their cover ratios, reducing the ratio of base to international reserves. Below we take changes in $BASE_{it} / RES_{it}$ as indicative of sterilization (either active or passive) by central banks.

4. *The ratio of international reserves to gold stocks*, $BASE_{it} / RES_{it}$. Under the gold exchange standard, central banks in many countries were allowed to hold "reserve currencies" (such as U.S. dollars and British pounds sterling) in lieu of gold. Hence, for the world as a whole, the ratio of international reserves to monetary gold exceeded one. During the early 1930s, fear of devaluation of the reserve currencies led many central banks to convert foreign exchange reserves into gold, implying a decline in the aggregate reserves-to-gold ratio (Eichengreen, 1990, ch. 10). In addition, several countries, France most notably, quite deliberately pursued a policy of eliminating foreign exchange reserves in favor of gold, even prior to the period of instability in the exchange market (see, e.g., Hawtrey, 1939, p. 138). We use the reserves-to-gold ratio below as an index of the effects of the liquidation of foreign exchange reserves on national and world money supplies.

5. *The quantity and "price" of gold*, $QGOLD_{it}$ and $PGOLD_{it}$. From the perspective of an individual country, with all else equal, an inflow of gold permitted an increase in the domestic money supply. An increase in the

price of gold in terms of domestic currency, that is, a devaluation, also permitted an increase in the domestic money supply, the physical quantity of gold stocks being held constant.

In summary, equation (1) provides a heuristic method for decomposing price changes in a given country into components due to

1. changes in the price level given the money stock, reflecting either changes in money demand or the disequilibrium adjustment of prices and money stocks under the gold standard;
2. changes in the money multiplier, reflecting conditions in the commercial banking system;
3. changes in the cover ratio, reflecting the degree to which the central bank sterilizes inflows or outflows of international reserves;
4. changes in the ratio of international reserves (inclusive of foreign exchange reserves) to gold, reflecting the liquidation of foreign exchange reserves; and
5. changes in the parity (the price of gold) or in physical gold stocks.

Equation (1) being a tautology, it naturally applies to all countries, both on and off the gold standard, and we will calculate and interpret these ratios for both groups of countries. The main difference that we expect to see between gold standard and nongold standard countries is that the latter—in principle at least—faced no constraints on their cover ratios.[4] Nevertheless, equation (1) should remain useful in interpreting the sources of changes in money stocks and price levels even in countries off gold. Further, countries that abandoned the gold standard (wholly or partially) continued in all cases to hold gold, so their policies remained quite relevant to those countries remaining on gold.

Equation (1) applies directly only to a single country. It will be useful to have a version of (1) that aggregates over countries, both so that we can compare the relative importance of various factors for monetary developments in the world as a whole, and so that we can account for possible compositional effects, such as the claim that gold stocks were "maldistributed" among countries.

To make (1) applicable to the world as a whole, let $p = \ln(P)$, $pm = \ln(P/M)$, $mb = \ln(M/BASE)$, $br = \ln(BASE/RES)$, $rg = (RES/GOLD)$, $qg = \ln(QGOLD)$, and $pg = \ln(PGOLD)$. Then equation (1) can be written more compactly (in logs) as

$$p_{it} = pm_{it} + mb_{it} + br_{it} + rg_{it} + qg_{it} + pg_{it}. \tag{2}$$

[4] It is interesting that countries did not necessarily use that freedom very aggressively. Eichengreen (1990, p. 250) writes: "Even most of the countries which went off the gold standard following the onset of the Great Depression maintained gold cover ratios not far different from those which had traditionally prevailed, either because of statutory requirements or out of concern to prevent depreciation due to lack of confidence."

Let ω_i be a time-invariant weighting factor which reflects the relative importance of economy i in the world economy, with $\sum_{i=1}^{n} \omega_i = 1$. (In the application, we use weights based on relative real GDPs in 1928.) Then, defining $p_t = \sum_{i=1}^{n} \omega_i p_{it}$, $pm_t = \sum_{i=1}^{n} \omega_i pm_{it}, \dots$, we can write a "world" version of equation (2) as

$$p_t = pm_t + mb_t + br_t + rg_t + qg_t + pg_t, \tag{3}$$

where the quantities now refer to weighted averages of the corresponding country quantities.

As mentioned, much contemporary discussion of the world "shortage" of monetary gold during the 1930s focused on the "maldistribution" of gold stocks among countries, rather than on any shortage in the total stock of monetary gold (which actually grew significantly during the decade). To separate monetary effects arising from the international distribution of gold from those arising from changes in the world stock of monetary gold, it is useful to take the decomposition implied by equation (3) one step further: For each country i at time t, break the log quantity of gold (in physical units) into two components: the country's log share of world monetary gold, s_{it}, and the log of the world monetary gold stock, g_t. That is,

$$qg_{it} = s_{it} + g_t.$$

Taking the weighted sum over all countries implies $qg_t = s_t + g_t$, where $s_t = \sum_{i=1}^{n} \omega_i s_{it}$, the weighted share, is an index of the "maldistribution" of gold. Note that s_t is approximately the covariance between country economic weights and log gold shares, so that lower values of s_t imply that the amount of gold countries are holding is disproportionate to their economic importance, for example, that gold is "maldistributed."

Using the definition $qg_t = s_t + g_t$, we rewrite equation (3) as

$$p_t = pm_t + mb_t + br_t + rg_t + s_t + g_t + pg_t. \tag{4}$$

Again, the presence of the terms s_t and g_t in (4) allows us to distinguish effects on the world price level arising from redistribution of the gold stock from those arising from changes in the total stock of monetary gold.

III. The Behavior of the Ratios of Prices to Money

In applying equations (2) and (4) to Depression-era data, we first consider the behavior of the ratio of prices to money in individual countries and in the "world" aggregate. Section IV takes up the determinants of money stocks.

The ratios of prices to money are shown for the world aggregate in Figure

2, and for each country in the sample in Figure 3. Price levels are measured alternatively by the WPI and the CPI for each country. The money stock is M1 or a close approximation (again, see the Data Appendix for more information on the construction of the data series).

As we have already seen (in the right panels of Figure 1 and the top right panel of Figure 2), both consumer prices and wholesale prices fell significantly between the beginning of the Depression and the spring of 1933, when they began to recover. When measured relative to the paths of money stocks, however, the trajectories of consumer and wholesale prices look rather different. As is evident in the bottom right panel of Figure 2 (for the world aggregate) or in Figure 3 (for individual countries), relative to M1, the declines in the CPI in the early stages of the Depression were typically rather modest. Equivalently, real money balances as measured by M1/CPI did not rise by very much. However, from late 1928 until the spring of 1931, wholesale prices fell precipitously, even when measured relative to money stocks; that is, M1/WPI rose substantially in virtually all the countries in our sample and for the world aggregate.

The specific values of these changes between June 1928 and June 1931— the first, critical stage of the Depression—are shown in Table 3, along with other relevant magnitudes. Again, the remarkable declines in wholesale prices in the early phases of the Depression are apparent. Even measured relative to money stocks, over this three-year period, wholesale prices fell by more than 35 log points in four countries and by more than 25 log points in six of the seven countries in the table. The weighted average of the decline in WPI/M1 across the countries in our sample was nearly 30 log points. In contrast, the weighted average of the decline in CPI/M1 over the three years was less than 6 log points. In Canada and France, consumer prices actually rose relative to money stocks during the 1928–1931 period.

Although it is beyond the scope of this chapter, the sources of the collapse of wholesale prices during the initial phase of the Depression are certainly worthy of additional investigation. We conjecture that factors both exogenous and endogenous to the state of the macroeconomy were responsible for the decline. For example, among causes exogenous to the business cycle, the post–World War I expansion in the world supply of commodities no doubt played a role, as stressed by Kindleberger (1973). (Prices of internationally tradable commodities made up a substantial share of wholesale price indexes during this period. That movements in national wholesale price indexes were being dominated by changes in the prices of internationally traded commodities seems particularly plausible for the 1928–1931 period, given the strong correlation of changes in the WPI across countries apparent in the first column of Table 3.) But it is also the case that commodity prices, and raw materials prices in general, often fall sharply in recessions; for example, these prices are endogenous to macro conditions. This

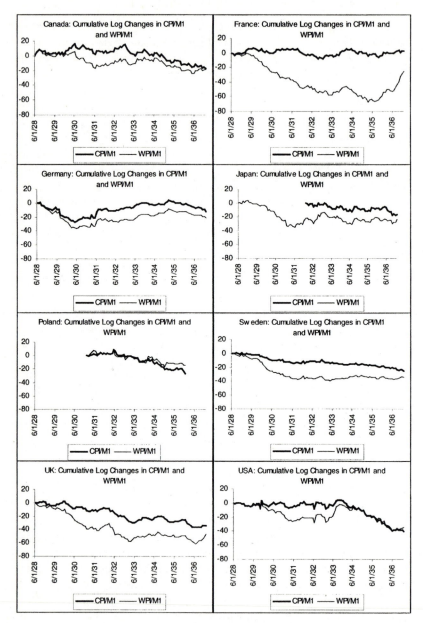

Figure 3. Ratios of Measures of the Price Level to the Money Stock by Country, 1928–1936. Values are cumulative log differences for the ratio of the price level (as measured by the CPI or the WPI) to the M1 money stock.

Table 3
Log Changes in Prices, Money, and Gold Stocks, 1928:6–1931:6

Country	WPI	WPI/M1	CPI	CPI/M1	M1	QGOLD
Canada	− 28.76	− 17.24	− 10.51	1.36	− 11.51	− 18.69
France	− 29.28	− 37.05	13.35	5.58	7.77	66.60
Germany	− 22.97	− 25.41	− 9.41	− 11.85	2.44	− 38.29
Japan	− 39.41	− 35.42	—	—	− 3.99	− 24.30
Sweden	− 31.68	− 36.51	− 9.07	− 13.90	4.83	3.34
UK	− 39.49	− 38.99	− 11.55	− 11.05	− 0.50	− 4.05
U.S.	− 33.24	− 25.67	− 12.14	− 4.57	− 7.57	20.75
World	− 32.38	− 29.19	− 8.68	− 5.59	− 3.19	7.68

Notes: The table shows the cumulative log change in each variable between 1928:6 and 1931:6, for seven countries and the world aggregate. The world aggregate excludes Poland due to missing data. See text for variable definitions.

strong cyclical sensitivity presumably reflects the fact that the prices of storable commodities exhibit some of the characteristics of asset prices, including "forward-looking" behavior and sensitivity to the level of interest rates, as well as the observation that the demand for commodities seems much more than unit elastic with respect to output. These observations notwithstanding, however, it seems likely that the collapse of wholesale prices between 1928 and 1931 had important nonmonetary causes.

Although the behavior of the wholesale price indexes is interesting, consumer prices are probably more relevant for the monetary issues that are the focus of this chapter. In particular, the CPI is the more appropriate deflator to use for measuring changes in the demand for real money balances, since households hold the bulk of the money supply. The CPI also gives more weight than does the WPI to domestic, nontraded goods and services, and so is probably the better index for measuring domestic price adjustment to international gold flows.

If we restrict our attention to changes in consumer prices relative to money stocks, then the absolute movements to be explained are much less dramatic than in the case of wholesale prices, as we have already noted. True, if we think of changes in the CPI as being decomposed into changes in M1 and changes in the ratio of the CPI to M1, then the latter can be quite important, as Table 3 illustrates. For example, during the crucial 1928–1931 period, consumer prices fell by more than 9 log points in both Germany and Sweden, despite the fact that the M1 money supply rose in both countries. In the United Kingdom, almost the entire decline (of over 11 log points) in consumer prices between June 1928 and June 1931 reflected a decline in the ratio of the British CPI to M1, rather than a decline in M1 itself. For the world aggregate, 5.6 log points of the total decline of

8.7 log points in consumer prices is accounted for by the decline in the ratio of CPI to M1.

Still, to say that CPIs fell more quickly than money stocks is only to say that real money balances rose in most countries over the three-year period. Looked at in that way, the behavior of consumer prices relative to money stocks does not appear particularly remarkable. For example, falling interest rates and inflation rates, as well as financial turmoil, can plausibly explain the relatively modest increases in real money holdings, although, of course, declines in real economic activity and associated reductions in transactions demands would have worked in the other direction.

The argument is sometimes made that unusual increases in money demand in a few countries exerted an important deflationary impact. Friedman and Schwartz (1963) noted that large declines in velocity occurred in both the United States and Canada during the early portion of the Depression, exacerbating the effects of contractions in the money stock. More recently, Field (1984) provided evidence that speculative activity on Wall Street increased the transactions demand for money in the United States in the period preceding the Depression; and Eichengreen (1992) and others have pointed to a possible role for poststabilization increases in money demand in France in generating gold inflows to that country. As we have noted, there is also the possibility that financial crises and deflation in certain countries raised money demand by increasing hoarding of currency. As is well known, in a closed economy, increases in money demand (from whatever source) imply contractionary (leftward) shifts in the LM curve. In open economies linked by a gold standard, exceptional increases in money demand in any one country will tend to drain gold from abroad, leading to deflationary pressures in all countries. France and the United States did indeed experience large gold inflows at the expense of other nations, as can be seen in the rightmost column of Table 3.

Did unusual increases in the demand for money in certain countries play a significant deflationary role in the early stages of the Depression? Table 3 provides relatively little support for this view. Real money balances in the United States (M1/CPI) rose by less than 5 log points over the three-year period beginning in mid-1928, a period that includes the major speculative boom on Wall Street. This observation suggests that the increase in the demand for money identified by Field was not especially important for the macroeconomy as a whole. In France, as Table 3 shows and we have already noted, real money balances actually *declined* between 1928 and 1931, which is inconsistent with the view that increases in French money demand were a primary source of the inflows of gold into that country during that period.

Finally, we note that Table 3 shows no obvious correlation between changes in real money demand and financial crisis. The largest increases in real money demand between 1928:6 and 1931:6 were in Sweden, Germany, and the United Kingdom. The United Kingdom and Sweden did not experience serious banking crises at any point during the Depression. Germany did have quite grave banking problems in the summer of 1931, just at the end of the period covered by Table 3. As Figure 3 shows, however, rather than increasing, real money balances dropped significantly in Germany in mid-1931, just as the banking panics took hold. So, to reiterate, there seems to be little evidence for a significant deflationary effect arising from unusual increases in money demand in particular countries.

Although there seems to be little reason to attribute CPI deflation to unusual increases in the demand for money, there does appear to be some evidence for the view that changes in prices relative to money stocks during the early years of the Depression may have reflected a process of disequilibrium adjustment, made necessary by inappropriate initial parities. The comparison of the United Kingdom and France is most instructive. A widely held view, both at the time among modern historians, is that at the official parities adopted upon the return to gold, the pound was overvalued and the franc was undervalued. If correct, this view would predict that the British would lose gold and experience deflation, while the French should gain gold and experience inflation. As is well known (and as Table 3 shows), this is precisely what happened. France gained massive amounts of gold during the period (see the last column of Table 3), and although most of this inflow was sterilized, the French money supply increased by about 8 log points. Britain lost gold, so that the nominal money supply declined slightly over the 1928:6–1931:6 period. Further, the difference in money growth between the two countries, about 8 log points, was considerably smaller than the difference in consumer price inflation: consumer prices rose in France by over 13 log points and fell in the United Kingdom by nearly 12 log points, a difference of 25 log points. This latter pattern is what would result from a disequilibrium adjustment process, if French real balances were initially above, and British real balances initially below, their long-run equilibrium levels.

To clarify this argument, it helps to work with equation (1). Rewrite (1) as

$$P_{it} = (P_{it} / M_{it})k_{it}(QGOLD_{it} * PGOLD_{it}), \tag{5}$$

where $k = (M / BASE)(BASE / RES)(RES / GOLD)$. Equation (5) applies to some country i in period t. An analogous equation applies to another country, j, in the same period. Taking the ratio of equation (5) as applied to country i to the same equation applied to country j, and noting that the nominal exchange rate e between the two countries is defined by $PGOLD_{jt} / PGOLD_{it}$, we can construct an expression for the real exchange rate between the two countries:

$$\frac{eP_{it}}{P_{jt}} = \frac{(P_{it} / M_{it})}{(P_{jt} / M_{jt})} \frac{k_{it}}{k_{jt}} \frac{QGOLD_{it}}{QGOLD_{ij}}. \tag{6}$$

For the sake of discussion, imagine that the real exchange rate defined by (6) is higher than its long-run equilibrium value (that is, think of country i as Britain and country j as France). Further, think of the ks (which depend on policy regimes and institutional factors) as being more or less fixed. Then equation (6) shows two means by which the real exchange rate can adjust toward its long-run equilibrium value. These are (1) decreases in the relative price-to-money ratios in England and France, and (2) decreases in British gold holdings relative to French holdings. The first of these, as we noted, will be operative only if initial real money balances are below equilibrium levels in England and above equilibrium levels in France. Empirically, both mechanisms appear to have been at work in the 1928–1931 period.

To summarize, the question of whether there were significant deflationary forces at work during the 1928–1931 period, *other* than contractions in money stocks, depends on which measure of the price level one has in mind. Wholesale price indexes fell far more rapidly than money stocks in the early stages of the Depression, in large part reflecting sharp declines in the prices of internationally traded commodities. The extent to which the fall in commodity prices was the result of factors exogenous or endogenous to contemporaneous and anticipated macroeconomic conditions remains to be determined, and would be an interesting topic for future research. It seems likely, though, that at least some significant part of the decline in wholesale prices was non-monetary in nature.

The behavior of consumer price indexes, in contrast, appears largely explainable by declining money stocks, coupled with modest increases in the demand for real balances. In addition, the disequilibrium adjustment of price levels, in response to the initial choices of parities and the international distribution of gold holdings, may account for some of the behavior of prices conditional on money stocks. However, there is little evidence for the view that unusually large increases in the demand for money in the United States, France, or other countries exerted a major deflationary impact.

IV. The Behavior of Money Stocks

In the previous section, we saw that, at least in the case of consumer price indexes, the destructive deflation of the early 1930s does not appear to have been attributable to any great degree to declines in price levels *conditional* on money stocks. Rather, the more plausible interpretation is that the general deflation was primarily the result of falling (or very slowly growing) money supplies. The sixth column of Table 3, labeled "M1," makes this point most dramatically. During the period 1928:6–1931:6, which is prior to the major banking and exchange rate crises of the period, nominal money stocks actually shrunk in four of the seven countries listed. Indeed, for the "world" weighted average, nominal M1 money stocks declined by over 3 log points between June 1928 and June 1931, despite a weighted-average increase of almost 8 log points in national gold stocks over the same period.[5] Nominal money stocks rose in Germany (by a total of 2.44 log points over the three-year period) and in Sweden (by 4.83 log points), but these must be judged to be very slow rates of money growth. Only in France, where M1 increased by a cumulative 7.77 log points between mid-1928 and mid-1931, was money growth more nearly in a "normal" range. We take these data to be generally supportive of Hamilton's (1987) thesis that monetary tightness played an important role in even the earliest stage of the Depression. Of course, following the upheavals of 1931, money stocks in many countries dropped even more precipitously, as we discuss further below.

Why did money stocks behave so perversely? To try to shed some light on this question, in this section we apply the decomposition described in Section II to M1 money stocks (or near-equivalents), first for the individual countries in our sample, and then for the aggregate of individual countries. Our objective is to identify the factors quantitatively most responsible for the collapse of national and world money supplies during the Depression.

The basic results are displayed graphically in Figures 4 and 5 and in tabular form in Tables 4 and 5. Figure 4 shows the behavior of the M1 money stock and its component ratios for all eight countries in our sample, while Figure 5 presents the analogous decomposition for the "world" aggregate (Poland is omitted). Table 4 presents the same information for selected quarters for the four economically most important countries (France, Germany, the United Kingdom, and the United States), and Table 5 gives the results for the world aggregates. Note that the decompositions of changes in the "world" money stock in Figure 5 and in Table 5 include the gold distribution effect discussed in Section II. Table 4 also includes central bank discount rates for reference. Except for the discount rates given in Table 4, data are reported in terms of the cumulative change in each variable, in log points, relative to June 1928. Data in the tables are for the last month of the quarter; taking quarterly averages instead would not materially affect the results.

To conserve space, our discussion here focuses on Tables 4 and 5. The corresponding figures are left to the reader's inspection.

France

Data for the French money stock and its components are summarized in part *a* of Table 4. The most remarkable feature of the French data is the contrast,

---

[5] Total world monetary gold stocks grew by 21 log points over the same period. The difference between 21 and 8 reflects the increasing "maldistribution" of monetary gold, as discussed below.

a.   CANADA

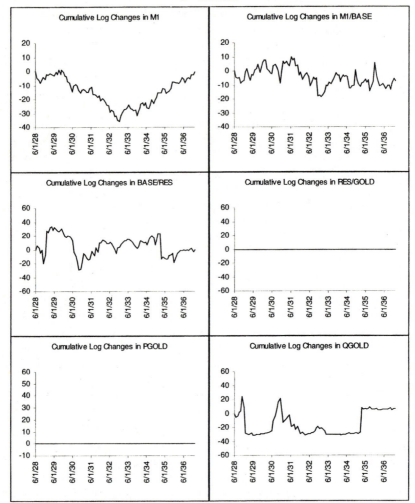

Figure 4. Components of Changes in the Money Stock by Country, 1928–1936. The cumulative change in the log of M1 is decomposed into components for each country in the sample. See text for definitions of the variables.

throughout the sample period, between the large gold inflows to the country and the small increases (or even decreases) in the nominal stock of money. For example, by the end of 1932, the French gold stock had increased by 105 log points relative to mid-1928, but the M1 money stock had increased by only 5 log points.

b. FRANCE

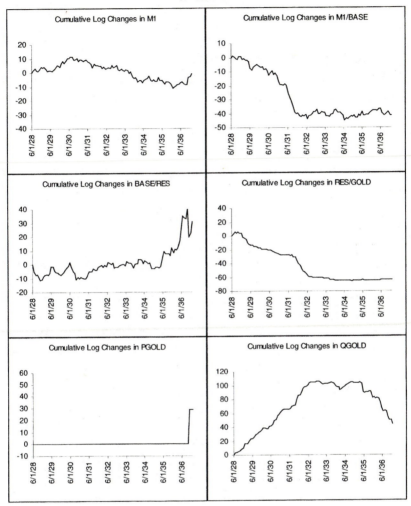

Figure 4. (*cont.*)

Part a of Table 4 shows that two factors helped to explain both the large gold inflows and the failure of those inflows to affect domestic money and prices in France. First, as required by laws enacted during the period of monetary stabilization and reform, the Bank of France actively sought to replace its existing foreign exchange reserves with gold reserves (see, e.g., Eichengreen, 1990, Chapter 10). This exchange of foreign assets for gold is reflected in a decline of 62 log points in the ratio of French international

c.   GERMANY

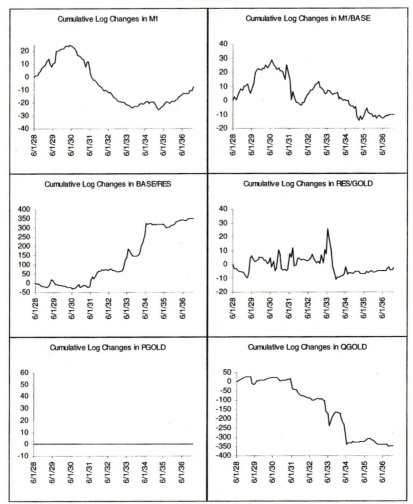

Figure 4. (*cont.*)

reserves to gold holdings between June 1928 and the end of 1932. Indeed, comparison of the *RES / GOLD* and *QGOLD* columns shows that this replacement of foreign exchange by gold can account for approximately half of the increased holdings of gold by the Bank of France. Importantly, as Eichengreen and others have stressed, since the substitution of an equal amount of gold for foreign exchange did not increase France's total international reserves, this component of the gold inflow had no direct effect on the domestic money supply.

d. JAPAN

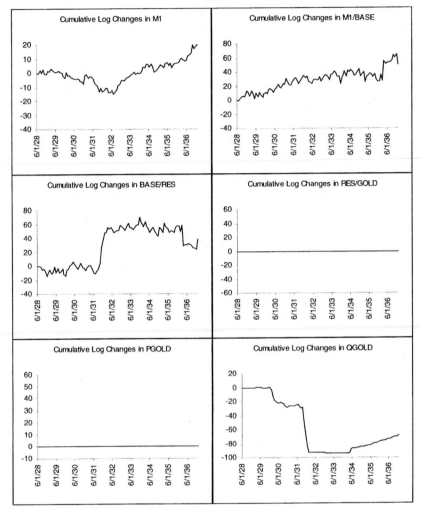

Figure 4. (*cont.*)

The second major element offsetting the effects of gold inflows to France, as shown in the table, was the sustained decline in the money multiplier, M1 / BASE. Although the major French banks emerged from the Depression relatively unscathed, regional and other small banks experienced significant difficulties (Bernanke and James, 1991), which probably accounts for the French public's switch from deposits to currency, particularly during 1931. The falling money multiplier combined with the Bank of France's

e. POLAND

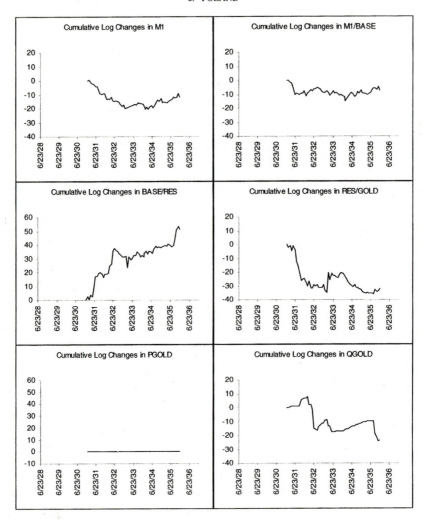

Figure 4. (*cont.*)

movement from foreign exchange reserves to gold accounts for essentially
the entire nullification of the effects of the gold inflows on the domestic
money supply.

What about the discretionary component of French monetary policy, such
as it was? The Bank of France was roundly criticized by the British and
others for its deflationist policies. The table suggests, however, that given *the
French commitment to the gold standard,* and to exclusive reliance on gold

f. SWEDEN

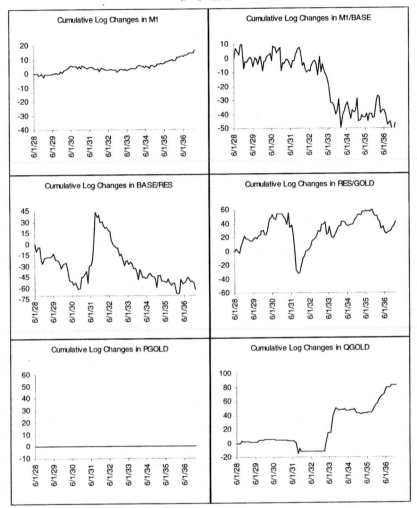

Figure 4. (*cont.*)

reserves, the actions of the Bank of France are difficult to fault. First, the Bank of France conducted policy almost entirely according to the gold standard's "rules of the game." This can be seen in the relative stability of the ratio of the monetary base to international reserves (the *BASE / RES* column). For example, at the end of 1933, the ratio of base to reserves in France was virtually identical to what it had been in mid-1928.

Second, within the general constraints of the gold standard, there is some

g.   UNITED KINGDOM

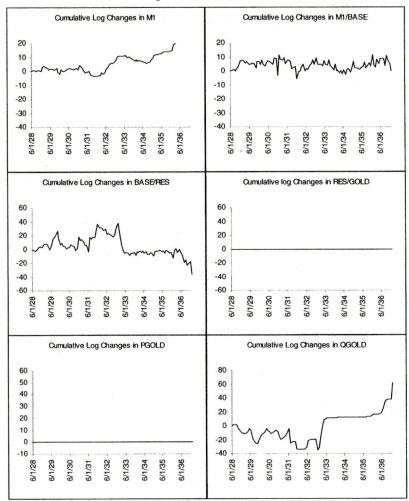

Figure 4. (*cont.*)

evidence that the Bank of France did what it could to provide countercyclical monetary policies. If we use the ratio of monetary base to international
reserves (*BASE / RES*) as a policy indicator, the table shows that the French
attempted to ease policy significantly during 1931, in the face of financial
crises abroad and declining output at home—an impression confirmed by
the decline in the central bank discount rate from 3.5 percent at the end of
1929 to 2.0 percent by the fall of 1931.

Additional evidence on the degree of French adherence to the "rules of

h.   UNITED STATES

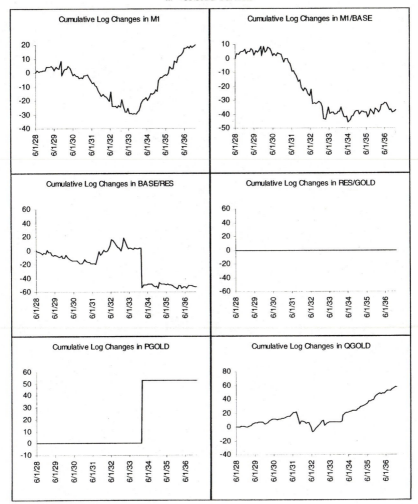

Figure 4. (*cont.*)

the game" is provided by Table 6. For each of the four economically most important countries, the table shows the results of regressions of monthly changes in the domestic monetary base against inflows and outflows of international reserves during the month.[6] According to the common view of the

[6] International reserves included foreign exchange reserves as well as gold for France and Germany and gold only for the United Kingdom and the United States (which did not employ foreign exchange reserves). We found no evidence that the French and German monetary bases reacted differently to the two components of their international reserves.

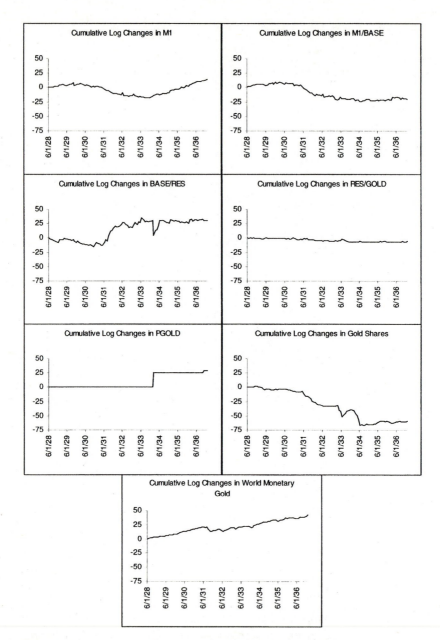

Figure 5. Components of Changes in the World M1 Money Stock, Seven-Country Averages, 1928–1936. The cumulative change in the weighted average of log M1 is decomposed into corresponding weighted components. Poland is omitted due to insufficient data. See Data Appendix for the weights used; see text for definitions of the variables.

Table 4
Determinants of the Money Stock in Four Countries, 1928:II–1936:IV

a. France

		M1	M1/BASE	BASE/RES	RES/GOLD	PGOLD	QGOLD	Disc. (%)
1928	II	0.00	0.00	0.00	0.00	0.00	0.00	3.5
	III	1.74	−0.52	−7.11	3.90	0.00	5.48	3.5
	IV	4.04	1.00	−10.85	4.09	0.00	9.81	3.5
1929	I	2.39	−1.70	−7.43	−4.98	0.00	16.49	3.5
	II	1.52	−7.30	−1.52	−13.04	0.00	23.38	3.5
	III	2.93	−6.14	−5.76	−15.88	0.00	30.71	3.5
	IV	4.12	−6.37	−7.89	−17.90	0.00	36.28	3.5
1930	I	6.78	−8.42	−4.08	−19.11	0.00	38.39	3.0
	II	10.37	−12.68	1.65	−20.44	0.00	41.84	2.5
	III	8.98	−12.07	−6.41	−23.87	0.00	51.32	2.5
	IV	8.29	−16.46	−10.15	−26.51	0.00	61.42	2.5
1931	I	8.28	−19.75	−10.16	−27.85	0.00	66.05	2.0
	II	7.77	−25.68	−5.01	−28.14	0.00	66.60	2.0
	III	3.75	−34.00	−3.01	−30.88	0.00	71.65	2.0
	IV	5.18	−39.82	−2.00	−39.52	0.00	86.52	2.5
1932	I	3.11	−41.50	−1.82	−51.04	0.00	97.47	2.5
	II	3.03	−43.80	1.55	−58.83	0.00	104.10	2.5
	III	5.22	−40.12	0.95	−60.41	0.00	104.80	2.5
	IV	5.02	−37.34	−1.85	−61.00	0.00	105.21	2.5
1933	IV	−3.80	−37.13	0.29	−64.77	0.00	97.81	2.5
1934	IV	−5.23	−41.38	−2.89	−65.09	0.12	104.01	2.5
1935	IV	−11.07	−37.77	8.26	−64.28	0.12	82.60	5.0
1936	IV	−1.17	−41.51	30.82	−63.87	29.14	44.25	2.0

b. Germany

		M1	M1/BASE	BASE/RES	RES/GOLD	PGOLD	QGOLD	Disc. (%)
1928	II	0.00	0.00	0.00	0.00	0.00	0.00	7.0
	III	3.48	3.69	−10.09	−4.13	0.00	14.00	7.0
	IV	8.49	7.40	−20.08	−5.81	0.00	26.97	7.0
1929	I	13.78	11.80	−13.28	−10.00	0.00	25.25	6.5
	II	10.25	7.64	5.29	5.97	0.00	−8.64	7.5
	III	20.18	21.33	−9.89	2.77	0.00	5.96	7.5
	IV	21.48	21.68	−14.28	4.96	0.00	9.12	7.0
1930	I	24.10	25.25	−22.27	3.09	0.00	18.03	5.0
	II	23.94	26.80	−30.53	4.82	0.00	22.84	4.0
	III	19.74	24.18	−17.14	−4.66	0.00	17.36	4.0
	IV	15.17	20.78	−19.62	7.87	0.00	6.13	5.0
1931	I	7.55	15.00	−14.77	−3.55	0.00	10.87	5.0
	II	2.44	14.53	18.37	7.82	0.00	−38.29	7.0
	III	−1.95	2.75	43.62	−1.18	0.00	−47.15	8.0
	IV	−6.55	−2.35	66.06	4.78	0.00	−75.04	7.0

Table 4 (*cont.*)

b. Germany

	M1	M1/BASE	BASE/RES	RES/GOLD	PGOLD	QGOLD	Disc. (%)
1932 I	− 10.30	− 1.67	74.09	3.65	0.00	− 86.36	7.0
II	− 12.05	5.05	71.52	3.19	0.00	− 91.81	5.0
III	− 15.56	9.21	67.31	4.11	0.00	− 96.19	5.0
IV	− 18.67	13.22	61.20	1.90	0.00	− 94.99	4.0
1933 IV	− 22.57	5.74	149.27	− 9.03	0.00	− 168.56	4.0
1934 IV	− 21.09	− 4.62	315.86	− 5.20	0.01	− 327.14	4.0
1935 IV	− 18.86	− 10.58	320.01	− 5.45	0.01	− 322.85	4.0
1936 IV	− 7.90	− 10.41	349.76	− 2.69	0.01	− 344.56	4.0

c. United Kingdom

	M1	M1/BASE	BASE/RES	RES/GOLD	PGOLD	QGOLD	Disc. (%)
1928 II	0.00	0.00	0.00	0.00	0.00	0.00	4.5
III	0.17	0.15	− 0.53	0.00	0.00	0.56	4.5
IV	0.12	7.18	2.74	0.00	0.00	− 9.81	4.5
1929 I	2.78	5.62	7.27	0.00	0.00	− 10.10	5.5
II	1.50	4.42	3.51	0.00	0.00	− 6.43	5.5
III	0.79	5.25	20.66	0.00	0.00	− 25.12	6.0
IV	− 1.80	6.84	6.46	0.00	0.00	− 15.10	5.0
1930 I	− 0.18	4.53	4.22	0.00	0.00	− 8.93	3.5
II	2.08	7.10	2.78	0.00	0.00	− 7.81	3.0
III	1.07	4.76	4.49	0.00	0.00	− 8.18	3.0
IV	1.18	− 3.02	18.10	0.00	0.00	− 13.90	3.0
1931 I	1.53	7.63	10.55	0.00	0.00	− 16.65	3.0
II	− 0.50	7.61	− 4.06	0.00	0.00	− 4.05	2.5
III	− 2.85	1.74	18.38	0.00	0.00	− 22.97	6.0
IV	− 3.35	− 5.42	36.06	0.00	0.00	− 33.99	6.0
1932 I	− 1.06	2.95	29.94	0.00	0.00	− 33.94	3.5
II	1.50	1.44	22.06	0.00	0.00	− 22.00	2.0
III	5.57	5.36	19.81	0.00	0.00	− 19.61	2.0
IV	7.88	9.34	33.34	0.00	0.00	− 34.80	2.0
1933 IV	7.13	4.54	− 9.13	0.00	0.00	11.73	2.0
1934 IV	9.33	6.51	− 9.71	0.00	0.01	9.33	2.0
1935 IV	14.66	11.38	− 13.22	0.00	0.01	16.49	2.0
1936 IV	25.29	0.13	− 36.32	0.00	0.01	61.46	2.0

d. United States

	M1	M1/BASE	BASE/RES	RES/GOLD	PGOLD	QGOLD	Disc. (%)
1928 II	0.00	0.00	0.00	0.00	0.00	0.00	4.49
III	1.22	4.14	− 3.45	0.00	0.00	0.53	4.83
IV	1.70	6.28	− 4.95	0.00	0.00	0.37	4.83

Table 4 (*cont.*)

d. United States

	M1	M1/BASE	BASE/RES	RES/GOLD	PGOLD	QGOLD	Disc. (%)
1929 I	4.24	4.83	−2.75	0.00	0.00	2.16	4.87
II	1.65	2.32	−6.50	0.00	0.00	5.82	5.00
III	2.65	5.44	−9.92	0.00	0.00	7.13	5.08
IV	1.70	8.26	−10.97	0.00	0.00	4.41	4.80
1930 I	4.43	7.70	−11.71	0.00	0.00	8.43	4.26
II	−1.83	1.61	−14.72	0.00	0.00	11.28	3.81
III	−2.69	3.64	−17.17	0.00	0.00	10.84	3.40
IV	−4.19	0.28	−16.89	0.00	0.00	12.41	3.37
1931 I	−1.75	−0.29	−16.63	0.00	0.00	15.16	3.08
II	−7.57	−9.67	−18.65	0.00	0.00	20.75	2.81
III	−9.60	−12.62	−12.64	0.00	0.00	15.65	2.81
IV	−17.15	−20.88	−4.48	0.00	0.00	8.21	3.58
1932 I	−17.69	−22.37	−1.91	0.00	0.00	6.58	3.45
II	−13.76	−22.31	15.95	0.00	0.00	−7.40	3.45
III	−24.12	−32.32	7.77	0.00	0.00	0.43	3.36
IV	−24.51	−31.96	−0.59	0.00	0.00	8.04	3.36
1933 IV	−27.41	−38.22	3.58	0.00	0.00	7.23	2.92
1934 IV	−13.21	−37.55	−54.84	0.00	52.67	26.51	2.46
1935 IV	7.10	−36.97	−55.74	0.00	52.67	47.14	1.91
1936 IV	20.19	−37.42	−52.79	0.00	52.67	57.74	1.91

Notes: For each country and each variable, the table shows the cumulative log change of the variable relative to 1928:6. Changes are calculated from the last month in the quarter. See text for variable definitions; "Disc." is the central bank discount rate.

"rules of the game," changes in the base should move in the same direction as reserve flows (that is, the coefficients on both increases and decreases in reserves should be positive), with magnitudes approximately equal to the inverse of the cover ratio. Table 6 presents results for subsamples in which each country was on and off the gold standard, according to dates provided by Bernanke and James (1991); see the notes to the table for additional information. France, of course, was on the gold standard throughout the sample period. The results shown in Table 6 are representative of what we found when we included lags of reserve changes on the right side and when we added error correction terms to the regressions.

Table 6 shows that the response of the French monetary base to reserve flows was of the right sign (positive) and statistically significant with respect to both inflows and outflows of reserves. Of the four countries for which results are reported, France is the only one for which this holds true. There is some evidence of asymmetry of response in the French case; for example,

Table 5
Determinants of the World Money Stock, 1928:II–1936:IV

	M1	M1/BASE	BASE/RES	RES/GOLD	PGOLD	SHARE	TOTGOLD
1928 II	0.00	0.00	0.00	0.00	0.00	0.00	0.00
III	1.08	2.84	−4.61	−0.31	0.00	0.78	2.38
IV	2.29	5.98	−7.88	−0.19	0.00	1.27	3.11
1929 I	5.03	5.75	−3.34	−1.83	0.00	−0.13	4.58
II	2.74	2.81	−1.99	−0.07	0.00	−3.70	5.69
III	4.94	6.87	−4.36	−0.79	0.00	−3.87	7.08
IV	4.10	8.64	−8.36	−0.51	0.00	−3.67	8.01
1930 I	6.32	8.87	−8.99	−0.94	0.00	−3.29	10.67
II	3.52	5.80	−11.61	−0.45	0.00	−3.43	13.21
III	2.26	6.56	−12.48	−2.26	0.00	−4.57	15.01
IV	0.38	3.01	−11.37	−0.55	0.00	−7.48	16.77
1931 I	0.69	3.19	−10.93	−2.71	0.00	−8.22	19.36
II	−3.19	−1.38	−8.53	−0.96	0.00	−13.33	21.01
III	−6.19	−6.86	3.26	−3.63	0.00	−16.26	17.30
IV	−10.99	−12.43	16.33	−3.44	0.00	−25.51	14.07
1932 I	−11.52	−12.98	19.53	−4.41	0.00	−30.24	16.57
II	−9.91	−12.47	26.77	−5.16	0.00	−32.51	13.46
III	−14.82	−15.50	21.09	−4.98	0.00	−32.81	17.38
IV	−14.82	−13.96	17.87	−5.25	0.00	−33.47	19.99
1933 IV	−17.13	−18.88	28.35	−7.23	0.00	−39.57	20.21
1934 IV	−9.19	−20.27	25.39	−6.43	25.72	−64.97	31.38
1935 IV	1.80	−20.43	25.48	−6.41	25.72	−60.10	37.54
1936 IV	13.64	−21.03	29.67	−6.04	28.56	−59.40	41.88

Notes: For the world aggregate, the table shows the cumulative log change in each variable relative to 1928:6. Changes are calculated from the last month in the quarter. See text for variable definitions. Poland is excluded from the world aggregate due to missing data.

it appears that outflows of reserves were sterilized by the Bank of France to a greater extent than inflows. Also, the magnitudes of the estimated responses are less than one, consistent with the view that the French acted to dampen rather than amplify the effects of reserve changes on the domestic money supply.[7]

In summary, in comparison to the other countries represented in Table 6, France made the most serious efforts to obey the "rules of the game" (although, admittedly, even they fell well short of the textbook ideal). This is not to claim that French monetary policies were not bad, even disastrous,

[7] In principle, the "rules of the game" required central banks to "lean" in the direction of gold flows, so that one franc of increased reserves should have led to more than one franc of base money. As discussed by Eichengreen (1990, Chapter 10), however, the 1928 Bank Law prohibited the Bank of France from performing the open-market operations necessary to amplify the effects of reserve flows.

Table 6
Monetary Policy and the "Rules of the Game" (dependent variable: change in the monetary base)

On gold

	France, 1928:7–1936:8		Germany, 1928:7–1931:5		U.K., 1928:7–1931:7		U.S., 1928:7–1933:1	
Constant	−64.32	(215.4)	8.325	(29.57)	0.008	(3.793)	22.94	(33.49)
Increase in reserves	0.717	(0.140)	−0.260	(0.250)	−0.286	(0.906)	−0.067	(0.612)
Decrease in reserves	0.330	(0.105)	0.034	(0.122)	0.098	(0.467)	−0.035	(0.288)

Off gold

			Germany, 1931:9–1936:12		U.K., 1931:11–1936:12		U.S., 1934:4–1936:12	
Constant	—		13.97	(16.03)	1.868	(2.386)	45.09	(73.89)
Increase in reserves	—		−1.152	(0.847)	0.268	(0.229)	0.685	(0.541)
Decrease in reserves	—		−0.124	(0.207)	0.624	(0.717)	6.741	(16.19)

Notes: The table shows the results of regressing the change in the monetary base on contemporaneous inflows and outflows of international reserves (gold for countries that did not hold foreign exchange reserves). "On gold" and "off gold" subsamples are based on break dates given by Bernanke and James (1991), with two months before the break and two months after the break dropped from the subsamples. In addition, for the United States the period between suspension of the gold standard and the formal devaluation is excluded. Numbers in parentheses are standard errors.

for the world as a whole: in particular, the large gold inflows induced by the conversion of foreign exchange and the switch by French citizens from deposits to currency put major pressure on other gold standard countries to tighten their monetary policies. However, the damage done by French policies lay to a much greater degree in the government's choice of monetary regime—its commitment to the gold standard, with minimal use of foreign exchange reserves—than in the Bank of France's implementation of that regime.

Germany

Monetary developments in Germany are summarized in part b of Table 4. These seem to fall naturally into four phases. In the first phase, from the beginning of our sample period until the middle of 1930, Germany experienced strong rates of money growth, about 24 log points cumulatively over the two-year period. This growth in the money stock largely reflected gold inflows (presumably the result of high German discount rates in 1929 and the confidence generated by agreement on the Young Plan and loan in April 1930), as well as increases in the money multiplier. It is interesting that this money growth occurred despite strong restraining influences by the Reichsbank. Note particularly the very sharp decline (of more than 30 log points) in the ratio of the monetary base to international reserves during this period, reflecting aggressive sterilization of gold inflows.

The second phase, from 1930:II to 1931:II, corresponds to the first year of the term of Heinrich Brüning, who held power from March 1930 to May 1932. Between 1930:II and 1931:II, German M1 dropped a remarkable 21.5 log points. Temin (1989, p. 31) characterizes this contraction as the result of the relentlessly deflationary policies of Brüning, but part b of Table 4 suggests a somewhat more complex story. The proximate causes of the fall in German M1 in this period were two: first, ongoing gold losses, which sharply accelerated when the financial crisis began in June 1931; and second, significant declines in the money multiplier, which occurred even before the onset of the financial crisis. Neither of these factors seems attributable to excessively tight monetary policy per se. Indeed, the behavior of *BASE / RES* during 1930:II-1931:II in Germany suggests a very significant attempt by the monetary authorities to offset contractionary influences. The behavior of the discount rate tells a similar story, as the rate was lowered by 2 percentage points during 1930, before rising again in the face of gold losses and financial crisis. Finally, the regressions in Table 6 show that prior to 1931:II, the Reichsbank generally tried to insulate the domestic monetary base from inflows and outflows of reserves.

The third phase in Germany begins with the banking panics of June 1931 and runs through the end of 1932. To our eyes at least, this is the period in which German monetary policy was most inept. Unlike the cases of France and the United States, the effects of the banking crisis on the money multiplier in Germany were transitory; by the end of 1932, the ratio M / BASE had returned to nearly what it was prior to the panics. Gold losses, though severe through 1932:I, slowed considerably for the rest of 1932 despite a declining discount rate. So in all, one would have expected the monetary situation to have stabilized in Germany in 1932. The puzzle is that the Reichsbank, though under no effective obligation to allow gold reserves to determine its money stock, did not sterilize gold outflows between the end of 1931 and the end of 1932. Indeed, over that period, as part b of Table 4 shows, the ratio of Germany's monetary base to its international reserves actually fell by about 5 log points, as gold holdings fell by 20 log points. The result—despite the helpful recovery of the money multiplier—was a fall in M1 of about 12 log points between 1931:IV and 1932:IV, an economically disastrous outcome.[8]

The final phase for Germany begins with the accession of Hitler in January 1933 and continues through the end of our sample period. M1 fell by an additional 4 log points in 1933, but subsequently Germany followed reflationist policies. M1 grew modestly in 1934 and 1935, and substantially in 1936. The striking feature of this money growth is that it occurred despite large ongoing gold and foreign exchange outflows and a significant decline in the money multiplier. In other words, German monetary policy under Hitler severed itself entirely from the traditional constraints of the international monetary system in the pursuit of domestic objectives. German production began a sustained recovery in early 1933 (refer back to Figure 1).

United Kingdom

The United Kingdom (part c of Table 4) experienced essentially zero nominal money growth between mid-1928 and the end of 1930. As the table shows, this monetary tightness was largely the result of gold losses, which in turn may have stemmed from the initial overvaluation of the pound discussed earlier. Discount rate increases were used to try to stabilize the situation in 1929, at the same time that gold outflows were partially sterilized (for example, the ratio BASE / RES was permitted to increase). The quarter 1929:III is particularly striking in this regard; compare the change in the discount rate with the change in the ratio of monetary base to reserves.

Although money growth remained flat, during 1930 and the first part of 1931, British monetary policy was more focused on domestic objectives than on following the "rules of the game," as part c of Table 4 makes clear. The

---

[8] On the Reichsbank's unwillingness to sterilize gold outflows, see the quote from Eichengreen in note 4.

fourth, seventh, and eighth columns of the table show that even as British gold stocks remained well below 1928 levels, the Bank of England both lowered the discount rate (from 6.0 percent in 1929:III to 2.5 percent in 1931:II) and sterilized the effects of gold outflows on the monetary base (compare the *BASE / RES* and *QGOLD* columns). Fortunately, banking problems in Great Britain remained minimal, and the money multiplier was stable throughout the period, in contrast to the three other countries covered in Table 4. Also, foreign exchange reserves were not an issue, as Britain was a reserve currency country and held only gold as reserves.

The British responded to the September 1931 crisis with discount rate hikes, but at the same time sterilized the gold outflows almost entirely (note that *BASE / RES* and *QGOLD* sum to approximately zero from mid-1931). Arguably, in this instance, our sterilization indicator, *BASE / RES*, is a better measure of the true stance of monetary policy than the discount rate. In the event, as we know, Britain was forced to suspend the gold standard in September 1931.

For the remainder of the period, the British data tell a relatively straightforward story. With the external constraint gone, money grew rapidly in 1932, by about 11 log points. However, money growth slowed in 1933 and 1934. What accounts for this slowdown in monetary expansion? Part c of Table 4 gives the impression that the Bank of England was focused on stabilizing the monetary base, rather than M1; again note that *BASE / RES* and *QGOLD* sum to approximately zero through 1935, implying that the nominal monetary base through 1935 was almost identical to what it was in mid-1928. With the base stable, changes in M1 through 1935 appeared to be driven largely by changes in the money multiplier, *M1 / BASE*, which fell between 1932:IV and 1934:IV.

The year 1936 saw large gold inflows to Great Britain, probably driven by growing political instability in continental Europe. It is interesting to note that the Bank of England only partially sterilized this inflow, allowing an increase in the monetary base of about 22 log points. Thus, even though the money multiplier dropped sharply in 1936, the British M1 money stock grew robustly. In its sterilization of gold outflows but not gold inflows, the Bank of England reverted to old gold standard–era habits of asymmetric adjustment, despite the fact that in 1936 gold flows should have been essentially irrelevant to British monetary policy.[9]

United States

The monetary data for the United States (part d of Table 4) are quite remarkable, and tend to underscore the stinging critique of the Fed's policy

---

[9] The regression results in Table 6 suggest that, to the contrary, after leaving gold the British sterilized inflows by more than they sterilized outflows. The estimated coefficients are not statistically significant, however.

choices by Friedman and Schwartz (1963). In particular, unlike all other major countries, the United States is the only country in which the discretionary component of policy (as opposed to the automatic responses required by the gold standard) was arguably significantly destabilizing.

The key column in the table is the one showing the ratio of monetary base to international reserves (BASE / RES). This ratio fell consistently in the United States from the beginning of our sample period (1928:II) through the second quarter of 1931. As a result, U.S. nominal money growth was precisely zero between 1928IV and 1929IV, despite both gold inflows and an increase in the money multiplier (M1 / BASE). The year 1930 was even worse in this respect: between 1929:IV and 1930:IV, nominal money in the United States fell by almost 6 log points, even as the U.S. gold stock increased by 8 log points over the same period. The proximate cause of this decline in M1 was continued contraction in the ratio of base to reserves, which reinforced rather than offset declines in the money multiplier. This tightening seems clearly inconsistent with the gold standard's "rules of the game," and locates much of the blame for the early (pre-1931) slowdown in world monetary aggregates with the Federal Reserve. Table 6 confirms that during the period in which the United States was on the gold standard, gold flows into and out of the United States were completely sterilized, and thus allowed to have no effect on the U.S. monetary base.

The years 1931 and 1932 were utter disasters for the United States in terms of monetary growth, with M1 dropping 13 log points in the former year and more than 7 log points in the latter. By this point, however— given the decision to remain on the gold standard after Britain left gold in September 1931—the Federal Reserve was in the grip of forces that may well have been too strong for it to control. As part d of Table 4 shows, about 150 percent of the monetary contraction between 1930:IV and 1932:IV was due to the sharp decline in the money multiplier, resulting from the series of banking crises (Friedman and Schwartz, 1963). In mid-1931 the Federal Reserve reversed its policy of sterilizing gold, raising the ratio of the monetary base to gold reserves by almost 35 log points between 1931:II and 1932:II. However, these actions were nearly nullified by gold outflows of over 28 log points during the same period. We do not want to take a stand here on the controversial issue of whether the Federal Reserve could have done more than it did in 1931–1932, but given these data and the commitment to the gold standard, it is understandable how U.S. monetary policymakers could have viewed expansion of the monetary base (for example, through open-market operations) as a futile exercise during this period.

Despite the suspension of the gold standard in March 1933 and official devaluation in April, U.S. M1 growth was negative for 1933 as a whole. Essentially, as part d of Table 4 shows, continuing declines in the money multiplier outweighed both gold inflows and an increase in the ratio of the

base to reserves. It is interesting that, like Germany and the United Kingdom, the United States did not immediately translate its newfound monetary independence into aggressive reflationist policies. A strong recovery in
both the real economy and the stock market took place in 1933 anyway,
which (as Temin, 1989, has noted) poses some challenge to a simpleminded
monetarist view of the effects of the United States' leaving the gold
standard.

In 1934, 1935, and 1936, the U.S. money stock grew rapidly. As part d of
Table 4 indicates, the Fed's policy during this period appears to have been to
"sterilize" the effects of the devaluation on the monetary base (note that the
fourth and seventh column sum to almost precisely zero for those three
years), while allowing gold inflows from Europe to expand the U.S. monetary base. This odd strategy suggests that U.S. policymakers were still to
some extent in the thrall of the gold standard framework after 1933, and
that (as Christina Romer, 1992, has suggested) U.S. monetary recovery was
due largely to the fortuitous gold inflows rather than to deliberate monetary
policies.

"World" Aggregate

The monetary developments within each of the major countries are to some
extent familiar. But how did these national developments contribute to the
worldwide declines in money? To answer this question it is useful to consider "world" aggregates (Table 5), which are weighted averages of data from
the four countries discussed above plus Canada, Japan, and Sweden.

The second column of Table 5 shows the behavior of aggregate nominal
M1 stocks. After rising from 1928:II through 1929:I, aggregate M1 was essentially flat for the subsequent year, and then began a sustained decline.
Measuring from year-end to year-end, we find that aggregate M1 declined
about 4 log points in 1930, about 11 log points in 1931, about 3 log points
in 1932, and a bit over 2 log points in 1933. Accelerating growth in world
M1 began in 1934: M1 grew about 8 log points in 1934, about 11 log points
in 1935 (when it finally regained its level of 1928), and about 12 log points
in 1936.

Although numerous factors contributed in varying degree to the collapse
in world money supplies, clearly a shortage of world monetary gold was *not*
responsible. As the rightmost column of Table 5 shows, the physical quantity of monetary gold held by these seven countries increased by 20 log
points between mid-1928 and the end of 1933, and by a cumulative 42 log
points by the end of 1936. Some of this increase was endogenous to the
rising price of gold in terms of goods, of course, as the incentives for gold
discovery increased, and gold flowed in from the "periphery" or was diverted
from nonmonetary uses. Nevertheless, we conclude that the gloomy predic-

tions of a secular gold shortage made in the early 1920s seem to have been far off the mark. Counteracting the growth in monetary gold stocks to some degree was the decline in the use of foreign exchange reserves, but this effect seems to have been quantitatively unimportant for aggregate M1 (see the *RES / GOLD* column of Table 5). The small effect arising from the flight from foreign-exchange reserves largely reflects the fact that the United States and several other countries in our sample had no significant foreign exchange reserves in the first place.

The factors that did contribute to monetary contraction varied by time period, as Table 5 shows.[10] Through 1930, a period in which the aggregate money stock was essentially flat, the main deflationary factor appears to have been the discretionary component of monetary policy, as measured by the ratio of monetary base to international reserves. Maldistribution of gold, as measured by *SHARE*, also had a negative impact, but this effect was more than outweighed by the increase in total monetary gold. Comparison with Table 4 shows that sterilization of gold inflows by the United States, Germany, and (to a lesser extent) France accounts for slow world money growth through 1930.

The nature of the contraction changed radically in the spring of 1931, however. The onset of banking crises led the money multiplier, M1 / BASE, to fall by more than 15 log points between the end of 1930 and the end of 1931, with further declines to follow. Even more significant quantitatively was the "maldistribution" effect, reflected by a drop of 18 log points in *SHARE* during 1931 and another 8-point drop in 1932. As Table 4 shows, the large inflows of gold to France (and the associated flows out of Germany and the United Kingdom) were the main source of the "maldistribution" effect. U.S. gold stocks remained relatively stable in contrast.

While these two factors were depressing aggregate M1, the discretionary component of monetary policy (as measured by the aggregate value of *BASE / RES*) turned highly expansionary, especially in Germany, Japan, and Sweden.[11] However, the partial decoupling of domestic money supplies from international reserves was insufficient to prevent substantial contraction in world M1 in 1931 and 1932, as Table 5 shows. As in the case of the United States, then, the story of the world monetary contraction can be summarized as "self-inflicted wounds" for the period through early 1931, and "forces beyond our control" for the two years that followed.

The world aggregates for the years 1933–1936 mask diverse country expe-

[10] In interpreting the following, the reader should keep in mind the heavy weight (about 50 percent) of the U.S. in the aggregate indexes.

[11] Of course, increases in the ratio of base to reserves can occur actively, as when the central bank undertakes open-market purchases, or more passively, as when gold outflows are sterilized. However, either case reflects a policy of disconnecting domestic monetary conditions from the quantity of international reserves.

riences, notably between countries on the gold standard and countries off it. In broad strokes, during this period devaluation (increases in the money price of gold) and expansionary monetary policies (as reflected in the ratio of base to reserves) overcame the depressing effects of continued "maldistribution" of gold and further declines in the money multiplier.

VI. Conclusion

This chapter proposes and carries out a simple method for decomposing the world deflation of the 1930s into its principal sources, including changes in holdings of real balances; changes in the money multiplier, usually associated with conditions in the banking sector; changes in the ratio of monetary base to reserves, an indicator of discretionary monetary policy and the degree of sterilization of reserves flows; changes in the use of foreign exchange reserves; changes in the distribution of gold among countries; changes in the world monetary gold stock; and changes in parities. The results reinforce some earlier findings in the literature and raise some new issue for further study. Probably our most important finding is the confirmation of the view that monetary forces played an important role in the world Depression in both its early and later stages. However, the sources of monetary contraction before and after the watershed year of 1931 were quite different. Prior to 1931, sterilization of gold inflows by surplus countries (notably the United States, but also to some extent France) was the principal deflationary factor. After the financial crises of 1931, however, as the situation spun out of control, sharp declines in money multipliers (reflecting problems in the commercial banking sector) and increasing "maldistribution" of gold played the largest roles. The discretionary component of monetary policy, as reflected in the ratio of monetary base to international reserves, was generally expansionary after 1931. However, except in those countries that abandoned gold and undertook aggressive reflationary policies, this change in policy stance was insufficient to counter the powerful deflationary forces that previous policy mistakes had unleashed.

Data Appendix

Wholesale Prices

Source: League of Nations, *Monthly Bulletin of Statistics*. Base year is 1929. All series are adjusted for base year changes and changes in composition of baskets as needed, using overlapping data from old and new series. Polish WPI data begin in January 1931.

Consumer Prices

Sources: For the United States, NBER *Macro History Dataset*, Series no. 04128: Consumer Price Index, All Items (BLS). For other countries, League of Nations, *Monthly Bulletin of Statistics*. Base year is 1929. All series are adjusted for base-year changes as needed. Geometric interpolation of quarterly data is used for France and for Sweden for June 1928–September 1931. The French CPI is for Paris; the Polish CPI is for Warsaw. Polish CPI data begin in January 1931; Japanese CPI data begin in January 1932.

Notes in Circulation

Sources: For the United States, Friedman and Schwartz (1963, Table A-1, col. 1, currency held by the public). For Canada, see Metcalf, Redish, and Shearer (1998) and web page referenced therein. For other countries, League of Nations, *Monthly Bulletin of Statistics*.

Bank Reserves

Sources: For the United States, Friedman and Schwartz (1963, Table A-2, col. 3, bank reserves). For Canada, see Metcalf, Redish, and Shearer (1998). For other countries, *Federal Reserve Bulletin*, "Condition of Foreign Central Banks," various issues.

Deposits

Sources: For the United States, Friedman and Schwartz (1963, Table A-1, col. 2, adjusted demand deposits in commercial banks). For Canada, see Metcalf, Redish, and Shearer (1998). For France, see Patat and Lutfalla ([1986] 1990, total deposits in commercial banks). For Germany and Japan, *Federal Reserve Bulletin* through 1931; League of Nations, *Monthly Bulletin of Statistics* thereafter. The series from the two sources are spliced, using ratios of overlapping values. Splices are also used to combine a revised deposit series for Japan (beginning in February 1934) with the earlier, unrevised series. Some missing monthly values for Germany (mostly December and January) are filled in by geometric interpolation. For Poland, data are available only after 1931, and are from League of Nations, *Monthly Bulletin of Statistics*. For Sweden, through 1931, the series is total deposits including savings and notice deposits in deposit banks (*Federal Reserve Bulletin*); after this date, the series used is deposits and checking accounts (League of Nations, *Monthly Bulletin of Statistics*). The two deposit series for Sweden are spliced, using ratios of overlapping values.

Gold Stocks

Source: Value of gold stocks (in dollars) from Board of Governors (1943, pp. 544–55). Quantities were calculated by dividing by the official U.S. gold price ($20.67 per ounce through January 1934, $35.00 per ounce subsequently).

Foreign Exchange Reserves

Japan, the United Kingdom, and the United States were not allowed to back their money with foreign exchange reserves (see League of Nations, *Legislation on Gold*, cited in Eichengreen, 1990, p. 248); hence we do not treat foreign assets held by these countries as international reserves. Canada did not have a central bank until 1935; prior to this time, data on Canadian foreign assets refer to net foreign positions of commercial banks. This series is volatile and sometimes negative; it does not appear appropriate to treat these holdings as international reserves. For the other four countries, foreign assets (from League of Nations, *Monthly Bulletin of Statistics*) are defined as follows: for Germany, cover assets only; for France, funds available at sight plus foreign bills and other short-term foreign assets; for Poland and Sweden, foreign assets.

Parities

Source: Board of Governors, 1943, pp. 528–35.

Discount Rates of Central Banks

Source: League of Nations, *Monthly Bulletin of Statistics*, end-of-month figures. Unavailable for Canada prior to March 1935. For the United States, discount rate is average rate earned by the 12 Federal Reserve Banks on the bills discounted.

Industrial Production

Source: League of Nations, *Monthly Bulletin of Statistics*. Quarterly data for the United Kingdom were interpolated to monthly by the method of Chow and Lin (1971), using monthly data on production of coal, pig iron, and steel. All series are adjusted for base-year changes. Japanese IP data begin in January 1930; Polish IP data begin in January 1931.

Country Weights

The weights for the construction of world aggregates (ω_i) are based on relative values of 1928 real GDP, derived from Maddison (1982, Tables A-2,

A-3, A-7). The weights are as follows: Canada, .030; France, .098; Germany, .158; Japan, .077; Sweden, .015; United Kingdom, .134; United States, .488. In figures where Japan is omitted, the weights are as follows: Canada, .032; France, .11; Germany, .17; Sweden, .016; United Kingdom, .145; United States, 0.528.

Seasonal Adjustment

M1 and base series were seasonally adjusted (in logs) by regression on monthly dummies, over the sample June 1928–December 1936 (January 1931–December 1935 for Poland).

References

Bernanke, Ben, and Harold James. 1991. "The Gold Standard, Deflation, and Financial Crisis in the Great Depression: An International Comparison." in R. G. Hubbard, ed., *Financial Markets and Financial Crises*. Chicago: University of Chicago Press.

Board of Governors of the Federal Reserve System, 1943. *Banking and Monetary Statistics*, Washington, D.C.: National Capital Press.

Choudhri, Ehsan, and Levis Kochin. 1980. "The Exchange Rate and the International Transmission of Business Cycles: Some Evidence from the Great Depression." *Journal of Money, Credit, and Banking* 12: 565–74.

Chow, Gregory, and An-loh Lin. 1971. "Best Linear Unbiased Interpolation, Distribution, and Extrapolation of Time Series by Related Series." *Review of Economics and Statistics* 53: 372–75.

Eichengreen, Barry. 1990. *Elusive Stability: Essays in the History of International Finance, 1919–1939*. Cambridge: Cambridge University Press.

———. 1992. *Golden Fetters: The Gold Standard and the Great Depression, 1919–1939*. New York: Oxford University Press.

Eichengreen, Barry, and Jeffrey Sachs. 1985. "Exchange Rates and Economic Recovery in the 1930s." *Journal of Economic History* 45: 925–46.

———. 1986. "Competitive Devaluation in the Great Depression: A Theoretical Reassessment." *Economics Letters* 22: 67–71.

Field, Alexander J. 1984. "Asset Exchanges and the Transactions Demand for Money, 1919–29." *American Economic Review* 74: 43–59.

Friedman, M., and A.J. Schwartz. 1963. *A Monetary History of the United States, 1863–1960*. Princeton, N.J.: Princeton University Press.

Hamilton, James D. 1987. "Monetary Factors in the Great Depression." *Journal of Monetary Economics* 19: 145–69.

Hawtrey, R. G. 1939. *The Gold Standard in Theory and Practice*. 4th ed. London: Longmans, Green.

Jonung, Lars. 1979. "Knut Wicksell's Norm of Price Stabilization and Swedish Monetary Policy in the 1930's." *Journal of Monetary Economics* 5: 459–96.

Kindleberger, Charles P. 1973. *The World in Depression, 1929–1939*. Berkeley: University of California Press.

Maddison, Angus. 1982. *Phases of Capitalist Development*. New York: Oxford University Press.

Metcalf, C., A. Redish, and R. Shearer. 1998. "New Estimates of the Canadian Money Stock, 1871–1967." *Canadian Journal of Economics* 31: 104–24.

Patat, J. P., and M. Lutfalla. [1986] 1990. *A Monetary History of France in the Twentieth Century*. Translated by P. Martindale and D. Cobham. London: Macmillan.

Romer, Christina. 1992. "What Ended the Great Depression?" *Journal of Economic History* 52: 757–84.

Sumner, Scott. 1991. "The Equilibrium Approach to Discretionary Monetary Policy under an International Gold Standard: 1926–1932." *The Manchester School of Economic and Social Studies* 59: 378–94.

Temin, Peter. 1976. *Did Monetary Forces Cause the Great Depression?* New York: Norton.

———. 1989. *Lessons from the Great Depression*. Cambridge: MIT Press.

Part Three

LABOR MARKETS

Five

The Cyclical Behavior of Industrial Labor Markets: A Comparison of the Prewar and Postwar Eras

WITH JAMES L. POWELL

1. Introduction

This paper compares the cyclical behavior of a number of industrial labor markets of the prewar (1923–39) and postwar (1954–82) eras. The methodology follows that of the traditional Burns and Mitchell (1946) business cycle analysis in at least two ways. First, the data employed are relatively disaggregated (we use monthly data at the two- or three-digit industry level). Second, we have not formulated or tested a specific structural model of labor markets during the cycle but instead concentrate on measuring qualitative features of the data. As did Burns and Mitchell, we see descriptive analysis of the data as a useful prelude to theorizing about business cycles. Thus, although the research reported here permits *no* direct structural inferences, it should be useful in restricting the class of structural models or hypotheses that may subsequently be considered.

The principal questions we study are also two in number. First, what are the means by which labor input is varied over the business cycle? We consider the intensity of utilization (as measured by gross labor productivity), hours of work per week, and number of workers employed. Both the timing and the relative magnitudes of the changes in these quantities over the cycle are examined. Second, what are the relationships over the cycle of output and labor input to measures of labor compensation? We look at the cyclical behavior of product wages and real weekly earnings as well as of real wages.

As might be expected, many of our findings are not novel; rather, they tend to support and perhaps refine existing perceptions of cyclical labor market behavior. However, we do reveal some interesting differences between the prewar and postwar periods in the relative use of layoffs and short

Reprinted from Robert J. Gordon, ed., *The American Business Cycle*, (Chicago: University of Chicago Press, 1986). Copyright © 1986 by the National Bureau of Economic Research. All rights reserved.

We thank Frank Brechling, Ken Rogoff, Larry Summers, and our discussants for useful comments.

hours in downturns and in cyclical movements of the real wage. Another finding is that labor productivity may behave in an anomalous manner in more severe recessions. Finally, a number of the familiar regularities are documented in a previously little-used data set, over an unusually long sample period, and by means of some alternative methods.

The paper is organized as follows: Section 2 reviews previous empirical work on the cyclical behavior of labor market variables. Sections 3 and 4 introduce and describe the data set used here. The behavior of key variables over the business cycle is analyzed by frequency domain methods in section 5 and by a time domain approach in section 6. Section 7 focuses on labor market phenomena in four particularly severe recessions. Results are summarized and conclusions drawn in section 8.

2. Previous Work: Some Regularities and Some Puzzles

There has been a great deal of empirical work that relates, sometimes directly and sometimes tangentially, to the cyclical behavior of labor markets. Without attempting an exhaustive survey, in this section we will try to summarize the major empirical findings of the literature. We will also include some brief discussion of how various authors have interpreted these findings. However, because the focus of this paper is description rather than structural analysis, the results we will present later do little to resolve existing disputes about interpretation.

The discussion of this section will be organized around the two questions of interest raised in section 1: the means by which labor input is varied over the cycle and the cyclical relationship of labor input and labor compensation. It might be said that by concentrating on these two questions, rather than on such phenomena as the frequency and duration of unemployment spells or cyclical variations in participation rates, we are emphasizing the "demand side" of the labor market at the expense of the "supply side." This imbalance is unfortunate but is dictated by the nature of the available prewar data.[1]

2.1. The Cyclical Pattern of Labor Utilization

The earliest empirical work on the variation of labor input over the cycle was done in the context of NBER business cycle research. Among the hundreds of data series whose business cycle patterns were painstakingly analyzed by Wesley Mitchell, and later by Mitchell and Arthur Burns, were a number of labor market variables. For example, Mitchell (1951) docu-

---

[1] This is not to say that no empirical work on cyclical aspects of labor supply exists for the prewar period; for a fascinating example, see Woytinsky 1942.

mented the high conformity of employment and weekly hours with output. (However, Mitchell was perhaps more interested in labor cost measures; see below.)

An early NBER finding was the strong tendency of weekly hours (that is, the length of the average workweek) to lead output and employment over the cycle (Moore 1955; Bry 1959). Weekly hours subsequently became a component of the NBER's well-known index of leading indicators. (For a relatively recent discussion and updating of this index, see Zarnowitz and Boschan 1975.) Other labor market variables identified as leading the cycle by the NBER included accession and layoff rates and initial claims for unemployment insurance (Shiskin 1961). Employment and unemployment were found to be coincident with the cycle.

Arguably the most important contribution of the NBER research program in this area was the classic paper by Hultgren (1960). With the purpose of investigating a hypothesis of Mitchell's about labor cost, Hultgren collected monthly data on output, aggregate hours worked, and payrolls for twenty-three industries. (The sample period was 1932–58.) With these and other data, Hultgren discovered that output per worker-hour is procyclical (or equivalently, that employment and hours worked vary relatively less over the cycle than does output).

The finding of procyclical labor productivity, or "short-run increasing returns to labor" (SRIRL), spawned a voluminous literature. Important early contributions were made by Kuh (1960, 1965), Okun (1962), Eckstein and Wilson (1964), and Brechling (1965). (Okun's famous "law" is, of course, SRIRL applied to the aggregate economy.) These and numerous other studies (including, notably, Ball and St. Cyr 1966; Masters 1967; Brechling and O'Brien 1967; and Ireland and Smyth 1967) found the SRIRL phenomenon to be ubiquitous: it occurs at both high and low levels of output aggregation, for both production and nonproduction workers, and in virtually all industrial countries.

Because of the neoclassical presumption of diminishing marginal returns to factors of production, SRIRL originally was perceived (and to some extent still is) as a deep puzzle. One favored explanation was that, because of the existence of specific human capital, firms "hoard" labor during downturns (Oi 1962; Solow 1968; Fair 1969); the hoarded labor is utilized more fully as demand recovers, giving the illusion of increasing returns. For empirical purposes, the labor hoarding model has become closely identified with a model in which increasing marginal costs of adjusting the labor stock induce the firm to move toward the desired level of employment only gradually (Brechling 1965; Coen and Hickman 1970); conceptually, however, the two models are not quite the same. Another popular explanation of SRIRL is that it is a reflection of unobserved (by the econometrician) variations in capital utilization rates that are associated with changes in labor input (Ireland and Smyth 1967; Lucas 1970; Solow 1973; Nadiri and Rosen 1973; Tatom 1980).

What is probably the most general current view is that SRIRL is the outcome of a complex dynamic optimization problem solved by the firm, in which labor is only one of a number of inputs, each with a possibly different degree of quasi-fixity. For example, Nadiri and Rosen (19973) emphasized that the rate at which employment will be varied depends not only on the costs of adjusting labor stocks but also on the costs of adjusting all other inputs (including inventories and rates of utilization); Morrison and Berndt (1981) showed that these interactions could result in the SRIRL phenomenon even if labor itself were a perfectly variable factor.

Overall, the research that followed Hultgren's original paper has made two valuable contributions to knowledge. First, from Brechling (1965) to Nadiri and Rosen (1973) to Sims (1974), there has been generated a wealth of empirical material on the sluggish short-run response of employment to output change and on the relationship over the cycle of employment to hours worked, inventories, and other factors of production. Second, the general dynamic optimization model of firm input utilization developed in this literature has proved to be a most useful and flexible research tool. (For example, it has permitted the incorporation of rational expectations; see Sargent 1978 or Pindyck and Rotemberg 1982.)

We may summarize the received findings on the cyclical behavior of labor inputs as follows: Employment and weekly hours are procyclical. Productivity is also procyclical; that is, employment and worker-hours vary less than output over the cycle. Finally, weekly hours lead output, while employment coincides with or possibly lags output over the cycle.

2.2. Labor Compensation over the Cycle

Although the qualitative behavior of labor inputs over the business cycle seems relatively well established, there is very little agreement about how to characterize the cyclical movements of labor compensation, especially of real wages. The debate about real wages began when Keynes (1936) conjectured that, again because of diminishing marginal returns, labor's marginal productivity and hence the real wage should be countercyclical.[2] Empirical studies by Dunlop (1938) and Tarshis (1939) purported to show that this conjecture was false; but these studies were in turn disputed (see Bodkin 1969 for references). The debate prompted Keynes (1939) to aver that countercyclical real wages were in fact not an essential implication of his theory.

Postwar research has done little to resolve the question of the cyclical

[2] Bodkin 1969 notes that the French economist Rueff made the same prediction in 1925.

behavior of real wages. One can find papers supporting procyclicality (Bodkin 1969; Stockman 1983), countercyclicality (Neftci 1978; Sargent 1978; Otani 1978; Chirinko 1980), and acyclicality (Geary and Kennan 1982). Altonji and Ashenfelter (1980) have argued that the best statistical model of the real wage is the random walk. It would not be much help for us to present a detailed comparison of these papers here. Instead, we simply list some of the major methodological issues that have arisen in this literature.

First, researchers have typically found that these results are sensitive to whether the nominal wage is deflated by an index of output prices, such as the wholesale price index or the producer price index or by a cost-of-living index such as the consumer price index. (See Ruggles 1940; Bodkin 1969; or Geary and Kennan 1982.) This does not seem unreasonable, since the wage divided by the output price (henceforth the "product wage") corresponds conceptually to the "demand price" of labor, while the wage deflated by the cost of living (henceforth the "real wage") corresponds to the "supply price"; it is not difficult to think of conditions under which the short-run behaviors of these two variables might differ. Unfortunately, however, the difference in behavior does not seem to vary systematically across studies.

Second, there is some dispute over whether the contemporaneous correlation of the real wage and output (or employment) is an interesting measure of the real wage's cyclical pattern. Neftci (1978) and Sargent (1978) have argued that, because of the complex dynamics of the wage/employment relationship, it is necessary to look at correlations at many leads and lags. (See also Clark and Freeman 1980.)

Finally, it has been founded that empirical results concerning the short-run behavior of wages may be particularly sensitive to aggregation biases, both when the aggregation is over individuals (Stockman 1983) and when it is over industries (Chirinko 1980).

The apparently very weak relationship of real wages and the business cycle has posed a problem for some prominent theories of cyclical fluctuations (or at least for simple versions of those theories; see, for example, Altonji and Ashenfelter 1980 and Ashenfelter and Card 1982). However, attempts to reconcile the low correlation of wages and the cycle with theories of short-run employment fluctuations have also led to a number of interesting lines of research: these include disequilibrium modeling of the cycle (Solow and Stiglitz 1968; Barro and Grossman 1971), contracting approaches that divorce wage payments and short-run labor allocations (see Hall 1980 for a discussion), Lucas's (1970) theory of capacity and overtime, and others.

Real and product wages are not the only measures of labor compensation whose cyclical behavior has been studied, although they have absorbed a large part of the research effort. Mitchell theorized in very early work that unit labor costs might play an important role in the business cycle; Hultgren's (1960, 1965) studies found that, in reasonably close correspondence to Mitchell's prediction, labor costs lag the cycle. Various other compensation measures were studied by the NBER analysts: nominal labor income, for example, was reported by Shiskin (1961) to be coincident with the cycle.

Another variable that has commanded some attention is the nominal wage. In an NBER Occasional Paper, Creamer (1950) studied monthly wage rates in a number of industries for 1919–31. (His aggregate wage rate series extended to 1935.) Creamer's most important conclusion was that nominal wage rates lagged business activity by nine months or more, a finding that some subsequent authors viewed as supporting the "stickiness" of wages. (Creamer also showed that the cyclical behaviors of an index of wage rates and of average hourly earnings were similar, a very useful result given the paucity of direct information on wage rates.) "Stickiness" was also a major issue for later students of the nominal wage: for example, Sachs (1980) has argued that wages became relatively more rigid after World War II, and Gordon (1982) has found United States postwar wages to be stickier than those of the United Kingdom and Japan. Gordon's result is the opposite of earlier characterizations by Sachs (1979) and others.

Overall, the question of how to characterize the cyclical behavior of labor compensation remains rather unsettled. This is unfortunate, given the central role of wages in much of macroeconomic theory.

3. The Data

This paper reassesses the qualitative empirical findings described in the previous section, with particular attention to possible differences between the prewar and postwar eras. This section introduces our data set and compares it briefly with what has been employed by others.

The data we use are monthly, roughly at the level of the "industry," and cover the time periods 1923–39 and 1954–82. We felt that the high-frequency data were necessary if short-run relationships were to be distinguished; the industry-level data were used both to reduce aggregation bias and to avoid reliance on the aggregate production indexes, which are poorly constructed for our purpose (see below). In contrast to our approach, few studies since Hultgren have used monthly, industry-level data (Fair 1969 is an important exception). Also, little recent work has used prewar data; the exceptions have typically looked only at annual, highly aggregated numbers.

There were many variables we could have chosen to study. Considerations of data availability and economic relevance led to the following short list (with mnemonic abbreviations):

IP   Industry output or production

EMP   Employment (number of production workers)

HRS   Hours of work per week (per production worker)

PROD Gross labor productivity = *IP*/(*EMP* × *HRS*)

WR   Average hourly earnings (nominal) divided by a cost-of-living index; the "real wage."

WP   Average hourly earnings divided by the industry wholesale output price; the "product wage"

EARN Real weekly earnings per production worker = *HRS* × *WR*.

In the analysis below, we concentrate not on the levels of these variables but on the log differences (roughly, the monthly growth rates). From now on, therefore, the mnemonic names just defined should be understood to denote log differences.

The variables above were collected for eight prewar manufacturing, eight postwar manufacturing, and three postwar nonmanufacturing industries. These industries are listed in table 1. Note that the eight prewar and postwar manufacturing industries are approximately a "matched set." This was done to facilitate comparison of the two eras. We did not have comparable prewar data for the three nonmanufacturing industries. However, we included these industries because they represent major sectors of the economy (mining, utilities, and construction) and because it seemed to us that nonmanufacturing industries have been slighted somewhat (relative to manufacturing industries) by students of the business cycle.

Some explanation should be given for the rather miscellaneous character of the manufacturing industries chosen. For the prewar period, the eight industries included represent the largest class for which complete and reasonably consistent data were available. In particular, our desire to have series on hours of work restricted us to industries regularly surveyed, beginning in the early 1920s, by the National Industrial Conference Board. The Bureau of Labor Statistics, which surveyed many more industries, did not collect hours data before 1932. Also, we included only industries whose output indexes were based on direct measures of physical output (e.g., number of automobiles) rather than on scaled-up input measures (e.g., man-hours). A wider selection of industries is available for the postwar period, of course, but because of the burden of collecting and entering the data, only those manufacturing industries "matching" the available prewar industries were used. In terms of employment or value added, the industries here studied made up about one-fifth of total manufacturing in the prewar era and about one-sixth of total manufacturing after the war.

A nice fringe benefit of using the Conference Board data rather than that from the Bureau of Labor Statistics (BLS) is that it gives us a prewar data

Table 1
Industries Included in Data Set

Prewar Industry Title	Postwar Industry Title (SIC Code)
Manufacturing industries (prewar and postwar data)	
1. Iron and steel (STEEL)	Blast furnaces and steel mills (331)
2. Automobiles (AUTOS)	Motor vehicles and equipment (371)
3. Meat-packing (MEAT)	Meat-packing plants (201)
4. Paper and pulp (PAPER)	Paper and allied products (26)
5. Boots and shoes (SHOES)	Footwear, except rubber (314)
6. Wool textiles (WOOL)	Weaving and finishing mills, wool (223)
7. Leather tanning and finishing (LEATH)	Leather tanning and finishing (311)
8. Lumber and millwork (excluding furniture (LUMBR)	Lumber and wood products (24)
9. All manufacturing industires (ALL MFG)	All manufacturing industries
Nonmanufacturing industries (post-war data only)	
10. NA (COAL)	Bituminous coal and lignite mining (12)
11. NA (ELECT)	Electric services (491)
12. NA (CONST)	Construction (no code)

set that has not been previously analyzed, except in a partial and desultory way by some earlier NBER studies. In particular, it is quite different from the data set used by Hultgren (1960).

A potential problem with studying only manufacturing industries that have more or less continuous identities since the 1920s is that it biases the sample toward older, often declining industries at the expense of new and growing fields. However, for the purpose of studying cyclical (as opposed to trend) behavior of labor market variables, this sample bias is probably not important. In particular, our informal comparisons of the declining manufacturing industries with the expanding manufacturing and nonmanufacturing industries did not reveal obvious differences in cyclical behavior.

For the purposes of comparison with the industry-level findings, we also analyzed prewar and postwar monthly data for aggregate manufacturing. Although these data obviously have broader coverage than the industry data, we have less confidence in the results using aggregates, for three reasons: (1) aggregation across industries introduces well-known cyclical biases; (2) the aggregate production indexes are heavily contaminated with input-based measures of output; and (3) the prewar output, price, and labor input series are not perfectly mutually consistent. (See the data appendix to this chapter for an explanation and for a more detailed discussion of all the data and their sources.)

4. Some Basic Statistics

Most of the analysis below follows the application of a deseasonalization process and the removal of means from the log-differenced series. As a preliminary step, this section looks at some features of the raw log differences.

Tables 2 and 3 present the means of the variables for each industry and for the prewar and postwar periods separately. The means are multiplied by 100 and thus can be interpreted approximately as percentage rates of growth *per month*.

Considering first the productivity column in table 2, we note that average prewar rates of productivity growth compared well with those of the postwar era. Rates of productivity growth were higher during 1923–39 than during 1954–82 in five of the eight manufacturing industries, as well as in aggregate manufacturing. The prewar rate of productivity growth reached rather exceptional levels in automobiles, paper and pulp, and iron and steel. The rapid expansion of prewar productivity observed in these data supports the view that the period between the world wars (particularly the 1920s) was a time of transformation of industrial technologies, leading to sharp reductions in costs; see Jerome (1934) and Bernstein (1960). In the postwar period, the best productivity performance among our manufacturing industries was by paper and allied products; best overall in the postwar sample was by electric services.

Productivity growth is, of course, definitionally equal to output growth minus the sum of employment and hours growth. Examining these constituents of productivity, we note first that the fastest prewar growth in output was experienced by automobiles and by paper and pulp; in the postwar period, paper took the output growth honors for manufacturing, with electric services again doing best overall. It appears that the high-output industries were also the high-productivity industries; the rank correlation between output growth and productivity growth is .945 for the eight prewar industries, .913 for the eleven postwar industries.

Despite the depression of the 1930s, employment growth in the prewar manufacturing industries studied tended to exceed that in their post-war counterparts (seven of eight cases); this was also true for the aggregates. This difference largely reflects serious long-term declines by a number of the postwar industries: in wool textiles, leather tanning and finishing, and footwear, prewar tendencies toward decline accelerated after the war; in iron and steel, prewar growth in employment changed to postwar shrinkage. The strongest employment growth in the sample took place in two postwar non-

Table 2

Monthly Rates of Growth (%) of Output, Employment, Weekly Hours, and Productivity

Industry	Period	IP	EMP	HRS	PROD
STEEL	1923–39	0.18	0.07	−0.25	0.35
	1954–82	−0.12	−0.26	−0.01	0.14
AUTOS	1923–39	0.34	0.07	−0.14	0.42
	1954–82	0.16	−0.09	0.00	0.25
MEAT	1923–39	0.04	0.05	−.08	0.07
	1954–82	0.18	0.02	−0.01	0.17
PAPER	1923–39	0.33	0.06	−0.12	0.39
	1954–82	0.33	0.03	0.00	0.29
SHOES	1923–39	0.01	−0.07	−0.14	0.22
	1954–82	−0.13	−0.22	−0.01	0.10
WOOL	1923–39	0.04	−0.08	−0.12	0.24
	1958–82	−0.14	−0.43	0.01	0.28
LEATH	1923–39	−0.09	−0.14	−0.10	0.15
	1954–82	−0.17	−0.29	0.00	0.12
LUMBR	1923–39	−0.07	−0.14	−0.10	0.17
	1954–82	0.18	−0.06	0.01	0.23
ALL MFG	1923–39	0.22	−0.01	−0.12	0.34
	1954–82	0.27	−0.02	0.00	0.29
COAL	1954–82	0.18	−0.13	0.06	0.26
ELECT	1954–82	0.48	0.11	0.00	0.36
CONST	1954–82	0.13	0.11	0.02	0.00

manufacturing industries (electric services and construction). As a whole, the employment column of table 2 is consistent with the often-noted secular fall in the fraction of total employment absorbed by manufacturing.

The behavior of the last component of productivity, hours of work, was quite different in the two sample periods. Weekly hours declined steadily during the prewar period in all industries, most precipitously in iron and steel (a notorious "long-hours" industry during the early 1920s, in which eighty-four-hour workweeks were not uncommon). This fall reflected changes in work organization during the 1920s (in a few cases as a response to the pressure of public opinion against long hours) and the "work sharing" of the depressed 1930s (sometimes initiated by employers, sometimes the result of New Deal legislation or union demands); see Zeisel (1958) for further discussion. In contrast, the postwar workweek was almost perfectly stable.

Finally, we may consider the mean rates of growth of the alternative measures of production worker compensation (table 3). It is interesting that,

Table 3
Monthly Rates of Growth (%) of Real Wages, Product Wages, and Real Weekly
Earnings

Industry	Period	WR	WP	EARN
STEEL	1923–39	0.31	0.29	0.06
	1954–82	0.16	0.10	0.15
AUTOS	1923–39	0.31	0.30	0.17
	1954–82	0.11	0.16	0.11
MEAT	1923–39	0.29	0.29	0.21
	1954–82	0.06	0.15	0.04
PAPER	1923–39	0.24	0.24	0.12
	1954–82	0.13	0.15	0.13
SHOES	1923–39	0.11	−0.01	−0.03
	1954–82	0.03	0.05	0.02
WOOL	1923–39	0.21	0.20	0.08
	1958–82	0.05	0.31[a]	0.06
LEATH	1923–39	0.27	0.25	0.17
	1954–82	0.05	0.03	0.05
LUMBR	1923–39	0.28	0.27	0.17
	1954–82	0.09	0.13	0.10
ALL MFG	1923–39	0.26	0.27	0.14
	1954–82	0.09	0.10	0.09
COAL	1954–82	0.12	−0.04	0.18
ELECT	1954–82	0.13	0.05[b]	0.13
CONST	1954–82	0.09	0.03	0.11

[a]Sample period is 1958–75.
[b]Sample period is 1958–82.

though productivity gains during the prewar period were larger than during the postwar period in only five of the eight manufacturing industries studied, real wage growth was significantly larger during the prewar in *all* eight industries, as well as in the aggregate. Prewar product wages also rose sharply, except in boots and shoes. Within the major sample periods, the rank correlation of real wage growth with productivity growth was .815 for the eight prewar industries, .864 for the eleven postwar industries. (Although these correlations are high, note that they are somewhat lower than the correlations of productivity and output growth reported above.) The large prewar growth in real wages was not fully reflected in increases in worker buying power, as the last column of table 3 shows; because of the sharp declines in hours of work, real weekly earnings rose much more slowly than real wages.

Turning from the first to the second moments, tables 4 and 5 contain the standard deviations of the raw log differences, multiplied by 100 so they can

Table 4

Standard Deviations (%) of Monthly Growth Rates of Output, Employment, Weekly Hours, and Productivity

Industry	Period	IP	EMP	HRS	PROD
STEEL	1923–39	13.40	4.70	6.85	8.00
	1954–82	16.09	11.53	2.25	7.06
AUTOS	1923–39	30.12	10.37	8.13	22.47
	1954–82	7.80	9.69	4.14	8.69
MEAT	1923–39	9.91	4.03	3.16	7.95
	1954–82	2.82	1.80	1.84	3.87
PAPER	1923–39	5.71	1.83	2.47	5.15
	1954–82	1.83	1.06	0.98	2.06
SHOES	1923–39	11.87	3.18	5.39	10.08
	1954–82	4.05	2.86	2.58	5.63
WOOL	1923–39	12.04	6.09	4.93	8.64
	1958–82	9.30	2.71	2.01	10.17
LEATH	1923–39	5.52	2.93	3.52	5.46
	1954–82	3.39	2.32	1.71	4.82
LUMBR	1923–39	6.80	5.63	4.88	6.79
	1954–82	2.85	2.47	1.87	3.62
ALL MFG	1923–39	4.70	2.36	2.59	2.92
	1954–82	3.28	1.36	1.17	2.58
COAL	1954–82	14.00	16.05	8.18	11.74
ELECT	1954–82	1.45	0.91	0.91	1.94
CONST	1954–82	7.88	6.17	2.87	5.25

be interpreted as percentages. We will not comment on these figures except to note, first, how surprisingly large the variability of the industry data often is and, second, that aggregation seems to reduce measured variability somewhat. To see how much of total variability was attributable to business cycles, we used a frequency domain technique to wipe out the variance associated with the high-frequency (seasonal) and the low-frequency (trending or long-wave) bands. The resulting standard deviations for five key variables are in table 6. Three facts are obvious from the table. First, the share of total variability of the data to be associated with business cycles is relatively small in both the prewar and postwar periods. Second, the business cycle has dampened considerably during the postwar period. Third, in most industries the cyclical variance of hours of work per week has, between the prewar and postwar periods, been reduced relatively more than that of employment.

This last observation, which is also confirmed in the raw data (table 4) and in section 7 below, is worth remarking on a bit further. Why have

Table 5
Standard Deviations (%) of Monthly Growth Rates of Real Wages, Product
Wages, and Real Weekly Earnings

Industry	Period	WR	WP	EARN
STEEL	1923–39	2.14	2.24	7.02
	1954–82	1.32	1.50	2.96
AUTOS	1923–39	1.90	2.24	8.32
	1954–82	1.69	1.87	5.21
MEAT	1923–39	2.24	4.81	3.25
	1954–82	1.29	4.05	2.43
PAPER	1923–39	1.30	2.14	2.43
	1954–82	0.83	3.61	1.36
SHOES	1923–39	2.70	2.47	5.41
	1954–82	0.95	1.80	2.60
WOOL	1923–39	2.14	2.97	4.79
	1958–82	1.06	1.48[a]	2.37
LEATH	1923–39	1.47	3.03	3.37
	1954–82	0.92	2.96	2.12
LUMBR	1923–39	4.14	4.74	5.25
	1954–82	1.32	1.99	2.37
ALL MFG	1923–39	1.24	1.48	2.55
	1954–82	2.30	2.34	2.69
COAL	1954–82	1.95	2.19	9.04
ELECT	1954–82	0.90	1.11[b]	1.44
CONST	1954–82	1.05	1.02	2.80

[a]Sample period is 1958–75.
[b]Sample period is 1958–82.

postwar employers relied relatively more heavily on layoffs, rather than on short workweeks, to reduce labor input in downturns? Two possible sources of the change are the greater postwar importance of unions and the advent of unemployment insurance programs. Union objective functions might be such that layoffs of a relatively small number of junior workers are preferred to a general reduction of hours. (Cross-sectional evidence that unions prefer layoffs was presented in Medoff 1979. Medoff also cited a study by Slichter, Healy, and Livernash 1960 claiming that unions, which initially approved of some work sharing, moved toward a preference for layoffs in the early postwar period.) Perhaps more important than unionism is the fact that in the United States, fully unemployed workers can receive government compensation but the partially unemployed cannot. See Baily (1977) for a formal analysis.

Table 6
Standard Deviations (%) of Monthly Growth Rates of Five Variables: Business
Cycle Frequencies (Twelve to Ninety-Six Months) Only

Industry	Period	IP	EMP	HRS	PROD	WR
STEEL	1923–39	3.96	1.59	1.73	1.53	0.59
	1954–82	2.28	1.05	0.48	1.15	0.27
AUTOS	1923–39	4.54	2.72	1.46	2.93	0.36
	1954–82	1.85	1.43	0.47	0.77	0.31
MEAT	1923–39	1.66	1.05	0.49	1.01	0.49
	1954–82	0.46	0.27	0.19	0.36	0.21
PAPER	1923–39	1.33	0.60	0.65	0.76	0.36
	1954–82	0.56	0.30	0.16	0.27	0.14
SHOES	1923–39	1.26	0.47	0.94	0.78	0.68
	1954–82	0.71	0.39	0.38	0.60	0.17
WOOL	1923–39	3.16	1.69	1.06	0.99	0.67
	1954–82	1.56	1.01	0.61	1.74	0.22
LEATH	1923–39	1.19	0.97	0.77	0.82	0.47
	1954–82	0.59	0.49	0.22	0.52	0.14
LUMBR	1923–39	1.75	1.48	0.85	1.19	0.70
	1954–82	0.87	0.61	0.21	0.44	0.23
ALL MFG	1923–39	1.53	0.97	0.67	0.48	0.33
	1954–82	0.60	0.39	0.15	0.21	0.20
COAL	1954–82	0.92	0.71	0.61	0.84	0.25
ELECT	1954–82	0.22	0.16	0.10	0.28	0.13
CONST	1954–82	0.69	0.75	0.21	0.77	0.15

5. Analysis in the Frequency Domain

We turn now to the study of these variables over the business cycle. To obtain characterizations of "typical" cyclical patterns, we subjected the data to both frequency domain and time domain analysis. In the frequency domain work we followed the approach suggested by Granger and Hatanaka (1964); in the time domain our analysis is in the spirit of Sims (1980). (There are, of course, close formal connections between these two approaches; this is evidenced by the similarity of the results obtained.) The results from the frequency domain will be discussed here. Those from the time domain are presented in section 6.

The data used in the frequency domain work (as well as in the time domain) were the deseasonalized log differences of the basic series. (Deseasonalization was done by the use of seasonal dummies; see our data appendix.) Each variable was analyzed separately by industry and for the prewar and postwar sample periods.

Spectra of these data showed power in the business cycle frequency range, but rarely were clear peaks apparent in that range. (Sargent 1979, 254, warns that this is to be expected.) We decided to investigate the properties of cycles with periods exceeding one year (so as to exclude remaining seasonal and other high-frequency influences) but shorter than eight years. (According to the NBER chronology, the longest business cycle in our sample—the one extending from 1929 to 1937—was eight years long.) For each industry/sample period, we calculated the coherences and phase relationships of the variables over the one- to eight-year band.

The coherences of six variables (the rates of growth of employment, weekly hours, productivity, real wages, product wages, and real weekly earnings) with the rate of growth of industry output over the business cycle range are reported in table 7. (Standard errors of the coherence estimates are also included. See the appendix for a description of how these were calculated.) Coherence is a measure of the degree of association of a pair of variables over a prescribed set of frequencies; a coherence of zero indicates the minimum association, a coherence of one the maximum. The table suggests that employment and hours bear the strongest relation to output over the business cycle. Productivity and earnings also are strongly related to output for most industries. The connection between the two wage measures and output is erratic across industries and, on the whole, is weaker; this is especially true in the postwar period. Note, however, that the coherences of wages and output appear to be statistically significant in both periods.

A particularly informative exercise in the frequency domain is the calculation of phase relationships. For a given frequency, think of variables as tracing out sine curves over time. Then the "phase lead" of variable A with respect to variable B is the number of months after A reaches a given point on its sinusoidal path that B reaches the corresponding point. We shall say a variable that has a phase lead with respect to output of near zero is "procyclical"; a variable whose phase lead with respect to output is approximately half the period of the full cycle is "countercyclical." (There are, however, some caveats to this interpretation of phase leads; see Hause 1971.)

The phase leads of six variables with respect to output growth, plus standard errors, are given in table 8. The phase leads are evaluated at the frequency with period of fifty-four months, the period at the center of the range considered. (See the appendix for more discussion.) We find that employment, hours, and earnings are roughly procyclical. Productivity is procyclical but slightly leading in the postwar period; its lead over output is greater in the prewar period. Hours typically leads, though by less than productivity, while employment consistently lags a few months behind output. Earnings is approximately coincident.

The interrelation of productivity, hours, output, and employment is essen-

Table 7
Coherences of Growth Rates of Six Variables with Growth Rate of Output

Industry	EMP	HRS	PROD	WR	WP	EARN
Prewar data						
STEEL	.828	.883	.915	.272	.230	.854
	(.060)	(.042)	(.031)	(.175)	(.179)	(.051)
AUTOS	.854	.583	.692	.252	.271	.568
	(.051)	(.125)	(.099)	(.177)	(.175)	(.128)
MEAT	.773	.657	.836	.541	.330	.292
	(.076)	(.107)	(.057)	(.134)	(.168)	(.173)
PAPER	.661	.870	.721	.610	.507	.836
	(.106)	(.046)	(.091)	(.119)	(.140)	(.057)
SHOES	.717	.836	.651	.098	.142	.794
	(.092)	(.057)	(.109)	(.187)	(.185)	(.070)
WOOL	.934	.878	.783	.449	.429	.797
	(.024)	(.043)	(.073)	(.151)	(.154)	(.069)
LEATH	.754	.742	.341	.473	.634	.823
	(.082)	(.085)	(.167)	(.147)	(.113)	(.061)
LUMBR	.749	.784	.276	.354	.659	.638
	(.083)	(.073)	(.175)	(.165)	(.107)	(.112)
ALL MFG	.935	.916	.567	.567	.607	.902
	(.024)	(.031)	(.128)	(.128)	(.119)	(.035)
Postwar data						
STEEL	.898	.895	.863	.527	.180	.829
	(.027)	(.028)	(.036)	(.102)	(.137)	(.044)
AUTOS	.912	.724	.479	.733	.578	.809
	(.024)	(.067)	(.109)	(.065)	(.094)	(.049)
MEAT	.592	.585	.618	.430	.706	.648
	(.092)	(.093)	(.087)	(.115)	(.071)	(.082)
PAPER	.911	.771	.856	.360	.735	.672
	(.024)	(.057)	(.038)	(.123)	(.065)	(.078)
SHOES	.714	.594	.503	.159	.094	.590
	(.069)	(.092)	(.106)	(.138)	(.140)	(.092)
WOOL	.418	.295	.586	.252	.573	.294
	(.127)	(.141)	(.101)	(.144)	(.123)	(.141)
LEATH	.620	.412	.416	.164	.368	.385
	(.087)	(.117)	(.117)	(.138)	(.122)	(.120)
LUMBR	.881	.845	.658	.378	.489	.779
	(.032)	(.040)	(.080)	(.121)	(.108)	(.056)
ALL MFG	.941	.839	.684	.378	.314	.693
	(.016)	(.042)	(.075)	(.121)	(.128)	(.073)
COAL	.603	.710	.331	.371	.063	.676
	(.090)	(.070)	(.126)	(.122)	(.141)	(.077)

Table 7 (*cont.*)

Industry	EMP	HRS	PROD	WR	WP	EARN
ELECT	.290	.359	.734	.287	.203	.413
	(.129)	(.123)	(.065)	(.130)	(.148)	(.117)
CONST	.568	.344	.384	.274	.507	.397
	(.096)	(.125)	(.121)	(.131)	(.105)	(.119)

Note: Bandwidth is twelve to ninety-six months. Standard errors are given in parentheses.

tially stable between the prewar and postwar periods and, except for the introduction of some subtleties in timing, is consistent with earlier findings. In conjunction with the dynamic model of the firm discussed in section 2, this interrelation suggests a simple economic interpretation: cycles are dominated by demand changes. Firms anticipating an increase in demand respond first by increasing nonlabor inputs and asking for more work effort; this increases productivity. As demand strengthens, hours of work expand. Finally, as the increase in demand assumes greater permanence, firms make the hiring and training investments needed to add to the work force. This story is hardly original (see, for example, Baily 1977), and we emphasize again that we have done no explicitly structural test. Still, it is interesting that this interpretation seems at least to be consistent with the facts for so many disparate industries, and for both the prewar and postwar eras.

This stability across industries and sample periods is not shared by the relationship of wages and output. There seems to be a definite difference between the prewar and postwar behavior of wages. Let us concentrate on real, rather than product, wages. During the prewar period, real wages lagged output significantly—not quite enough to be called countercyclical, but still "half out of phase."[3] (A well-known example of this is the positive growth of real wages in 1931–32, even as output and employment plunged.) In contrast, during the postwar period real wages were nearly in phase (procyclical), even leading the cycle in some industries.

Why did the cyclical behavior of real wages change between the prewar and postwar periods? A satisfactory answer to this question would require an explicit structural model, which we do not attempt in this paper. However, we do present a simple heuristic example suggesting that this change may be related to one of our earlier findings, that layoffs have become relatively more important than work sharing in the postwar period.

Suppose that, because of fixed costs, workers can hold only one job at a time. (This example will generalize as long as an individual's work effort is not infinitely divisible among employers.) Then the labor market is cleared not by the hourly wage, but by the total utility available to the worker in a

[3] This is reminiscent of Creamer's (1950) result for nominal wage rates. See section 2.

Table 8
Phase Leads of Growth Rates of Six Variables with Respect to Growth Rate of Output, in Months

Industry	EMP	HRS	PROD	WR	WP	EARN
Prewar data						
STEEL	−4.7	1.8	2.3	−5.3	−0.3	1.2
	(1.11)	(0.9)	(0.7)	(5.7)	(6.9)	(1.0)
AUTOS	−0.5	10.4	−2.9	−10.6	−6.0	9.8
	(1.0)	(2.3)	(1.7)	(6.2)	(5.8)	(2.4)
MEAT	−6.0	2.2	4.6	−22.2	−7.6	−5.1
	(1.3)	(1.9)	(1.1)	(2.5)	(4.7)	(5.3)
PAPER	−7.3	2.4	2.3	−19.3	26.5	−0.5
	(1.8)	(0.9)	(1.6)	(2.1)	(2.8)	(1.1)
SHOES	−6.3	−2.4	9.0	−11.5	9.0	−3.0
	(1.6)	(1.1)	(1.9)	(16.6)	(11.3)	(1.2)
WOOL	−2.6	2.1	2.7	−15.8	24.7	−0.6
	(0.6)	(0.9)	(1.3)	(3.2)	(3.4)	(1.2)
LEATH	−5.7	2.8	11.1	−14.6	26.5	−0.7
	(1.4)	(1.5)	(4.5)	(3.0)	(1.9)	(1.1)
LUMBR	−3.8	2.0	11.2	−19.1	27.0	−0.7
	(1.4)	(1.3)	(5.7)	(4.3)	(1.9)	(2.0)
ALL MFG	−3.9	2.3	9.3	−11.6	−19.5	−0.3
	(0.6)	(0.7)	(2.4)	(2.4)	(2.1)	(0.8)
Postwar data						
STEEL	−2.8	1.1	2.2	3.1	9.3	1.6
	(0.6)	(0.6)	(0.7)	(2.0)	(6.6)	(0.8)
AUTOS	−2.5	4.5	5.0	3.6	3.9	4.1
	(0.5)	(1.2)	(2.2)	(1.1)	(1.7)	(0.9)
MEAT	−4.1	2.3	1.8	0.1	−1.6	1.3
	(1.7)	(1.7)	(1.6)	(2.6)	(1.2)	(1.4)
PAPER	−4.4	2.1	3.9	7.2	10.0	3.5
	(0.6)	(1.0)	(0.7)	(3.2)	(1.1)	(1.3)
SHOES	−5.9	1.6	3.8	−7.6	11.9	0.8
	(1.2)	(1.7)	(2.1)	(7.6)	(12.9)	(1.7)
WOOL	−3.4	−1.0	1.5	4.9	24.3	0.5
	(2.8)	(4.1)	(1.8)	(4.9)	(2.0)	(4.1)
LEATH	−2.3	3.5	1.7	−5.4	12.4	1.8
	(1.5)	(2.7)	(2.7)	(7.3)	(3.1)	(2.9)
LUMBR	−3.9	2.0	6.4	−1.2	25.7	1.0
	(0.7)	(0.8)	(1.4)	(3.0)	(2.2)	(1.0)
ALL MFG	−2.4	2.1	4.4	0.7	8.4	1.6
	(0.5)	(0.8)	(1.3)	(3.0)	(3.7)	(1.3)
COAL	−5.1	−0.1	9.1	−10.4	−21.3	−1.7
	(1.6)	(1.2)	(3.5)	(3.0)	(19.2)	(1.3)

Table 8 (*cont.*)

Industry	EMP	HRS	PROD	WR	WP	EARN
ELECT	− 16.0	− 0.3	1.9	2.8	− 5.4	1.3
	(4.0)	(3.2)	(1.1)	(4.1)	(4.9)	(2.7)
CONST	− 4.2	4.2	5.0	11.6	12.3	6.7
	(1.8)	(3.3)	(2.9)	(4.3)	(2.0)	(2.8)

Note: Bandwidth is twelve to ninety-six months. Standard errors are given in parentheses.

job. Assume that workers get utility from total real compensation Y and disutility from hours of work per week H. If, for simplicity, the marginal utilities of income and leisure are taken to be constant, then instantaneous utility at time t, U_t, can be written as

$$U_t = Y_t - \alpha H_t, \tag{1}$$

where α is a parameter.

To retain their labor forces, firms must provide workers with (Y_t, H_t) combinations such that workers' utility equals or exceeds $\overline{U}$, the (exogenous) utility level obtainable elsewhere in the economy. Assuming for purposes of this example that business cycles are regular since waves and the $\overline{U}$ is procyclical, we can write

$$\overline{U}_t = \overline{U}_0 (1 + a \sin t), \tag{2}$$

where $\overline{U}_0$ is average obtainably utility and a is a positive parameter measuring the cyclical sensitivity of $\overline{U}$.

Firms' choices about which (Y_t, H_t) combinations to offer (from among those combinations that satisfy the external utility constraint) will arise from a maximization calculation that takes into account the nature of the production function, the existence of specific human capital or adjustment costs, and so forth. For this heuristic example we do not explicitly specify the firm's maximization problem but simply assume (realistically) that its outcome will imply a procyclical workweek:

$$H_t = H_0 (1 + b \sin t), \tag{3}$$

where H_0 is the average workweek over the cycle and b measures the workweek's cyclical sensitivity. Equation (3) is to be interpreted as a reduced form; the parameter b may well depend on the other parameters in the problem.

The three equations just given, plus the assumption that real earnings are just high enough to meet the external utility constraint, imply that the cyclical behavior of real earnings per worker is

$$Y_t = (\overline{U}_0 + \alpha H_0) + (a + \alpha b) \sin t. \tag{4}$$

Average earnings Y_0 equal $\overline{U}_0 + \alpha H_0$.

In this example, the measured "real wage" W_t is just Y_t/H_t. Under what conditions will the measured wage be procyclical (i.e., have a positive sensitivity to the exogenous cycle)? It is easy to show that the necessary and sufficient condition for real wage procyclicality is

$$a > b. \tag{5}$$

That is, wages are procyclical if reservation utility has a greater sensitivity to the cycle than do hours of work.

It is difficult to say what has happpened over time to the cyclical sensitivity of reservation utility; perhaps reservation utility has become less cyclical in the postwar period, which would work against the present argument. However, in section 4 we introduced evidence that b, the cyclical sensitivity of hours, has fallen in the postwar era. The example shows that, everything else being equal, reduced cyclical sensitivity of hours tends to be associated with greater observed procyclicality in real wages. Thus, two of the novel findings of this paper—that hours have become less procyclical and that real wages more procyclical in the postwar period—may be related.

An important question is whether the cyclical relationships described in table 7 and 8 are the same in long and short business cycles. Closely related is whether it is useful to study "reference cycles." Burns and Mitchell frequently measured timing relationships in terms of "stages" of a standard "reference cycle" instead of in calendar times. For this to be worthwhile, it must be the case that cyclical lead/lag relationships are roughly constant fractions of the cycle length rather than constant when measured in calendar time; that is to say, phase angles must be constant across business cycle frequencies.

Some insight on this question is provided by table 9. That table gives the estimates of the phase leads of the six variables for the deseasonalized high-frequency band (two to twelve months); for short cycles (one to two years); and for long cycles (two to eight years). (The business cycle band was broken up in that particular way because there are approximately as many frequencies with periods between twelve and twenty-four months as there are with periods between twenty-four and ninety-six months.) Also reported for each variable are the results of a statistical test for constancy of phase angles between short and long business cycles. Inspection of table 9 suggests two observations.

First, while not much systematic emerges in the high-frequency band, the qualitative pattern of leads and lags is the same in the short and long business cycles ranges (the b and c rows in the table). For example, productivity still leads the cycle, employment still lags.

Second, there appears to be a bit of support for the "reference cycle" construction (and, by implication, for the "time deformation" approach to cycles recently suggested by Stock 1983). The hypothesis of constant phase

Table 9
Phase Leads of Growth Rates of Six Variables with Respect to Growth Rate of Output, in Months

Industry		EMP	HRS	PROD	WR	WP	EARN
Prewar data							
STEEL	(a)	−0.4	0.0	0.2	−1.9	2.5	−0.1
	(b)	−1.6	0.6	0.8	2.2	2.4	0.8
	(c)	−5.0	2.1	2.5	−13.8***	−13.5***	−0.4
AUTOS	(a)	0.3	0.5	−0.2	−1.4	−1.2	0.4
	(b)	−0.3	4.1	−0.9	−2.2	−1.2	4.0
	(c)	0.1	6.6	−3.6	−15.3	−9.4	5.0*
MEAT	(a)	−1.0	−0.1	0.2	−2.0	−1.2	−0.2
	(b)	−2.2	0.6	1.1	−8.2	−5.5	0.2
	(c)	−5.8	23.9***	10.4***	−16.1	0.3***	−18.9***
PAPER	(a)	−1.4	−0.6	0.3	−3.0	−2.4	−0.9
	(b)	−3.1	0.7	0.8	−7.1	−8.9	0.1
	(c)	−4.5	3.4	2.7	−18.1	27.8	−2.7
SHOES	(a)	−0.3	−0.1	0.1	2.8	2.6	0.1
	(b)	−1.9	−0.9	3.0	−7.4	4.4	−1.1
	(c)	−8.6	−1.1	9.8	−5.0	0.6	−2.3
WOOL	(a)	−0.6	−0.1	0.4	−2.6	−3.4	−0.3
	(b)	−0.6	0.6	0.6	−5.3	−8.9	0.2
	(c)	−4.4	2.9	5.3	−17.5	25.6	−3.5
LEATH	(a)	0.0	−0.1	0.0	1.9	−3.3	0.2
	(b)	−2.4	0.8	3.5	−4.9	8.8	0.1
	(c)	−3.2	4.0	18.7	−15.9	29.5	−4.0
LUMBR	(a)	−0.4	0.6	−0.1	−2.6	−3.0	0.4
	(b)	−1.8	0.4	4.6	−7.4	−8.8	−0.5
	(c)	−1.3***	5.7	−0.9*	−5.7	28.8	0.8
ALL MFG	(a)	−0.5	−0.1	0.6	3.4	−3.2	−0.1
	(b)	−1.7	0.6	2.3	−3.9	−7.2	0.0
	(c)	−3.3*	3.4	19.9***	−12.8	−20.0	−0.7
Postwar data							
STEEL	(a)	−0.4	0.0	0.1	0.7	0.9	0.1
	(b)	−0.9	0.1	0.5	0.8	0.8	0.3
	(c)	−3.3	2.9***	4.4*	4.7	17.6	3.4
AUTOS	(a)	−0.2	−0.1	1.7	−0.2	−0.1	−0.1
	(b)	−0.8	1.5	1.6	1.2	2.0	1.4
	(c)	−2.7	4.6	6.1	3.9	−0.7*	4.3
MEAT	(a)	−1.3	0.1	0.0	−0.6	−0.4	−0.1
	(b)	−1.3	0.9	0.5	1.0	−0.2	0.9
	(c)	−4.9	1.9	2.4	−5.6*	−2.4	−1.5

Table 9 (*cont.*)

Industry		EMP	HRS	PROD	WR	WP	EARN
PAPER	(a)	0.4	−0.6	0.0	2.7	−2.0	−0.4
	(b)	−1.2	0.3	1.0	−2.8	3.1	0.1
	(c)	−5.5	3.6	5.8*	8.7	12.0	5.8*
SHOES	(a)	0.3	0.5	0.1	1.0	1.2	0.5
	(b)	−1.9	0.9	0.6	−3.5	5.3	0.5
	(c)	−6.7	0.8	8.3	−5.6	10.9	0.1
WOOL	(a)	0.0	0.1	0.0	0.5	2.5	0.1
	(b)	−1.9	−1.9	0.5	1.0	−5.2	0.5
	(c)	−2.2	3.7	0.8	7.1	25.2**	4.6
LEATH	(a)	0.7	0.7	−0.1	0.7	1.8	0.7
	(b)	−0.4	1.5	−0.1	−3.3	−8.5	0.7
	(c)	−3.2	3.0	4.2	−2.6	13.3	1.7
LUMBR	(a)	−0.2	0.1	0.0	0.4	1.2	0.3
	(b)	−1.4	0.7	1.3	−2.6	−7.7	0.2
	(c)	−6.2	0.8	18.7***	−8.5	29.1	0.2
ALL MFG	(a)	−0.0	0.2	0.1	0.6	0.7	0.1
	(b)	−0.7	0.0	1.0	−1.8	2.8	−0.7
	(c)	−2.9	4.7***	9.5**	5.7**	9.3	9.5**
COAL	(a)	−0.2	−0.2	0.1	−2.7	−1.6	−0.2
	(b)	−1.1	−0.3	0.7	−3.7	−3.2	−1.1
	(c)	−6.2	0.8	18.7***	−8.5	29.0	0.2
ELECT	(a)	2.1	0.7	−0.1	−2.2	0.6	0.3
	(b)	−5.7	1.1	0.3	−3.3	−4.4	−0.8
	(c)	−16.5	−9.0*	3.1	8.5***	−0.1	5.2
CONST	(a)	0.0	0.2	0.0	−3.4	−3.1	0.2
	(b)	−0.8	1.6	0.6	7.0	5.6	3.2
	(c)	−6.7	1.5	8.5	4.9***	10.3**	4.0

Note: Asterisks denote significance of *t*-tests of difference of phase angles between frequency bands (b) and (c), at marginal significance levels of .10 (*), .05 (**), and .01 (***).

(a) Bandwidth: two to twelve months. (b) Bandwidth: twelve to twenty-four months. (c) Bandwidth: twenty four to ninety-six months.

angles between short and long business cycles, which is implied by the reference cycle approach, is not usually rejected by the data. (Exceptions are the prewar meat-packing industry and, to some extent, aggregate manufacturing in both the prewar and postwar periods.) Thus, assuming that leads and lags are proportional to cycle length does not seem unreasonable. On the other hand, it should be noted that this evidence in favor of reference cycles may possibly be spurious: as an example in Hause (1971) shows, two variables with a fixed distributed lag relationship in the time domain may also exhibit a phase relationship that is roughly proportional to the period of the cycle.

The observations we have made so far apply to more or less all the industries in the sample, with a few distinctions drawn between the patterns visible in the prewar period and those in the postwar era. We had hoped to be able to make more cross-sectional distinctions (e.g., like the finding of Nadiri and Rosen 1973 that input responses are much more rapid in durable goods industries). Unfortunately, much less cross-sectional variation than we expected was evident when we grouped the industries in the obvious ways.

To see if the industries might be grouped by the nature of their cyclical behavior, we estimated the coherences and phases between industry outputs and the aggregate index of output, for the prewar and postwar periods separately. These are presented in table 10. An odd result is that almost all the phase leads are positive; this may be due to the inclusion of input-based measures of output in the aggregate index. The coherence estimates suggest that cyclical influences became relatively less important for the industries in the postwar period. There is also a tendency in the postwar sample for durable goods industries to exhibit a relatively higher coherence with the cycle than nondurable goods industries. However, except for meat-packing, there is surprisingly little evidence of this pattern in the prewar period. Overall, cross-sectional differences still seem less significant than cross-sectional similarities.

6. Analysis in the Time Domain

To complement the frequency domain analysis of the data, we employed time domain methods, primarily vector autoregressions (VARs). Separate VARs, using twelve monthly lags of four variables (output, hours, employment, and real wages), were estimated for each of the prewar and postwar industries and for the aggregates. The data were the same centered and seasonalized log differences described in section 5. As in Sims (1980), the estimated VARs were used to do three things. First, we looked at the statistical significance of blocks of coefficients in order to search for patterns of causality (in the Granger sense). Second, we calculated the percentages of the forecast errors attributable to (triangularized) innovations in the right-hand-side variables, for four forecast horizons. Finally, the implied impulse/response diagrams were examined for systematic timing relationships among the variables. We briefly discuss each of these exercises.

Table 11 summarizes the results of the Granger-causality F-tests. There is one matrix for each dependent variables. In each matrix, the rows designate the industry to which the VAR applies, the columns give the block of independent variables being tested. One, two, or three asterisks in a given cell of

Table 10
Coherences and Phase Leads of Growth Rates of Output in Each Industry with
Respect to Growth Rate of "All Manufacturing" Output

Industry	Period	Coherence (SE)	Phase Lead (SE)
STEEL	1923–39	94.7 (2.0)	1.3 (0.6)
	1954–82	64.6 (8.2)	0.2 (1.4)
AUTOS	1923–39	78.0 (7.4)	−4.1 (1.3)
	1954–82	78.6 (5.4)	0.2 (1.0)
MEAT	1923–39	19.5 (18.2)	1.2 (8.2)
	1954–82	26.2 (13.2)	4.8 (4.5)
PAPER	1923–39	86.7 (4.7)	2.3 (0.9)
	1954–82	79.7 (5.2)	1.2 (0.9)
SHOES	1923–39	73.9 (8.6)	6.7 (1.5)
	1954–82	46.4 (11.1)	4.9 (2.3)
WOOL	1923–39	80.1 (6.8)	3.5 (1.2)
	1954–82	31.9 (13.9)	1.4 (3.9)
LEATH	1923–39	75.0 (8.3)	0.6 (1.4)
	1954–82	38.8 (12.0)	3.7 (2.9)
LUMBR	1923–39	88.0 (4.3)	1.0 (0.9)
	1954–82	73.9 (6.4)	5.3 (1.1)
COAL	1954–82	28.4 (13.0)	−5.4 (4.1)
ELECT	1954–82	44.7 (11.3)	−2.1 (2.4)
CONST	1954–82	57.4 (9.5)	6.3 (1.7)

Note: Bandwidth is twelve to ninety-six months.

a matrix implies that the twelve monthly lags of the independent variable jointly "explain" the dependent variable (for the given industry and period) at the .10, .05, or .01 level of significance. No asterisks in a cell implies that the joint contribution of all lags of the given regressor is not significant at the .10 level.

Table 11 suggests that, for all industries taken together:

1. Output growth tends to be relatively exogenous (in the Granger sense), at least in comparison with the growth rates of employment and hours. (Thus hours may be a "leading indicator" without having incremental predictive value for output. See Neftci 1979.) Output seemed to be much more "persistent" in the postwar period, in the sense that lagged growth rates of output became much stronger predictors of the current growth rate.

2. Hours and employment are rarely found to be Granger exogenous;

Table 11
VAR F-Tests

Dependent Variables	Industry	Independent Variables			
		IP	HRS	EMP	WR
Prewar data					
IP	STEEL	**	*		***
	AUTOS	***		***	
	MEAT		**		**
	PAPER			**	
	SHOES	***	**		*
	WOOL	*		***	
	LEATH		*		
	LUMBR	***	***		***
	ALL MFG	***			
HRS	STEEL	***	***	***	***
	AUTOS		***		
	MEAT		**	*	*
	PAPER	***	*		*
	SHOES	***	***	***	
	WOOL	***	**	***	
	LEATH	***	***	***	
	LUMBR	**	***		
	ALL MFG	***	*	***	
EMP	STEEL	*			
	AUTOS	***	***	**	*
	MEAT	**	**		
	PAPER	**		**	
	SHOES	**	**	***	
	WOOL	***		***	
	LEATH	***		**	
	LUMBR	**		**	
	ALL MFG	**	*		
WR	STEEL				
	AUTOS		**		
	MEAT				
	PAPER			**	**
	SHOES	**	**		
	WOOL				
	LEATH	**			
	LUMBR	***	*	*	***
	ALL MFG			*	

Table 11 (*cont.*)

Dependent Variables	Industry	Independent Variables			
		IP	HRS	EMP	WR
Postwar data					
IP	STEEL	*			
	AUTOS	*		***	
	MEAT	***	**		*
	PAPER	***		**	***
	SHOES	***	***	**	
	WOOL	***	***		
	LEATH	***	**		
	LUMBR	***		***	***
	ALL MFG	***	**	***	
	COAL	***		*	
	ELECT	***			***
	CONST	***			**
HRS	STEEL	**	***	**	
	AUTOS		***		
	MEAT	**	***		**
	PAPER	***	***	*	
	SHOES	***	***	***	
	WOOL	*	***	***	***
	LEATH		***	**	*
	LUMBR		***		
	ALL MFG	***	***	**	
	COAL	***	***	*	**
	ELECT		***		
	CONST		***		
EMP	STEEL	***	**		
	AUTOS	***	**	***	
	MEAT	***		**	
	PAPER	***	***	***	
	SHOES	**	***	***	
	WOOL	***	***	***	***
	LEATH		***	***	
	LUMBR	***		***	**
	ALL MFG	***		**	
	COAL	*		***	
	ELECT		**	***	
	CONST			***	
WR	STEEL				***
	AUTOS	***		***	***

Table 11 (*cont.*)

Dependent Variables	Industry	Independent Variables			
		IP	HRS	EMP	WR
	MEAT	*			**
	PAPER				***
	SHOES		**		***
	WOOL		*		***
	LEATH				***
	LUMBR			**	
	ALL MFG				***
	COAL				***
	ELECT	**		***	***
	CONST				***

Note: F-tests whose outcomes are reported are tests of the joint significance of all twelve lags of the independent variable in the explanation of the dependent variable. (All variables are in growth rates.) *F-test significant at .10 level. **F-test significant at .05 level. ***F-test significant at .01 level.

they respond both to each other and to output. The two variables are also found to be persistent, in the sense just defined, in both the prewar and postwar samples. The persistence of employment will be an appealing finding for supporters of the view that there are "adjustment costs" to changing employment. Are there also adjustment costs to changing hours of work? The data seem consistent with this.

3. The real wage seems to vary nearly independently of the three other variables, neither consistently predicting nor being predictable by them. A remarkably strong finding about the real wage is that, like output, its persistence significantly increased between the prewar and postwar periods.

The results of the forecast error decomposition exercise are given in Table 12. To save space, we report results for three industries only: iron and steel (a durable good industry), paper and pulp (nondurables), and leather tanning and finishing (semidurables). Results for the manufacturing aggregates are also reported. The prewar and postwar forecast error decompositions are placed side by side in the table, for easier comparison. Also note that, since the growth in productivity is just a linear combination of the growth in output, hours, and employment (all of which were included in the VARs), it is possible to report decompositions for this variable as well.

As the reader familiar with these methods is aware, the attribution of forecast error at different horizons to the (triangularized) innovations in the

Table 12
Percentages of Forecast Error k Months Ahead Produced by Each Innovation
(prewar/postwar)

Forecast Error	k	Triangularized Innovation			
		IP	HRS	EMP	WR
Iron and steel					
IP	6	89/91	2/3	3/5	6/1
	12	79/87	5/4	4/6	13/2
	24	66/85	8/5	5/8	21/2
	48	63/85	8/5	6/8	23/2
EMP	6	31/55	1/1	63/41	5/3
	12	29/52	4/6	59/39	8/4
	24	29/51	5/7	53/38	12/4
	48	29/51	6/7	51/38	15/4
HRS	6	40/43	40/52	19/4	2/1
	12	41/41	34/50	19/7	7/2
	24	40/41	31/49	17/8	12/2
	48	39/41	31/49	17/8	13/2
WR	6	3/4	3/8	6/1	88/86
	12	6/6	5/9	7/4	82/82
	24	8/6	6/9	8/4	78/81
	48	8/6	7/9	8/4	77/81
PROD	6	57/76	29/10	3/12	11/2
	12	49/74	30/10	5/13	16/2
	24	40/73	30/11	7/14	24/3
	48	39/73	30/11	7/14	24/3
Paper and pulp					
IP	6	83/92	3/2	10/5	4/0
	12	75/83	6/3	11/7	8/7
	24	71/80	8/3	12/7	10/9
	48	71/80	8/3	12/7	10/9
EMP	6	21/31	1/5	72/62	6/2
	12	19/30	5/6	68/57	8/7
	24	19/30	5/6	65/55	11/10
	48	19/30	5/6	65/54	11/10
HRS	6	30/11	61/86	3/2	6/2
	12	32/14	56/80	4/3	8/3
	24	32/14	54/79	4/4	10/4
	48	32/14	54/79	4/4	10/4
WR	6	9/1	10/2	2/2	80/96
	12	13/2	10/3	8/3	69/93

Table 12 (*cont.*)

Forecast Error	k	Triangularized Innovation			
		IP	HRS	EMP	WR
	24	13/3	10/4	10/3	67/91
	48	13/3	10/4	10/3	66/91
PROD	6	50/64	26/18	19/17	5/1
	12	45/60	27/16	20/18	8/6
	24	43/58	26/17	19/18	12/8
	48	43/58	26/17	19/18	12/8

Leather tanning and finishing

Forecast Error	k	IP	HRS	EMP	WR
IP	6	84/90	5/3	8/5	3/2
	12	80/87	8/5	7/5	4/3
	24	78/85	10/7	8/5	5/4
	48	78/85	10/7	8/5	5/4
EMP	6	21/8	8/9	69/82	2/2
	12	23/8	9/10	65/78	4/4
	24	29/8	9/10	58/78	4/4
	48	29/8	10/10	56/78	5/4
HRS	6	19/3	69/89	7/3	6/5
	12	21/5	65/84	8/6	6/6
	24	23/5	61/82	9/6	7/7
	48	24/5	60/81	9/6	7/7
WR	6	8/3	12/1	7/3	72/92
	12	14/4	14/3	8/5	64/88
	24	16/5	16/3	9/5	59/87
	48	16/5	16/3	9/5	58/87
PROD	6	24/58	36/14	37/26	3/1
	12	33/55	34/17	30/25	4/3
	24	34/54	34/17	28/25	4/4
	48	35/53	34/17	28/25	4/4

All manufacturing firms

Forecast Error	k	IP	HRS	EMP	WR
IP	6	94/93	1/2	3/4	2/1
	12	77/86	8/4	8/7	7/3
	24	71/82	12/6	10/9	7/3
	48	70/80	12/6	11/10	7/4
EMP	6	64/59	1/2	33/39	2/0
	12	57/57	9/3	31/39	3/2
	24	54/57	11/4	30/38	5/2
	48	53/56	11/4	31/38	5/2

Table 12 (*cont.*)

Forecast Error	k	Triangularized Innovation			
		IP	HRS	EMP	WR
HRS	6	51/22	38/74	9/4	1/1
	12	47/21	38/71	12/5	2/3
	24	46/22	37/68	14/6	4/4
	48	46/22	37/68	14/6	4/4
WR	6	7/2	5/3	11/1	77/94
	12	7/3	9/3	14/2	70/92
	24	13/14	9/3	15/2	62/91
	48	14/4	9/3	16/2	61/91
PROD	6	22/18	41/47	36/34	2/1
	12	22/18	39/44	34/35	5/3
	24	20/19	39/42	35/36	5/3
	48	21/19	39/42	35/36	5/3

regressors is not invariant to the ordering of the variables. The ordering used here (and for the construction of the impulse/response diagrams below) is as follows: (log differences of) output, hours, employment, real wages. Given that the data are monthly and that forecast horizons up to forty-eight months are studied, the choice of ordering is not likely to be crucial to the results.

The pattern of relationships suggested by table 12 is, perhaps not surprisingly, very similar to that revealed by the *F*-tests reported in table 11. Note, for example, that the relatively exogenous output variable (*IP*) is shown in table 12 to be largely "self-caused," even at the four-year forecast horizon. (This tendency seems to be even greater in the postwar period than in the prewar.) Hours and employment are fairly sensitive to output innovations except, for some reason, in the postwar leather industry. The "persistence" of both hours and employment is apparent; this persistence increases markedly for hours in the postwar era. The productivity variable is largely driven by innovations in output, especially in the postwar period, although productivity's other components (employment and hours) also play a role.

Again, a most striking finding is the relationship (or lack of a relationship) between real wages and the other variables. Innovations in the real wage appear to have virtually no predictive power for output, employment, and weekly hours; and in the other direction, no variable except the real wage itself is of much use in forecasting the real wage. This essential independence of the real wage and the other variables is more pronounced in the postwar period.

The final exercise in the time domain was the use of the estimated VARs to generate impulse/response (IR) diagrams. These diagrams show the movement over time of each variable in the VAR in response to a (triangularized) innovation to one of the regressors. (The response of productivity to innovations in the other variables was also analyzed.) The ordering of the variables was the same as in the forecast error decompositions above. Since the data are in log differences, we printed out cumulative response diagrams; this allowed us to interpret the patterns in terms of log levels. These diagrams were useful for gaining a qualitative appreciation of "typical" short-run patterns in the data.

The number of industries, variables, and sample periods meant that there were potentially hundreds of IR diagrams to study. We chose to look carefully only at the three representative industries (iron and steel, paper, leather); we also looked closely at construction. The reader will be burdened with only a few sample IR diagrams (see figs. 1 and 2). These show the forty-eight month response pattern of (the log levels of) output, hours, employment, real wages, and productivity to a one standard deviation innovation in output growth in the iron and steel industry. Figure 1 a–d covers the prewar period; figure 2 a–d covers the postwar period. The path of output is included in each diagram, for reference.

From our examination of all the IR diagrams, we drew the following conclusions:

1. Generally, the IRs reinforce the characterization of the cycle obtained in the frequency domain. For example, the conclusion of section 5 that productivity is highly coherent with output and that it tends to lead the cycle by a few months emerges distinctly from the IR diagrams; this is true no matter which disturbance term provides the initial shock. Similarly, the high coherence and the lead/lag patterns for hours and employment found by frequency domain techniques recur almost exactly in the IRs. Figure 1a, b, d and 2a, b, d are here perfectly representative.

2. As the frequency domain analysis was less clear about the cyclical characteristics of the real wage, so it is the case in the time domain. The pictures show a real wage behavior that is not very stable across industries and that is also sensitive to the source of the initial shock, especially in the prewar sample. However, as in section 4, there still appear to be noticeable differences between prewar and postwar wage movements. (See figs. 1c and 2c.) During the postwar period, in the cases when there is a visible relationship between output and wages, the IRs show the real wage to be a roughly coincident, procyclical variable. In the prewar data, the real wage is usually "half out of phase," either lagging (the typical response to output shocks; see fig. 1c) or leading (when there is an employment shock). There is also an interesting contrast between the prewar and postwar periods with regard to the effect of a wage shock on the rest of the system: a prewar wage shock

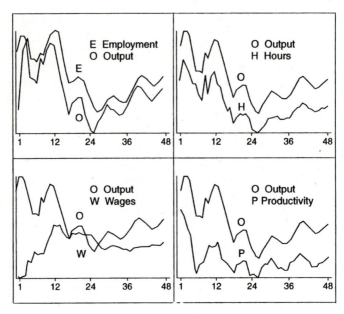

Figure 1. Response of Log Levels to Innovation in Output Growth: Prewar, Iron and Steel

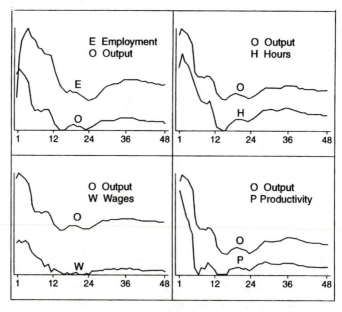

Figure 2. Response of Log Levels to Innovation in Output Growth: Postwar, Iron and Steel

tends to result in declining output and employment, whereas a wage shock in the postwar sample typically has just the opposite effect.

3. Finally, the diagrams show a postwar decline in cyclical variability (given a "typical" shock), which is consistent with several findings already discussed. Output and real wages in particular (reflecting their increased "persistence"?) are much less prone to gyrations in the postwar sample.

7. Four Major Recessions

The analysis so far has been "democratic" in its use of the data, allowing every sample observation equal weight in the calculations. This is consistent with the view that business cycles are realizations of stationary stochastic processes. An alternative view is that serious recessions or depressions are "special" occurrences, governed by different laws of probability than the "normal" parts of the sample. In the spirit of this alternative view, this section looks briefly at the behavior of labor market variables during four major downturns—two prewar and two postwar.

The four downturns studied are 1929:3 to 1933:1, 1937:2 to 1938:2, 1973:4 to 1975:1, and 1981:3 to 1982:4. Note that, except for the first, the recessions are of comparable length. (The peak and trough quarters are from the official NBER chronology.) For each of the four downturns, table 13 gives (for each of the seven labor market variables studied) the ratio of the average value of the *level* of the variable in the trough quarter to its average value in the preceding peak quarter. (The data are detrended and deseasonalized.) The purpose of this is to get a rough measure of the behavior of these variables in individual major recessions. (Alternatives would have been to construct multistage Burns/Mitchell "reference cycles" or to look at all quarters of the downturns. We experimented with both of these but did not find them much more informative.)

A preliminary point that should be made is that the designated peaks and troughs are based on aggregate economic variation, which may not coincide exactly with the industry-level cycles. Nevertheless, there is obviously a strong correlation between aggregate and industry output: in table 13 the trough-to-peak ratio for (detrended) production exceeds one only four times in thirty-eight cases.

The trough-to-peak ratios for most of the variables displayed in table 13 do not seem too far out of line with our findings of previous sections. Employment and hours display their strong procyclicality throughout. As in section 4, we see again here that postwar employers seemed to rely more on layoffs than on short workweeks as the means of reducing labor input in the trough, whereas prewar employers relied relatively more heavily on part-time work. Real wages show little systematic peak-to-trough change, which is indicative of the low coherence of real wages and output. Product wages are more

Table 13
Trough-to-Peak Ratios of Seven Variables for Four Selected Recessions

Industry	Cycle	IP	EMP	HRS	PROD	WR	WP	EARN
STEEL	I	.17	.50	.56	.62	.91	.84	.50
	II	.36	.72	.65	.77	.95	.92	.62
	III	.87	.96	.95	.95	1.00	.81	.95
	IV	.57	.68	.96	.87	.99	1.05	.94
AUTOS	I	.18	.40	.76	.58	.99	.88	.75
	II	.36	.49	.85	.86	1.02	.90	.87
	III	.60	.74	.93	.88	.95	.92	.88
	IV	.96	.87	1.01	1.10	.97	.97	.97
MEAT	I	.91	.77	.95	1.25	.95	1.50	.90
	II	1.07	.93	1.03	1.12	.99	1.12	1.02
	III	.97	.98	.99	1.00	1.01	1.17	1.00
	IV	.90	.96	1.00	.94	.94	.94	.94
PAPER	I	.59	.74	.79	1.01	.99	.87	.79
	II	.71	.87	.86	.95	1.06	1.13	.91
	III	.74	.88	.95	.89	.96	.82	.91
	IV	.98	.95	.99	1.05	1.02	1.02	1.01
SHOES	I	.79	.89	.92	.96	.99	.95	.91
	II	.82	.93	.73	1.20	1.00	1.02	.73
	III	.81	.87	.91	1.03	.95	.98	.86
	IV	.87	.91	.98	.97	1.00	1.01	.98
WOOL	I	.62	.73	.88	.95	.94	1.23	.83
	II	.44	.68	.80	.80	1.01	1.21	.81
	III	.47	.57	.71	1.16	.91	1.23	.65
	IV	.77	.77	.82	1.22	.99	NA	.82
LEATH	I	.76	.80	.91	1.04	.98	1.43	.89
	II	.71	.79	.85	1.06	1.03	1.23	.87
	III	1.03	.99	.99	1.06	.95	1.24	.94
	IV	.88	.90	1.01	.97	1.02	1.07	1.03
LUMBR	I	.32	.42	.74	1.04	.92	1.13	.68
	II	.67	.86	.87	.89	1.02	1.22	.88
	III	.75	.78	.94	1.01	.96	1.21	.91
	IV	1.10	.99	1.02	1.09	1.01	1.06	1.02
ALL MFG	I	.50	.72	.79	.89	.96	1.01	.76
	II	.62	.73	.81	1.05	.97	1.04	.78
	III	.81	.88	.96	.96	.97	.88	.93
	IV	.90	.90	.99	1.01	.99	1.02	.98
COAL	III	1.05	1.20	1.01	.87	.96	.68	.97
	IV	.83	.84	.91	1.09	1.02	1.02	.93

Table 13 (*cont.*)

Industry	Cycle	IP	EMP	HRS	PROD	WR	WP	EARN
ELECT	III	.96	.98	.97	1.00	.96	.80	.94
	IV	.93	1.00	1.01	.93	1.02	1.00	1.02
CONST	III	.78	.87	.98	.92	.94	.89	.92
	IV	.99	.93	.98	1.09	1.00	1.04	.98

Note: The variables from which the ratios are formed are detrended, deseasonalized, quarterly averages of levels (not growth rates). Peak and trough quarters are from the official NBER chronology. I: 1933:1/1929:3. II: 1938:2/1937:2. III: 1975:1/1973:4. IV: 1982:4/1981:3.

variable than real wages; they also show some tendency to countercyclicality. Weekly real earnings, as would be predicted, are clearly procyclical.

A variable that is somewhat puzzling is productivity. The standard finding that productivity is procyclical implies that its trough-to-peak ratio should be less than one. This ratio is actually below one in only about half of the thirty-four cases in which output declines between peak and trough. Productivity is most procyclical in the heavy durable goods industries (iron and steel, automobiles); in the other industries productivity is more likely to rise than fall, peak to trough.

A partial explanation of these results may follow from our earlier finding that productivity, though essentially procyclical, may lead the cycle by a number of months. Thus productivity at the output peak has already fallen from its highest level, while at the output trough it has already begun to recover. (A similar observation is made by Gordon 1980.) The recovery of productivity in the trough may also be particularly strong in very deep recession, in which financial pressure on firms increases the costs of hoarding labor or permitting inefficient production. These considerations serve at least to reduce this new productivity puzzle, though they probably do not eliminate it.

Putting aside the productivity question, table 13 does suggest that there are qualitative similarities between major recessions and less dramatic economic fluctuations. This should be encouraging to forecasters and policymakers, whose tasks would be impossible if every severe fluctuation were essentially a unique event.

8. Conclusion

This exercise in "measurement without theory" has supported some existing perceptions about the cyclical behavior of labor markets and has uncovered a few additional facts. To summarize the most important findings:

1. Procyclical labor productivity (SRIRL) appears to be present in every industry, in both the prewar and postwar periods. (This paper is the first to document SRIRL for the pre-1932 period, as far as we know.) However, in confirming this standard empirical result, we have found two qualifications. First, productivity is a leading, rather than coincident, variable. Second, SRIRL may be less pronounced in major recessions.

2. Weekly hours and employment are strongly procyclical. Hours lead output, whereas employment lags. Our evidence that employment is lagging rather than coincident is somewhat novel; otherwise these observations replicate previous results.

3. A new findings is that there has been an increased reliance in the postwar period on layoffs, rather than short workweeks, as a means of reducing labor input.

4. The relationship of the real wage to other variables over the business cycle is weak, and it has been weaker in the postwar period. On the question whether any cyclical sensitivity of the real wage exists at all, the results from the frequency domain analysis are much more affirmative than those for the time domain. The difference between the two approaches probably arises because the frequency domain analysis blocks out some high-frequency interference that the time domain analysis does not; this permits the frequency domain approach to recover a relationship at business cycle frequencies that is less apparent in the time domain. The noisiness of the wage/employment relationship in the time domain may explain the inability of Geary and Kennan (1982) to reject the hypothesis that these two series are independent.

5. To the extent that the real wage is related to the cycle, there seems to be a definite difference between its prewar and its postwar behavior. The real wage was procyclical (essentially coincident) in the postwar period but "half out of phase" (usually lagging) in the prewar. This difference has not been noticed before for real wages, although Creamer (1950) found that nominal wages lagged the cycle in the early prewar period.

6. The relationship of product wages to the cycle is, if anything, weaker and more erratic than that of real wages. Real weekly earnings are strongly procyclical in both major samples.

7. Cyclical variation is a relatively small part of the total variation of the labor market variables. (A similar finding is in Bernanke 1983.) The postwar data exhibit more stability (i.e., less total variance and less business cycle variance). They also are more serially persistent than the data from the earlier period, which may be interpreted either as being consistent with Sachs' (1980) finding of greater rigidity or as simply reflecting a more stable economy.

We hope that this and similar analyses will lead to a better understanding of the cyclical behavior of labor markets. However, we emphasize once again that this research is intended to be a complement to, not a substitute for, structural modeling of these phenomena.

Appendix

Sources

The sources of the *prewar* industry data used in this study are as follows:

1. Earnings, hours, and employment data are from Beney (1936) and Sayre (1940). These data are the result of an extensive monthly survey conducted by the National Industrial Conference Board (NICB) from 1920 until 1947.

   All the industries in the sample paid at least part of their work force by piece rates (see *Monthly Labor Review* 41 [September 1935]:697–700). No correction was made for this.
2. Industrial production data are from the Federal Reserve Board. See "New Federal Reserve Index of Industrial Production," *Federal Reserve Bulletin* 26 (August 1940):753–69, 825–74.
3. Wholesale price indexes are from the Bureau of Labor Statistics (BLS). See the following publications of the United States Department of Labor: *Handbook of Labor Statistics* (1931 ed., bulletin 541; 1936 ed., bulletin 616; 1941 ed., bulletin 694) and *Wholesale Prices 1913 to 1927* (Washington, D.C.: Government Printing Office, 1929, bulletin 473). For the automobile industry we merged two BLS series of motor vehicle prices. Neither series covered 1935; the price series on all metal products was used to interpolate the automobiles price series for that year.
4. The consumer price series is from Sayre (1948).

All basic data were seasonally unadjusted. The span of the prewar sample is January 1923 to December 1939. Although some of the data exist before 1923, there are two major problems with extending the sample further back: some of the industrial production data are missing, and there is a six-month gap in the NICB survey in 1923. The December 1939 stop date was chosen to avoid considering the many special features of the wartime economy.

The sources of the *postwar* industry data are as follows:

1. Earnings, hours, and employment data are from *Employment and Earnings, United States* (Bureau of Labor Statistics).
2. Industrial production indexes for industries 1–10 are from the Federal Reserve Board (see Board of Governors, Federal Reserve Board, *Industrial Production, 1976*. Updates are from the *Federal Reserve Bulletin*, and some unpublished series were obtained directly from the board.)

The output index for construction was obtained by dividing the value of new construction (as reported by the *Survey of Current Business* [SCB]) by the Department of Commerce construction cost index (also available in the SCB).

3. Wholesale prices are again from the Bureau of Labor Statistics. See *Wholesale Prices and Price Indexes, 1963* (BLS bulletin 1513), *Producer Price Indexes*, and the *Monthly Labor Review*.

4. The consumer price series used to calculate real wages is the Department of Labor's consumer price index (all items, wage earners and clerical workers, revised).

Again, the basic data are seasonally unadjusted. The span of the postwar sample is 1954–82, except for the wool textile industry, where the data begin in January 1958. Adequate data on output prices (and therefore on product wages) are missing for wool textiles after 1975 and for electric services before 1958.

The *total manufacturing* series were as follows:

1. For the prewar period, output was measured by the industrial production index for manufacturing. Employment, hours, and earnings data come from the National Industrial Conference Board, as reported in Beney (1936) and Sayre (1940). The NICB series are based on twenty-five major manufacturing industries; the coverage is similar but not identical to that of the industrial production index. The manufacturing output price, used only in the construction of the product wage variable, is the BLS wholesale price index for nonagricultural, nonfuel goods. Again the coverage is similar but not identical to that of the IP index.

2. For the postwar period, again the IP index for manufacturing is used to measure output. Employment, hours, and earnings data are for manufacturing production workers; the output price is the wholesale price index for total manufacturers. Those data are from "Business Statistics and the *Survey of Current Business* and, as far as we can tell, are mutually consistent.

Stationarity

The log-differenced data series appeared in general to be stationary. We arrived at this conclusion by studying the autocorrelations and partial autocorrelations of the log-differenced data and by testing for the presence of trend shifts and higher-order trend terms in the log levels. Rejections of stationarity were sufficiently infrequent and weak that, for the sake of uniform treatment of the data, we decided to ignore them.

Reduction of High-Frequency Noise

The spectra of most of the series exhibited considerable power in the higher frequencies; high-frequency noise (primarily seasonality) may interfere with the analysis of the data at business cycle frequencies. To reduce this noise, we regressed each log-differenced series against constant, seasonal dummies and (where applicable) dummy variables for strike periods. (There was no pooling of regressions across industries or between the two major sample periods. There also appeared to be no need to allow for shifts of the regression coefficients within subsamples.) The residuals from these regressions, "cleaned" of much of the very high- and low-frequency noise of the original series, were treated as the basic data in the frequency and time domain analyses.

Details of Frequency Domain Calculations

The entries of tables 7 through 10 were constructed by simple averaging of the finite Fourier transforms, evaluated at evenly spaced intervals on $(0, \pi)$, for each data series. Since the prewar and postwar sample sizes differed, the frequencies corresponding to the "business cycle" varied as well; thus each calculation involved averages of about 7% (that is, $1/12$–$1/96$) of the number of periodogram ordinates calculated for each variable.

Table 6 gives square roots of the cumulated periodogram ordinates (between twelve and ninety-six months) for each variable. These calculations (and those in the remaining tables) will not be affected by the seasonal or strike adjustments made for the log-differenced data.

Standard errors for the sample coherence $\hat{\rho}$ and phase $\hat{\theta}$ between each pair of variables were computed using the following formulas, adapted from Hannan (1970, chap. 7):

$$[SE(\hat{\rho})]^2 = v^{-1/2}(1 - \hat{\rho}^2),$$

and

$$[SE(\hat{\theta})]^2 = v^{-1/2}\left(\frac{1 - \hat{\rho}^2}{\hat{\rho}^2}\right)^{1/2},$$

where v is twice the number of periodogram ordinates in the 12–96 month range. Since these expressions are derived from the asymptotic behavior of finite Fourier transforms, the resulting confidence intervals are only approximate and will be poorly behaved for $\hat{\rho}$ near zero or one; still, the standard errors are useful guides to the precision of the estimates.

The estimated phase leads of tables 8 through 10 were expressed in months by dividing the estimated phase angle $\hat{\theta}$ (and its standard error) by the frequency corresponding to the period in the center off the bandwidth considered. That is, the phase leads calculated for the 12–96, 2–12, 12–24, and 24–96 month bandwidths correspond to cycles with period lengths 54, 7, 18, and 60 months, respectively. These period lengths are uniformly higher than the period lengths corresponding to the average frequency in the bandwidth (which is, for example, about $2/(1/12 + 1/96) = 21.33$ months for the 12–96 month bandwidth). Since the coherences and phase angles are implicitly assumed to be constant within each frequency band, the phase lead for any frequency in the interval can be obtained by rescaling; that is, to obtain a phase lead for a "typical" 20 month cycle, the reported phase lead (and its standard error) for the 12–24 month bandwidth can simply be multiplied by 20/18. The tests of equality of phase angles in table 10.9 do not use the "scaled" phase leads above; rather, t-statistics for the difference in phase angles are constructed directly from the standard error formulas reported above (and use the large-sample independence of the phase estimates for the prewar and postwar periods).

All calculations were carried out using the RATS statistical package (see Doan and Litterman 1981). Other, more theoretical references to frequency domain methods are the texts by Hannan (1970) and Anderson (1971).

References

Altonji, Joseph, and Orley Ashenfelter. 1980. Wage movements and the labour market equilibrium hypothesis. *Economica* 47 (August):217–45.

Anderson, T. W. 1971. *The statistical analysis of time series.* New York: John Wiley.

Ashenfelter, Orley, and David Card. 1982. Time series representations of economic variables and alternative models of the labour market. *Review of Economic Studies* 49 (special issue):261–82.

Baily, Martin Neil. 1977. On the theory of layoffs and unemployment. *Econometrica* 45 (July):1043–63.

Ball, R. J., and E. B. A. St. Cyr. 1966. Short-term employment functions in British manufacturing industry. *Review of Economic Studies* 33 (July):179–207.

Barro, Robert J., and Herschel I. Grossman. 1971. A general disequilibrium model of income and employment. *American Economic Review* 61 (March):82–93.

Beney, M. Ada. 1936. *Wages, hours, and employment in the United States, 1914–1936.* New York: National Industrial Conference Board.

Bernanke, Ben S. 1983. On the sources of labor productivity variation in U.S. manufacturing, 1947–1980. *Review of Economics and Statistics* 65 (May):214–24.

Bernstein, Irving. 1960. *The lean years: A history of the American worker, 1920–1933.* Boston: Houghton-Mifflin.

Bodkin, Ronald G. 1969. Real wages and cyclical variations in employment: A re-examination of the evidence. *Canadian Journal of Economics* 2 (August):353–74.

Brechling, F. P. R. 1965. The relationship between output and employment in British manufacturing industries. *Review of Economic Studies* 32 (July):187–216.

Brechling, F. P. R., and P. O. O'Brien. 1967. Short-run employment functions in manufacturing industries: An international comparison. *Review of Economic Studies* 99 (August):277–87.

Bry, Gerhard. 1959. The average workweek as an economic indicator. Occasional Paper 69, National Bureau of Economic Research.

Burns, Arthur F., and Wesley C. Mitchell. 1946. *Measuring business cycles*. New York: National Bureau of Economic Research.

Chirinko, Robert. 1980. The real wage over the business cycle. *Review of Economics and Statistics* 62 (August):459–61.

Clark, Kim B., and Richard B. Freeman. 1980. How elastic is the demand for labor? *Review of Economics and Statistics* 62 (November):509–20.

Coen, Robert M., and Bert G. Hickman. 1970. Constrained joint estimation of factor demand and production functions. *Review of Economics and Statistics* 52 (August):287–300.

Creamer, Daniel. 1950. Behavior of wage rates during business cycles. Occasional Paper 34, National Bureau of Economic Research.

Doan, T. A., and R. B. Litterman. 1981. *RATS user's manual, version 4.1*. Minneapolis: VAR Econometrics.

Dunlop, John T. 1938. The movement of real and money wage rates. *Economic Journal* 48 (September):413–34.

Eckstein, Otto, and Thomas A. Wilson. 1964. Short-run productivity behavior in U.S. manufacturing. *Review of Economics and Statistics* 46 (February):41–54.

Fair, Ray C. 1969. *The short-run demand for workers and hours*. Amsterdam: North-Holland.

Geary, Patrick T., and John Kennan. 1982. The employment–real wage relationship: An international study. *Journal of Political Economy* 90 (August):854–71.

Gordon, Robert J. 1980. The "end-of-expansion" phenomenon in short-run productivity behavior. Working Paper 427, National Bureau of Economic Research.

Granger, C. W. J., and M. Hatanaka. 1964. *Spectral analysis of economic time series*. Princeton: Princeton University Press.

Hall, Robert E. 1980. Employment fluctuations and wage rigidity. *Brookings Papers on Economic Activity* 1:91–124.

Hannan, E. J. 1970. *Multiple time series*. New York: John Wiley.

Hause, John C. 1971. Spectral analysis and the detection of lead-lag relations. *American Economic Review* 61 (March):213–17.

Hultgren, Thor. 1960. Changes in labor cost during cycles inproduction and business. Occasional Paper 74, National Bureau of Economic Research.

———. 1965. *Costs, prices, and profits: Their cyclical relations*. New York: National Bureau of Economic Research.

Ireland, J. J., and D. J. Smyth. 1967. Short-term employment functions in Australian manufacturing. *Review of Economics and Statistics* 49 (November):537–44.

Jerome, Harry. 1934. *Mechanization in industry*. New York: National Bureau of Economic Research.

Keynes, John Maynard. 1936. *The general theory of employment, interest, and money*. London: Macmillan.

———. 1939. Relative movements of real wages and output. *Economic Journal* 49 (March):34–51.

Kuh, Edwin. 1960. Profits, profit markups, and productivity. Joint Economic Committee Paper 15. Washington, D.C.: Government Printing Office.

———. 1965. Cyclical and secular labor productivity in United States manufacturing. *Review of Economics and Statistics* 97 (February):1–12.

Lucas, Robert E., Jr. 1970. Capacity, overtime, and empirical production functions. *American Economic Review* 60 (May):23–27.

Masters, Stanley H. 1967. The behavior of output per man during recessions: An empirical study of underemployment. *Southern Economic Journal* 33 (January):388–94.

Medoff, James L. 1979. Layoffs and alternatives under trade unions in U.S. manufacturing. *American Economic Review* 69 (June):380–95.

Mitchell, Wesley C. 1951. *What happens during business cycles.* Cambridge, Mass.: Riverside Press.

Moore, Geoffrey H. 1955. Business cycles and the labor market. *Monthly Labor Review* 78 (March):288–92.

Morrison, Catherine J., and Ernst R. Berndt. 1981. Short-run labor productivity in a dynamic model. *Journal of Econometrics* 16 (August):339–65.

Nadiri, M. Ishaq, and Sherwin Rosen. 1973. *A disequilibrium model of demand for factors of production.* New York: Columbia University Press.

Neftci, Salih N. 1978. A time-series analysis of the real wages–employment relationship. *Journal of Political Economy* 86 (April):281–91.

———. 1979. Lead-lag relations, exogeneity, and prediction of economic time series. *Econometrica* 47 (January):101–13.

Oi, Walter Y. 1962. Labor as a quasi-fixed factor. *Journal of Political Economy* 70 (December):538–55.

Okun, Arthur M. 1962. Potential GNP: Its measurement and significance. In *Proceedings of the Business and Economics Section*, 98–104. Washington, D.C.: American Statistical Association.

Otani, Ichiro. 1978. Real wages and business cycles revisited. *Review of Economics and Statistics* 60 (May):301–4.

Pindyck, Robert S., and Julio J. Rotemberg. 1982. Dynamic factor demands and the effects of energy price shocks. Research Paper, Massachusetts Institute of Technology.

Ruggles, Richard. 1940. The relative movements of real and money wage rates. *Quarterly Journal of Economics* 55 (November):130–49.

Sachs, Jeffrey. 1979. Wages, profits, and macroeconomic adjustment: A comparative study. *Brookings Papers on Economic Activity* 2 (1979):269–319.

———. 1980. The changing cyclical behavior of wages and prices: 1890–1976. *American Economic Review* 70 (March):78–90.

Sargent, Thomas J. 1978. Estimation of dynamic labor demand schedules under rational expectations. *Journal of Political Economy* 86 (December):1009–44.

———. 1979. *Macroeconomic theory.* New York: Academic Press.

Sayre, R. A. 1940. Wages, hours, and employment in the United States, 1934–1939. *Conference Board Economic Record* 2 10 (March):115–37.

———. 1948. *Consumers' prices, 1914–1948.* New York: National Industrial Conference Board.

Shiskin, Julius. 1961. Signals of recession and recovery. Occasional Paper 77, National Bureau of Economic Research.

Sims, Christopher A. 1974. Output and labor input in manufacturing. *Brookings Papers on Economic Activity* 3 (1974):695–728.

———. 1980. Macroeconomics and reality. *Econometrica* 48 (January):1–48.

Slichter, Sumner H., James J. Healy, and E. Robert Livernash. 1960. *The impact of collective bargaining on management.* Washington, D.C.: Brookings Institution.

Solow, Robert M. 1968. Distribution in the long and short run. *Proceedings of a conference held by the International Economics Association at Palermo*, ed. Jean Marchal and Bernard Ducrois. New York: St. Martin's Press.

———. 1973. Some evidence on the short-run productivity puzzle. *Development and planning: Essays in honour of Paul Rosenstein-Rodan*, ed. Jagdish Bhagwati and Richard Eckaus. London: Allen and Unwin.

Solow, Robert M., and Joseph E. Stiglitz. 1968. Output, employment, and wages in the short run. *Quarterly Journal of Economics* 82 (November):537–60.

Stock, James H. 1983. Economic models subject to time deformation. Ph.D. diss., University of California at Berkeley.

Stockman, Alan C. 1983. Aggregation bias and the cyclical behavior of real wages. Research Paper, University of Rochester.

Tarshis, Lorie. 1939. Changes in real and money wages. *Economic Journal* 49 (March):150–54.

Tatom, John A. 1980. The "problem" of procyclical real wages and productivity. *Journal of Political Economy* 88 (April):385–94.

Woytinsky, W. S. 1942. *Three aspects of labor dynamics.* Washington, D.C.: Committee on Social Security–Social Science Research Council.

Zarnowitz, Victor, and Charlotte Boschan. 1975. Cyclical indicators: An evaluation and new leading indexes. *Business Conditions Digest* 15 (May):v–xix.

Zeisel, Joseph S. 1958. The workweek in American industry, 1850–1956. *Monthly Labor Review* 81 (January):23–29.

Six

Employment, Hours, and Earnings in the Depression: An Analysis of Eight Manufacturing Industries

SEISMOLOGISTS LEARN MORE FROM one large earthquake than from a dozen small tremors. On the same principle, the Great Depression of the 1930's would appear to present an important opportunity for the study of the effects of business cycles on the labor market. In no other period for which we have data do output, labor input, and labor compensation exhibit such severe short-run variations.

Despite this apparent opportunity, modern econometric analyses of labor markets have typically made little use of pre-World War II data. There are some significant exceptions. In the class of papers that assume continuous labor market equilibrium, the best known example is by Robert Lucas and Leonard Rapping (1969). This influential piece was followed by Michael Darby (1976), who basically supported the Lucas-Rapping approach, and by Joseph Altonji and Orley Ashenfelter (1980) and Altonji (1982), who were critical of it. Among papers that allow for market disequilibrium, work by Harvey Rosen and Richard Quandt (1978) and Ashenfelter (1980) should be noted.[1] However, none of the papers cited, I think it is fair to say, is the definitive study of 1930's labor markets. They have in common at least two deficiencies in this regard.

First, all of this work has employed annual and highly aggregated data. This reflects the fact that none of the papers is focused on the 1930's per se but include prewar data only as part of a longer-period study. Since none of the papers uses data from before 1929, any conclusion drawn about the prewar period is based on at most a dozen or so observations.

Second, the papers are limited in their capacity to rationalize the movements of a number of key labor market time-series. For example, none of them addresses the radical fluctuations in the length of the workweek which occurred during the depression, a phenomenon which the present research

Reprinted with permission from *American Economic Review*, vol. 76 (March 1986), 82–109.

I thank participants in workshops at Stanford, MIT, Harvard, Chicago, Carnegie-Mellon, Rochester, Princeton, and Pennsylvania for comments on the first draft of this paper. Numerous colleagues were also helpful. The Center for Economic Policy Research and the Hoover Institution provided support.

[1] Martin N. Baily (1983) gives an interesting discussion of labor markets in the 1930's, but does not estimate a structural econometric model.

will argue is a quite important part of the overall story. As is documented in my forthcoming paper with James Powell and my working paper (1985), variations in the workweek contributed nearly as much as did changes in employment to the overall variance in labor input during this period (in the manufacturing industries studied)—in contrast to the postwar period, during which employment change was the much more important factor. Workweek reductions were also surprisingly persistent: in the iron and steel industry, hours of work (which were about fifty-five hours per week during the late 1920's) did not average as much as forty hours weekly in any year from 1932 to 1939, and for long periods were considerably less.

Perhaps more significant, and more puzzling, than the behavior of the workweek, was the behavior of the real wage. My paper with Powell showed, for the industry data set used also in this paper, that real wages were typically countercyclical during the prewar period. This countercyclicality is equally apparent if indexes of wage rates[2] are used instead of average hourly earnings to measure real wages; it seems to have held for the manufacturing sector as a whole (Alan Stockman, 1983) as well as, for individual industries. The tendency of real wages to rise despite high unemployment was especially striking during the major depression cycle (1929–37): real wages rose during the initial downturn (1930–31). They rose sharply again in 1933–34 and 1937, despite unemployment rates of 20.9 percent in 1933, 16.2 percent in 1934, and 9.2 percent in 1937 (according to Darby's correction of Stanley Lebergott's 1964 figures). In contrast, my paper with Powell found some evidence of real wage procyclicality in similar data for the postwar period.

Why real wages should rise when the demand for labor is presumably very low[3] is difficult for any existing approach, equilibrium or disequilibrium, to explain: On the equilibrium side, Lucas arid Rapping (1972) admitted in a reply to Albert Rees (1970) that their model could not explain the relation of wages and employment for the period from 1933 until the war; they did claim success for 1929–33. However, as Rees (1972) noted in his rejoinder, even this more restricted claim requires that the negative effects of falling nominal wages and prices on labor supply in 1929–33 strongly dominate the positive effect of the steadily rising real wage.

How could deflation have reduced labor supply even though real wages were rising? The original Lucas-Rapping explanation appears to be that falling nominal wages and prices depressed current labor supply by raising

---

[2] The data on wage rates, available for the first six industries and through August 1931 only, are from Daniel Creamer (1950).

[3] Throughout I will maintain the premise (with which I believe most economists would agree) that prewar business cycles were characterized primarily by fluctuations in the aggregate volume of labor demanded, rather than in the volume of labor supplied. It is, of course, not difficult to explain countercyclicality in the real wage when labor supply is fluctuating.

workers' expectations of inflation (expectations are assumed to be adaptive in the log of the price level) and lowering *ex ante* real interest rates. In light of Lucas (1972), an alternative rationale for this effect of deflation is that workers mistakenly interpreted the fall in money wages as a (local?) decline in real wages. The first explanation is hard to maintain, both on quantitative grounds and also given that, *ex post*, real interest rates in 1930–33 were the highest of the century. The second explanation relies on an extremely slow diffusion of information about wages and prices. In either case, it seems unlikely that the impact of falling nominal wages and prices would be strong enough and persistent enough to explain the data.[4]

The disequilibrium, or Keynesian, explanation for the behavior of real wages in the 1930's (at least in 1930–33) is that nominal wage "stickiness" and the sharp deflation combined to create an unplanned increase in real wages; higher real wages forced firms up their labor demand curves, adding to unemployment.[5] Now it cannot be denied that money wages are more inertial than prices (in the sense that they exhibit less high-frequency variation), although the economic interpretation of this fact is in dispute. Indeed, the present paper will conclude that the inertia of nominal wages must be given some role in the explanation of real wage behavior. However, the problem with the Keynesian story as a complete explanation, in my view, is the *degree* of unexplained wage rigidity that must be accepted in order to fit this model to the facts. For example, for their 1930–73 sample, Rosen and Quandt estimated that up to four years are required to eliminate *half* of an initial discrepancy between the actual wage and its equilibrium path;[6] presumably, the same model estimated on prewar data would yield smaller if not negative speeds of real wage adjustment. Such slow rates of adjustment are incompatible with what we know of the institutions and practices prevalent in most prewar labor markets.[7]

---

[4] Darby estimates an equilibrium model that does better than the model of Lucas and Rapping in explaining the 1930's. This model is discussed and reinterpreted in Section III below.

[5] The Keynesian story does not have a very satisfactory answer to why firms prefer laying off workers to cutting the wage, although some theoretical attempts (relying, for example, on adverse-selection problems) have been made in that direction. The sticky-wage story is also not very useful for explaining 1933–39, when real wages rose despite high unemployment and *rising* prices.

[6] Rosen and Quandt's 1978 paper postulated sticky real (rather than nominal) wages. In their 1985 work, they estimated a sophisticated disequilibrium model in which sticky nominal wages are assumed; they again found very slow speeds of wage adjustment.

[7] In particular, for most sectors during the prewar period (including manufacturing, the subject of this study), barriers to rapid wage adjustment following economic shocks were much lower than they are today. Factors that gave firms a relatively free hand with respect to wages (and with respect to the employment relationship in general) included: the quiescence of the labor movement between the early 1920's and the latter New Deal; the fall in average skill levels which followed the introduction of mass production techniques; the ample supplies of unskilled and low-skilled workers; the low level of government intervention in labor relations; and the lack of a social consensus about the nature of workers' rights. See my 1985 paper for

The present paper gives a new empirical analysis of Depression-era labor markets, with particular attention to rectifying the two problems just cited. First, instead of aggregate annual data, I employ monthly data for each of eight manufacturing industries. I also extend the sample period back to 1923, which gives more than 200 time-series observations for each industry. This previously unexploited data set (described in more detail in Section II and in the Appendix) appears to be a rich source of information.

Second, to search for an improved explanation of the behavior of labor market variables over this period, in this paper I depart from the standard equilibrium and Keynesian models in favor of a different and somewhat eclectic approach. The basis of my analysis is a model in which, as in Lucas (1970), firms may vary the number of hours each employee works per period (the intensive margin) as well as the number of people employed (the extensive margin). In combination with other, more conventional elements (including slow, but not glacial, adjustment of nominal wages to price changes), this model is able to deliver a reasonably successful explanation of the behavior of workweeks, real wages, and other important variables such as employment. The basic model may also be of independent theoretical and empirical interest; see Section I, Part G.

A caveat to the above is that this paper focuses on the labor market, not on the economy on the whole; thus, the offered "explanations" of labor market variables are only partial, in that they take the paths of industry outputs as given. The partial equilibrium approach was adopted for theoretical and econometric simplicity; it also has the advantage of producing results which are not dependent on a specific explanation of prewar fluctuations in aggregate demand. (However, I note here my view that it was the monetary and financial collapse of 1930–33 that gave the depression its unusually severe character; see my 1983 paper.)

The paper is organized as follows: Section I introduces a simple model of the labor market which builds on elements of Lucas (1970). An empirical analysis which uses this model as the starting point, but also incorporates a number of additional features, is discussed in Section II. Section III considers an alternative, more dynamic specification of the supply side of the model.

I. The Supply and Demand for Workers and Hours of Work: A Model

The model which contributes the basic elements of the analysis of this paper is described in a short article by Lucas (1970). The distinctive feature of Lucas's setup is that he assumes that firms can vary not only the number of

further discussion and references. Also recommended is the excellent book by Irving Bernstein (1960).

workers (and of machines) that they employ, but also the number of hours per period in which the workers (and machines) work, that is, the "work-week." In equilibrium in this model, the manner in which changes in total labor input are divided between variations in workweeks and changes in employment depends on the nature of the production function and on worker preferences. Since, as has been noted, large fluctuations in workers' weekly hours were a prominent feature of depression labor markets, the explicit determination of workweeks in Lucas's analysis makes his model (or a related one) a natural candidate for use in the present context. As a bonus, Lucas showed that his model places no restriction on the cyclical behavior of (average) real wages; thus this model is also (at least) not inconsistent with the observed countercyclical pattern of wages. Indeed, it will be shown in the analysis below that conditions that promote cyclical sensitivity of the workweek may also increase the tendency toward real wage counter-cyclicality. Thus, there appears to be a previously unsuspected connection between the puzzling aspects of the two time-series.

In what follows I set out a simple, static model in the spirit of Lucas's paper.[8] This model, in conjunction with some additional elements (including elementary dynamics), is the basis for the estimation reported below.

A. Setting

Since my data are for individual manufacturing industries, for concreteness in what follows I will consider the supply and demand of labor for a "primary" (manufacturing) sector. Each primary sector is to be thought of as being surrounded by its own "secondary" or alternative sector, in which people work at agriculture, trade, or services, or are not formally employed. The demand for the output of primary sectors is assumed to be more cyclically sensitive than the demand for secondary-sector output. (This assumption appears to be reasonable for most manufacturing industries.) Primary sectors are also assumed to be separated on some dimension (geographical or otherwise) from other primary sectors and thus do not compete directly with each other for workers. (This last assumption seems to be realistic for the 1930's; while there was much movement of workers between manufacturing and the secondary sector, few workers moved from one manufacturing sector to another. See, for example, E. Wight Bakke, 1940, p. 242.)

To reemphasize: discussions below of the supply or demand for labor refer *only* to the primary sector. The secondary, less cyclical sector is not explicitly modeled.

---

[8] It should be made clear that Lucas is not to be implicated for the details of what follows, which differ substantially from his paper. Yakir Plessner and Shlomo Yitzhaki (1983) employ a model similar to that below.

B. *The Supply Side*

In this model I shall be concerned with the determination of both 1) the length of the workweek, and 2) the number of workers employed, not just the total number of hours worked. Thus, on the supply side, I shall have to consider both the willingness of the individual worker to increase hours of work *and* the sensitivity of the participation rate to the returns available in the primary sector. Let us first examine the supply the hours of work by an individual worker, worker *i*. I will characterize the individual's supply curve of hours indirectly, through a function describing his reservation level of earnings for each level of hours worked. (This is the analogous construct to Lucas's 1970 wage schedule, $w(s)$.) Let E_{it} be the nominal earnings received by worker *i* in period *t*, H_{it} be the number of hours worked by *i* in *t*, and θ_{it} be a set of unspecified exogenous indicators known to worker *i* in *t*. Let COL_t be the period *t* cost of living, which will be assumed for now to be public knowledge. Now define the *earnings function*

$$E_{it}(H_{it}, COL_t, \theta_{it}) \tag{1}$$

to be the minimum (nominal) earnings necessary to induce worker *i* to work H_{it} hours (in the primary sector) in period *t*, given the cost of living COL_t and indicators θ_{it}.

I have begun by introducing the earnings function to emphasize that it is a very general concept, well-defined for almost any specification of the worker's preferences and environment. However, I will here make a number of restrictive assumptions in order to derive the earnings function for a specific, particularly simple case. I assume first that the worker has a temporally separable utility function, with within-period utility

$$U_i = U_i(C_{it}, \overline{H} - H_{it}), \tag{2}$$

where C is consumption and $\overline{H} - H$, the complement of hours of work, is leisure. I assume also that the worker cannot borrow or lend, but simply consumes his earnings each period ($C_{it} = E_{it}/COL_t$). With these two assumptions I rule out some complexities that occur when workers can intertemporally substitute consumption and leisure (but see Section III below). Finally, suppose that the worker has a reservation level of utility U_{it}^* which he is able to obtain in the secondary or alternative sector. (Here, U_{it}^* is the datum affecting the worker's labor supply, i.e., $\theta_{it} = U_{it}^*$.) In this case the earnings function can be constructed period by period; it is defined by

$$U_i(E_{it}(H_{it}, COL_t, U_{it}^*)$$
$$/COL_t, \overline{H} - H_{it}) = U_{it}^* \tag{3}$$

for $H_{it} > 0$; $E_{it} = 0$, otherwise. That is, the earnings function is an indifference curve in (E, H) space. With normal curvature assumptions on the

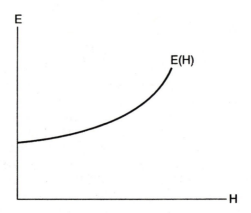

Figure 1. The Earnings Function

utility function, (3) implies that the earnings function will be increasing and convex in hours, as well as increasing in the reservation level of utility. (See Figure 1.)

An important feature of the earnings function defined in (3) is that there is a discontinuity at zero hours: no payment is required to induce zero hours, but the earnings function is positive as hours approach zero from the right. The implicit assumption underlying this feature is that a worker who works any positive amount of hours in the primary sector must leave the secondary sector completely, that is, there is no moonlighting. Although the existence of the jump at zero hours is important for obtaining countercyclical real wages, it should be emphasized that the no-moonlighting assumption is much stronger than I need. With moonlighting, the earnings function will take lower values for small H than is suggested by (3), because workers will be able to make use of the extra time; however, as long as there is any fixed cost associated with moving between jobs, or simply a cost of going to work, the discontinuity at zero in the earnings function will exist.

Consider now the second component of labor supply, the supply of individual workers (i.e., the primary sector participation rate). I model labor supply to the primary sector as increasing in the utility level offered by that sector. This can be motivated simply as follows. Assume that workers are alike in their productivity and in their utility functions, but that they differ in their secondary sector opportunities (or in other factors that affect reservation utility, such as dislike for primary-sector types of work). Specifically, let

$$U_{it}^* = \gamma_t \Omega_i, \tag{4}$$

where γ_t is a purely time-dependent scalar and Ω_i is an individual-specific constant. The distribution function of Ω_i in the population is $G(\Omega_i)$;

$G(0) = 0$ and $G(\infty) = \overline{N}$, where $\overline{N}$ is the total population of potential workers. Assume that the reservation utilities of individual workers are private information, so that workers must be treated identically.[9] Then, if the primary sector wishes to employ N workers, it must provide each worker with a utility equal to at least $\gamma_t G^{-1}(N)$. Alternatively, the supply curve of workers in period t, $N_t^s(U_t^*, \gamma_t)$, can now be defined by

$$N_t^s(U_t^*, \gamma_t) = G(U_t^*/\gamma_t). \tag{5}$$

The total cost to the primary sector of employing N workers for H hours each in period t can be written

$$NE(H, COL_t, \gamma_t G^{-1}(N)). \tag{6}$$

Per worker earnings E can now be seen to depend positively on the level of primarysector employment N and the index of alternative opportunities γ, as well as on hours of work H and the cost of living COL.[10]

C. The Demand Side

I now examine the behavior of the representative firm in the primary sector, firm j. The price of the firm's output is taken as given;[11] thus, to calculate the firm's derived demand for labor, I need only to specify the production function.

The usual specification of the production function assumes that employment and the number of hours each employee works enter multiplicatively, for example, as

$$Q_{jt} = F(L_{jt}, X_{jt}), \tag{7}$$

where Q_{jt} is the output of firm j in t, L_{jt} is total worker-hours (i.e., $L_{jt} = N_{jt}H_{jt}$, where N_{jt} is firm employment and H_{jt} is the length of the workweek), and X_{jt} is a vector of nonlabor inputs. However, as Martin Feldstein (1967) and Sherwin Rosen (1968) have noted, the assumption that employment

[9] Since workers have identical utility functions and productivity, there is no opportunity for firms to induce self-selection among workers, as in Andrew Weiss (1980).

[10] The expression for total labor cost (6) assumes that primary-sector firms pay workers just enough to make the marginal worker indifferent between the primary and secondary sector. An alternative assumption, suggested by the "efficiency wage hypothesis" (see, for example, Janet Yellen, 1984), is that firms avoid the costs of continuous monitoring of employees by paying more than the minimum required earnings (thus giving employed workers a surplus), then firing workers caught shirking in random "spot checks." This alternative assumption. which could easily be incorporated into the present framework, has the advantage of being able to explain such phenomena as the long queues at employment offices and the extreme reluctance of the employed to leave their jobs.

[11] That is, firms are assumed to be competitive in output markets. This is admittedly not such a good assumption for some of the industries studied. See the discussion of the model simulations below.

and hours worked enter multiplicatively may not be a good one. For example, lengthening the workweek by a given percentage may affect output differently than increasing the number of workers by the same percentage.[12] Since here I particularly want to focus on the distinction between hours of work and the number of workers, I follow Feldstein in specifying the production function as

$$Q_{jt} = F(N_{jt}, H_{jt}, X_{jt}). \tag{8}$$

This is more general than (7) if the assumption is maintained that (say, for technological reasons) each worker in the firm has a workweek of the same length.

The profit-maximization problem for firm j can be written

$$\max_{\{N, H, X\}} pF(N_j, H_j, X_j) - N_j E(H_j, COL, U^*) - r(X_j), \tag{9}$$

where p is the output price, $r(X_j)$ is the cost of X_j, and the time subscripts are suppressed. The reservation utility of the marginal worker, U^*, depends on sectoral employment N, not firm employment N_j, and is parametric to the firm; its determination will be discussed in a moment.

The relevant first-order conditions are

$$pF_N = E \tag{10}$$

$$pF_H = N_j E_H \tag{11}$$

where now the capitalized subscripts denote differentiation (with respect to firm-specific variables) and the notation has been abbreviated further, in the obvious way. Equation (10) says that the firm should hire extra workers up to the point that their marginal revenue product each week just equals their weekly earnings. Equation (11) says that the marginal benefit of increasing the length of the firm's workweek H_j should be set equal to the marginal cost, which is the number of workers employed times the increment to their earnings required to get them to work the extra time.

The second-order conditions, which are set out explicitly in my 1985 paper, are assumed to hold.

This treatment of the number of employees and the length of the shift as separate inputs allows for an explicit analysis of firm preferences for, say, layoffs instead of work sharing as a way of reducing labor input when demand falls. For example, by standard methods it can be shown that, under a reasonable additional assumption, the firm's level of employment and its workweek will depend positively on its output price, with the associated elasticities related to the shapes of both the production function and the

[12] Lengthening the workweek may have diminishing returns because of increased worker fatigue; increased employment does not increase fatigue but will typically dilute the capital-labor ratio. See Feldstein for further discussion.

earnings function. (See my 1985 paper, p. 13.) Thus, we may expect firms to react to depressed demand with both layoffs and work sharing, as indeed they did in the depression.[13] Similarly, it can be shown (under the same auxiliary assumption), that the firm's demand for workers and for hours per employee will decrease as reservation utility U^* rises (see my 1985 paper, pp. 13–14).

D. Sectoral Equilibrium

Determination of equilibrium employment and hours in the primary sector is now straightforward. It has been shown that the supply of employment increases with the level of utility U^* available in the primary sector, while the demand for employment can be expected to decrease with U^*. If there are n firms in the primary sector, the equilibrium level of reservation utility, call it U^{**}, satisfies

$$N_t^s(U_t^{**}, \gamma_t) = \sum_{j=1}^{n} N_{jt}^d(U_t^{**}, p_t). \tag{12}$$

This level of utility is just enough to make the marginal worker indifferent between the secondary and primary sectors; inframarginal workers obtain a surplus in equilibrium.

Given U^{**}, p, and the N_j's, we may think heuristically of firms choosing hours of work H_j according to condition (11). (Of course, strictly speaking everything is determined simultaneously.) This is represented in Figure 2, which shows H_j^* being chosen at the level where the per capita total revenue curve (pF/N_j, written as a function of H_j) is parallel to the earnings function. Since the earnings function is an indifference curve, workers do not care what level of hours the firm chooses: Different firms in the industry (if they have different production functions) may well choose different workweeks in equilibrium. Indeed, since "wages" are simply average hourly earnings, and since earnings functions are not rays through the origin (recall the discontinuity at zero), firms using different workweeks may also be paying different wages in equilibrium. This result, which would be paradoxical in the traditional model, poses no problem here; workers comparing jobs look not at the wage but at the total utility (the combination of earnings and hours of work) available.

Although workers are indifferent about which point on the earnings function is selected by the firm, Figure 2 suggests an interesting observation. Note that a ray from the origin (OA) intersecting the earnings function at

[13] This single-period rationalization of the layoff vs. work-sharing decision ignores an important dynamic element, i.e., the differential costs of adjusting work forces and shift lengths. This will be incorporated in the empirical model below.

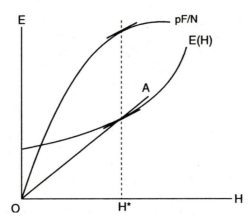

Figure 2. The Determination of H^*

H_j^* in this case cuts through the earnings function from below. This illustrates the possibility that the average wage (E/H) may exceed the marginal wage (E_H) at the equilibrium level of hours. Thus, workers would happily work more hours at the *average* wage. That they are "constrained" not to do so is not the result of any market failure or disequilibrium, but of the difference between the marginal and average wage.

E. Countercyclical Real Wages

It is straightforward to generate countercyclical real (average) wages in this setup. Since the primary sector is by assumption cyclically sensitive, declining aggregate demand will cause the relative price of its output to fall. Without loss in generality, assume that the cost of living COL is unchanged while the output price p falls.

If N_j and H_j are normal inputs, firm (and industry) usage of both will fall as demand falls. For the moment, ignore the decline in N_j and consider only the effects of falling H_j:

Falling hours of work can be represented as a movement to the left on the earnings function (compare Figure 1). The reduced demand for hours will unambiguously reduce the *marginal wage*, E_H. However, the effect of failing hours on the *average* wage (and the average real wage, since COL is fixed) is ambiguous. The necessary condition for average wages to rise as hours fall is that the elasticity of earnings with respect to hours be less than one. This would be satisfied, for example, if U^* is not close to zero and the marginal disutility of labor does not increase quickly (i.e., the earnings function is close to linear, with a positive intercept). To anticipate, the empirical results do typically confirm that this elasticity is less than one.

The intuitive story underlying countercyclical real wages is as follows. A fall in industry demand causes employers to shorten the workweek. Workers will be benefited by the shorter hours of work, but will dislike the reduction in weekly earnings arising from short workweeks. The rate at which firms can reduce weekly earnings as the workweek falls depends on workers' preferences and reservation utilities. Especially at low levels of work and earnings, when consumption is highly valued relative to leisure, it may not he possible to cut weekly earnings as sharply as hours and still meet the reservation utility constraint. Thus the wage (i.e., hourly earnings) may rise even as labor demand and workweeks fall.

The iron and steel industry, as described by Carroll Daugherty et al. (1937) provides an illustration of these points. The workweek dropped extremely sharply during the 1930's in this industry. This occurred both because firms found it efficient to cut production by running certain operations only part time, and because firms' desires to maintain their work forces relatively intact led them to adopt "staggered" or "spread-work" schedules under which many workers worked only a few days a week (pp. 163–65). The problem posed by short workweeks for most workers was the obtaining of a basic sufficiency of income. It was estimated that in 1932–33 the weekly earnings of the average steelworker (not to mention the lowest paid) were less than half of that needed to reach a standard of "minimum health and decency" for a family of four (pp. 155–57). Moreover, "in most iron and steel communities there [were] few other opportunities for supplemental employment and income" (p. 167). Firms must have recognized that their ability to keep cutting total earnings as the workweek shortened was limited, since if workers could not attain a subsistence level in the mill town they would be forced to try elsewhere. Thus real hourly earnings in iron and steel rose, or fell relative slightly, as the workweek was cut.

The above discussion has emphasized the possibility that, *ceteris paribus*, a reduction in the workweek may tend to raise the real wage. This effect of falling hours of work will be offset to the degree that lower demand for industry output also results in lower primary-sector employment N. Declining demand for employment, as well as any reduction in secondary-sector opportunities which result from the general downturn, will lower the equilibrium reservation utility level U^{**}. Lower U^{**} translates into a downward shift of the earnings function, which implies lower average wages for a given H. The net impact of the decline in the demand on average wages will depend on the relative strength of the various influences. In general, as in Lucas (1970), the cyclical behavior of the wage will be unrestricted.

An interesting implication of this analysis is that economies which rely more heavily on short workweeks (rather than employment reductions) as a way of reducing labor input are more likely to have countercyclical real wages. Using the same data as this paper, plus a matched data set for the postwar period, my paper with Powell verified that depression-era manufacturing industries did indeed exhibit both a greater relative reliance on variations in the workweek and greater countercyclicality in wages than did their postwar counterparts.

F. Skilled and Unskilled Workers

Until now I have assumed that workers are alike with respect to the production process. Empirically, it may well be the case that the changing skill mix over the cycle is of some importance. I consider this issue briefly now.

Suppose there are two types of workers, skilled and unskilled. Assuming that skilled and unskilled workers have systematically different opportunities in the secondary sector, or that they differ in number, they will have different supply functions. We can write the two supply functions in a given period, in the obvious analogy to (5), as $N_1^s(U_1^*, \gamma_1) = G_1(U_1^*/\gamma_1)$ and $N_2^s(U_2^*, \gamma_2) = G_2(U_2^*/\gamma_2)$, where the indexes 1 and 2 denote skilled and unskilled workers, respectively, and time and firm subscripts are suppressed. The corresponding earnings functions for the two groups are $E_i(H_i, U_i^*)$ where $U_i^* = \gamma_i G_i^{-1}(N_i)$ and $i = 1,2$. Normally, if $H_1 = H_2$, we expect to observe only N_i such that $E_1 > E_2$; that is, skilled workers earn more than unskilled.

On the demand side, assume that skilled and unskilled workers must be used in fixed coefficients, but that the ratio of skilled to unskilled falls as the length of the workweek (a proxy for the scale of production) expands. (See Rosen and references therein for evidence supporting this assumption.) Specifically, assume that if a firm is running the factory H hours per week, then a fraction $g_1(H)$ of its workers must be skilled and a fraction $g_2(H)$ unskilled, where $g_1 + g_2 = 1$ and $g_1(H)$ is decreasing in H. Then the firm's production function can still be written as in (8). Moreover, under the assumption that the skilled and unskilled must work the same number of hours, it is possible to write an average earnings function for the firm

$$\overline{E}(H, COL, U_1^*, U_2^*) = \sum_{i=1}^{2} g_i(H)E_i(H, COL, U_i^*), \tag{13}$$

where as before the U_i^* depend on total sectoral employment but are parametric to the firm.

The firm's optimization problem is not substantially complicated by the extension to skilled and unskilled workers (under the convenient assumptions that have been made). The firm finds optimal hours and total employment in precisely the same manner as in Part C above, except that the average earnings function $\overline{E}$ defined in (13) is used in place of the simple earnings function E. The division of employment into skilled and unskilled is then found by applying the ratios $g_1(H^*)$ and $g_2(H^*)$ to the optimal level of total firm employment.

The point of this digression is to highlight the effect of the changing skill mix on the properties of the empirically observed, average earnings function $\bar{E}$. Earnings functions defined for workers with identical utilities and productivities, for example, the E_1 and E_2, must be increasing, convex functions of hours, for $H > 0$. However, since the low-skilled and low-earnings fraction of the workforce varies procyclically, the *average* earnings function $\bar{E}$ will be flatter and have a lower elasticity than *either* E_1 or E_2 taken separately. This has two implications. First, the empirically observed earnings function may not be convex in hours.[14] Second, as was shown above, a lower elasticity of the earnings function increases the probability of observing countercyclical real wages. Thus cyclicality of the skill mix may be an additional factor contributing to the solution of the wage puzzle.

G. Implications for the Standard Approach

The model set forth in the preceding parts of this section may seem outlandish to users of the standard labor market model (in which total worker-hours supplied and demanded are simply written as functions of the real wage). I believe, however, that the present model has a stronger prior claim than does the standard approach to being the correct way to model aggregate labor markets. The problem with the standard model is that, contrary to its major premise, workers are in fact typically not able to vary their labor supply continuously with respect to a parametric real wage; instead, they must choose among "packages" of total compensation, hours of work, and other job attributes offered by employers, The economic reason for the prevailing arrangement, as suggested above, is that there are usually economies or diseconomies of "bundling" of worker-hours. Supplying one hour of work each to eight different employers is not the same to a worker as supplying eight hours to a single employer. Similarly, employers are not indifferent between receiving one hour of work from eight different workers and receiving eight hours from one worker. As long as economies or diseconomies of bundling worker-hours exist, the standard model cannot be literally correct.

Inappropriate use of the standard model can lead to misconceptions. For example, the debate between supporters and defenders of the Lucas-Rapping intertemporal substitution approach has centered on the time series properties of the real wage (see, for example, Altonji and Ashenfelter). However, if the approach of the present paper is correct, rather than the standard

---

[14] It should be noted that that convexity of the earnings function is not necessary for the second-order conditions to hold. The earnings function estimated below is log linear, i.e., earnings is concave in hours: empirically, this seemed to work best.

model, then the behavior of the real wage is largely irrelevant to that debate.

Another example concerns the estimation of labor supply elasticities. Suppose workers have identical utility functions, given by

$$U = (E_t/COL_t) - \phi H_t. \tag{14}$$

That is, the marginal utility of consumption (equal to real earnings) and the marginal disutility of hours of work are constant. The labor supply elasticities of these workers (in the conventional sense) are infinite. But what will researchers using aggregate data and assuming the standard model find? Suppose that the model of the present paper actually applies, and that reservation utilities U_{it}^* are distributed in the population as assumed in Part B above. Then it is easy to show that the aggregate real wage w_t is given by

$$w_t = (\gamma_t G^{-1}(N_t)/H_t) + \phi. \tag{15}$$

Note that $\partial w/\partial N > 0$, $\partial w/\partial H < 0$. The observed relationship between worker-hours and the wage thus depends on whether N or H is more variable. Suppose, at one extreme, that the workweek is institutionally fixed: then the econometrician regressing total worker-hours against the wage will find a positive (although not infinite) elasticity, since all variation in worker-hours is attributable to changes in employment. At the other extreme, suppose that workweeks but not employment vary: then the estimated aggregate labor supply curve will be *backward bending*. The econometrician may well be concerned about the "instability" over time of his estimates, and their lack of relation to labor supply elasticities found in micro-level panel data. The problem, however, does not lie with data or identification problems, but with the use of the wrong model.

II. Empirical Implementation

This section begins with a brief description of the data used in this study. It then specifies an empirical model and reports the results of its estimation for each of the eight manufacturing industries. The estimated model is based closely on the analysis of the previous section but contains substantive additional elements as well.

A. *Data*

The data set constructed for this research includes, for each of eight manufacturing industries, *monthly* observations on the following variables: 1) production; 2) the (wholesale) price of output; 3) employment (of wage earners); 4) hours of work per week (per wage earner); and 5) average hourly

Table 1
Industries Included in the Data Set

Industry (mnemonic)	Wage Earners[a]		Value-Added[b]	
	Thousands	% Total Mfg.	$Millions	% Total Mfg.
1. Iron and Steel (*IRON*)	419.6	5.02	1622.8	5.40
2. Automobiles (*AUTOS*)	226.1	2.70	1315.0	4.37
3. Meat Packing (*MEAT*)	122.5	1.46	460.5	1.53
4. Paper and Pulp (*PAPER*)	128.0	1.53	482.8	1.61
5. Boots and Shoes (*SHOES*)	205.6	2.46	450.9	1.50
6. Wool Textiles (*WOOL*)	179.6	2.15	414.8	1.38
7. Leather Tanning and Finishing (*LEATH*)	49.9	0.60	143.7	0.48
8. Lumber and Mill-work[c] (*LUMBER*)	509.2	6.09	1088.5	3.62
Total	1840.5	22.01	5979.0	19.89

[a]Number of wage earners, and percentage of wage earners in all manufacturing employed in the industry, 1929; from Solomon Fabricant (1942, Appendix B).

[b]Millions of dollars of value-added, and percentage of all manufacturing value-added originating in the industry, 1929; from Fabricant (1940, Appendix C).

[c]Furniture is excluded.

earnings (of wage earners). The sample period runs from January 1923 to December 1939. The data from the 1920's were included so that the depression might be studied in a broader context, including a period of "normalcy." It is unfortunate that it was impossible to extend the sample even further back (see the Appendix).

The eight manufacturing industries covered, with measures of their relative importance, are listed in Table 1. The industries are diverse with respect to type of output (producers of durables, nondurables, and semidurables are represented), market structure, stage of development, geographical location, and the skill composition and demographics of the labor force. The choice of industries was not arbitrary; this was the largest set for which complete and reasonably consistent data series could be found. In particular, the desire to have series on weekly hours restricted me to industries regularly surveyed, beginning in the early 1920's, by the National Industrial

Conference Board. (The Bureau of Labor Statistics, which surveyed many more industries, did not collect hours data before 1932.) Also, a number of candidate industries were eliminated by the requirement that the industrial production series be based on a measure of the physical volume of output (for example, tons of iron), not inputed by using measures of inputs.[15]

Additional discussion of the data is contained in the Appendix. Also see my paper with Powell and my 1985 paper.

B. Specification of the Supply Side

The supply side in this model is summarized by the earnings function faced by each primary sector (manufacturing industry), as in equation (6). Average weekly nominal earnings received by wage earners in an industry have been shown to depend on four elements:

1) the length of the industry workweek H (now assumed to be the same for all firms);
2) industry employment N;
3) factors affecting workers' reservation utilities, γ;
4) the cost of living COL.

Hours and employment for each industry and the economywide cost of living are directly observed. The most difficult problem is to identify monthly determinants of workers' reservation utilities. Two factors which I expected to be important here were the level of government relief and the strength of the labor movement. As measures of these factors I constructed two (monthly) variables, EMERGWORK and UNIONPOWER. (A list of all variables used in estimation is given in Table 2.) EMERGWORK is the log of the number of "emergency workers" employed by the federal government, including all of the major work relief programs. UNIONPOWER attempts to capture the resurgence of the labor movement after the favorable legislation of the New Deal. This variable is set equal to zero until May 1935, the month the Wagner Act was passed. (The labor movement was extremely weak between the beginning of the sample period and 1935, as has been noted.) Starting with May 1935, UNIONPOWER is set equal to the cumulative number of man-days idled by strikes (in the economy as a whole).[16] The idea here is that strikes are an investment in the capital good of union credibility, which in turn affects the level of earnings workers are

---

[15] Aggregate industrial production indices are heavily contaminated by input-based measures of output. For this reason I obtained estimates only at the industry level, not for all manufacturing.

[16] Economywide rather than industry series are used primarily because of lack of data. Arguably, however, union successes in individual industries had "spillover" effects on industries not directly involved. (But see fn. 22 below.)

Table 2
Definitions of Variables Used in Estimation

Variable	Definition
COL	Cost-of-living index
EARN	Nominal weekly earnings (per wage earner)
$\widetilde{EARN}$	Nominal weekly earnings, less intercept; see (17)
EMERGWORK	"Emergency workers" hired under the New Deal
EMP	Employment of wage-earners
EMPLF	EMP—LABORFORCE
HCOST	Marginal cost of HRS; see (24)
HRS	Weekly hours of work (per wage earner)
INTERCEPT	Intercept in earnings equation; see (17)
LABORFORCE	Aggregate labor force (Lebergott), interpolated
NRA	National Recovery Act dummy
P	Industry output price
PAY	Nominal weekly earnings deflated by product price
Q	Real production (not deseasonalized)
QSEAS	Purely seasonal component of real production
Q-QSEAS	Deseasonalized real production
t	Time
UNIONPOWER	Cumulative man-days idled by strikes; = 0, May 1935

Note: All variables except COL, EMERGWORK, LABORFORCE, NRA, t, and UNION-POWER are defined separately for each of the eight industries. Other than NRA, INTER-CEPT, t, and UNIONPOWER, variables are in logarithms.

able to demand. (There is in fact a close correlation in this period between strike activity and the major new union recognitions and contracts that were achieved.)

The basic earnings functions that I estimated was of the form

$$\widetilde{EARN}_t = \alpha_0 + \alpha_H HRS_t + \alpha_E EMPLF_t$$
$$+ \alpha_W EMERGWORK_t$$
$$+ \alpha_U UNIONPOWER_t$$
$$+ \alpha_N NRA_t + COL_t + \alpha_t t \qquad (16)$$

where

$$\widetilde{EARN}_t = \log(earnings - cost\ of\ living \times INTERCEPT) \qquad (17)$$

and where the variables are as in Table 2. Equation (16) says that the log of nominal weekly earnings (less an intercept term, to be discussed in a moment) is a positive function of the log of hours worked per week, HRS; a positive function of the log of industry employment (normalized by national labor force), EMPLF; a positive function of workers' reservation utilities, as measured by EMERGWORK and UNIONPOWER; and is related one-for-one to the log of the current cost of living COL (i.e., there is no money illusion or imperfect information about price levels). Also included in the equation are a time trend (to capture secular influences on reservation utilities, such as demographics or wealth accumulation); and a dummy for the National Recovery Act period of September 1933–May 1935 (NRA), during which legislation affecting wages and hours may have had a direct impact on earnings.

The dependent variable of (16), which is defined in (17), is not simply the log of nominal weekly earnings, but the log of nominal weekly earnings less an expression which is constant when measured in real terms. This is in order to conform to a basic element of the theory, that there is a discontinuity in the earnings function at zero; that is, workers require some minimum pay "just to come to work." I did not expect to be able to estimate a value of the constant term INTERCEPT from the data, since sample values of hours worked are never very near zero and the earnings function is likely to be nonlinear in a relatively unrestricted way. Instead, for each industry I arbitrarily set INTERCEPT equal to the real value of six hours' pay at the rate paid in June 1929; that is, the "fixed cost of coming to work" was assumed to be equal to one hour's real pay for each day in the standard workweek. The exact value chosen for INTERCEPT was not at all crucial; I tried values from zero to twelve hours' pay without affecting the qualitative nature of the results.

Equation (16) was estimated, and was found to " work" fairly well empirically, in the sense that the estimated coefficients were of the right sign and were statistically significant. However, the estimated equations also had low Durbin-Watson statistics and did not perform particularly well in simulations. After some examination of the data, I recognized that the restriction in (16) that nominal earnings must be directly proportional to the current cost of living is not a good one. If this constraint were correct, it would imply that the high-frequency variation of earnings should be similar to that of the cost of living. In fact, the usual result that nominal labor compensation variables are "smoother" than price-level variables holds in these data.

To capture this smoothing effect, I assumed that nominal earnings respond only to the "permanent" component of cost-of-living changes, in the sense of John Muth (1981). That is, nominal earnings are proportional not to COL but to COL*, where COL* is defined by

$$COL_t^* = \lambda_p COL_t + (1 - \lambda_p)COL_{t-1}^*. \tag{18}$$

Alternative interpretations of this assumption are that earnings are set each period on the basis of adaptive forecasts of the cost of living (compare Lucas and Rapping, 1969); or that costs of rapidly adjusting wage rates cause employers to attempt to smooth out the effects of cost-of-living changes (see Julio Rotemberg, 1982).

The final earnings function therefore was (16), with COL_t^* replacing COL_t. A Koyck transformation of this equation, using (18), yields an observable model. Nonlinear estimation methods were used so that estimates of the original parameters α_H, α_E, α_W, α_U, α_N, α_t, and λ_p could be obtained. These results are discussed in conjunction with the demand-side results below.

C. Specification of the Demand Side

The primary constituent of the demand side of the model is the production function F. To obtain a specific functional form for F, I assumed that employment and hours of work aggregate as a generalized CES:

$$Q_t = B(\alpha e^{g_N t}N_t^{-\rho} + (1 - \alpha)e^{g_H t}H_t^{-\rho})^{(-k/\rho)}, \qquad (19)$$

where B, α, ρ, k, g_N, and g_H, are parameters. This formulation allows for nonconstant returns to scale and factor-augmenting technical change. Explicit dependence of output on the capital stock and other nonlabor factors is suppressed because of lack of data; the hope is that these effects can be adequately represented, for the purposes of our short-run and medium-run analyses, by the exponential trend terms. (I experimented with quadratic as well as linear exponential trends in the estimation, without a significant effect on the results.) The expression (19) was chosen basically because it rationalizes simple log-linear relationships that have been shown to be empirically successful in other applications. Note however, that if the capital stock follows a time trend, then (19) is more general than some standard specifications, for example, the Cobb-Douglas form estimated by Feldstein.

With this specification, the first-order condition for employment (10) can be written as

$$n_t^* = \beta_{n0}^* + \beta_{nq}^* u q_t - \beta_{ne}^*(e_t - p_t) + \beta_{nt}^* t, \qquad (20)$$

where n^* is the log of employment; q is the log of output; $e - p$ is the log of weekly earnings divided by the output price; and the coefficients β^* depend on the production function parameters in a straightforward way.

The variable n_t^* may be thought of as the desired level of employment in period t; that is, it is the level of employment that exactly satisfies the first-order condition. We may suspect, however, that (20) will not be successful empirically, because costs of adjustment will prevent this relation from holding instantaneously (especially in monthly data, such as these). A possible response to this is to make the underlying model explicitly dynamic and solve the resulting maximum problem, as in Thomas Sargent's study (1978). Such an approach can become extremely complicated, however; and, as Sargent noted, it is not likely to reduce the need for auxiliary *ad hoc* assumptions. Here I follow the bulk of the previous work in simply assuming gradual adjustment of employment toward the desired level. That is, if n_t^* is the desired level of employment defined by the first-order condition, I assume that firms adjust actual employment n_t according to

$$n_t - n_{t-1} = \lambda_n(n_t^* - n_{t-1}), \tag{21}$$

where λ_n is the speed of adjustment. Given (21), a Koyck transformation of (20) gives an equation for actual employment of the form:

$$n_t = \beta_{n0} + \beta_{nq}q_t - \beta_{ne}(e_t - p_t) + \beta_{nt}t + \beta_{nn}n_{t-1}, \tag{22}$$

where $\beta_{ni} = \lambda_n\beta_{ni}^*$, $i = 0, q, e, t$, and $\beta_{nn} = (1 - \lambda_n)$.

Similarly, using the first-order condition (11) for desired hours of work, and making the reasonable assumption that there may also be costs to rapid adjustment of the length of the workweek,[17] we obtain

$$h_t = \beta_{h0} + \beta_{hq}q_t - \beta_{hc}(hcost_t) + \beta_{ht}t + \beta_{hh}h_{t-1}, \tag{23}$$

where h is the log of average hours worked per week, $hcost$ the log of the marginal cost of hours of work (as obtained from the earnings function; see below), and the coefficients are defined by the obvious analogies to the employment case, with λ_h the rate of adjustment of hours of work.[18]

Equations (22) and (23) may be viewed as representative-firm demand functions for employment and hours of work (length of the workweek). In both cases demand is positively associated with the level of production and negatively related to a cost variable. Except for the inclusion of the cost variables and the specification of separate equations for employment and hours, (22) and (23) are quite conventional short-run labor demand functions; see for example Frank Brechling (1965), Robert Ball and E. B. A. St. Cyr (1966), N. J. Ireland and D. J. Smyth (1967), and the survey in Ray Fair (1969), as well as Lucas and Rapping (1969).

In the construction of empirical versions of (22) and (23), several practical issues had to be addressed:

1) A basic question was the treatment of seasonality, which is fairly significant in these data. Fair has argued against deseasonalization in this context, on the grounds that the factors which explain cyclical movements in employment, etc., should also explain seasonal movements. There is also some danger that deseasonalization may introduce spurious relationships or obscure genuine ones. For these reasons the data were not deseasonalized prior to estimation, and seasonal dummies were not used in the equations. (Note that leaving in seasonal fluctuations causes an essentially spurious deterioration in fit.) I did, however, allow for the possibility that employ-

---

[17] These include the costs of reorganizing production schedules and of inducing workers to rearrange their personal schedules.

[18] For simplicity I have assumed that the adjustment of hours depends only on the difference between actual and desired hours, not on the difference between actual and desired employment (and similarly, for the adjustment of employment). Arguments made in M. Ishaq Nadiri and Rosen (1973) would favor the relaxation of this restriction.

ment and hours demand might respond differently to the seasonal and non-seasonal components of production, as follows. For each industry I constructed a variable QSEAS, the "seasonal component of production," as the residual of the deseasonalization of industry output. I then allowed QSEAS and Q − QSEAS (the seasonally adjusted component of production) to enter the demand for workers and hours equations with separate coefficients.

2) At an early stage of my analysis of this data set, I looked at the cross correlations, at various leads and lags, of the log-differences of output and the labor market variables (employment, hours, earnings). My concern was, given that the data are monthly and that the output and labor variables are from different sources, that there might be an alignment problem. This examination revealed little potential difficulty, except in the relation of the employment and output series: For a few industries, employment seemed more strongly related to output one month ahead than to current output. Given that the other labor series lined up with output, this seemed likely to reflect a genuine economic phenomenon, for example, hiring in advance of production, rather than a data alignment problem. In any case, for the employment demand equations, I allowed both current and one-month-ahead production to enter. (Since both seasonal and nonseasonal production were used, this gave a total of four output variables in these equations.) Actual one-month-ahead nonseasonal production was instrumented for rather than treated as exogenous in the estimation of the employment demand equations; thus its estimated coefficients may be interpreted as measuring the impact of one-month-ahead forecasts of output (rather than actual future output) on current employment. One-month-ahead seasonal production was taken to be exogenous, on the grounds that the recurring seasonal component should be perfectly forecasted.

The inclusion of one-month-ahead output did not appear necessary in the hours demand equation.

3) The marginal cost of extending the workweek one hour, HCOST, was defined for the empirical application by

$$HCOST = EMP + \widetilde{EARN} - HRS - P, \tag{24}$$

where $\widetilde{EARN}$ is defined by (17) and P is the industry output price. This follows directly from (11) and the form of the earnings function (16). (HCOST is actually proportional to, not equal to, the marginal cost of increasing the workweek; the factor of proportionality will be absorbed into the estimated coefficient of HCOST.)

The marginal cost of adding a worker, PAY, is simply given by EARN − P; note that the intercept of the earnings function has no bearing on the construction of this cost variable.

4) Industry codes drawn up under the National Recovery Act imposed some direct constraints on firm employment and hours decisions, for exam-

ple, through the worksharing provisions. To allow for this, in the estimation the dummy variable NRA was added to both the employment and hours demand equations.

These considerations, in conjunction with equations (22) and (23), allow the specification of employment demand and hours demand equations that can be estimated for each industry. (For a list of the independent variables in these two equations, see the lefthand columns of Tables 3 and 4, and the variable definitions in Table 2.) The results of this estimation will be discussed in Part D below, following a digression on the identification problem.

C. Identification

The earnings equation and the two demand equations form a simultaneous system, which raises the standard estimation issues of identification and the availability of instruments. It was evident in this case that, as is often true, a strict application of the criteria for valid instruments would leave no instruments (except the constant and time), no identification, and no hope of proceeding further. In particular, it is difficult to come up with measured exogenous variables that are highly correlated with the fluctuations in the demands for industry outputs.[19]

After some consideration, I made the tactical decision to treat industry output as exogenous in estimation. Although the assumption of output exogeneity is not ideal, there are a few arguments in its favor (beyond the obvious one of necessity): First, there are many precedents (Lucas and Rapping, 1969, and virtually all papers in the traditional literature on the short-run demand for labor make this assumption). Second, and more important, treating output as exogenous seems likely to provide considerable identifying power at a relatively low cost in induced bias. Given the maintained presumption that fluctuations in aggregate labor demand, rather than labor supply, dominated prewar business cycles, the correlation of industry output with disturbances to the industry production function and earnings equations should be relatively small.

Besides output, other variables treated as exogenous included the cost of living and the government policy variables (NRA, UNIONPOWER, and EMERGWORK). Also, at some risk of bias in the presence of serial correlation, I treated lagged employment, workweeks, and earnings as predetermined variables. Given all of these assumptions, the three estimated equations are well-identified, both in the formal sense and in the sense that sharp estimates are obtained in the sample. However, it should not be for-

---

[19] The money supply might seem to be a possible exception to this statement. I did experiment with this variable. However, its correlation with industry variables in monthly data is sufficiently low that it is of not much value as an instrument.

gotten that, given that some of the variables treated as exogenous are at best only approximately so, the results below should be interpreted with caution.

I did not attempt to enhance the degree of identification by imposing the cross-coefficient restrictions implied by the structural derivations of the various equations. My reason was that, because of the aggregation of the data, there is no serious reason to believe that such cross-equation restrictions will hold. The demand equations, for example, were derived for a hypothetical individual firm and will not literally apply (because logarithms do not add) to the industry-level data at hand. The strongest justifiable assumption, I believe, is that the qualitative magnitude and sign relationships survive the aggregation process; this is the assumption that underlies my interpretations of the results.

Note that, given that the previous assumptions make the cross-coefficient restrictions inessential to identification, failure to impose them at worst may cause a small loss in efficiency. This is not a serious issue, given the size of the data set.

D. Estimation Results

We proceed now to the estimates. The results of estimating the demand equations are in Tables 3 and 4; the earnings function results are in Table 5. Two-stage least squares (2SLS) was used to correct for simultaneity bias (for the earnings equations, nonlinear 2SLS was used). Instruments and variables treated as endogenous are given in the Appendix. Each equation was estimated separately for each industry.

The employment and hours demand equations are modest extensions of the conventional formulation and should be uncontroversial; they will be discussed first. (See Tables 3 and 4.) The estimates suggest the following.

First, there appear to be significant costs of adjustment (or some other source of inertia) for both employment and weekly hours of work; that is, the lagged value of the dependent variables shows up as highly significant in every case. We would expect employment to be more inertial than hours of work, and this is confirmed by the estimates in every industry except automobiles. The rates of adjustment implied by the estimates are rather rapid: on average, the industries are able to eliminate about one-quarter of the gap between actual and desired employment each month, and nearly one-half of the gap between actual and desired hours.

For both employment and hours demand, the cost variables (PAY and HCOST) enter with the expected negative signs for each industry (except for one case, in which the coefficient of PAY is effectively zero). However, the statistical significance of the cost variable in the employment demand equation is low for some industries. The low significance of PAY is possibly due to the use of monthly data, which may obscure the presumably slow

Table 3
Industry Demands for Workers (dependent variable: EMP_t)

Independent Variables	IRON	AUTOS	MEAT	PAPER	SHOES	WOOL	LEATH	LUMBER
EMP_{t-1}	.740	.610	.916	.881	.720	.578	.771	.684
	(19.6)	(11.3)	(16.7)	(42.5)	(13.2)	(11.8)	(19.2)	(16.1)
PAY_t	-.135	-.134	-.094	-.046	-.202	-.229	-.008	-.204
	(-3.70)	(-1.04)	(-1.98)	(-1.59)	(-1.87)	(-2.82)	(0.16)	(-2.91)
$Q_{t+1} - QSEAS_{t+1}$	.123	.450	.918	.179	-.033	.002	.046	.216
	(1.69)	(5.39)	(1.87)	(1.27)	(-0.32)	(0.02)	(-0.26)	(1.39)
$QSEAS_{t+1}$	.102	.343	.124	.039	.220	.286	.147	.279
	(1.94)	(4.94)	(1.90)	(0.98)	(8.12)	(2.61)	(2.36)	(3.50)
$Q_t - QSEAS_t$	.058	-.125	-.532	-.050	.240	-.008	.236	.071
	(1.94)	(-2.06)	(-.137)	(-0.37)	(1.86)	(-0.11)	(1.37)	(0.42)
$QSEAS_t$	.081	-.160	-.016	.082	-.030	.393	.160	.172
	(1.47)	(-2.35)	(-0.23)	(2.01)	(-1.03)	(5.10)	(2.55)	(1.73)
NRA_t	.010	.035	.026	.019	.018	-.002	.015	-.024
	(1.04)	(1.48)	(1.40)	(2.72)	(1.85)	(-0.16)	(2.38)	(-1.04)
Durbin-Watson	1.46	1.79	1.81	2.11	1.90	1.91	1.65	1.55
Sum of output coefficients	.364	.508	.494	.250	.397	.673	.497	.737
	(6.71)	(6.69)	(3.68)	(4.76)	(4.74)	(8.06)	(6.69)	(7.34)

Notes: Sample: January 1923–December 1939; estimation was by 2SLS. See Table 2 for variable definitions; instruments are given in the Appendix. Estimates of the constant and the trend term are not reported. The *t*-statistics are shown in parentheses.

Table 4
Industry demands for Hours of Work (dependent variable: HRS_t)

Independent Variables	IRON	AUTOS	MEAT	PAPER	SHOES	WOOL	LEATH	LUMBER
HRS_{t-1}	.560	.761	.521	.612	.397	.512	.562	.381
	(14.0)	(11.0)	(10.6)	(14.5)	(5.58)	(10.1)	(10.0)	(5.83)
$HCOST_t$	−.312	−.162	−.116	−.056	−.509	−.334	−.217	−.159
	(−7.76)	(−2.85)	(−6.88)	(−2.51)	(−6.42)	(−7.82)	(−5.22)	(−3.70)
$Q_t - QSEAS_t$	.323	.131	.196	.220	.474	.242	.130	.254
	(12.4)	(4.01)	(7.11)	(8.70)	(7.50)	(9.17)	(5.05)	(7.44)
$QSEAS_t$	.231	.062	.111	.162	.160	.348	.263	.357
	(3.99)	(1.96)	(5.01)	(3.49)	(3.29)	(5.31)	(3.63)	(5.70)
NRA_t	−.041	−.010	−.016	−.026	.047	−.042	−.007	−.062
	(−3.40)	(−0.53)	(−2.34)	(−4.86)	(3.06)	(−3.95)	(−0.80)	(−4.61)
Durbin-Watson	1.99	1.57	1.73	1.80	1.47	1.44	1.49	1.54
Sum of output coefficients	.553	.193	.307	.382	.634	.590	.394	.611
	(8.17)	(3.42)	(7.54)	(7.06)	(6.42)	(7.65)	(4.94)	(6.89)

Notes: See Table 3.

substitution between workers and other factors of production. The effect of the cost variable in the hours demand equation, in contrast, tends to be large and is in each case highly statistically significant. The lower inertia of hours of work and its greater sensitivity to short-run cost changes suggest that workweeks will lead employment in cyclical downturns; this conforms to the findings of Geoffrey Moore (1955), Gerhard Bry (1959), and myself and Powell.

The effect of production on input demand is broken down, for employment, into the effects of current "seasonal" production, current nonseasonal production, and seasonal and nonseasonal production one month in the future. Not too much systematic emerges from this breakdown; in particular, employment in some industries seems to depend most strongly on current output, while other industries hire "one-month ahead." However, although a few negative signs are scattered through the estimated effects of components of production on employment, the total estimated effects of output on employment are, as expected, positive and strongly significant. (See the last row in Table 3.) In conjunction with the estimated speeds of adjustment, the estimated output effects confirm in some cases, although not all, the familiar finding of short-run increasing returns to labor.[20]

In the hours equation, it was necessary to consider only current output effects. As can be seen from Table 4, both the seasonal and nonseasonal components of production, and of course their sum, have a strongly significant, positive effect on hours of work. Shortrun increasing returns to this factor appear to exist for all industries.

The final estimated parameters show the effects of the NRA codes on industry demands for labor inputs. The results imply that, for the most part, the NRA tended to increase employment and reduce hours. This is consistent with one of the legislation's explicit goals, which was to increase employment through "work-sharing." It also helps to explain the persistence of part-time work during the post-1933 recovery.

The residual serial correlation in the two demand equations appears to be relatively low, although it must be remembered that the Durbin-Watson statistic will be biased by the presence of the lagged dependent variables. (Calculated values of Durbin's h-statistic, which corrects for the lagged dependent variable problem, implied that the hypothesis of no serial correlation could be rejected for each equation; however, this statistic gives no information about the extent of serial correlation.) Reestimation of the de-

---

[20] The "total output effect" coefficients in the last row of Table 3 (and Table 4) actually double count the effect of an output increase on employment (or hours), since they represent the effect of a simultaneous increase in adjusted output and the (multiplicative) seasonal adjustment factor. Short-run increasing returns exists when the sum of the coefficients on either seasonal or nonseasonal output alone, divided by one minus the coefficient on the lagged endogenous variable, is less than one.

mand equation using Fair's method gave qualitatively similar results. I also estimated the two demand equations for each industry jointly, so that contemporaneous correlation of residuals could be accounted for; this led to virtually identical results. For computational reasons, I did not attempt to estimate any equation for all industries simultaneously.

In tests for stability across the 1920's and 1930's subsamples, five of the eight employment equations and four of the eight hours equations failed at the .05 significance level. This is not really surprising, given the stark differences in the economic environments of the two periods. When the demand equations are estimated for the subsamples separately, however, they do not look grossly different. In particular, estimates for the 1930's subsample, as well as for 1923–29 and 1923–33, have the right signs and look very much like the whole-sample results.

Overall, the estimated labor demand equations seem reasonably successful, certainly of sufficient quality to use in simulation exercises. They also lend some support to the treatment of employment and hours as "separate" factors of production.

Estimates of the earnings equations, which make up the "supply side" of the model, are given in Table 5. The estimated parameters are those defined in equations (16) and (18): The most important of these are α_E and α_H, which capture the sensitivity of earnings to employment (normalized by the labor force) and to hours of work, and λ_p, which measures the speed of adjustment to cost-of-living changes. I have reported separate estimates for 1923–33 (which avoids the effects of New Deal legislation; i.e., $\alpha_N = \alpha_U = \alpha_w = 0$) and for the whole period.

If we look first at the results for 1923–33, we find that overall the results conform closely to the predictions of the theory. First, for a given level of weekly hours there is typically a strong positive relationship between earnings and employment. This is interpretable as a supply relationship; that is, to induce more workers to enter an industry, firms must increase the utility value of the earnings-hours packages they offer. Second, the elasticity of earnings with respect to hours of work is highly significant, positive, and typically less than one;[21] as argued above, finding this elasticity to be less than one is consistent with countercyclicality of real wages. Finally, nominal earnings adjust only partially to current changes in the cost of living; for the 1923–33 sample, the average rate of adjustment is about 17 percent per month. Although this is a significant amount of "stickiness," it is much less than is usually assumed by Keynesians.

One industry that looks somewhat different from the others is auto-

---

[21] Actually, the estimated coefficient α_H measures the elasticity of earnings less the intercept, not earnings itself, to hours. The elasticity of earnings to hours is strictly less than α_H and is less than one for each industry except automobiles.

Table 5
Earnings Functions

1. Sample: January 1923–June 1933

Estimated Parameter	IRON	AUTOS	MEAT	PAPER	SHOES	WOOL	LEATH	LUMBER
α_E	.352	.048	.202	.496	1.111	.285	.267	.364
	(4.13)	(0.98)	(2.71)	(2.95)	(5.76)	(4.95)	(3.07)	(3.33)
α_H	.951	1.172	.648	.869	.784	.737	1.010	.817
	(11.8)	(22.1)	(8.79)	(7.43)	(7.53)	(9.22)	(17.8)	(4.16)
λ_P	.127	.173	.188	.078	.204	.175	.145	.320
	(3.19)	(2.99)	(3.88)	(2.57)	(3.30)	(3.97)	(3.40)	(4.52)
Durbin-Watson	1.99	1.82	1.96	2.16	2.09	1.97	2.25	2.20

2. Sample: January 1923–December 1939

Estimated Parameter	IRON	AUTOS	MEAT	PAPER	SHOES	WOOL	LEATH	LUMBER
α_E	.320	.004	.118	.419	.317	.326	.252	.369
	(4.08)	(0.14)	(1.85)	(2.84)	(2.46)	(5.76)	(3.90)	(4.28)
α_H	1.030	1.203	.713	.913	.983	.697	.966	.698
	(18.9)	(27.0)	(8.52)	(11.8)	(12.2)	(9.13)	(18.1)	(4.76)
α_N	.029	.020	.009	.008	.053	.057	.040	.036
	(1.47)	(1.25)	(0.53)	(0.64)	(2.38)	(3.11)	(3.73)	(0.98)
α_U	.229	.183	.210	.137	−.250	.117	.097	.030
	(2.42)	(1.61)	(4.00)	(2.23)	(−1.60)	(1.63)	(2.32)	(0.24)
α_W	−.069	−.131	.163	.007	.008	−.035	.045	.020
	(−0.88)	(−1.94)	(2.64)	(0.17)	(0.08)	(−0.47)	(1.03)	(0.17)
λ_P	.129	.073	.204	.095	.068	.163	.157	.217
	(3.84)	(2.22)	(4.81)	(3.27)	(1.97)	(4.45)	(4.50)	(4.60)
Durbin-Watson	1.83	1.84	2.03	2.20	1.95	1.97	2.10	2.32

Notes: Estimation was by NL2SLS. See text for parameter definitions; instruments are given in the Appendix. Estimates of the constant and trend term are not reported. The estimates of α_U and α_W are multiplied by 10^5 and 10^4, respectively, for legibility. The t-statistics are shown in parentheses.

mobiles. For both sample periods, the measured sensitivity of earnings to employment is low, while the sensitivity of earnings to hours is the highest of any industry. The earnings function for the automobile industry was even more striking when it was reestimated without an imposed intercept (i.e., EARN rather than $\widehat{EARN}$ was used as the dependent variable). In that case, for both sample periods, the elasticity of earnings with respect to employment was almost exactly zero and the elasticity of earnings with respect to hours was almost exactly one. This result (which was quite different from what was obtained for the other industries) would be consistent with an industry policy of setting a flat wage rate, which is not changed even when the workweek changes, and of rationing the available jobs among applicants. It is worth noting in this connection that Henry Ford was a prominent maverick of this time in wage and employment policies; a fixed, high wage plus job rationing might not be a bad description of his announced strategy for improving worker motivation.

The estimates of the basic parameters for the whole sample (the bottom half of Table 5) are fairly similar to those for 1923–33, although the rate of adjustment of earnings to prices is estimated to be under .1 in three cases (instead of in just one case for 1923–33). The major difference is that the equation for the 1923–39 period also incorporates estimates of the effects of the New Deal on earnings. Briefly, the estimates show, first, that the NRA codes had relatively small but positive effects on weekly earnings. Second, the expansion of union power after the Wagner Act appears to have had a strong positive impact on earnings, raising weekly earnings by about 10 percent or more in six of the industries. (In lumber, the effect of unionization appears to have been positive but negligible; in boots and shoes, workers suffered significant pay *cuts* during the late New Deal.)[22] Finally, government employment programs appear to have had little systematic effect on the earnings of those privately employed in manufacturing.[23]

For both the short and long samples, diagnostic checks did not seem to

[22] Horace Davis notes: "Another significant point [regarding the decline in shoe industry wages], as bearing on the year 1937, was the checking of the unionization drive in shoes at the very time when unionism was getting established in several other manufacturing industries for the first time" (1940, p. 98). The unusual decline in shoe industry wages after 1937 probably also accounts for the very different estimates of α_E in the 1923–33 and the 1923–39 samples.

[23] Henning Bohn suggested that agricultural earnings, an additional measure of workers' alternative opportunities, might belong in the industry earnings functions; so I tried this. Monthly agricultural wage rates (nominal, without board) are reported for each quarter in the sample in R. A. Sayre (1940); I interpolated this series and divided by the cost of living to obtain a monthly series on real agricultural earnings. Reestimated earnings functions including this variable looked quite similar to those reported in Table 5. The estimated coefficient of agricultural earnings was typically found to be positive, as predicted by the theory, but of only moderate magnitude and statistical significance. An exception was the lumber industry, for which agricultural wages appear to have had an important influence on earnings.

indicate important amounts of serial correlation. Because of this, and because the nonlinear version of Fair's method imposes some computational costs, I did not make any serial correlation correction.

I performed some additional diagnostic analyses of the estimated equations. Of these, the most interesting were within-sample simulations of the complete model. Space does not permit a full reporting here of these experiments (see my 1985 paper for more detail); but I will note that, in dynamic simulations of both 1930–33 and the New Deal era, the model did quite well overall (according to a number of criteria) in tracking the major variables. In particular, the model simulations did a creditable job of tracking the real wage in each of the eight industries, the tendency of real wages to rise even as output and employment fall being clearly exhibited.

Three factors contributed to the model's ability to simulate counter-cyclicality in wages: namely, the tendency in this model for wages to be countercyclical when workweeks are cyclically sensitive, as was discussed above; the assumed inertia in nominal wages (important in 1930–33); and unionization effects (important after 1935). In order to obtain an idea of the relative importance of nominal wage inertia in the determination of real wages in the critical 1930–33 period, I conducted the following experiment. I ran the simulations of 1930–33 again, this time assuming perfect adjustment of nominal earnings to the cost of living ($\lambda_p = 1$). All other coefficients were unchanged. I found that, first, although a rising real wage was still predicted by the simulations, the ability of the simulations to track the actual real wage deteriorated significantly for most of the industries. In several cases the root mean square error of simulation increased by one-half or more; also, the maximum real wage over the period predicted by the simulations tended to be quite a bit lower than what was actually attained. Thus, although not the whole story, a degree of nominal wage inertia seems to be an essential element in the explanation of real wage behavior in the early depression. There was also, however, a rather surprising second finding from these simulations: the assumption of perfect wage adjustment to the cost of living had virtually no effect on the ability of the model to track employment and hours. Indeed, on average, fits improved slightly. Thus, despite the importance of lagged adjustment for explaining observed real wage behavior in this period, this phenomenon may not have had great allocative significance.

Perhaps as interesting as the successes of the model in simulations were its occasional failures. For example, the model did not predict a strong attempt in 1932 by the steel and automobile industries to preserve their workforces through pronounced work-sharing strategies (i.e., a sharp cut in hours of work coupled with significantly increased employment). Another problem was that the model simulations tended to understate somewhat the degree of nominal inertia of wages during the first six to nine months of 1931. The first problem probably reflects the oligopolistic nature of the two particular industries, and their resulting ability to deviate from competitive behavior in the short run; the second difficulty no doubt results from the assumption that the sensitivity of wages to cost-of-living changes was the same in all periods, rather than being dependent on recent price behavior. (Since the 1920's were a period of stable prices, presumably the sensitivity of wages to prices was in fact less in the early 1930's than later on.) Significantly, however, these deviations from the projected paths were in each case quite transitory, with the simulated variables returning to their predicted paths in a year or less. Thus, although these failures suggests ways of improving the model, they do not appear to present fundamental difficulties.

III. A Dynamic Labor Supply Equation

A possible objection to the supply side of the model developed and estimated in this paper is that it is rather static in nature. I have made strong assumptions (that workers cannot borrow or lend, and that they have intertemporally separable utility functions) in order to avoid consideration of the intertemporal substitution of leisure and consumption. In addition, the implicit assumption that there are no mobility costs to moving between the secondary and primary sectors implies that workers need consider only current returns (and not long-run returns) when deciding whether to change sectors. Only the partial adjustment of nominal earnings to cost-of-living changes (in the estimated earnings functions) induces a modest dynamic element.

Although developing a more explicitly dynamic representation of this paper's model of labor supply is not particularly difficult conceptually, there are some substantial problems of empirical implementation. Rather than tackle those here, I propose to do something more limited: I will try to show that one of the more empirically successful models of depression-era labor supply, the intertemporal substitution model of Darby, can be reinterpreted as a dynamic version of the supply model in this paper. Estimates of a Darby-type model on these data will then be presented. The reasonableness of these estimates, it will he argued, constitutes evidence that the present paper's model of labor supply could survive the transition to a more dynamic specification.

Darby's model of labor supply is an extension of the basic Lucas-Rapping (1969) formulation. Lucas and Rapping argued, it will be recalled, that labor supply (i.e., worker-hours, normalized by the number of households) should depend 1) *positively* on the current returns to working; 2) *negatively* on the long-run, or "normal" returns to working; and 3) *negatively* on the ratio of the normal to the current price level.

The reasoning should be familiar. 1) High current returns to work increase labor effort by improving the rate of exchange between work and consumption. 2) High long-run returns to work depress current labor supply by making it more profitable to substitute present for future leisure. 3) Finally, assuming that nominal interest rates do not adjust fully to inflation, an increase in the ratio of the normal to the current price level lowers labor supply by leading workers to anticipate lower real rates of interest.

An important issue in this context, and one that I do not believe has been adequately addressed by the intertemporal substitution literature, is how to measure the returns from working. Lucas and Rapping, and most other authors, have assumed that the real wage is a good proxy for these returns. However, as was discussed in the introduction, this assumption makes it hard to explain labor supply behavior in the 1930's.[24] One of a number of contributions made by Darby was the substitution of full-time-equivalent earnings (FTE)[25] for the wage as the measure of the returns to work. Darby showed that using earnings instead of wages significantly improved the capacity of the model to fit the 1930's.

What is the rationale for using earnings rather than wages as a measure of the returns to work? Darby's argument was that, because the NRA codes required shorter workweeks, actual hours of work either were underreported by firms (leading to an upward bias in the measurement of hourly wages) or, possibly, were rationed. For these reasons he expected average earnings per FTE employee to "more accurately reflect the development of wages in the 1930s" (p. 10) than the official wage series.

A problem with Darby's argument is that the NRA codes were in effect for less than two years, but the substitution of earnings for wages seems to be empirically preferable for the entire prewar period. (See Darby's paper, and the results below.) An alternative explanation for the superiority of the earnings variable follows from the analysis of the present research. It has been suggested here that, in an environment where hours of work are not constant, the correct measure of the returns to working is neither wages nor earnings but the total utility of the earnings-hours package offered by the job, perhaps measured relative to the utility of remaining in the secondary sector. An obvious problem, however, is that this utility is not observable to the econometrician thus we might ask which, if any, of the observables is likely to be correlated with the total utility of a job. The wage is not a good choice; as has been shown at length, wages and the utility of a job can easily

[24] It may be noted also that estimation of a Lucas-Rapping-type model using these data (equations (25)–(27) below with the real wage in place of real earnings) yielded a number of wrong signs and a generally poorer fit than the Darby real earnings version.

[25] The FTE earnings variable used by Darby is essentially identical to actual average earnings for most industries, including manufacturing. That is, the variable reflects actual rather than normal workweeks. See the *Survey of Current Business*, June 1945, pp. 17–18.

move in opposite directions. However, in the case where fluctuations in employment are due primarily to variations in demand rather than supply (the probable situation in the 1930's), the utility from holding a job and earnings will be highly correlated. This is straightforward to show. Increased demand in the primary sector, which increases the equilibrium utility of workers, will also typically both move the equilibrium earnings function upward and increase hours of work. Thus increased primary-sector demand will also increase earnings. The explanation for the superiority of Darby's specification, therefore, is simply that earnings are a good proxy for the total utility of holding a job, and wages are not.

These considerations suggest that estimating a model in the spirit of Darby on the present data set may be a valuable exercise. I specify an empirical model as

$$
\begin{aligned}
EMP_t &\times HRS_t - LABORFORCE_t \\
&= \beta_0 + \beta_1(EARN_t - COL_t) \\
&\quad + \beta_2(EARN_t - COL_t)^* \\
&\quad + \beta_3(COL_t^* - COL_t) \\
&\quad + \alpha_N NRA_t + \alpha_U UNIONPOWER_t \\
&\quad + \alpha_W EMERGWORK_t + \alpha_t t
\end{aligned}
\tag{25}
$$

$$
\begin{aligned}
(EARN_t - COL_t)^* &= \lambda_P(EARN_t - COL_t) \\
&\quad + (1 - \lambda_P)(EARN_{t-1} - COL_{t-1})^*
\end{aligned}
\tag{26}
$$

$$
COL_t^* = \lambda_P COL_t + (1 - \lambda_P)COL_{t-1}^*
\tag{27}
$$

where an asterisk denotes the "permanent" or long-run component of a variable. (Variables definitions are given in Table 2.)

Equation (25) is a labor supply equation, of the general form first written down by Lucas and Rapping (1969). The dependent variable is total worker-hours supplied to an industry, normalized by Lebergott's aggregate labor force estimates. (Lebergott's annual data were linearly interpolated to obtain a monthly series.) Equation (25) follows the discussion above in specifying that the supply of worker-hours to an industry depends differentially on the current and longrun returns to working (where the returns to work are measured by real weekly earnings), as well as on the ratio of the long-run to current cost of living. The use of earnings to measure the returns to work reflects Darby's innovation. By the logic of the intertemporal substitution model, the expected signs of the coefficients are $\beta_1 > 0$, $\beta_2 < 0$, and $\beta_3 < 0$.

The labor supply equation (25) also contains terms reflecting New Deal government actions. The expected signs of the coefficients are: for α_N, ambiguous (since the NRA codes increased employment but reduced hours); for α_U, negative (since unionization should restrict labor supply below competitive levels; and for α_W, negative (since increased public works programs should reduce the supply of labor to industry). A time trend is also included.

Equations (26) and (27) follow Lucas and Rapping in assuming that the permanent components of returns and the cost of living are updated adaptively, with the same "rate of learning" applying in both cases. Constants and trends are excluded from (26) and (27); if included they would be absorbed into the constant and trend of the estimated equation, with no effect on the important estimated parameters.

Using (26) and (27), the labor supply equation (25) can be transformed so that only observable variables appear (see Lucas and Rapping). The use of a nonlinear estimation procedure permits the recovery of the original parameters of (25) to (27).

The results of estimating the system (25)–(27) are reported in Table 6. The estimation method was (nonlinear) two-stage least squares, used to correct for simultaneity bias. (Instruments are listed in the Appendix.) The sample was January 1923–December 1939; estimates obtained for the sample ending before the New Deal, which set $\alpha_U = \alpha_W = \alpha_N = 0$, are also reported. The Durbin-Watson statistics are for the Koyck-transformed equations.

The most important result in Table 6 is that the estimate of β_1, which measures the elasticity of worker-hours supplied to earnings, is positive and highly significant in every case. There is also a remarkable uniformity across industries and sample periods of the magnitude of this estimated parameter. This is consistent with the idea that (25) is a true supply curve in which earnings are acting as a proxy for the total utility from working.[26]

The estimates of β_2 are also all positive, although magnitudes and statistical significance vary. The finding that β_2 is positive, that is, that higher long-run returns to work increase labor supply, is the opposite of the prediction of the intertemporal substitution model. An explanation of this finding is available, if we are willing to reinterpret (25). Recall that these estimates have been obtained from industry-level, not aggregate, data. At the level of the industry, labor supply depends not only on the decisions of workers already "in" the sector (for example, already living in the mill town), but also on the number of workers that can be drawn from the rest of the economy. If there are mobility costs to switching sectors, higher long-run returns in an industry will *increase* the industry's labor supply, by making it more worthwhile for workers to incur the fixed costs of entering the sector. Thus it might be argued that long-run earnings belong in (25) because of

---

[26] The positive and significant estimates of β_1, it should be noted, did not simply reflect the fact that weekly hours is a constituent of both the dependent variable and weekly earnings. Reestimates using employment as the dependent variable instead of worker-hours also yielded positive and highly significant values for $\hat{\beta}_1$.

Table 6
Dynamic Labor Supply Equation

Estimated Parameter	IRON	AUTOS	MEAT	PAPER	SHOES	WOOL	LEATH	LUMBER
Sample: January 1923–June 1933								
β_1	1.78	1.63	1.77	1.45	1.04	2.10	1.21	1.80
	(8.25)	(11.1)	(6.98)	(8.51)	(12.1)	(10.1)	(11.1)	(3.24)
β_2	0.03	2.29	2.99	0.30	0.29	0.42	2.92	0.26
	(0.08)	(3.43)	(0.97)	(0.41)	(0.83)	(0.67)	(2.31)	(0.58)
β_3	−0.95	−0.66	−2.55	−1.51	−0.74	−2.69	−1.24	−3.12
	(−0.74)	(−0.46)	(−3.32)	(−3.55)	(−1.24)	(−2.15)	(−2.47)	(−1.53)
λ_P	.137	.148	.093	.071	.184	.199	.095	.351
	(2.57)	(3.49)	(1.59)	(2.30)	(3.17)	(3.26)	(2.72)	(4.24)
Durbin-Watson	2.02	1.85	1.81	2.06	2.04	2.23	1.86	2.08
Sample: January 1923–December 1939								
β_1	1.43	1.99	1.86	1.38	1.38	2.24	1.31	1.59
	(16.3)	(10.5)	(7.54)	(12.5)	(15.2)	(14.8)	(12.9)	(8.28)
β_2	0.52	2.61	4.11	0.79	0.10	0.67	3.01	0.52
	(2.05)	(3.34)	(1.62)	(1.71)	(0.23)	(1.25)	(3.35)	(1.46)
β_3	−1.93	−0.32	−3.11	−1.64	0.07	−2.01	−1.53	−4.21
	(−2.74)	(−0.21)	(−4.39)	(−5.97)	(0.12)	(−2.35)	(−4.17)	(−3.99)
α_N	−.021	.085	−.003	.011	.020	.032	−.009	−.046
	(−0.49)	(0.98)	(−0.06)	(0.65)	(0.62)	(0.66)	(−0.42)	(−0.87)
α_U	−.035	−.102	−.088	−.030	−.051	−.009	−.027	.023
	(−1.56)	(−2.57)	(−2.04)	(−1.92)	(−3.24)	(−0.43)	(−1.98)	(1.00)
α_W	.142	.098	−.149	.019	−.145	.157	.065	−.211
	(0.86)	(0.31)	(−0.87)	(0.28)	(−1.10)	(0.89)	(0.76)	(−1.03)
λ_P	.128	.170	.094	.081	.136	.165	.107	.174
	(3.90)	(3.89)	(2.49)	(3.68)	(2.76)	(4.03)	(3.99)	(4.52)
Durbin-Watson	1.85	1.79	1.82	2.13	2.21	2.07	1.93	2.20

Notes: See Table 5: only exception is [that] estimates of α_U and α_W are multiplied by 10^4 for legibility.

their relevance to worker mobility decisions, not for any reason of intertemporal substitution.

This alternative interpretation of (25) is an attractive one, and not simply because it rationalizes $\beta_2 > 0$. A drawback of the intertemporal substitution hypothesis as a model of 1930's labor supply is that it assumes perfect capital markets. This assumption appears at variance with the tremendous disarray of the financial sector in the depression, and the resulting large difference between lending and borrowing rates for consumers.[27] In contrast, the mobility-cost interpretation of (25) does not require perfect capital markets; indeed, under this interpretation (25) is consistent with the Section I model of this paper, with its no-borrowing, no-lending assumption.

With respect to the effects of the New Deal, Table 6 finds the same result as the estimated earnings function in Table 5: namely, that the legislation-supported unionization drive was the most important New Deal change in labor markets. In contrast to the NRA codes and government work programs, which had little systematic impact, unionization appears to have had a strong effect in a number of industries.

Overall, the Darby-type specification seems to work well in these data. If the interpretation of this specification that I have given is accepted, this bodes well for the development of a more explicitly dynamic version of this paper's model of labor supply.

IV. Conclusion

This paper has employed monthly, industry-level data in a study of Great Depression labor markets. The framework of analysis was a model in which, as in Lucas (1970), both firms and workers are concerned with the distinction between the number employed and the number of hours each worker works. In the context of the depression, this distinction appears to be an important one; and, in conjunction with additional empirical elements, this model does a rather good job of explaining the behavior of the key time-series. This raises the possibility that the decomposition of aggregate labor supply into participation rates and hours per worker may be important for understanding other macroeconomic episodes as well.

A limitation of this analysis is its partial equilibrium nature: output is treated as exogenous. A really satisfactory analysis of the 1930's would have to consider labor markets, product markets, and financial markets in a simultaneous general equilibrium. This should be pursued in future research.

---

[27] See my 1983 article. The failure of the perfect capital markets assumption may explain the difficulty the intertemporal substitution model has in explaining the path of consumption in the 1930's (Altonji).

Appendix

The sources of the data used in this study are as follows.

1) Earnings, hours, and employment data are from M. Ada Beney (1936) and R. A. Sayre (1940). These data are the result of an extensive monthly survey conducted by the National Industrial Conference Board from 1920 until 1947.

   All of the industries in the sample paid at least part of their workforce by piece rates (see the *Monthly Labor Review*, September 1935, pp. 697–700). No correction was made for this. This should not create any problem of interpretation, as long as the speed at which the piecework tasks were executed did not vary much in the short run.

2) Industrial production data are from the Federal Reserve Board. See "New Federal Reserve Index of Industrial Production," *Federal Reserve Bulletin*, August 1940, pp. 753–69 and 825–74.

3) Wholesale price indexes are from the Bureau of Labor Statistics. See the following publications of the U.S. Department of Labor: *Handbook of Labor Statistics* (Bulletin 541, 1931; Bulletin 616, 1936; Bulletin 694, 1941), and *Wholesale Prices 1913 to 1927* (Bulletin 473, 1929). For the automobile industry I merged two BLS series of motor vehicles prices. Neither series covered 1935; the price series on all metal products was used to interpolate the automobiles price series for that year.

4) The consumer price series is from Sayre (1948).

5) The *NRA* dummy is set equal to one for all months from September 1933, when the first NRA industry codes went into effect, until May 1935, when the Act was declared unconstitutional. The monthly data on mandays idle due to strikes (used in the construction of the *UNIONPOWER* variable) are from the Bureau of Labor Statistics (Bulletins 651 and 694). The data series for total federal emergency workers, which include the WPA, the CCC, and other programs, is from the National Industrial Conference Board (NICB) *Economic Almanac* for 1941–42.

The span of the sample is January 1923 to December 1939. Although some of the data exist before 1923, there are two major problems with extending the sample further back. 1) Some of the industrial production data are missing and cannot be constructed. 2) There is a six-month gap in the NICB survey in 1922. The December 1939 stop date was chosen so as to avoid consideration of the many special features of the wartime economy.

The variables treated as endogenous and the additional instruments used in estimation in the principal equations are as follows. 1) *Demand for workers equation:* PAY_t and $QADJ_{t+1}$ are taken to be endogenous. ($QADJ_{t+1}$ is treated as endogenous because of the measurement error problem created when a future value of a variable is used in place of a forecast. See the text.) Additional instruments are $QADJ_{t-1}$, HRS_{t-1}, $UNIONPOWER$, and the current value and two lags of the cost-of-living variable COL. 2) *Demand for hours of work equation*. The endogenous variable is the cost variable, $HCOST_t$. Additional instruments are EMP_{t-1}, $UNIONPOWER_t$, and the current value and two lags of COL. 3) *Earnings equation*. Endogenous variables are EMP_t and HRS_t. Instruments were the current and two lagged values of production Q and current and two lagged values of COL. Because it was observed earlier that current employment was highly correlated with one-month-ahead production in some industries, I also used as an instrument a forecast of one-month-ahead production based on a univariate autoregression. 4) *Dynamic labor supply, or "Darby," equation*. Endogenous variable is $EARN_t$. Instruments are the same as in the earnings equation above.

References

Altonji. Joseph, "The Intertemporal Substitution Model of Labour Market Fluctuations: An Empirical Analysis," *Review of Economic Studies*, Special Issue 1982, 49, 783–824.

────── and Ashenfelter, Orley, "Wage Movements and the Labour Market Equilibrium Hypothesis," *Economica*, August 1980, 47, 217–45.

Ashenfelter, Orley, "Unemployment as Disequilibrium in a Model of Aggregate Labor Supply," *Econometrica*, April 1980, 48, 547–64.

Baily, Martin N., "The Labor Market in the 1930's," in James Tobin, ed., *Macroeconomics, Prices, and Quantities*. Washington: The Brookings Institution, 1983.

Bakke, E. Wight, *The Unemployed Worker: A Study of the Task of Making a Living Without a Job*, New Haven: Yale University Press, 1940.

Ball, Robert J. and St. Cyr, E. B. A., "Short-Term Employment Functions in British Manufacturing Industry," *Review of Economic Studies*, July 1966, 33, 179–207.

Beney, M. Ada, *Wages, Hours, and Employment in the United States, 1914–1936*, New York: National Industrial Conference Board, 1936.

Bernanke, Ben, "Nonmonetary Effects of the Financial Crisis in the Propagation of the Great Depression," *American Economic Review*, June 1983, 73, 257–76.

──────, "Employment, Hours, and Earnings in the Depression: An Analysis of Eight Manufacturing Industries," Working Paper No. 1642, NBER, June 1985.

────── and Powell, James, "The Cyclical Behavior of Industrial Labor Markets: A Comparison of the Pre-War and Post-War Eras," in R. J. Gordon, ed., NBER Conference Volume on Business Cycles, forthcoming.

Bernstein, Irving, *The Lean Years: A History of the American Worker, 1920–1933*, Boston: Houghton-Mifflin, 1960.

Brechling, Frank P. R., "The Relationship Between Output and Employment in British Manufacturing Industries," *Review of Economic Studies*, July 1965, 32, 187–216.

Bry, Gerhard, "The Average Workweek as an Economic Indicator," Occasional Paper No. 69, NBER, 1959.

Creamer, Daniel, "Behavior of Wage Rates During Business Cycles," Occasional Paper No. 34, NBER, 1950.

Darby, Michael R., "Three-and-a-Half Million U.S. Employees Have Been Mislaid: Or, an Explanation of Unemployment, 1934–41," *Journal of Political Economy*, February 1976, *84*, 1–16.

Daugherty, Carroll R. et al., *The Economics of the Iron and Steel Industry*, New York: McGraw-Hill, 1937.

Davis, Horace B., *Shoes: The Workers and the Industry*, New York: International Publishers, 1940.

Fabricant, Solomon, *The Output of Manufacturing Industries, 1899–1939*, NBER, New York: Arno Press, 1940.

———, *Employment in Manufacturing, 1899–1939*, NBER, New York: Arno Press, 1942.

Fair, Ray C., *The Short-Run Demand for Workers and Hours*, Amsterdam: North-Holland, 1969.

Feldstein, Martin, "Specification of the Labour Input in the Aggregate Production Function," *Review of Economic Studies*, October 1967, *34*, 375–86.

Ireland, N. J. and Smyth, D. J., "Short-Term Employment Functions in Australian Manufacturing," *Review of Economics and Statistics*, November 1967, *49*, 537–44.

Lebergott, Stanley, *Manpower in Economic Growth: The American Record Since 1800*, New York: McGraw-Hill, 1964.

Lucas, Robert E., Jr., "Capacity, Overtime, and Empirical Production Functions," *American Economic Review Proceedings*, May 1970, *60*, 23–27.

———, "Expectations and the Neutrality of Money," *Journal of Economic Theory*, April 1972, *4*, 103–24.

——— and Rapping, Leonard A., "Real Wages, Employment, and Inflation," *Journal of Political Economy*, September/October 1969, *77*, 721–54.

——— and ——— "Unemployment in the Great Depression: Is There a Full Explanation?," *Journal of Political Economy*, January/February 1972, *80*, 186–91.

Moore, Geoffrey H., "Business Cycles and the Labor Market," *Monthly Labor Review*, March 1955, *78*, 288–92.

Muth, John F., "Optimal Properties of Exponentially Weighted Forecasts," in Robert E. Lucas, Jr. and Thomas Sargent, *Rational Expectations and Econometric Practice*, Minneapolis: University of Minneapolis Press, 1981.

Nadiri, M. Ishaq and Rosen, Sherwin, *A Disequilibrium Model of Demand for Factors of Production*, NBER, New York: Columbia University Press, 1973.

Plessner, Yakir and Yitzhaki, Shlomo, "Unemployment and Wage Rigidity: The Demand Side," *Oxford Economic Papers*, July 1983, *35*, 202–12.

Quandt, Richard E. and Rosen, Harvey S., "Unemployment, Disequilibrium and the Short-Run Phillips Curve: An Econometric Approach," Working Paper No. 1648, NBER, June 1985.

Rees, Albert, "On Equilibrium in Labor Markets," *Journal of Political Economy*, March/April 1970, *78*, 306–10.

———, "Real Wages and Inflation: Rejoinder," *Journal of Political Economy*, January/February 1972, *80*, 192.

Rosen, Harvey S., and Quandt, Richard E., "Estimation of a Disequilibrium Aggregate Labor Market," *Review of Economics and Statistics*, August 1978, 60, 371–79.

Rosen, Sherwin, "Short-Run Employment Variation on Class-I Railroads in the U.S., 1947–1963," *Econometrica*, July/October 1968, 36, 511–29.

Rotemberg, Julio, "Sticky Prices in the United States," *Journal of Political Economy*, December 1982, 90, 1187–211.

Sargent, Thomas, "Estimation of Dynamic Labor Demand Schedules Under Rational Expectations," *Journal of Political Economy*, December 1978, 86, 1009–44.

Sayre, R. A., "Wages, Hours, and Employment in the United States, 1934–1939," *Conference Board Economic Record*, March 28, 1940, 2, 115–37.

———, *Consumers' Prices, 1914–1948*, New York: National Industrial Conference Board, 1948.

Stockman, Alan C., "Aggregation Bias and the Cyclical Behavior of Real Wages," research paper, University of Rochester, 1983.

Weiss, Andrew, "Job Queues and Layoffs in Labor Markets with Flexible Wages," *Journal of Political Economy*, June 1980, 88, 526–38.

Yellen, Janet C., "Efficiency Wage Models of Unemployment," *American Economic Review Proceedings*, May 1984, 74, 200–05.

Seven

Unemployment, Inflation, and Wages in the American Depression: Are There Lessons for Europe?

WITH MARTIN PARKINSON

ANALYSTS OF THE CONTEMPORARY European unemployment problem (Robert J. Gordon, 1988, being the most recent) have with some frequency drawn comparisons with the experience of the 1930s. In one sense, this comparison is unwarranted: While today's European unemployment is a serious matter, its impact on human welfare is an order of magnitude less than what was wrought by the Great Depression. From a scientific perspective, however, the possibility that analogous mechanisms generated persistent unemployment in the 1930s and the 1980s makes the comparison an interesting one.

In this paper, we consider whether the American experience of the 1930s can teach us anything about three "puzzles" raised by the current European unemployment problem. These widely discussed issues are: 1) the persistence of high unemployment (equivalently, the apparent failure of the economy's homeostatic, or self-correcting, mechanisms); 2) the apparent lack of impact of high unemployment on the rate of inflation (the "floating NAIRU"); and 3) the phenomenon of increasing real wages despite high unemployment ("real wage rigidity"). We focus here on the manufacturing sector, where the data are best; obviously, extensions to other sectors would be desirable.

The comparison of America in the 1930s and Europe in the 1980s reveals some important differences; most strikingly, in the dynamics of unemployment. The persistence of unemployment in the 1930s reflected to a much greater degree a sequence of large destabilizing shocks (in 1929–33 and 1937–38), and much less a low-level equilibrium trap, than does modern European unemployment. The self-correcting tendencies of the 1930s economy were probably much stronger than is generally acknowledged.

However, the depression era confirms the modern observation that the level of unemployment has little independent influence on the rate of inflation—an observation that, we argue, is consistent with macro theory. The

Reprinted with permission from *AER Papers and Proceedings*, Vol. 79 (May 1989), 210–14.

We thank the Olin Foundation for support. Brad De Long, our Princeton colleagues, and members of the Berkeley macro history seminar provided helpful suggestions.

experience of the 1930s also supports the impression of students of the European situation that political factors are important in the process of real wage determination.

I. The Dynamics of Interwar Employment

How should we characterize the behavior of U.S. manufacturing employment during the 1930s? One thing that is certain is that, after contracting sharply between 1929 and 1933, manufacturing employment did not simply stabilize at a low level (as seems to have occurred recently in Europe). Between 1933 and 1937, employment in U.S. manufacturing rose by 3.4 percent per *quarter*, total labor hours by 4.4 percent per quarter, and output by 5.0 percent per quarter. The recession of 1937–38 was followed by another strong recovery: Quarterly growth rates for manufacturing employment, hours, and output in 1938–40 were 1.8, 2.8, and 4.9 percent, respectively.

An important question is whether the large fluctuations in interwar employment were due to a self-correcting tendency of the economy, as suggested by natural rate theory, or whether they were instead the product of a highly volatile economy with no endogenous stabilizing mechanism. A useful econometric framework for studying this question is the error correction model:

Let n_t^* be the (log of) the "normal" or "full-employment" level of employment. Then a simple error-correction model for (the log of) actual employment n_t, is given by

$$\Delta n_t = \text{constant} + a(L)\,\Delta n_t + b\,(n_{t-1}^* - n_{t-1}) + Z_t c + e_t \tag{1}$$

where Δ is the difference operator, $a(L)$ is a lag operator intended to reflect short-run dynamics in employment, Z_t is a list of stationary variables affecting employment growth, and e_t is a stationary error term. The error-correction term, $b(n_{t-1}^* - n_{t-1})$, captures any tendency of employment to move toward its normal level after a displacement; the value of the error-correction parameter b, together with the values of the autoregressive parameters defining $a(L)$, determines the speed with which this return to normal occurs. If b is strictly positive, then n and n^* are cointegrated; that is, lapses from full employment may be persistent but they ultimately disappear. If b is zero, then n and n^* may not be cointegrated, and actual and full employment may drift permanently apart.

We estimated (1) using quarterly averages of monthly U.S. manufacturing employment data, for the period 1924:2–1941:4. The manufacturing labor force (n^* in this application) was taken to be the total U.S. labor force, as estimated by Stanley Lebergott (1964), times the fraction of the U.S. labor force employed in manufacturing in 1929:1. Four lags of actual employment growth and seasonal dummies were included. For Z_t we used the current and once-lagged value of "unexpected inflation" as a measure of aggregate demand shocks. (Unexpected inflation was measured as the residual from a prediction equation for inflation, estimated on pre-1930 data and using lagged inflation and commercial paper rates as predictors.) When unexpected inflation is put in (1), that equation becomes what might be called an *error-correction Phillips curve* (ECPC). The ECPC collapses to a conventional, static, expectations-augmented Phillips curve if $b = 1$, $a(L) = 0$, and $c(L) = c$; but in general, the ECPC allows for richer employment dynamics than a standard Phillips curve.

Two main results emerge from the estimation. First, unexpected inflation enters the equation with the right (positive) sign and with high statistical significance.[1] Second, the error-correction parameter b is estimated to be .15, with a marginal significance of .06 under the null of no cointegration of n and n^*.[2] Together with the estimates of $a(L)$ (which are small and negative), this estimate of b implies rather rapid movement of the economy toward full employment. For example, after a negative disturbance to the steady state, the economy is estimated to make up over half of the difference between actual and full employment in the first three quarters after the shock. Similar results are obtained 1) when unexpected inflation is defined as the residual of a prediction equation estimated over the entire sample; 2) when the real value of the liabilities of failing banks was used in the place of unexpected inflation (as an alternative measure of macro shocks); and 3) when unanticipated changes in real government spending or the deficit were added to (1). The results are also unchanged when actual rather than "unexpected" inflation is included in (1), and there is not much to choose between the two specifications. We will return to the significance of this last finding in a moment.

Can it really be that the 1930s U.S. economy was a "natural rate" economy, rather than a "low-level trap" economy (as it has most usually been characterized)? To dispute this conclusion, one has to argue either that the 1929–33 and 1937–38 downturns were endogenous developments in the labor market, not the result of outside forces; or, that the periods of strong recovery (particularly 1933–37) were due only to policy or other exogenous developments.[3] However, the first of these potential arguments is unreason-

---

[1] The marginal significance is .002. We did not correct for the bias in the standard error which arises because unexpected inflation is the residual from a first-stage regression, but it is unlikely that this correction would change the basic result.

[2] The *t*-statistic is 2.55. However, under the null the "*t*-statistic" may not have a standard distribution, since if n and n^* are not cointegrated and are individually not stationary, then $n - n^*$ will not be stationary. The marginal significance level was therefore estimated by a small Monte Carlo study (100 replications).

[3] Econometrically, the first hypothesis corresponds to setting $Z_t = 0$ in (1); the second, to

able; particularly for 1929–33, it is easy to identify forces outside the labor market that depressed the economy. The second argument may bear further investigation. Our own view at present is that the New Deal is better characterized as having "cleared the way" for a natural recovery (for example, by ending deflation and rehabilitating the financial system), rather than as being the engine of recovery itself.

There are qualifications to the view that self-correcting mechanisms were strong in the depression era. It cannot be denied, for example, that long-term unemployment was very important in the 1930s, and it may be that other sectors showed less "bounce" than manufacturing. But the contrast with modern Europe, where employment has stagnated despite the apparent absence of new shocks, seems marked.

II. The Floating NAIRU

What is called the "floating NAIRU" by Gordon is the phenomenon of continuing inflation despite unemployment above the natural rate. This phenomenon describes both recent Europe and New Deal America: Prices in the United States rose about 20 percent between President Roosevelt's inauguration and the 1937 recession (but were flat for the rest of the decade).

But is the floating NAIRU really a puzzle? In fact, the standard equation employed by NAIRU proponents, which makes the inflation rate the dependent variable and the deviation of unemployment from it normal level the independent variable, is not implied by any well-articulated theory. Theory suggests instead that inflation will be determined by current and expected money supply and demand. Inflation surprises or (in models in which superneutrality fails) inflation itself may then have effects on employment.[4] That is, it is inflation rather than employment that should be the independent variable. This theoretically preferred formulation also appears to be preferred empirically: As discussed above, our estimates of variants of equation (1) are consistent with the existence of significant effects of either unanticipated or anticipated inflation on employment during the interwar period.

When we follow the theory and look to monetary conditions, it is not at all difficult to explain the behavior of the price level in the New Deal.

---

making one element of Z_t a dummy equal to one for 1933–37. Either change makes it impossible to reject $b = 0$ at the .10 significance level, once a correction is made for the nonstandard distribution of the estimate of b.

[4] The Fischer-Taylor contract model or the Lucas aggregate supply curve implies that unanticipated inflation or deflation will affect employment, as do "debt-deflation" theories. For a model potentially relevant to the depression in which superneutrality fails, see J. Bradford De Long and Lawrence Summers (1986).

President Roosevelt was a strong believer in the importance of "reflation"; shortly after his inauguration he initiated a new, expansionary monetary regime which included, besides direct monetary expansion, abandonment of the gold standard and rehabilitation of the banking system. The higher inflation this created may have had some positive effects of its own on the recovery process, for example, by reducing debt burdens and eliminating deflationary expectations;[5] but no paradox is implied by the simultaneous existence during the New Deal of high inflation and a high level of unemployment. Presumably monetary conditions also explain continued inflation in Europe today.

None of this resolves the puzzle of why unemployment in Europe has remained so high in the 1980s. But this discussion does suggest that, in the analysis of protracted high unemployment, we should pay less attention to price level adjustment and more attention to the real factors inhibiting recovery.

III. Real Wage "Rigidity"

It has often been noted that real wages in Europe seem to have been little affected by the level of unemployment. Similarly, in the United States, the 1930s were a period of robust real wage growth. (This growth, we emphasize, was a secular phenomenon, unrelated to the transient spikes in real wages induced by unanticipated deflation in 1931–32.)

This behavior of real wages cannot be explained in a vacuum, but must be related to several other trends in labor markets that developed in the depression decade.

First, there was a significant decline over the period in average hours of work per week. Shorter workweeks were initiated because firms chose to use "work sharing" as a labor hoarding device, and possibly also because firms were concerned that too many layoffs might create pressure for some sort of company-sponsored unemployment compensation. The reduction in workweeks was reinforced by legislation, unionization, and changing employment practices later in the decade.

Second, productivity growth during the 1930s was remarkably strong. An interesting feature of this productivity growth is that it occurred despite absolute declines in the capital stocks of most industries. (Indexes of employment-capital ratios in 1937 for industries for which we have constructed data, taking 1929 = 100, are as follows: steel, 123.5; textiles, 167.1; petroleum refining, 99.5; autos, 139.9; leather, 182.1; lumber, 122.7; rubber,

[5] The expectational effect is emphasized by Peter Temin and Barrie Wigmore (1988). For a contemporary account of Roosevelt's monetary regime change, see National Industrial Conference Board (1934).

158.6; paper and pulp, 122.3.) American productivity growth in the 1930s, perhaps unlike some of the recent productivity growth in Europe, was not the result of capital deepening.

Third, industrial unionism achieved major successes during the New Deal period, organizing some important industries, winning concessions from previously organized industries, and more than doubling membership.

Finally, as documented in Sanford Jacoby's (1985) excellent book, there were significant changes in the employment practices of most firms during this period, most of them positive from the point of view of the worker. These included a reduction of the authority of the foreman, stronger guarantees of employment stability, formalized grievance procedures—and higher wages.

How do all of these labor market trends fit together? A critical element in the story is surely the political environment. The landslide election of President Roosevelt was a signal of changing public attitudes about government intervention in the economy. Along with the monetary and financial reform mentioned above, the New Deal also brought substantial labor market legislation. The direct effect of the new laws was actually rather uneven: The NIRA codes, for example, had a large effect on real wages in a few industries, such as leather and textiles, but little impact in others. Similarly, the direct effects of government-assisted unionization differed across industries. However, the indirect effect of President Roosevelt's program was to convince employers that they would have to change employment practices in a way perceived to be more favorable to labor, or else risk the possibility that legislation or legislation-supported unions would enforce even more radical changes.

This political change was an important factor in each of the labor market trends mentioned above. For example, hours legislation and union agreements helped to institutionalize the shorter workweeks originally put in effect by firms. As is discussed in Bernanke (1986), to the extent that workers have a reservation level of weekly earnings (as opposed to a reservation hourly wage), falling workweeks will induce upward pressure on average hourly earnings. Similarly, government policies supported the trend to unionization and helped "convince" employers that they should adopt more liberal labor policies. Both of these trends led to higher real wages.

Perhaps the most interesting issue, though, has to do with why productivity grew during the decade, despite the weakness in capital investment. One hypothesis is that the conventional rhetoric of the time, which said that higher wages and better treatment of labor would improve productivity, was actually correct. In this view, government action and the union threat may have induced employers, grudgingly, to adopt a profitable course; namely, for the first time on a widespread basis, to pay "efficiency wages." The view that the New Deal represents a transition period to an efficiency wage regime may help explain not only the real wage growth of the period, but the increase in productivity as well.

IV. Conclusion

The New Deal era, 1933–41, was a period of general economic growth, set back only by the 1937–38 recession. This economic growth occurred simultaneously with a real wage "push" engineered in part by the government and the unions. As we normally think of higher real wages as depressing aggregate supply, how can these two developments be consistent? If the "transition to efficiency wage" hypothesis is true, part of the answer may be that the higher wages to some extent "paid for themselves" through increased productivity of labor. Probably more important, though, is the observation that with imperfectly competitive product markets, output depends on aggregate demand as well as the real wage. Maybe Herbert Hoover and Henry Ford were right: Higher real wages may have paid for themselves in the broader sense that their positive effect on aggregate demand compensated for their tendency to raise costs.[6]

What about Europe? There are some parallels with the 1930s, notably the irrelevance of the unemployment level to the determination of inflation and the political aspects of real wage growth. But there are also large enough differences to make inferences about policy treacherous. In particular, President Roosevelt's inflationary policies beginning in 1933 probably helped increase employment because they were part of a financial rehabilitation program, and because it was important to reverse the deflationary expectations of the previous years; it does not necessarily follow that inflating would help Europe today. Similarly, the real wage increases of the New Deal may not have hurt recovery, because of their positive effects on productivity and aggregate demand. But again, we certainly would not want to conclude that higher real wages in Europe would be beneficial.

References

Bernanke, Ben S., "Employment, Hours, and Earnings in the Depression: An Analysis of Eight Manufacturing Industries," *American Economic Review*, March 1986, 76, 82–109.

---

[6] The aggregate demand argument does not require the assumption (which is inconsistent with lifecycle theory) that workers have systematically higher marginal propensities to consume. The existence of capital market restrictions on borrowing against future labor income, plus the assumption that workers perceived their incomes in the depression as being below their permanent incomes, is sufficient.

De Long, J. Bradford and Summers, Lawrence H., "Is Increased Price Flexibility Stabilizing?," *American Economic Review*, December 1986, 76, 1031–44.

Gordon, Robert J., "Back to the Future: European Unemployment Today Viewed from America in 1939," *Brookings Papers on Economic Activity*, 1:1988, 271–304.

Jacoby, Sanford M., *Employing Bureaucracy: Managers, Unions, and the Transformation of Work in American Industry, 1900–1945*, New York: Columbia University Press, 1985.

Lebergott, Stanley, *Manpower in Economic Growth: The American Record Since 1800*, New York: McGraw-Hill, 1964.

National Industrial Conference Board, *The New Monetary System of the United States*, New York, 1934.

Temin, Peter and Wigmore, Barrie A., "The End of One Big Deflation," Working Paper No. 503, MIT, October 1988.

Eight

Procyclical Labor Productivity and Competing Theories of the Business Cycle: Some Evidence from Interwar U.S. Manufacturing Industries

WITH MARTIN PARKINSON

I. Introduction

Since its discovery by Hultgren (1960), the procyclical behavior of average labor productivity, also known as short-run increasing returns to labor (SRIRL), has achieved the status of a basic stylized fact of macroeconomics. The ubiquitous nature of procyclical productivity has been confirmed by studies at levels of aggregation ranging from the firm to the national economy, and for a variety of countries and sample periods.

Much of the original research on procyclical productivity was undertaken during the 1960s and early 1970s, contributions being made by Brechling (1965), Kuh (1965), Ball and St. Cyr (1966), Solow (1968), Fair (1969), and Sims (1974), among others. More recently, attention has been refocused on SRIRL in the context of research on real business cycles (Prescott 1986*b*) and by the work of Fay and Medoff (1985), Hall (1987, 1988*a*, 1988*b*), Rotemberg and Summers (1988), and Chirinko (1989). The reason for the renewed interest in SRIRL is that, as has become increasingly clear, the choice of explanation of SRIRL effectively entails a choice among some leading contemporary models of the business cycle.

Three major explanations for SRIRL have been advanced: technology shocks, true increasing returns, and labor hoarding. Each explanation is closely associated with a competing model of the cycle.

The *technology shocks* explanation is favored by the competitive real business cycle approach, as exposited by Prescott (1986*b*). In the real business cycle model, changes in technology are the driving force behind cyclical fluctuations, and intertemporal substitution in labor supply is a key propaga-

Reprinted with permission from *Journal of Political Economy*, vol. 99, no. 31 (1991). Copyright © 1991 by The University of Chicago. All rights reserved.

We thank the referee for useful comments. Financial support from, respectively, the National Science Foundation and the Australian Treasury is gratefully acknowledged. Views expressed are our own and should not be attributed to the Treasury.

tion mechanism. Labor productivity is procyclical in the real business cycle model, despite the assumption of diminishing marginal returns to labor input, because booms are periods in which technological conditions are particularly favorable. Labor input rises in booms to take advantage of this opportunity to be especially productive and thus to earn a real wage that is temporarily high.

The idea that SRIRL reflects *true increasing returns* in the production function (for a fixed level of technology) has been advocated by Hall (references noted above). Supporting evidence has been presented by Ramey (1987), Chirinko (1989), and others. Thus Hall characterizes business cycles as movements along a fixed production function, while Prescott argues that the production function itself shifts over the cycle. Genuine increasing returns are the essential component of models that characterize the cycle as a period of optimal bunching of production. Increasing returns usually imply a noncompetitive industry market structure, although this is not necessarily the case if the increasing returns are external to the firm (Murphy, Shleifer, and Vishny 1989). We shall focus below on the case in which the increasing returns are internal to the firm but shall comment briefly on the external increasing returns case.

The traditional explanation for SRIRL is *labor hoarding*, arising from the quasi fixity of labor (Becker 1962; Oi 1962; Rosen 1968). This is the explanation usually embraced by Keynesians. The idea is that, if the labor force cannot be costlessly adjusted in the short run, it may pay firms to smooth labor input over the cycle (i.e., "hoard" labor in downturns).[1] With hoarded labor, firms utilize labor more intensively in booms than in recessions; this variable utilization over the cycle creates the illusion of increasing returns.[2] The labor hoarding explanation is attractive to Keynesians because it allows the observation of SRIRL to be reconciled with the Keynesian view that most cycles are demand driven, without abandoning the assumption of diminishing returns in the production function. An additional connection between labor hoarding and the Keynesian approach has recently been provided by Rotemberg and Summers (1988), who show that labor hoarding may in some cases be a consequence of price rigidity.

Because the competing theories' explanations for SRIRL are so clearly differentiated and because choosing among these theories is of such great

---

[1] An alternative to costly adjustment as a motivation for labor hoarding is that there is some fixed quantity of "overhead labor," whose presence is necessary for operation of the production process. If some overhead labor is counted with production workers, what appears to be SRIRL may be observed in the data even though true marginal costs are constant or increasing. We emphasize the costly adjustment motive in this paper, but we return to the issue of overhead labor in the conclusion.

[2] It should be noted that labor hoarding does not necessarily imply procyclical productivity. Additional necessary conditions are that the intensity of labor utilization can be varied and that the firm finds it profitable in the short run to substitute increases (decreases) in the rate of labor utilization for increases (decreases) in measured employment or hours of work.

practical importance, evidence from any source on the reason we observe SRIRL should be welcome. In this paper we study the SRIRL phenomenon in a sample of U.S. manufacturing industries drawn from the interwar period (1923–39). This is a period, obviously, of extreme cyclical variation. More important, there is a potential identifying restriction that we are much more willing to apply to this period than to the postwar era; specifically, we believe that it is quite unlikely that the preponderance of interwar cyclical variation (at least during the 1930s) was due to technological shocks to the production functions of individual manufacturing industries. Under this restriction, if the real business cycle theory is true, SRIRL should have been much less pronounced in the Depression era than in the postwar era. We find, on the contrary, that labor productivity was, if anything, more procyclical before World War II than after. In our view, and as is explained in more detail below, this constitutes a strong rejection of the technological shock theory of SRIRL and, consequently, of the real business cycle approach.

This leaves two potential explanations of SRIRL in the interwar data, true increasing returns and labor hoarding. We propose two tests for distinguishing between these explanations. Both tests are based on the idea that, if there are true increasing returns (and if nonlabor inputs are held fixed), current industry output and current industry labor input should be "sufficient statistics" for each other; that is, given current industry output, no other variable should help predict the contemporaneous level of industry labor input, and vice versa. Using these tests, we can reject pure increasing returns in favor of labor hoarding for some of the industries in our sample but not others. We are thus unable to draw any sweeping conclusions about the relative importance of increasing returns and labor hoarding in interwar industry; it may simply be the case that both of these factors help explain the observation of interwar SRIRL.

The rest of the paper is organized as follows: Section II describes a simple common framework for thinking about alternative explanations of short-run increasing returns to labor. Section III briefly describes the interwar data set. That SRIRL holds for the interwar period is documented in Section IV. Section V discusses the implications of this finding for the technological shocks hypothesis, and Section VI takes up increasing returns and labor hoarding. Section VII presents conclusions.

II. Alternative Explanations for SRIRL: A Common Framework

Recent work on SRIRL for the most part has been couched in terms of explaining the behavior of the "Solow residual," or output minus factor-share-weighted inputs. However, only under the competitive real business cycle approach does the Solow residual have a straight-forward economic interpretation (as a measure of disembodied technical progress); under the alternative approaches, the Solow residual does not correspond to any fundamental economic concept. We find it clearer, therefore, to avoid the Solow residual altogether and to use the more primitive analytical framework of the production function itself. We show in this section that the alternative explanations of SRIRL can be expressed in simple econometric terms as alternative interpretations of an estimated regression coefficient in a production equation.

Consider the Cobb-Douglas production function

$$Q_t = A_t K_t^\alpha N_t^\beta, \tag{1}$$

where Q is value-added production,[3] A is an indicator of Hicks-neutral technical progress, and K and N are measures of capital and labor input. We make no presumption of constant returns to scale. If there is a distinction between the ex ante and ex post production functions, as in the "putty-clay" model, equation (1) is the ex post production function.

Direct estimation of (1) would be complicated by nonlinearity and the likelihood of nonstationarity; we therefore take logs and difference. Equation (1) becomes

$$q_t = \alpha k_t + \beta n_t + \epsilon_t, \tag{2}$$

where lowercase letters denote log differences and $\epsilon = \Delta \ln A$. In the estimation below we add a constant term to (2) so that the mean of ϵ is zero.

Under competition and constant returns, the parameter β would equal labor's share. However, ordinary least squares (OLS) estimates of (2) on time-series data typically yield estimated values of β much larger than labor's share. Indeed, estimates of β frequently equal 1.0 or greater, implying that the rate of growth of average labor productivity, $q - n$, is procyclical (increasing in n). This is the SRIRL puzzle.

The alternative explanations of SRIRL given in the Introduction can be interpreted as explanations of why the OLS estimate of β in equation (2) exceeds the observed income share received by labor.

1. According to the competitive real business cycle theory, the true value of β equals labor's share. However, OLS estimates of β are biased upward because of a positive correlation between the independent variable n and the error term ϵ in (2). This correlation arises because when productivity growth is temporarily high (ϵ is large), it is optimal also to increase labor input (n is high). More formally, the bias of the OLS estimate is $\rho_{n\epsilon}\sigma_\epsilon/\sigma_n$, where $\rho_{n\epsilon}$ is the correlation of n and ϵ, and σ_n and σ_ϵ are their standard deviations. If intertemporal substitution in labor supply causes $\rho_{n\epsilon}$ to be positive, the bias term will be positive.

---

[3] In our empirical application we have series on only total physical output, not value added. We must therefore assume that, while capital and labor may be substitutable for each other, the capital-labor aggregate is used in fixed proportions with materials.

2. Under an increasing returns approach and with no significant technological shocks, the OLS estimate of β is a correct estimate of the technological parameter β in equation (2).[4] In this view, the estimate of β exceeds
one because there are true increasing returns. With a monopolistic or a
monopolistically competitive market structure, labor's share in this case is
$\beta(1 - \theta) < \beta$, where $\theta(0 < \theta < 1)$ is the inverse elasticity of the demand
for the firm's output.

3. With labor hoarding, (2) is misspecified in that an unobserved factor of
production, labor effort or labor utilization, is omitted from the right side of
the equation. In this approach, the true production function is not (2) but

$$q_t = \alpha k_t + \beta n_t + \delta e_t + \epsilon_t, \tag{3}$$

where e is the growth rate of labor effort.[5] Omission of the effort terms
implies that the expected value of the OLS estimate of β will be $\beta + \delta\gamma$,
where γ is the coefficient on n from the regression of e on k and n. Presumably $\delta > 0$ (more effort leads to more output) and $\gamma > 0$ (if firms respond to
more demand both by requiring more effort in the short run and by using
more measured labor input, then growth in effort and measured labor input
will be positively correlated). Therefore, the bias term is positive, and the
estimated value of β will exceed the true value.

Labor's share when there is labor hoarding will depend in a complicated
way on factors such as worker's compensation for effort, the rate of employment adjustment, and market structure; but again labor's share should normally be below the estimated value of β.

The goal of this paper is to try to distinguish among these three interpretations of the SRIRL finding, using data from the interwar period. We
briefly discuss these data before turning to the analysis.

III. Data

Most studies of SRIRL have used postwar data (a notable exception is the
original Hultgren [1960] paper; see also Bernanke and Powell [1986]). In
this paper, we examine relatively disaggregated interwar data.

---

[4] Strictly speaking, the variance of the productivity shock ϵ cannot be zero since then the
estimated production function (2) would have to fit the data perfectly. Since we do not expect
to see a perfect fit, we must allow for $\text{var}(\epsilon) > 0$; ϵ must then be interpreted as measurement
error or as unpredictable production variations uncorrelated with employment in order for the
OLS estimate of β to be unbiased. Alternatively, if $\text{var}(\epsilon)$ is small relative to the variance of
product demand and labor supply shocks, which also affect equilibrium employment, the OLS
estimate of β will be only slightly biased.

[5] An alternative interpretation of e is that it is the weighted change in utilization of both
capital and labor.

The data we use are quarterly (aggregated up from monthly),[6] are roughly at the level of the two-digit manufacturing industry, and cover the period 1923:1–1939:4. (Most of the data are not available before 1923; after 1939, war production seriously affected the composition of industrial outputs, rendering questionable the assumption that the same production function applied.) Industry-level data rather than measures for total manufacturing were used to reduce aggregation bias and to allow us to avoid those industries whose production indices are based on scaled-up input measures rather than on direct measures of physical output. We carried out all analyses for both a 1924–39 sample period (the first year of data is reserved to allow for differencing and lags) and a 1929–39 sample period (in order to isolate the experience of the Depression).

Data for the whole 1923–39 sample were found for the following eight industries, which are similar to those used by Bernanke (1986): (1) iron and steel and their products; (2) lumber and allied products; (3) automobiles; (4) petroleum refining; (5) textiles and their products; (6) leather and its products; (7) rubber and allied products; and (8) pulp, paper, and allied products. We also used data for two additional industries for the period 1932–39: (9) stone, clay, and glass and their products and (10) nonferrous metals and products.

Collectively, these 10 industries accounted for about one-fifth of interwar manufacturing employment. Additional information about these industries is presented in table 1.

The basic data in this study refer to output and labor input in each industry; other types of data used are described below at the relevant points. Output was measured by components of the Federal Reserve index of industrial production. Labor input in each industry is measured as total hours of work (employment times average weekly hours). The principal source for data on employment and hours is the Bureau of Labor Statistics (BLS),[7] supplemented by the *Monthly Labor Review* and the National Industrial Conference Board data provided in Beney (1936). All data used in this paper are available on request. Further details on the sources of the data and adjustments made appear in Parkinson (1990), also available on request.

---

[6] We temporally aggregated in the hope that it would reduce the effects of possible measurement error or temporal misalignments of data series from different sources. None of our results depends in any crucial way on this aggregation.

[7] See in particular BLS bulletin no. 610, "Revised Indexes of Factory Employment and Payrolls, 1919–1933" (February 1935) and updates in BLS mimeos "Revised Index Numbers of Factory Employment and Pay Rolls" (September 1938) and "Index Numbers of Factory Employment and Pay Rolls" (May 1940).

Table 1

Labor's Share, Industry Size, Average Employment, and Concentration Ratios for Sample Industries in 1935

Industry	Labor's Share	Number of Establishments	Average Employment*	Concentration Ratio†
Steel	.477	8,105	108	.394
Lumber	.504	16,127	36	.109
Autos	.486	946	410	.739
Petroleum	.307	395	196	.361
Textiles	.542	22,847	74	.136
Leather	.528	3,506	89	.232
Rubber	.433	466	246	.619
Pulp	.378	779	163	.167
Stone, clay, glass	.381	5,846	41	.376
Nonferrous metals	.404	5,411	40	.385

*Yearly average employment of wage earners; excludes salaried personnel and proprietors. These data and the data on labor's share and the number of establishments are taken from the 1937 and/or 1939 *Biennial Census of Manufactures*.

†Four-firm concentration ratio, defined as the proportion of industry value added attributable to the four largest (by value added) firms in the industry. These ratios were calculated from data contained in *The Structure of the American Economy*, U.S. National Resources Committee (1939).

IV. SRIRL in the Interwar Period

In this section we document the existence of SRIRL in our sample of interwar U.S. manufacturing industries.

Estimation of equation (2) requires data on output and on capital and labor inputs for each industry. As described in Section III, data on output and labor input are available on a monthly basis; we have aggregated them up to quarterly. Capital stock data, however, are much harder to come by.

We constructed industry capital stock series using data from Creamer, Dobrovolsky, and Borenstein (1960) and Dewhurst et al. (1955). Our procedure was to combine benchmark industry capital stock estimates, available for 1929 and 1937, with annual gross investment figures to obtain annual industry capital stocks; quarterly estimates were then made by interpolation. Unfortunately, however, estimation of the log-differenced production function (2) using these constructed series yielded estimates of the coefficient on the capital stock that were never statistically significant and often had the wrong sign. Presumably this reflected the low quality of the capital stock data, especially at higher frequencies. Alternatively, if there was persistent excess capacity throughout the period, it is possible that the size of industry capital stocks was (on the margin) irrelevant to industry production rates. In any case, in subsequent regressions we excluded the capital stock series, allowing any trend growth in capital to be picked up by the industry-specific constant terms.[8] It is important to note that the estimated coefficients on labor input were essentially the same with or without inclusion of the capital series.[9]

Results from OLS regressions of the growth rate of industry output on the growth rate of industry labor input and a constant (and with capital input excluded) are shown in table 2. (Seasonal dummies were also included here and in subsequent regressions.) Column 1 of the table shows the estimated coefficient on labor input (β) for the whole sample period (1924:1–1939:4). Column 2 shows the estimated coefficient when the sample period is restricted to the Depression period (1929:1–1939:4). For comparison, column 5 shows the estimated labor input coefficient for the same industries (or for as close a match as the data permitted) over the postwar period. (Ignore cols. 3 and 4 for now.) As in the case of the interwar industries, output for the postwar industries is measured by the Federal Reserve industrial production index, and labor inputs come from the BLS; sample periods are given in the notes to the table. The reported standard errors were calculated using the method suggested by Wooldridge (1989) and are robust to heteroskedasticity and serial correlation.[10] Conventional OLS standard errors (not reported) were generally similar to the robust standard errors; in the few cases in which they were different, the qualitative conclusions were not affected.

The principal message of table 2 is that SRIRL was a common feature in the interwar period.[11] Of the 10 industries in the sample, only two (petroleum refining and leather) have estimated values of β less than one. For each of the eight industries with estimated values of β greater than one, the difference between the estimated β and labor's share in value added, shown in table 1, is highly statistically significant. The finding of interwar SRIRL does not depend on the inclusion or exclusion of the 1920s: The estimates from the full interwar sample and from the 1929–39 subsample are quite close.

Another striking feature of table 2 is the similarity of the estimates be-

---

[8] Gross investment rates were of course very low during the Depression, so the trend in the capital stock was probably negative for most industries.

[9] At the suggestion of the referee, we also repeated our analyses using growth in a combined capital-labor aggregate, with capital and labor weighted by 1935 industry factor shares, in place of growth in labor input. The coefficients on labor input implied by this alternative procedure were in all cases virtually identical to those reported here.

[10] Wooldridge's method is similar in spirit to those suggested earlier by White (1984) and others; its principal advantage is computational simplicity.

[11] A similar result was found by Bernanke and Powell (1986).

Table 2
Estimates of the Labor Input Coefficient

| Industry | Ordinary Least Squares | | Instrumental Variables | | Postwar Ordinary Least Squares, 1955–88 |
	1924–39 (1)	1929–39 (2)	1924–39 (3)	1929–39 (4)	(5)
Steel	1.53 (.17)	1.51 (.17)	1.48 (.19)	1.45 (.18)	1.66 (.10)
Lumber	1.11 (.04)	1.07 (.05)	1.06 (.04)	1.01 (.04)	.86 (.05)
Autos	1.26 (.15)	1.21 (.15)	1.33 (.21)	1.20 (.21)	1.05 (.06)
Petroleum*	.36 (.10)	.42 (.07)	.96 (.40)	.80 (.38)	−.04 (.03)
Textiles	1.03 (.12)	1.09 (.17)	1.34 (.28)	1.12 (.36)	1.03 (.13)
Leather	.61 (.10)	.58 (.08)	.69 (.08)	.71 (.08)	.83 (.03)
Rubber	1.21 (.06)	1.21 (.07)	1.30 (.10)	1.27 (.10)	.98 (.06)
Pulp	1.10 (.10)	1.11 (.10)	1.04 (.09)	.99 (.09)	1.04 (.38)
Stone, clay, glass	—	1.11 (.07)	—	.99 (.11)	.94 (.10)
Nonferrous metals	—	1.38 (.03)	—	1.18 (.10)	1.23 (.07)

Note: Data are quarterly. Standard errors are in parentheses. All regressions include a constant and three seasonal dummy variables. The sample periods for the interwar regressions are 1924:1–1939:4 for cols. 1 and 3 and 1929:1–1939:4 for cols. 2 and 4 (1933:1–1939: 4 for stone, clay, and galss and nonferrous metals). The sample period for the postwar regression, col. 5, is 1958:2–1988:4 for pulp). The instruments for the instrumental variables regessions are the current value and one lagged value of the log differences of real government expenditure, the currency/deposit ratio, and real deposits of failed banks.

*Using monthly data for the postwar regession results in a cofficient of .07 with a standard error of .04. Using quarterly data and adding dummy variables for each oil shock, for the 1969 and 1980 oil industry strikes and the post-1964 change in the trend of industry employment, and allowing for changes in the seasonal pattern after each shock change this coefficient to −.06 with a standard error of .04.

tween the interwar and postwar sample periods. Despite obvious differences in the economic environments of the two periods, important product and process innovations, and an imperfect match in industry definitions, the correlation between the full interwar and postwar estimates of industry β's is .90; the rank correlation is .82. It should also be noted that the unweighted mean of the interwar β's is slightly higher than that of the postwar era, 1.07 to 0.96.

We conclude overall that there is strong evidence for SRIRL in interwar manufacturing data and that there is little difference in this regard between the Depression decade and the interwar sample as a whole, or between the interwar period and the postwar period.

V. The Technological Shocks Hypothesis

We now consider how our findings for the interwar period bear on the three alternative explanations for the general SRIRL phenomenon outlined in Section II, beginning with the technological shocks hypothesis.

We would argue that the finding of SRIRL (estimated $\beta > 1$) in the interwar period is a serious problem for the technological shocks explanation of SRIRL, as advocated by the real business cycle school. Our reasoning is as follows: No one, including the real business cycle school, seriously maintains that the Great Depression was caused primarily by technological shocks to industry production functions.[12] To the extent that the large fluctuations in output and employment that occurred were due to other types of shocks (e.g., shocks to aggregate demand or to factor supplies), under the maintained real business cycle assumptions, SRIRL should not have been manifest in the Depression period. Instead, diminishing returns to labor should have been observed. But as we have seen, SRIRL was at least as strong in the interwar period as in the postwar period, contradicting this basic real business cycle prediction.

This point can be restated in terms of the discussion of Section II. Recall that, under the technological shocks hypothesis, the bias in the estimate of β is proportional to σ_ϵ/σ_n, where σ_ϵ and σ_n are the standard deviations of the growth rates of technology and labor input, respectively.[13] We can observe directly from the data that the standard deviation of quarterly labor input growth σ_n was on the order of two to three times larger in the inter-

---

[12] See, e.g., Prescott (1986a, p. 29). Bernstein (1987) suggests that, while the interwar period as a whole was characterized by considerable and widespread innovative activity, technical change in the Depression decade itself was restricted to a small number of industries. Parkinson (1990) reviews the available material on technical change in the specific industries studied here and concludes that while innovations certainly occurred during the Depression, their scope was relatively modest. This is consistent with the low rate of gross investment during the 1930s. In any case, *negative* technological shocks would be needed to explain the sharp falls in output and employment that occurred during the Depression.

[13] The factor of proportionality is $\rho_{n\epsilon}$, the correlation of labor supply response to technology shocks. The magnitude of this correlation depends on the willingness of workers to substitute intertemporally and on the expected persistence of productivity shocks, with less persistent shocks causing a stronger response. Although we cannot say what workers believed ex ante, the Depression of course turned out to be an extremely persistent shock, so that if anything $\rho_{n\epsilon}$ would make it even more difficult for the technology shocks hypothesis to explain the presence of SRIRL in the interwar data.

war data than in the postwar data, depending on the industry. Thus, under the assumption that the true β's were similar in the two eras (and labor shares in fact have not changed very much), the technological shocks hypothesis can explain the finding of interwar SRIRL only by asserting that the standard deviation of technological change σ_ϵ also was two to three times larger in the interwar data than in the postwar data. This amounts to explaining the Depression by a large exogenous increase in technological variability, which we believe is historically implausible.

A possible real business cycle rebuttal is that many of the real shocks that contributed to the Depression—including shocks to the payments and credit systems, political instability in Europe, tariff wars, falling agricultural prices, sectoral "imbalances" caused by World War I, and New Deal policies affecting price and wage setting—might be construed broadly as "productivity shocks," if not technological shocks in the literal sense. Under this interpretation, an explanation of interwar SRIRL can be offered that is in the spirit of the real business cycle explanation for postwar SRIRL, namely, that other types of real shocks played the role of more narrowly defined technological shocks in the interwar period.

To be clear, we should emphasize that we do not deny that real shocks were important for the Depression (obviously they were) or even that it might be possible to construct an equilibrium model that explains the Depression as a response to those shocks. The issue here is instead whether the real shocks that occurred during the Depression can explain the observation of SRIRL in a way consistent with the real business cycle approach. *To do so, it would be necessary for these shocks to have had their effects primarily by changing the amount of industry outputs producible by given levels of capital and labor inputs; that is, they would have to have been "ϵ-like" shocks, where ϵ is the error term in (2).* Again, to the extent that real shocks had their effects in other ways—by changing labor supply, the structure of product or labor markets, or the expected marginal productivity of new capital goods, for example—they should have induced countercyclical rather than procyclical variation in labor productivity.[14] In terms of the econometric discussion, real shocks that raise σ_n but not σ_ϵ will not lead us to find SRIRL in the data.

Might the real shocks that occurred during the 1930s have been the functional equivalents of technological shocks to industry production functions? One can think of some possible stories: For example, it might be conjectured that trade restrictions affected the cost or availability of intermediate

---

[14] In particular, some existing classical explanations of the Depression would not in general be consistent with both diminishing returns and the observation of SRIRL. Consider, e.g., the explanation of Lucas and Rapping (1969), which argues that workers misperceived the real wage and thus reduced labor supply. Under maintained real business cycle assumptions, this induced movement *back along* the diminishing returns production function should have led to countercyclical labor productivity rather than procyclical productivity as observed.

inputs; substitution away from intermediate inputs toward labor would show up as negative productivity shocks in our empirical analysis, given that we must measure output as total production rather than as value added. However, while this is a theoretical possibility, the direct evidence for a disruptive effect of trade restrictions is weak: In particular, the Smoot-Hawley tariff of 1930 primarily affected imports of agricultural goods and finished manufactures, not intermediates (Eichengreen 1986). Indeed, because of the worldwide glut of raw materials and commodities, the real prices of most imported intermediates (inclusive of tariffs) fell during the Depression.

Another potential source of not strictly technological productivity shocks is the breakdown in the early 1930s of the monetary and financial system, which many writers on the Depression have argued was important. In principle, money and credit can be thought of as substitutes for other inputs, implying that disturbances to the payments and credit mechanisms might reduce labor productivity.[15] However, Bernanke (1983), citing Lutz (1945), argued that in the United States most larger firms (which would make up an important share of output and employment in our sample) entered the 1930s with more than sufficient cash and liquid reserves to finance working capital needs;[16] a similar conclusion was reached by Hunter (1982). On this basis, Bernanke concluded that, at least in the United States, financial effects must have worked to a greater extent by reducing aggregate demand, including the demand for new investment, rather than by affecting the quantity of output producible with given quantities of capital and labor inputs. To the degree that credit and monetary factors affected the demand for rather than the supply of current output, under the maintained real business cycle assumptions they should have induced diminishing rather than increasing returns to labor.

We conclude that it is unlikely that the economic shocks of the interwar period entered industry production functions in the way required by the broad version of the technological shocks hypothesis. But even if future research should identify shocks of this form, there is an additional problem for the "real but not strictly technological" shocks story. This problem is how to explain the high cross-sectional (across industry) correlation of the estimated β's between the interwar and postwar sample periods. To rationalize this similarity, it would have to be the case that the real shocks hitting individual industrial production functions in the interwar period accounted for about the same percentage of employment variation in each industry as genuine technological shocks hitting industrial production functions did in the postwar period. In other words, even though the shocks hitting produc-

---

[15] King and Plosser (1984) formalize this idea.

[16] Lutz's sample of large firms included the major firms in (among other industries) automobiles, iron and steel, building materials, chemicals, petroleum, and textiles, all of which overlap to some degree with industries used in our study.

tion functions in the interwar period (e.g., credit shocks) were presumably of a nature qualitatively different from the corresponding shocks in the post-war period, the real business cycle hypothesis requires that the bias term for each industry, $\rho_{n\epsilon}\sigma_\epsilon/\sigma_n$, was nevertheless approximately the same before and after the war. This would be extremely coincidental.

Our discussion so far has concerned the interpretation of OLS estimates of industry production functions. A more direct way to test the technological shocks hypothesis is to reestimate the production functions using instrumental variables. If our instruments are correlated with industry employment and output but uncorrelated with industry technological shocks, and if the technological shocks hypothesis is true, then instrumental variables estimates of the labor input coefficient β should be much lower (closer to labor's share) than the OLS estimates.

Instrumental variables estimates of β for each industry for the 1924–39 and 1929–39 sample periods are reported in table 2, columns 3 and 4. The instruments used to obtain the reported estimates were the current values and one lag each of real government expenditure, the currency/deposit ratio, and the real deposits of failed banks, all in log differences.[17] Our choice of these variables is consistent with what we take to be the dominant view among economic historians, that policy mistakes—including mismanagement of the gold standard, failure to defend the banking system and the money supply, and procyclical fiscal policy—were major causes of the Great Depression in the United States. These instruments surely are not strongly exogenous, but they plausibly have very weak contemporaneous correlation with shocks to industrial production functions. Robust standard errors calculated by the method of Wooldridge (1989) are reported; again, these were generally quite similar to the conventional standard errors.

As can be seen from table 2, the instrumental variables estimates of β differ relatively little from the OLS estimates.[18] This was also true when both broader and narrower instrument sets were used, as an earlier version of the paper reported. Indeed, Hausman specification tests comparing the OLS and instrumental variables estimates almost never can reject the hypothesis that the OLS regressions are not misspecified; for the instrumental variables estimates reported in table 2, no misspecification could be rejected at the 10 percent level only for the petroleum refining industry, which was

[17] Data sources for instrumental variables are as follows: Government spending data come from Firestone (1960). The currency/deposit ratio is calculated from Friedman and Schwartz (1963). Deposits of failed banks come from the *Federal Reserve Bulletin* and are deflated by the consumer price index due to Sayre (1948).

[18] Indeed in a number of industries the instrumental variables estimates are larger than the OLS estimates. This contradicts the implication of the technology shocks hypothesis that the OLS bias should be positive, suggesting instead the presence of some factor such as classical measurement error. (We thank Jerry Hausman for pointing this out to us.)

not one of the eight SRIRL industries. Once again, we find little support for the technological shocks hypothesis in the interwar data.[19]

VI. Increasing Returns versus Labor Hoarding

If we put aside technological shocks as an explanation for SRIRL, we are still left with the two possibilities of increasing returns and labor hoarding. In trying to discriminate between these explanations, we relied on the observation that, if the increasing returns hypothesis is true, then the production function relationship (2) is well specified; but if the labor hoarding view is true, equation (2) suffers from an omitted variable problem (compare eqq. [2] and [3]) since it ignores the rate of labor utilization. This suggests testing the increasing returns hypothesis against the labor hoarding alternative by checking whether variables that are "fundamentally" extraneous, but that might be correlated with utilization rates, can be statistically excluded from estimated production functions.

As a first test of this type, for each industry we regressed output growth on labor input growth, a constant, seasonal dummies, and a set of aggregate business cycle indicators. As we have just argued, if there are true increasing returns, industry labor input should be a "sufficient statistic" for industry output, and the cyclical indicators should not appear in the production function.[20] On the other hand, if there is labor hoarding and the cyclical indicators are sufficiently correlated with the omitted utilization term, the cyclical indicators will enter the estimated production function significantly. Further, to the extent that the cyclical indicators are good proxies for utilization rates, the estimated coefficients on labor input should be closer to the true production function coefficients (thus lower in magnitude, presumably) when the cyclical indicators are included.

There are several reasons to think that cyclical indicators will be corre-

[19] Overfitting in the first stage, a potential pitfall in the comparison of OLS and instrumental variables estimates, is not an issue here: For the latter, first-stage R^2's were in an intermediate range (usually between .4 and .6), and no misspecification was found even when more minimal sets of instruments were used. Also, in this application, the Hausman test can be implemented by regressing labor input growth against the instruments, then entering the fitted and residual values from this regression separately in a regression for output growth; the Hausman test amounts to a test of whether the estimated coefficients on fitted and residual labor input growth in the second-stage output growth regression are the same. When we implemented the test this way, we found the estimated coefficients on fitted and residual labor input growth to be individually highly significant and very similar in magnitude, a result that would not be expected if overfitting were a problem.

[20] If one assumes that the increasing returns are internal to the industry (see below). This argument would also be complicated by the presence of aggregate productivity shocks. At this point we maintain the hypothesis that productivity shocks can be neglected in the interwar period.

lated with unobserved variations in utilization if labor hoarding is in fact important. For example, suppose that fluctuations in industry demand due to changes in cyclical conditions have different persistence properties than changes in industry demand due to idiosyncratic sectoral shocks. Then labor-hoarding firms will optimally respond to cyclical and sectoral demand shocks with different combinations of employment and utilization adjustment, and aggregate cyclical indicators will contain information about industry utilization rates. Another possibility is that an industry's costs of adjusting the labor force depend on aggregate labor market conditions; again, in general, this would tend to create a correlation between cyclical indicators and industry labor utilization rates.[21]

The results of this exercise are contained in table 3. Two sets of cyclical indicators were used. Set 1 (corresponding to col. 1 of the table) included current and once-lagged growth rates of real government spending, the currency/deposit ratio, and the deposits of failed banks; these are the same variables used as instruments in table 2. Set 2 (corresponding to col. 2) included all variables in set 1 plus current and once-lagged growth rates of the consumer price index and the Federal Reserve aggregate industrial production index. The numbers reported in the two columns of table 3 are the estimated labor input coefficients when cyclical indicators were included, with Wooldridge standard errors in parentheses. The regressions in which joint exclusion of the cyclical indicators from the production function can be rejected at conventional significance levels are indicated by asterisks.

The results depend on which set of cyclical indicators is used. With the narrower set, set 1, exclusion of the indicators from the production function is rejected in only three of the 10 industries (albeit at the 1 percent significance level in each case). Further, comparing the results from set 1 with those reported in table 2, column 1, we see that the estimated values of the labor input coefficient are not systematically lowered when the indicators in set 1 are included, as would be expected if there is labor hoarding and the cyclical indicators proxy for utilization rates. In contrast, with the broader set of indicators, set 2, the cyclical indicators cannot be excluded from the production function in six of the 10 industries (four at the 1 percent significance level); in each of these industries, the estimated value of the labor input coefficient is reduced, as the labor hoarding view predicts.[22]

The results seem moderately favorable to labor hoarding, at least when the broader set of cyclical indicators is used. However, a rationalization of the results of table 3 that does not rely on labor hoarding is that the appearance of cyclical indicators in industry production functions is evidence of

---

[21] We thank the referee for this second point.

[22] When only the contemporaneous growth rate of aggregate industrial production was added to the production function equation, it entered significantly in four industries.

Table 3
Estimates of the Labor Input Coefficient When Business Cycle Indicators Are Included

	Cyclical Indicators	
Industry	List 1 (1)	List 2 (2)
Steel	1.56**	.54**
	(.13)	(.30)
Lumber	1.16	1.04
	(.06)	(.13)
Autos	1.24	1.21
	(.20)	(.26)
Petroleum	.26	.06**
	(.13)	(.07)
Textiles	.95	.61**
	(.12)	(.16)
Leather	.58	.44
	(.12)	(.15)
Rubber	1.16**	1.12**
	(.06)	(.15)
Pulp	1.14	.78*
	(.13)	(.21)
Stone, clay, glass	1.21	.96
	(.06)	(.33)
Nonferrous metals	1.53**	.52*
	(.05)	(.47)

Note: Data are quarterly. Standard errors are in parentheses. All regressions include a constant and three seasonal dummy variables. The sample period for all regressions is 1924:1–1939:4 except for stone, clay, and glass and nonferrous metals, for which it is 1933:1–1939:4. Cyclical indicator list 1 includes the current value and one lagged value of the log differences of real government expenditure, the currency/deposit ratio, and real deposits of failed banks. Indicator list 2 is list 1 plus the current and first lagged values of the log differences of the consumer price index and aggregate manufcturing production.

*The null hypothesis that all cyclical indicators can be excluded is rejected at the 5 percent significance level.

**The null hypothesis is rejected at the 1 percent significance level.

external (to the industry) increasing returns. Indeed, this is how Caballero and Lyons (1989) interpreted a very similar set of results for postwar data. We find it hard to imagine external economies large enough to account for our results, however, and are thus more inclined to favor the labor hoarding interpretation of our estimates.

As a second test of increasing returns versus labor hoarding, we examined the dynamic response of industry labor input to changes in industry production by regressing current labor input growth on current and lagged output growth, a constant, and seasonal dummies. If there are costs of adjusting labor input, as required by our specification of the labor hoarding hypothesis, firms are likely to respond to changes in demand for output by increasing effort requirements in the short run and adjusting measured labor input only gradually.[23] In an industry without adjustment costs, in contrast, labor input should adjust immediately when there is a change in demand and should therefore depend only on current and not lagged output. This test is similar in spirit to the last one, in that again we are testing for labor hoarding by checking whether a variable that is "extraneous," but that is potentially informative about utilization rates, can be statistically excluded from the contemporaneous relationship between output and labor input; in this case the extraneous variable is lagged output growth.

For each industry and for the full interwar sample period, table 4 reports the estimated coefficients on current and lagged output growth, with Wooldridge standard errors in parentheses. Both OLS and instrumental variables estimates are presented, with the instruments in the latter regressions the same as those used in table 2. We interpret a significant estimated coefficient on lagged output in this regression as evidence for lagged adjustment of labor input and thus for labor hoarding. In the OLS estimates, five of the eight SRIRL industries have coefficients on lagged output that are economically and statistically significant; in the instrumental variables estimates, the statistical significance of one of these five industry coefficients becomes marginal. Since the data are quarterly, the estimates thus suggest a significant lag in employment adjustment for a majority of the SRIRL industries, which favors the labor hoarding hypothesis. On the other hand, the correlation between industries exhibiting lagged adjustment of labor input to output and those for which cyclical indicators enter the production function is not particularly good: Only three SRIRL industries (steel, rubber, and stone, clay, and glass) pass both tests for labor hoarding.

VII. Conclusion

This paper has documented that manufacturing industries in the interwar period exhibited short-run increasing returns to labor or procyclical labor productivity, to a degree very similar to what has been observed in the postwar period; indeed, the industry-by-industry pattern of SRIRL is very similar between the two periods. We have argued that this finding is troublesome for the technology shocks explanation of procyclical productivity

[23] Gradual adjustment would be expected if there was uncertainty about the permanence of the demand change or if costs of adjustment are convex.

Table 4
Elasticity of Total Labor Input Growth with Respect to Current and Lagged Output Growth

Industry	Ordinary Least Squares		Instrumental Variables	
	q_t	q_{t-1}	q_t	q_{t-1}
Steel	.46	.20	.48	.31
	(.02)	(.01)	(.04)	(.04)
Lumber	.74	.11	.85	.13
	(.07)	(.03)	(.06)	(.07)
Autos	.52	−.04	.69	.01
	(.06)	(.03)	(.10)	(.09)
Petroleum	.35	.13	.79	.21
	(.09)	(.13)	(.45)	(.24)
Textiles	.48	.03	.60	.10
	(.06)	(.08)	(.11)	(.09)
Leather	.78	.14	1.21	.37
	(.15)	(.10)	(.15)	(.19)
Rubber	.61	.20	.62	.31
	(.04)	(.06)	(.04)	(.04)
Pulp	.66	.16	.81	.18
	(.06)	(.05)	(.08)	(.08)
Stone, clay, glass	.73	.18	.80	.20
	(.03)	(.04)	(.05)	(.08)
Nonferrous metals	.63	−.01	.66	.02
	(.04)	(.04)	(.03)	(.10)

Note: Data are quarterly. Standard errors are in parentheses. All regressions include a constant and three seasonal dummy variables. The sample period for both regressions is 1924:1–1939:4 except for stone, clay, and glass and nonferrous metals, for which it is 1933:1–1939:4. The instruments used in the instrumental variables regression are the current value and one lagged value of the log differences of real government expenditure, the currency/deposit ratio, and real deposits of failed banks.

(and thus for the real business cycle hypothesis). To explain interwar SRIRL in a way consistent with the technology shocks hypothesis, it must be argued either that changes in industrial technologies caused the Depression or that the real (nontechnological) shocks of the 1930s just happened to generate a cross-sectional pattern of SRIRL very similar to that created by true technological shocks in the postwar period. We find these arguments to be implausible. Additional evidence against the technological shocks hypothesis is provided by instrumental variables estimates of industry production functions, which are very similar to the OLS estimates.

While we rule out technological shocks as an explanation for interwar

SRIRL, the distinction between industries for which labor hoarding is the key factor and those for which increasing returns are dominant is less clear-cut. We devised a set of simple statistical tests that treat increasing returns as the null hypothesis and labor hoarding as the alternative; unfortunately, these tests do not always reject increasing returns or always fail to reject it. It may be that both explanations have some validity, with weights that differ by industry.

It may also be that our inconclusive results are due to the use of a nonexhaustive set of explanations. An alternative explanation of SRIRL that we have not explicitly considered (primarily because it does not fit conveniently into our Cobb-Douglas organizing framework) is the overhead labor hypothesis. This hypothesis (which may be taken as an alternative rationalization of labor hoarding) assumes that there is a fixed group of workers whose presence is necessary for the firm to produce any positive amount of output. Over a range of production levels, which depends on the number of overhead workers and the rate at which returns to variable labor input diminish, the presence of overhead workers can create the illusion of increasing returns. Exploring this possibility is a useful direction for future research.[24]

References

Ball, Robert J., and St. Cyr, E. B. A. "Short Term Employment Functions in British Manufacturing Industry." Rev. Econ. Studies 33 (July 1966): 179–207.

Becker, Gary S. "Investment in Human Capital: A Theoretical Analysis." J.P.E. 70, no. 5, pt. 2 (October 1962): 9–49.

Beney, M. Ada. Wages, Hours, and Employment in the United States, 1914–1936. New York: Nat. Indus. Conf. Board, 1936.

Bernanke, Ben S. "Nonmonetary Effects of the Financial Crisis in Propagation of the Great Depression." A.E.R. 73 (June 1983): 257–76.

———. "Employment, Hours, and Earnings in the Depression: An Analysis of Eight Manufacturing Industries." A.E.R. 76 (March 1986): 82–109.

Bernanke, Ben S., and Powell, James L. "The Cyclical Behavior of Industrial Labor Markets: A Comparison of the Prewar and Postwar Eras." In The American Business Cycle: Continuity and Change, edited by Robert J. Gordon. Chicago: Univ. Chicago Press (for NBER), 1986.

Bernstein, Michael A. The Great Depression: Delayed Recovery and Economic Change in America, 1929–1939. New York: Cambridge Univ. Press, 1987.

[24] If overhead workers are primarily nonproduction workers, then the overhead labor hypothesis is consistent with the observation that the ratio of nonproduction to production workers rose during the Depression (U.S. Bureau of Labor Statistics 1957). However, a key issue is whether a significant amount of overhead labor is included in the category of production workers; if not, this hypothesis cannot explain the results of this paper since we measure labor input by production workers only.

Brechling, Frank P. R. "The Relationship between Output and Employment in British Manufacturing Industries." *Rev. Econ. Studies* 32 (July 1965): 187–216.

Caballero, Ricardo J., and Lyons, Richard K. "The Role of External Economies in U.S. Manufacturing." Manuscript. New York: Columbia Univ., 1989.

Chirinko, Robert S. "Non-Convexities, Labor Hoarding, Technology Shocks, and Procyclical Productivity: A Structural Econometric Approach." Manuscript. Chicago: Univ. Chicago, 1989.

Creamer, Daniel; Dobrovolsky, Sergei P.; and Borenstein, Israel. *Capital in Manufacturing and Mining: Its Formation and Financing.* Princeton, N.J.: Princeton Univ. Press (for NBER), 1960.

Dewhurst, J. Frederic, et al. *America's Needs and Resources: A New Survey.* New York: Twentieth Century Fund, 1947; 2d ed., 1955.

Eichengreen, Barry J. "The Political Economy of the Smoot-Hawley Tariff." Working Paper no. 2001. Cambridge, Mass.: NBER, August 1986.

Fair, Ray C. *The Short-Run Demand for Workers and Hours.* Amsterdam: North-Holland, 1969.

Fay, Jon A., and Medoff, James L. "Labor and Output over the Business Cycle: Some Direct Evidence." *A.E.R.* 75 (September 1985): 638–55.

Firestone, John M. *Federal Receipts and Expenditures during Business Cycles, 1879–1958.* Princeton, N.J.: Princeton Univ. Press (for NBER), 1960.

Friedman, Milton, and Schwartz, Anna J. *A Monetary History of the United States, 1867–1960.* Princeton, N.J.: Princeton Univ. Press (for NBER), 1963.

Hall, Robert E. "Productivity and the Business Cycle." *Carnegie-Rochester Conf. Ser. Public Policy* 27 (Autumn 1987): 421–44.

———. "Increasing Returns: Theory and Measurement with Industry Data." Manuscript. Stanford, Calif.: Stanford Univ., 1988 (*a*).

———. "The Relations between Price and Marginal Cost in U.S. Industry." *J.P.E.* 96 (October 1988): 921–47. (*b*).

Hultgren, Thor. *Changes in Labor Cost during Cycles in Production and Business.* Occasional Paper no. 74. New York: NBER, 1960.

Hunter, Helen Manning. "The Role of Business Liquidity during the Great Depression and Afterwards: Differences between Large and Small Firms." *J. Econ. Hist.* 42 (December 1982): 883–902.

King, Robert G., and Plosser, Charles I. "Money, Credit, and Prices in a Real Business Cycle." *A.E.R.* 74 (June 1984): 363–80.

Kuh, Edwin. "Cyclical and Secular Labor Productivity in United States Manufacturing." *Rev. Econ. Statis.* 47 (February 1965): 1–12.

Lucas, Robert E., Jr., and Rapping, Leonard A. "Real Wages, Employment, and Inflation." *J.P.E.* 77 (September/October 1969): 721–54.

Lutz, Friedrich A. *Corporate Cash Balances, 1914–43: Manufacturing and Trade.* New York: NBER, 1945.

Murphy, Kevin M.; Shleifer, Andrei; and Vishny, Robert W. "Building Blocks of Market Clearing Business Cycle Models." Working Paper no. 3004. Cambridge, Mass.: NBER, June 1989.

Oi, Walter Y. "Labor as a Quasi-fixed Factor." *J.P.E.* 70 (December 1962): 538–55.

Parkinson, Martin L. "Cyclical Aspects of Labor Market Behavior in the Macroeconomy." Ph.D. dissertation, Princeton Univ., 1990.

Prescott, Edward C. "Response to a Skeptic." *Fed. Reserve Bank Minneapolis Q. Rev.* 10 (Fall 1986): 28–33. (*a*).

———. "Theory ahead of Business Cycle Measurement." *Fed. Reserve Bank Minneapolis Q. Rev.* 10 (Fall 1986): 9–22. (*b*).

Ramey, Valerie. "Non-convex Costs and the Behavior of Inventories." Manuscript. La Jolla: Univ. California, San Diego, 1987.

Rosen, Sherwin. "Short-Run Employment Variation on Class-I Railroads in the U.S., 1947–1963." *Econometrica* 36 (July/October 1968): 511–29.

Rotemberg, Julio J., and Summers, Lawrence H. "Labor Hoarding, Inflexible Prices, and Procyclical Productivity." Working Paper no. 2591. Cambridge, Mass.: NBER, May 1988.

Sayre, Robert A. *Consumers' Prices, 1914–1948.* New York: Nat. Indus. Conf. Board, 1948.

Sims, Christopher A. "Output and Labor Input in Manufacturing." *Brookings Papers Econ. Activity*, no. 3 (1974), pp. 695–728.

Solow, Robert M. "Distribution in the Long and Short Run." In *The Distribution of National Income: Proceedings of a Conference Held by the International Economic Association*, edited by Jean Marchal and Bernard Ducros. New York: St. Martin's, 1968.

U.S. Bureau of Labor Statistics. "Nonproduction Workers in Factories, 1919–56." *Monthly Labor Rev.* 80 (April 1957): 435–40.

White, Halbert. *Asymptotic Theory for Econometricians.* Orlando, Fla.: Academic Press, 1984.

Wooldridge, Jeffrey M. "A Computationally Simple Heteroskedasticity and Serial Correlation Robust Standard Error for the Linear Regression Model." Manuscript. Cambridge: Massachusetts Inst. Tech., 1989.

Nine

Nominal Wage Stickiness and Aggregate Supply in the Great Depression

W I T H   K E V I N   C A R E Y

I. Introduction

The problem of explaining why the world economy collapsed in the 1930s has provided a difficult challenge to economists for more than six decades. Thus, it is particularly exciting that in the last few years there has developed something of a new consensus about the sources of the Great Depression. The distinctive claim of this emerging view—which is based on the research of a number of scholars and has been given an authoritative treatment by Eichengreen [1992]—is that the proximate cause of the world depression was a structurally flawed and poorly managed international gold standard.

A brief synopsis of the "gold standard theory" of the Depression is as follows. For a variety of reasons, including among others of desire of the Federal Reserve to curb the U.S. stock market boom, monetary policy in several major countries turned contractionary in the late 1920s—a contraction that was transmitted worldwide by the gold standard [Hamilton 1987, 1988; Temin 1989].[1] What was initially a mild deflationary process began to snowball when the banking and currency crises of 1931 instigated an international "scramble for gold." Sterilization of gold inflows by surplus countries, substitution of gold for foreign exchange reserves, and runs on commercial banks all led to increases in the gold backing of money and, consequently, to sharp, unintended declines in national money supplies

Reprinted with permission from The Quarterly Journal of Economics, vol. III, no. 3 (August 1996), 853–83. Copyright © by the President and Fellows of Harvard College and the Massachusetts Institute of Technology.

We thank Ilian Mihov for research assistance, and Olivier Blanchard, Bo Honore, James Powell, Peter Temin, Mark Watson, and two anonymous referees for comments. The National Science Foundation provided research support.

[1] In its emphasis on monetary factors the gold standard theory is complementary to the seminal analysis of Friedman and Schwartz [1963]. However, in its focus on the international finance and international political economy aspects of the story, the new view adds an important dimension that was not fully explored by Friedman and Schwartz.

[Bernanke 1995]. Monetary contractions in turn were strongly associated with falling prices, output, and employment. Effective international cooperation could in principle have permitted a simultaneous monetary expansion despite gold-standard constraints, but disputes over reparations and war debts and the insularity and inexperience of the Federal Reserve, among other factors, prevented this outcome. As a result, individual countries were able to escape the deflationary vortex only by unilaterally abandoning the gold standard and reestablishing domestic monetary stability, a process that dragged on in a halting and uncoordinated manner until France and the other Gold Bloc countries finally left gold in 1936 [Eichengreen and Sachs 1985].

The gold standard theory's main contribution is that it largely solves what might heuristically be called the "aggregate demand puzzle" of the Depression: namely, why did sharp declines in nominal aggregate demand take place nearly simultaneously in so many countries in the early 1930s? As we have noted, the theory's answer is that aggregate demand was depressed by a (largely unplanned) monetary contraction, which was transmitted around the world by the gold standard. However, the gold standard theory leaves unsolved the corresponding "aggregate supply puzzle," namely, why were the observed worldwide declines in nominal aggregate demand associated with such deep and persistent contractions in real output and employment? Or, in the language of contemporary macroeconomics, how can we explain what appears to be a massive and very long-lived instance of monetary nonneutrality?

Explicitly or implicitly, most proponents of the gold standard theory have invoked "sticky" nominal wages as the reason for the protracted real impact of the monetary contraction. However, in contrast to the attention paid to the determinants of aggregate demand, recent research on the Depression has included very little analysis of aggregate supply in general or the sticky-wage assumption in particular. In the introduction to his 1992 book, Eichengreen alludes to the issue as follows: "However devastating this initial disturbance [the deflationary shocks], one would think that at this point the self-equilibrating tendencies of the market would come into play. Wages and other costs should have fallen along with prices to limit the rise in unemployment and the decline in sales. They did so only modestly" [pp. 15–16]. Eichengreen goes on to sketch a brief but intriguing explanation, based on the notion of coordination failure, for why wages and other costs failed to adjust. But he does not return to develop this explanation in the main part of the text, and the rest of the 450-page volume makes only a few passing references to the issue of wage adjustment.

In the context of the Great Depression, the relatively uncritical acceptance of the sticky-wage assumption is surprising. During the 1930s many forces that Keynesian economists commonly point to as conducive to slow wage adjustment appeared relatively weak in most countries: union power was at a low ebb; government's role in labor markets was generally more limited than today; price declines were too large and well publicized for money illusion to be widespread; and the existence of an army of the unemployed must have significantly reduced workers' bargaining power. Given these conditions, it would seem reasonable to expect wage adjustment to be fairly rapid. At the same time it must be conceded that something prevented the world's economies from adjusting to the deflationary shocks of the 1930s, and there is a dearth of alternatives.[2] Thus, the solution to the aggregate supply puzzle of the Depression remains very much an open issue.

The purpose of this paper is to reexamine, from a comparative international perspective, the empirical evidence on the role of wage stickiness in the Depression. We take as our starting point the important work of Eichengreen and Sachs [1985, 1986].[3] Section II begins by recapitulating a key bit of evidence offered by Eichengreen and Sachs in support of a role for wage stickiness in the Depression: a cross-sectional regression (using data from ten industrialized countries for the year 1935) of industrial production against the real wage. As we discuss further below, under the maintained assumption that cross-sectional differences in economic performance as of 1935 were due primarily to differences in gold-standard (monetary) policies, this simple regression has the important strength that it identifies a component of the aggregate supply relation. On the other hand, as we also discuss, the Eichengreen-Sachs regression is subject to a number of potentially important criticisms, both substantively economic and more narrowly econometric.

Section III presents new estimates of the link between output and wages that attempt to address the problems with the original Eichengreen-Sachs results and to clarify the role of wage stickiness in the Depression. We use a larger data set than they did, covering 22 countries over the period 1931–

---

[2] In a related paper Bernanke and James [1991] survey the aggregate supply puzzle and investigate the role of financial crises as a mechanism through which deflation induced declines in real output. Although they find evidence for financial crisis as a transmission mechanism, the strongest effects are limited to a subset of countries and to the 1931–1932 period. Thus, some additional factors are probably required to account for the entire real effect of monetary contraction and deflation. In our estimates below, we attempt to control for banking crises and (indirectly) for debt-deflation and similar effects operating through the price level.

[3] Although we focus on the Eichengreen-Sachs evidence, which is the best known, there have been a few other comparative studies of the period. Newell and Symons [1988] estimate "labor demand equations" for Europe, for the United Kingdom, and Scandinavia separately, and for the United States, in which employment is regressed on the real wage and the real interest rate for the period 1923–1938. Many of the econometric issues we raise in this paper apply to the Newell-Symons results as well. Bernanke and James [1991] look at the links between real wages and output using a data set similar to ours, but their focus is on the role of financial crises in transmitting deflationary shocks rather than on wages. Numerous articles have studied wage stickiness within a single country (usually the United States). However, single-country studies lack the identifying power that cross-country differences in gold-standard policies bring to comparative analyses.

1936. We deal with residual simultaneity bias, using aggregate demand shifters as instruments, and make a number of other econometric corrections. We also allow for dynamic influences (by incorporating lagged dependent variables) and account for other factors (such as banking panics and work stoppages) that may have affected aggregate supply. We augment our analysis of the relationship among wages, prices, and output by estimating wage adjustment equation, which provides information on how quickly nominal wages responded to changes in the price level and in unemployment rates. Finally, we provide joint estimates of the aggregate supply and wage adjustment equations, imposing cross-equation restrictions.

Despite the many modifications, our findings broadly concur with the original conclusions of Eichengreen and Sachs. The econometric evidence offers reasonably strong support for the hypothesis that slowly adjusting nominal wages helped propagate monetary shocks in the Depression. This empirical finding leaves open the deep question of why wages did not adjust more quickly in the interwar period. Section IV summarizes the findings, makes some conjectures about why wage adjustment in the Depression appears to have been so slow, and gives suggestions for future research.

II. Aggregate Supply in the Depression: The Eichengreen-Sachs Evidence

Many of the key elements of the gold standard theory of the Depression were originally set out in two important papers [1985, 1986] by Eichengreen and Sachs, hereinafter E-S.[4] The 1985 E-S paper is the basic statement of their view that the interwar gold standard was the principal carrier of the deflationary virus, and that devaluation or abandonment of the gold standard—rather than being a counterproductive or even hostile (i.e., "beggar-thy-neighbor") act—was in fact the essential first step to national and world economic recovery.

The primarily historical mode of analysis in E-S [1985] is complemented by the theoretical analysis of their 1986 article, which lays out a simple two-country model. The main contribution of this model is to extend the conventional Mundell-Fleming framework to incorporate the links between gold reserves and the money supply under a gold standard. For our purposes here, the key part of that model is the two-equation "aggregate supply block:"

$$q_t = -\alpha(w_t - p_t) \tag{1}$$

$$w_t = \overline{w}, \tag{2}$$

---

[4] These papers in turn built on themes raised by (among others) Warren and Pearson [1933], Haberler [1976], and Choudhri and Kochin [1980].

where q is real output, w is the nominal wage rate, p is the price level, and subscripts indicate the time period. All variables are in logs and the constant term in equation (1) is omitted. Equation (1) states that the output supplied by industry depends negatively on the real wage, which firms treat as parametric. We refer to equation (1) as the output supply equation, to distinguish it from the aggregate supply equation, in which the price level is the only contemporaneous endogenous variable appearing on the right-hand side. Equation (2) is the wage adjustment equation, which describes the evolution of the nominal wage. Here this equation is trivial, since, for expositional purposes, E-S made the extreme assumption that the nominal wage is exogeneously fixed. We relax this assumption in Section III below.

Substituting (2) into (1) yields the aggregate supply equation of the E-S model:

$$q_t = -\alpha(\overline{w} - p_t). \tag{3}$$

As is conventional, the aggregate supply equation (3) implies a positive-sloping relationship between output and the price level, given the nominal wage. In postulating (3), E-S adopt the traditional Keynesian view that price increases raise aggregate supply by lowering the real wage faced by firms.[5]

In the empirical portion of their 1985 paper, E-S focused on the differences between the countries that abandoned the gold standard at a relatively early stage (notably the Sterling Bloc, consisting the Great Britain and her trading partners, which left gold subsequent to the 1931 crises) and those countries that remained on gold until the collapse of the system in 1935 and 1936 (the Gold Bloc, led by France).[6] Consistent with their view that monetary contraction enforced by the gold standard was the principal source of the Depression, they found that countries that left gold early enjoyed much more rapid recoveries than those that stayed on gold, and that this difference in performance was associated with earlier reflation of money stocks and price levels in the countries leaving gold (see Bernanke and James [1991] and Bernanke [1995] for detailed evidence on these points).

As a test of their hypothesis about the role of wages in aggregate supply

---

[5] This traditional view is currently out of favor, on the grounds that it supposedly predicts a strong countercyclicality of real wages, while empirically real wages in the postwar United States appear to be acyclical or procyclical. In fact, (3) implies real-wage countercyclicality only if aggregate demand shocks are dominant. As we will see, real wages were indeed countercyclical in the interwar period, consistent with the gold standard theory's interpretation of events. The postwar U. S. experience can be reconciled with (3) if one accepts that both aggregate demand and aggregate supply shocks have hit the U. S. economy since 1945.

[6] Of course, to some extent the decision to leave gold was determined by economic conditions. However, political and philosophical considerations appear to have been at least as important. See Bernanke [1995, pp. 11–12] for a discussion of why endogeneity of the exchange-rate regime is unlikely to weaken the basic E-S argument.

determination, E-S presented a cross-sectional regression (using data from ten industrial countries for the year 1935) of industrial production (measured as an index, 1929 = 100) against a constant and the real wage (also measured as an index, 1929 = 100). Under this assumption that the differences among countries in 1935 were due primarily to differences in monetary policies (which shift the aggregate demand curve), this regression should identify the aggregate supply curve, equation (3) above. Their estimated equation was

$$\text{Ind. Prod.}_{1935} = \quad 175.2 - 0.598 \text{ (Real wage}_{1935}) \quad \bar{R}^2 = .50;$$
$$(t = 7.39) \ (t = 3.14)$$

i.e., E-S found a strong negative relationship across countries between output and real wages, as predicted by (3). In addition, a plot of their data (their Figure 2, p. 938) confirms their claim that adherence to the gold standard was strongly associated with high real wages and depressed output. The countries that fall in the high-real-wage, low-output region of their figure are all countries that remained on gold well beyond 1931 (France, Belgium, the Netherlands, and Italy), while the countries with low real wages and higher output were members of the Sterling Bloc that left gold early (Finland, Denmark, Sweden, the United Kingdom, and Norway).

Our Figure 1 expands the E-S sample by showing industrial production and real wage data (both measured relative to 1929 = 100) for 22 relatively industrialized countries, for each year from 1931 through 1936 (i.e., all years in which there were a significant number of countries both on and off the gold standard). Countries in the sample, with mnemonic abbreviations, are listed in Table 1. Included in the sample are all countries for which annual aggregate nominal wage series of 1929–1936 were published by the International Labor Organization,[7] and for which we could also find matching output and price level data. Industrial production and wholesale price indices (used to deflate the wage series) are from the League of Nations (*Statistical Year Book*, various issues), except for Argentine IP data, which are from Thorp [1984]. The choice of a wholesale price index as a deflator (as in E-S) is dictated by data availability. In Figure 1 countries that were on the gold standard for more than half the year in a given year are designated by capi-

---

[7] In various issues of its *Yearbook*. The exception is the United States, for which wage data were taken from Beney [1936]. Wages are for the industrial sector; in some countries, related sectors such as mines and transport are included. We used hourly wage series for all workers wherever possible. However, for two countries, Japan and Norway, we only had series for daily earnings. (A partial hourly wage series for Japan exhibited behavior similar to the daily earnings series.) We did not use any weekly or monthly earnings data in order to avoid confounding changes in hourly pay with changes in workweeks, which were common during the Depression.

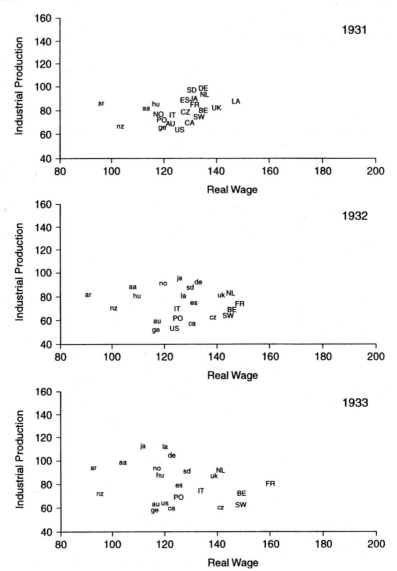

Figure 1. Industrial Production and Real Wages in 22 Countries, 1931–1936

tal letters; countries off the gold standard in a given year are indicated by lowercase letters.[8]

[8] Following Bernanke and James [1991], we define "off the gold standard" loosely to encompass any major deviation from the gold standard's rules of operation, such as imposing foreign exchange controls or devaluing. See Bernanke and James [Table 2.1, p. 37] for dates of changes in countries' policies with respect to the gold standard.

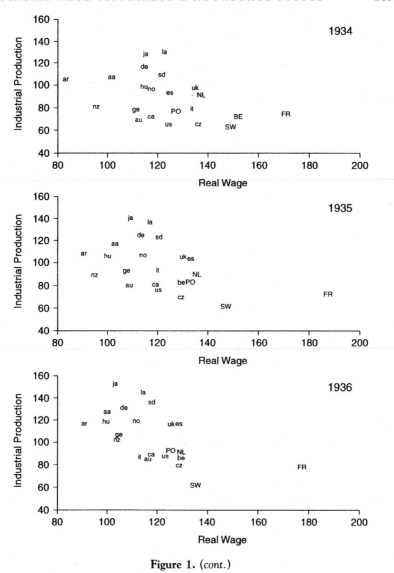

Figure 1. (*cont.*)

Figure 1 has several interesting features. First, note the countercyclicality of real wages in the great majority of countries. Real wages during 1931–1934 (the worst part of the slump) were between 20 percent and 40 percent higher than in 1929 in most countries, the result of sharp declines in price levels not accompanied by comparable falls in nominal wages. In contrast, by 1936 real wages in most countries had dropped significantly (as prices

Table 1
Countries Included in This Study

Country	Mnemonic
1. Argentina	AR
2. Australia	AA
3. Austria	AU
4. Belgium	BE
5. Canada	CA
6. Czechoslovakia	CZ
7. Denmark	DE
8. Estonia	ES
9. France	FR
10. Germany	GE
11. Hungary	HU
12. Italy	IT
13. Japan	JA
14. Latvia	LA
15. Netherlands	NL
16. New Zealand	NZ
17. Norway	NO
18. Poland	PO
19. Sweden	SD
20. Switzerland	SW
21. United Kingdom	UK
22. United States	US

rose and nominal wages fell), to a range centered at about 10 percent higher than 1929. At the same time that real wages fell, world output and employment grew substantially from Depression-era lows. This pattern of output, wages, and prices over time is consistent with the E-S interpretation of the link between wages and aggregate supply.

Also apparent in Figure 1 is the evolving cross-sectional relationship between output and real wages. At the beginning of the period (particularly in 1931), little cross-sectional variation in the two variables can be seen. From the perspective of the E-S hypothesis, this lack of variation may be ascribed to the fact that, as of 1931 or 1932, most countries were either on the gold standard or had recently left it, and thus had experienced similar shocks to aggregate demand. However, as gold standard (and hence monetary) policies diverged over time, cross-sectional variations in the state of aggregate demand increased, and the negative relationship of output and real wages became apparent. For the later years, particularly 1935 and 1936, the scatter plots show a downward-sloping relationship between output and the real wage similar to that found by E-S. Further, the countries we have added to the data set conform in almost all cases to the E-S observation that Gold Bloc countries (such as Switzerland and Poland) had high real wages and low output, while countries that abandoned gold early on (Japan, Australia, New Zealand, and Argentina, for example) had lower real wages and higher production by the middle of the decade. Thus, in general, the cross-sectional pattern displayed in Figure 1 also seems supportive of the E-S view.

In summary, the E-S evidence, as simple as it is, has two important strengths. First, it demonstrates that cross-country differences in monetary policy during the Depression era (associated with membership or nonmembership in the gold standard) provide an unusually good opportunity to identify the aggregate supply curve. Second, the basic E-S regression discussed above—as well as the extended data set displayed in Figure 1— appears consistent (at least) with the role for sticky wages postulated in the E-S model of the Depression.

Nevertheless, there are a number of substantive criticisms that can be made of the E-S approach. In the rest of this section we describe four general weaknesses of the E-S evidence. In Section III we provide new estimates of the determinants of aggregate supply in the interwar period that address each of these weaknesses.

A. The Eichengreen-Sachs Evidence: A Critique

Potential reservations about the E-S empirical results include the following.

1. *Small sample size.* As has already been stressed, the E-S regression uses data for only one year and ten countries. Below we present estimates employing our larger data set.

2. *Simultaneity bias.* We have emphasized E-S's insight that—under the maintained assumption that differences in national economic performance during the Depression can be attributed primarily to differences in the state of aggregate demand—cross-sectional data may be used to identify aggregate supply relationships. However, strictly speaking, their use of an OLS regression requires the assumption that 100 percent of the observed cross-sectional variation be due to aggregate demand factors, and 0 percent to factors shifting aggregate supply. This assumption, besides being rather implausible a priori, is difficult to square with the absence of a downward-sloping relationship between output and real wages in 1931 and 1932. Hence, it seems worthwhile to explicitly incorporate aggregate demand shifters as instruments, in order to identify the aggregate supply relationships and eliminate remaining simultaneity bias.

3. *Specification issues.* This simple specification utilized by E-S raises a number of concerns. First, the output supply equation (equation (1)) used by E-S does not acknowledge the possibility that other factors might have

affected supply, given the real wage. We introduce additional supply shifters in Section III below. Second, the output supply equation used by E-S contains no dynamic element; in particular, no allowance is made for the possibility of adjustment costs in output. Third, the assumption that the nominal wage is exogenously fixed is obviously oversimple (and counterfactual). Below we present estimates of wage adjustment equations that allow nominal wages to respond to changes in the price level and the unemployment rate.

4. *The wage effect versus the price effect.* The E-S evidence (and Figure 1) makes clear that there was an inverse cross-sectional relationship between output and real wages during the Depression era, especially in 1933–1936. However, it is important to ask whether there are any alternative explanations for this observed relationship besides sticky nominal wages.

It seems to us that explanations of the output-real wage relationship not involving nominal shocks and nonneutrality, i.e., purely "real" explanations, can largely be ruled out. Adverse technology shocks would induce low, not high, real wages in depressed countries. Spending reductions due strictly to real factors, plus imperfect competition and countercyclical markups, could in principle reproduce the observed patterns. But we are not aware of any plausible story of why these declines in spending should have affected so many disparate countries around the world nearly simultaneously, and in particular why they should have been more persistent in countries remaining on the gold standard. Similarly, negative labor supply shocks could in principle generate both high real wages and falling output; but again, there is no reason why labor supply shocks should have hit only Gold Bloc countries after 1931 and not the countries that abandoned gold. Further, the observed changes in output and the real wage are simply too large in magnitude to be comfortably reconciled with a labor supply story.[9]

Although the evidence for a nonverticle aggregate supply curve in the Depression era is strong, it is important to note that the E-S regression of output on the real wage cannot be itself distinguish whether the nonverticality of the aggregate supply curve in the interwar period is due to imperfect adjustment of nominal wages, or to some other connection between the prices and aggregate supply (such as debt-deflation, for example).[10] For a thought experiment that illustrates this point, suppose that it were the case that (1) the nominal wage data consisted entirely of measurement error, uncorrelated with anything else, and (2) falling prices caused output to de-

---

[9] We do not mean to deny, however, that labor supply conditions, e.g., the power of unions or the extent of unemployment insurance, might have affected the speed of nominal wage adjustment and levels of employement.

[10] Bernanke and James [1991] discuss several nonwage channels through which falling prices may affect output.

cline, but for some reason other than an increase in the (correctly measured) real wage. Under these assumptions the real wage variable in the E-S regression would simply equal the price variable plus noise, and the estimated coefficient on the real wage would be a (downward-biased) estimate of the impact of falling prices on output. In this thought experiment the link between deflation and output would be erroneously attributed to the real wage channel, even though by assumption there is no real wage effect.

Ideally, this identification problem would be dealt with by specifying the alternative channels linking prices and output and including the appropriate proxies in the regression along with the real wage. However, if there are missing data, measurement errors, or uncertainties about the nature of the alternative channels, there may be a bias toward finding a real wage effect even if none exists. To distinguish effects on output operating through wages and other effects operating solely through prices, in the estimates of the output supply equation reported in the next section we allow nominal wages and prices to enter separately, and then test whether their estimated coefficients are equal and opposite, as should be the case if only wage effects are operative.

III. Depression-Era Aggregate Supply Relationships: New Estimates

The shortcomings of the E-S evidence described above lead us to undertake a more comprehensive econometric analysis of interwar aggregate supply relationships. We present, in turn, new estimates of the output supply equation, which relates output supplied by firms to the real wage; estimates of the wage adjustment equation, which describes the adjustment of nominal wages to prices and other factors; and joint estimates of the aggregate supply equation (relating output to the price level) and the wage adjustment equation. In each case our main interest is to assess empirically whether slow adjustment of nominal wages was an important factor in the Depression.

All of our estimates utilize the panel data set described in the previous section (22 countries, 1931–1936; data for 1929 and 1930 are available for use when lagged data are needed). Reflecting the panel nature of the data, each estimated equation includes country fixed effects and year dummies. Year dummies—the most flexible way of allowing for time effects—were employed after more parsimonious ways of allowing for time variation, such as trend terms, were tried and statistically rejected. The use of free year dummies implies that the identifying power in the following estimates is obtained essentially only from cross-sectional variation, albeit for each year in the sample.

A. *The Output Supply Equation*

For estimation purposes we replace the E-S output supply equation, equation (1), with the following:

$$q_t = -\alpha_W w_t + \alpha_p P_t + \delta q_{t-1} + X_t\beta + \varepsilon_t^q. \tag{4}$$

Equation (4) incorporates a number of generalizations to the E-S output supply equation. First, we allow nominal wages and prices to enter the equation separately. Then we test the restriction, implicit in the E-S specification, that the coefficients α_W and α_p are equal. As discussed in the previous section, this procedure allows us to separate aggregate supply effects entering through nominal wages from other effects working through the price level alone. This approach puts a higher burden of proof on the sticky-wage channel, since separate wage effects will be identified only if there are autonomous shocks to nominal wages, and if the wage data are not excessively noisy. Since we do generally find important wage effects, this conservative approach is appropriate.

Second, (4) introduces lagged output into the output supply equation. The addition of this variable is motivated by the presumption that there exist adjustment costs (in hiring or in reactivating facilities, for example) that prevent extremely rapid changes in national output. In the absence of a term in lagged output, the output supply equation implies that a decline of real wages to their normal level would induce a complete recovery of output within the year, no matter how severely depressed the economy is initially. This implication of omitting lagged output seems implausible. As is well-known, however, inclusion of the lagged dependent variable may result in inconsistent estimates if there is serial correlation in the error term. To deal with this problem, we employ a nonlinear least squares (NLLS) procedure to obtain consistent estimates of both the serial correlation coefficient (assumed to be common to all countries) and the coefficient on lagged output.[11]

Third, the new term $X_t\beta$ in (4) reflects the possibility that other factors besides the real wages (and the time and country fixed effects) shift the output supply equation. In our estimates we include two additional regressors in equation (4).

1. Bernanke and James [1991] found that a dummy variable indicating periods of banking panics, which they constructed from qualitative historical evidence, was an important explanator of output. Banking panics could shift the supply equation if they disrupted normal flows of credit to firms. To

---

[11] The technique is to write the estimated equation in quasi-differenced form, which produces a specification with white noise error and regression coefficients that are nonlinear functions of the serial correlation coefficient and the parameters of the original equation. The NLLS procedure imposes the nonlinear restrictions and obtains consistent and efficient estimates of all parameters.

capture this effect, we include their dummy variable PANIC in some of the regressions reports below. Bernanke and James based this variable on a chronology of banking crises, reported in their paper. For each year and country, PANIC equals the number of months that the banking system was "in crisis." Periods of crisis are dated as starting from the onset of severe banking problems and ending either at some clear demarcation point (such as the U.S. bank holiday in March 1933) or, alternatively, after one year.

2. In a number of countries, production was affected by largescale strikes and lockouts. Thus, we also add to the output supply equation the number of days lost to industrial disputes per 1000 employees, or STRIKE (from various issues of the ILO's *Yearbook of Labor Statistics*).

While the inclusion of these additional regressors should reduce the omitted variables problem, it remains likely that other, unmeasured factors also shifted the supply relationship. Possibilities include technological changes, shifts in the composition of output or the workforce, government policies affecting labor supply or work rules, and simple mismeasurement of regressors, to name a few. Since shocks to the supply of output should affect current wages and prices, simultaneity bias is a potential problem and instrumental variables are needed to obtain consistent estimates of the supply relation.

As we have reiterated, the basic premise underlying the E-S interpretation of their own regression is that the output supply relation is identified by cross-sectional differences in aggregate demand conditions, which in turn are due primarily to differences in exchange rate and monetary policies. We followed this logic in constructing our instruments. First, we broke our sample into two sets of countries: those that abandoned gold in 1931 and those that remained on gold after 1931.[12] The countries that left gold had effective control of their own monetary policies for all or most of our sample period, so for those countries we treat the log of M1 (money and notes in circulation plus commercial bank deposits, both from the League of Nations *Yearbook*, various issues) as an exogenous aggregate demand shifter.

Countries that remained on gold, in contrast, did not have control of their own money supplies.[13] As specified in the E-S [1986] extension of the Mundell-Fleming model, in small countries on the gold standard, domestic

[12] Countries in our sample adhering to gold after 1931 included Belgium, France, Italy, the Netherlands, Poland, and Switzerland. The United States also remained on gold after 1931, but we treat it as a nongold country for reasons explained in the next note.

[13] The United States was at least a partial exception to this statement. Besides its great economic size, which limits the relevance of the usual "small country" model, the United States had at its disposal large gold reserves, which probably gave it a degree of potential control over its own money supply (although of course exactly how much control is in dispute). For these reasons we decided to treat the United States as a nongold country with an exogenous money supply in the estimation, even though it did not leave gold until 1933. We also experimented with treating France, the dominant force in the Gold Bloc, as a "large" country with an exogenous money supply. The results were not sensitive to this latter change.

aggregate demand instead depends on the domestic-currency price of imports (determined by the foreign price level and the gold content of the domestic currency) and the domestic interest rate (determined by the world interest rate through interest-rate parity). Accordingly, we used the log of an import price index and the central bank discount rate (taken from the League of Nations *Yearbook*, various issues) as instruments for gold standard countries during the years in the sample that they were on gold[14] The import price index for each country on the gold standard was constructed as a weighted average of the domestic-currency prices of imports from each trading partner, using 1929 import shares as weights.[15] For the portion of the sample period after each Gold Bloc country left gold, we used M1 as an instrument rather than the import price and the discount rate.[16]

For all countries we treated the lagged nominal wage and lagged output as predetermined, and we took the PANIC and STRIKE variables to be exogenous (more precisely, to be uncorrelated with the disturbance in the output supply equation).[17] Current and once-lagged values of the aggregate demand shifters were used as instruments, reflecting the fact that both current and lagged values of the price level appear in the NLLS specification that we use.

Before turning to the results, we must discuss one more technical issue, which relates to the treatment of panel data with fixed effects. In deriving the asymptotic properties of estimates and standard errors in this situation, it is generally assumed that the cross section is "large;" that is, asymptotic

[14] However, for readers concerned that imperfect capital markets or other factors might have broken the link between domestic and foreign interest rates, we note that the discount rate is a relatively poor instrument and its inclusion or exclusion has little bearing on the results.

[15] Import shares are from League of Nations [1938]. We ignored imports from countries not in our 22-country sample, which in general were a very small portion of the total. Of the countries in our sample, export data from Estonia, Latvia, and New Zealand were not available. In constructing import shares for Switzerland, we used 1932 rather than 1929 data because the latter included bullion trade for banking transactions. Domestic currency prices of imports were calculated as the exporting country's wholesale price index times of the value of the country's currency as a percentage of the 1929 gold parity [League of Nations, *Statistical Yearbook*, 1940/41]. German data on currency values are used in place of missing Austrian data; also, for Germany 1934–1936, we used the value of blocked marks (kreditsperrmark).

[16] If the abandonment of gold took place in the middle of a year, we weighted the two sets of instruments by the fraction of the year that the country was on and off the gold standard, respectively.

[17] Clearly, it is not literally correct that banking panics and labor unrest were independent of aggregate supply conditions. However, both of these variables have very sharp and largely unpredictable year-to-year movements, suggesting a significant random element. It is also likely that both variables reflect institutional and historical conditions only weakly related to the disturbance term in the output supply equation. For example, Bernanke and James [1991] point out that the incidence of banking panics was not well predicted by prior declines in output but instead largely reflected factors such as banking structure and national banking policies in the 1920s.

theory applies in the cross-sectional dimension. However, one may choose to regard the number of time units either as "large" (tending toward infinity) or "fixed." In the former case, our nonlinear instrumental-variables procedure, estimated with the variables in levels and with time and country dummies included, as consistent. Under the latter assumption, however, our procedure leads to inconsistent estimates due to correlation between the lagged dependent variable and the error term, which does not disappear for fixed T. The recommended procedure in the latter case is to difference the model and to use second and higher lags of the differenced lagged dependent variable as instruments (see Arellano and Bond [1991] for a recent discussion and application). Since in our case $T = 6$ (excluding two observations reserved for lags), the fixed-T assumption seems more appropriate. On the other hand, with noisy data, the use of twice-lagged and differenced data as instruments is likely to produce quite imprecise results. Further, the application of this technique requires the sacrifice of two more years of data, reducing the sample period to 1933–1936 inclusive. As a compromise, we present both estimates obtained in levels with explicitly estimated fixed effects (i.e., estimates based on the "large-T" assumption), as well as estimates obtained in a differenced specification with the appropriate lagged instruments (relevant under the "fixed-T" assumption).

We are now ready to turn to Table 2, which reports estimated versions of the output supply equation that include various combinations of the three additional regressors (PANIC, STRIKE, and lagged output). Results estimated with levels and country dummies are reported in Panel A, and results from the differenced specification are given in Panel B. We report point estimates and t-statistics for the coefficient on each regressor, as well as for the serial correlation coefficient. The final column of Table 2 indicates the p-value of the hypothesis that the nominal wage and the price level enter the equation with equal and opposite signs (i.e., $\alpha_W = \alpha_p$), with a small entry indicating that this hypothesis can be rejected.

The results are interesting. First, there is strong support for the inclusion of lagged output in the equation, indicating the existence of adjustment costs in production. In the presence of lagged output, the serial correlation coefficient is typically estimated to be insignificantly different from zero, and it is often negative.

Second, the auxiliary variables, PANIC and STRIKE, generally make contributions to the equation that are highly significant, both economically and statistically. For example, in the equation with all variables included (either line 4 or line 8), the estimated effect of a banking panic on output is about 1.0 percentage points *per month*, with a t-statistic of around four; i.e., the median-sized banking crisis, which under the Bernanke-James assumptions lasted twelve months, was associated with a loss of about twelve percentage points of output growth (Bernanke and James [1991] found an effect

Table 2
NLIV Estimates of the Output Supply Equation

Dependent variable: Industrial production (q)

A. Specification: Levels, country dummies
   Sample: 1931–1936

Independent Variables

	(1) w	(2) p	(3) q_{-1}	(4) PANIC	(5) STRIKE	$\hat{\rho}$	$\alpha_w = \alpha_p$?
1.	−1.423	1.581				0.428	0.714
	(2.21)	(3.78)				(2.88)	
2.	−1.163	1.102	0.363			0.181	0.812
	(2.42)	(2.74)	(1.99)			(0.64)	
3.	−0.601	0.679	0.574	−0.011		−0.089	0.608
	(3.31)	(4.34)	(6.91)	(4.56)		(0.63)	
4.	−0.531	0.714	0.464	−0.010	−0.75–05	0.163	0.361
	(2.42)	(3.85)	(3.84)	(4.29)	(3.58)	(0.81)	

B. Specification: Differences, correction for fixed-T bias
   Sample: 1933–1936

Independent Variables

	(1) w	(2) p	(3) q_{-1}	(4) PANIC	(5) STRIKE	$\hat{\rho}$	$\alpha_w = \alpha_p$?
5.	−1.049	0.890				0.059	0.732
	(1.74)	(2.70)				(0.32)	
6.	−1.272	0.835	0.425			−0.161	0.308
	(2.38)	(2.68)	(2.43)			(0.87)	
7.	−0.810	0.509	0.583	−0.011		−0.151	0.366
	(2.28)	(2.11)	(3.84)	(3.53)		(0.98)	
8.	−0.800	0.580	0.544	−0.010	0.41–05	−0.255	0.433
	(2.58)	(2.69)	(4.13)	(3.54)	(0.84)	(2.08)	

These regressions pool cross-sectional data and include time dummies. A nonlinear (quasi-differenced) specification is used to allow for consistent estimation of both the serial correlation coefficient and the coefficient on the lagged dependent variable. Absolute values of t-statistics are in parentheses. See the text for data definitions and instruments.

of similar magnitude). The coefficient of STRIKE is significant statistically ($t = 3.58$) and of reasonable magnitude in the levels specification with all variables included (line 4).[18] However, STRIKE's coefficient is insignificant

---

[18] To assess the magnitude of this coefficient, recall that STRIKE is measured as days lost per 1000 employees. Assuming for the sake of argument that the normal work-year is 250 days, then if the effect of strikes on output is simply proportional to time lost, the coefficient on

and of the wrong sign in the differenced specification (line 8), possibly because of the shortened sample period used in that specification.

The most important results relate to the effects of wage and price movements on output. Table 2 shows that, in all specifications, both the nominal wage and the price level enter the output supply equation significantly[19] and with the expected sign. The long-run elasticity of output with respect to the real wage (taking into account the presence of the lagged dependent variable) generally is estimated to exceed one. Further, as the last column shows, the hypothesis that wages and prices enter the equation with equal and opposite signs is never close to rejection, which is consistent with the view that prices affected output through only the real-wage channel (given that the effects of deflation operating through banking panics have been controlled for).

Thus, generalizations of the E-S regression including the use of a larger, panel data set; allowing for separate wage and price effects; allowing for additional output supply shifters and dynamic effects; using instruments to correct for simultaneity bias; and with additional econometric corrections, lead to results that support E-S's original interpretations of the data, that the inverse relationship of output and real wages reflects largely the effects of incomplete nominal wage adjustment in the presence of aggregate demand shocks.

B. The Wage Adjustment Equation

In their work E-S made the simplifying assumption that the nominal wage is literally rigid. For increased empirical realism we replace the simple E-S wage adjustment equation, (2), with the following:

$$w_t = \lambda_p p_t + \lambda_W w_{t-1} - \gamma u_t - \theta(\Delta u_t) + \epsilon_t^w. \tag{5}$$

In (5), λ_p measures the degree to which nominal wages respond to contemporaneous price movements, and λ_W, the coefficient on the lagged nominal wage, is a measure of nominal inertia.[20] If wages follow the partial adjustment mechanism usually assumed, then $\lambda_p + \lambda_W = 1$. We do not impose this condition but instead test for it. The partial adjustment mechanism typically presumes that the wage is adjusting toward a "desired" or

---

STRIKE should be 1/250,000, or .4E-5. in fact, the estimated value of this coefficient is .75E-5.

[19] The nominal wage enters with only marginal significance in line 5 ($t = 1.74$), but this is clearly not a good specification.

[20] Note that we assume that the wage adjustment rate is the same across countries. We did experiment with allowing the adjustment rate to depend on national union densities (for the eight or so countries for which union data are available), but we found no significant link between the speed of wage adjustment and the union variable. In taking rates of adjustment to be the same across countries, we must now implicitly ascribe cross-sectional differences in nominal wages conditional on prices to cross-sectional differences in the sequences of shocks to the wage adjustment equation.

equilibrium level. In (5), following much work on the Phillips curve for both the interwar and postwar periods, we allow the desired wage level to be affected by both the unemployment rate u and the change in the unemployment rate, Δu. Variations in the desired real wage over time and space are also accommodated by the time dummies and country fixed effects.

The new data required to estimate equation (5) are unemployment rates. Data on industrial unemployment rates for each year in the sample were available for 14 of the 22 countries in our sample.[21] Unemployment rates for the remaining eight countries were constructed by regressing the change in unemployment against the change in industrial employment for countries for which both series were available, then applying the estimated coefficients to employment data for countries with no unemployment data.[22] Estimates of the wage adjustment equation for the subsample of countries with noninterpolated unemployment data were similar to those reported below and are not given here to save space.

As in the case of the output supply equation, we use a nonlinear procedure to obtain consistent estimates in the presence of a lagged dependent variable and possible serial correlation, and use instruments to correct for simultaneity bias. Instruments include the aggregate demand shifters described above and lagged wages or lagged differenced wages, as appropriate. In equations including unemployment or differenced unemployment, lagged unemployment or lagged differenced unemployment are added to the instrument list.

The estimates of the wage adjustment equation are reported in Table 3. As in Table 2, Panel A contains estimates for the variables in levels with explicit fixed effects, and Panel B gives the results estimated in differences, with twice- and thrice-lagged differences of the lagged dependent variable as instruments. (We do not include the specification including differenced unemployment in Panel B, since that would require us to use a second difference of unemployment in estimation. The second difference of these unemployment data seems unlikely to contain much information.) The final column of Table 3 gives p-values for the hypothesis that the coefficients on the price level and the lagged nominal wage sum to one, as is implied by the partial-adjustment model.

---

[21] Unemployment data for eleven countries are reported in Eichengreen and Hatton [1988, Table 1.1, p. 6]; the original sources are Galenson and Zellner [1957] and Lebergott [1964]. Data for three more countries (Czechoslovakia, Japan, and Switzerland) were available from the ILO *Yearbook*. Substituting Darby's [1976] modified U. S. unemployment data for Lebergott's did not affect the overall results.

[22] Employment data are from the ILO *Yearbook*. As we fit changes in unemployment rates only, we cannot determine the mean level of unemployment for the eight countries with fitted data and simply normalize the mean level at zero. This normalization is inconsequential for our purposes, as the estimated equations all include country fixed effects.

Table 3
NLIV Estimates of the Wage Adjustment Equation

Dependent variable: Nominal wage (w)

A. **Specification: Levels, country dummies**
   Sample: 1931–1936

	Independent Variables					
	(1)	(2)	(3)	(4)		
	p	w_{-1}	u	Δu	$\hat{\rho}$	$\lambda_p + \lambda_w = 1?$
1.	0.278	0.438			0.252	0.074
	(2.54)	(2.04)			(0.92)	
2.	0.247	0.334	−0.192		0.450	0.040
	(2.13)	(1.57)	(1.00)		(1.67)	
3.	0.159	0.566	−0.162	−0.188	0.217	0.086
	(1.37)	(2.91)	(1.27)	(0.75)	(3.16)	
4.	0.394	0.185		0.288	0.484	0.006
	(2.10)	(0.76)		(0.94)	(2.13)	

B. **Specification: Differences, correction for fixed-T bias**
   Sample: 1933–1936

	Independent Variables				
	(1)	(2)	(3)		
	p	w_{-1}	u	$\hat{\rho}$	$\lambda_p + \lambda_w = 1?$
5.	0.329	0.284		−0.042	0.047
	(3.14)	(1.58)		(0.13)	
6.	0.278	0.272	−0.161	−0.171	0.005
	(2.70)	(1.99)	(1.09)	(0.52)	

See Table 2.

Two general conclusions can be drawn from Table 3. First, estimates of the wage adjustment equation appear to provide further evidence of nominal-wage stickiness. Nominal wages are found to depend on both current prices and lagged nominal wages with coefficients that lie between zero and one. The coefficients on the current price level are generally estimated to be in the vicinity of 0.2–0.4 and are typically six or seven standard deviations below one, the theoretical value if wages adjust completely within the year to aggregate demand shocks. Estimated coefficients on lagged nominal wages are significant or near-significant. Taken together, the results suggest a substantial degree of stickiness in wage adjustment. In particular, the hypothesis that wages adjust immediately to price changes arising from aggregate demand shocks ($\lambda_p = 1$, $\lambda_W = 0$) can always be rejected at $p = 0.000$ (not shown in the table). On the other hand, the restriction imposed by the partial-adjustment model of wages ($\lambda_p + \lambda_W = 1$) is also generally rejected, though not nearly so sharply, as shown by the last column of Table 3.

Second, a higher unemployment rate does seem to imply lower nominal wages, all else equal (see lines 2 and 6), although in these estimates the level of statistical significance is low (possibly because of poor instruments[23]). Interestingly, in the light of other results that have been obtained, the level of unemployment seems to be more relevant to wage determination in this sample than is differenced unemployment. Unemployment enters with greater statistical significance than differenced unemployment when both are included in the regression (line 3), although the coefficients are similar, and difference unemployment enters with the "wrong" sign when the level of unemployment is excluded (line 4).

C. *Joint Estimation of the Wage Adjustment and Aggregate Supply Equations*

To this point we have estimated the component equations of the aggregate supply block individually. We close this section by reporting estimates of the aggregate supply block as a whole, with cross-equation restrictions imposed and with allowance for correlation of contemporaneous equation residuals. This joint estimation is both more efficient and also permits direct estimates of the aggregate supply equation, as opposed to the output supply equation estimated above.

If we substitute the wage adjustment equation (5) into the output supply equation (4), we obtain the aggregate supply equation:

$$q_t = \alpha(1 - \lambda_p)p_t - \alpha\lambda_W uw_{t-1} + \alpha\gamma u_t + \delta q_{t-1} + X_t\beta + (\epsilon_t^q - \alpha\epsilon_t^w) \tag{6}$$

The aggregate supply equation links current output to the current price level, the output supply shifters (PANIC and STRIKE), and the lagged level of output (reflecting adjustment costs). Output is also affected by the lagged nominal wage and the current unemployment rate, through the effect of those two variables on the current nominal wage (we omit the differenced unemployment rate here). In (6) we have imposed the restriction $\alpha_W = \alpha_p = \alpha$, which is accepted by the data (Table 2), but we do not impose $\lambda_p + \lambda_W = 1$, which is generally rejected (Table 3).

Joint estimates of the parameters of the aggregate supply equation (6),

---

[23] In particular, lagged unemployment may be a poor instrument if, say because of serial correlation, it is not uncorrelated with the current disturbance to the nominal wage. In this case the likely bias in the estimate of the coefficient on unemployment is positive, which could help explain the relatively weak effect of unemployment on wages found in these estimates.

Table 4
Joint Estimation of Aggregate Supply and Wage Adjustment

		Parameter Estimates and t-Statistics			
		Levels Specification		Differences Specification	
Parameter		(A)	(B)	(C)	(D)
1.	α	−0.835	−0.611	−0.521	−0.480
		(5.57)	(4.47)	(1.37)	(1.57)
2.	δ	0.492	0.553	0.449	0.409
		(8.03)	(9.12)	(2.49)	(3.01)
3.	β_{CRISIS}	−0.009	−0.011	−0.010	−0.010
		(4.88)	(5.49)	(3.40)	(3.65)
4.	β_{STRIKE}	−0.65−05	−0.69−05	−0.59−06	−0.45−07
		(3.59)	(3.69)	(0.11)	(0.01)
5.	λ_P	0.207	0.012	0.335	0.238
		(2.26)	(0.09)	(3.30)	(2.21)
6.	λ_W	0.439	0.201	−0.001	0.066
		(2.01)	(2.13)	(0.01)	(0.43)
7.	γ	—	−0.693	—	−0.319
			(3.68)		(1.81)
Aggregate supply equation					
	$\bar{R}^2$	0.956	0.947	0.050	0.026
	D.W.	1.94	1.95	2.28	2.19
Wage adjustment equation					
	$\bar{R}^2$	0.911	0.903	0.402	0.448
	D.W.	2.06	2.09	1.87	1.95
	$\hat{\rho}^w$	0.314	0.723	—	—

See Table 2. These results are from joint estimation of the aggregate supply and wage adjustment equations, allowing for correlation between contemporaneous equation residuals. Parameters are defined as in equations (4)–(6) in the text. The bottom portion of the table reports individual-equation diagnostics.

and the wage adjustment equation (5), are provided in Table 4. Results are presented for both the levels and differences specifications, and both with and without inclusion of the unemployment rate in the wage adjustment equation. The instruments employed are the union of the instruments used for the output supply and wage adjustment equations separately. The correlation between contemporaneous residuals of the two equations is unrestricted. Based on the results of Tables 2 and 3, and for simplicity, we apply the serial correlation correction only for the wage adjustment equation (levels specification). Estimates of the serial correlation coefficient for that one case, as well as other equation diagnostics, are provided at the bottom of the table.

The results complement those already reported. In the levels specification, estimates are of the right sign and general magnitude, and are in almost all cases significant. The estimates allow us to reject the hypothesis of vertical aggregate supply (complete within-period adjustment of wages to the price level, i.e., $\lambda_p = 1$, $\lambda_W = 0$) with a high degree of confidence ($p = 0.000$). Interestingly, in this specification of role of unemployment in depressing nominal wages is found to be much larger and more statistically significant than it is when the wage adjustment equation is estimated by itself.

The differences specification (which, recall, is estimated for the 1933–1936 period) yields qualitatively similar results (with lower statistical significance, as expected), with two exceptions. First, as before, the STRIKE variable does not enter significantly in the differences specification. Second, and more importantly, nominal-wage effects (as reflected in the parameters α and λ_W) are smaller and less statistically significant. The latter result appears to be due to the fact that the log-difference of the wage is poorly predicted by the available instruments. However, because the coefficient λ_p is well identified in these estimates, the hypothesis of complete wage adjustment to price changes can still be rejected at $p = 0.000$.

As in Tables 2 and 3, the results reported in Table 4 omit estimated year effects, to save space. In brief, the time dummies are found to play very little role in the wage adjustment equation, either in terms of magnitude or statistical significance; a similar remark applies to the estimates of the wage equation in Table 3. Estimated year effects are more important in the aggregate supply equation (and similarly, in the output supply equations in Table 2). In these equations the time dummies capture what appears to be a fairly rapid increase in average potential output over the period 1931–1933, and a slower increase between 1933 and 1936. However, the estimated year effects capture little of the short-run variation in output (and, of course, none of its cross-country variation) and therefore do not account for a particularly large component of the overall explanatory power of our specification.

D. A Final Specification Issue: Aggregation Bias

This paper has shown that, all else equal, higher nominal wages were associated with lower real output during the 1931–1936 period. However, the wage data we have used are aggregate indexes, about whose construction we know less than we would like. We believe that in most cases these wage indexes were constructed by dividing aggregate payrolls by aggregate hours of work. If so, then there may be reasons to worry that our finding of a negative relationship between output and wages is spurious. First, if errors in measuring hours of work and output are positively correlated, as seems likely, then a spurious negative relationship between measured output and the measured wage will be induced. Second, a spurious negative relationship might also arise because of changes in the composition of the workforce over the cycle. For example, if employers were more likely to fire their low-skill, low-wage workers as output declined, then the aggregate wage would be observed to rise as output fell. A similar bias would result if employment losses in low-wage industries were greater than those in high-wage industries, although this seems empirically less likely.

We were able to address the aggregation issue by using occupational wage data, reported in various issues of the International Labor Organization's *Yearbook*. The ILO reported wage rates for a number of occupations within seven industries, for as many as nine countries. The numbers reported are clearly wage rates rather than average hourly earnings (one indication is that they sometimes remain unchanged for several years at a time). Another nice feature of these data is that the particular industries included span major sectors of the economy, including not only manufacturing but construction, utilities, transport, and government.

For each industry we chose an occupation which seemed representative and for which all the data were available (the list of occupations is available on request). After converting all wages into an index form (1929 = 100), for each country we constructed a nominal wage index as the simple average of the occupational wages. In principle, these wage indexes should avoid the aggregation problems alluded to above, since they are based on wage rates (not average hourly earnings) and are constructed using fixed weights.[24]

The bias hypothesis says that the aggregate ILO wage indexes used in this study should lie above the corresponding fixed-weight indexes in the periods of lowest output. Of the nine countries for which comparison was possible, this implication seems to be true only for Australia and Estonia. For Canada, the Netherlands, and Sweden, we found that the aggregate wage index is actually below the fixed-weight index at the low point of the Depression, while for Denmark, the United Kingdom, Italy, and to a slightly lesser extent France, the two wage indexes track closely. A regression of the aggregate wage index less the fixed-weight index against output, using country dummies, yields a coefficient on output of .041, with a t-statistic of 1.22. Hence the differential between the two indexes is found to be slightly procyclical, not countercyclical as would have to be the case to account for the observed negative relationship between output and the real wage. Thus, it does not appear that aggregation bias in the construction of the wage data is driving our results.

---

[24] However, the use of fixed-weight wage indexes does not correct for changes in worker quality, as when workers receive a demotion in lieu of a wage cut [Solon, Whatley, and Stevens 1993], nor does it correct for differences between official wage rates and actual wages paid.

IV. Conclusion

In concluding the paper, it is worth recapitulating the evidence that we have found in favor of a role for nominal-wage stickiness in the Depression.

First, like Eichengreen and Sachs [1985], we verified that during much of this period there existed a strong inverse relationship (across countries as well as over time) between output and real wages, and also that countries which adhered to the gold standard typically had low output and high real wages, while countries that left gold early experienced high output and low real wages. It does not appear that any purely real theory can give a plausible explanation of this relationship. Among theories emphasizing some type of monetary nonneutrality (i.e., a nonvertical aggregate supply curve), there are basically only two types: theories in which the price level affects output supply because of nominal-wage stickiness, and theories in which the price level affects output supply for some other reason. We find that, once we have controlled for lagged output and banking panics, the effects on output of shocks to nominal wages and shocks to prices are roughly equal and opposite. If price effects operating through nonwage channels were important, we would expect to find the effect on output of a change in prices (given wages) to be greater than the effect of a change in nominal wages (given prices). As we find roughly equal effects, our evidence favors the view that sticky wages were the dominant source of nonneutrality.

Second, we have estimated wage adjustment equations that measure the sensitivity of current nominal wages to lagged nominal wages and current prices (instrumented by aggregate demand shifters). If wages were flexible, then wages would respond proportionally to prices in the face of a (nominal) aggregate demand shock, and would be unrelated to lagged wages. We are able to reject the hypothesis that wages respond fully to current aggregate demand shocks, and are not partly determined by lagged wages, with a high degree of statistical confidence.

Typically, studies of wage stickiness face the difficult problem of ascertaining whether an observed tendency of wages to adjust slowly has allocational consequences. For example, wages might just be "installment payments" in efficient labor contracts [Hall 1980]. It is worth stressing that the gold standard theory of the Depression generates a strong identifying restriction which helps us circumvent this problem, namely, that the dominant source of variation across countries was differences in money stocks and hence in levels of aggregate demand. Under this identifying restriction—which is not available in most other periods or in single-country studies—the correlation across countries of high nominal wages and low output is interpretable as an allocational effect of sticky wages. The Depression-era results should therefore be of interest to macroeconomists generally and not only to historians.

Our findings suggest several topics worthy of further investigation. First, the nature of our data set—panel data with many more countries than time periods—has led us to focus on cross-sectional relationships between output and real wages. More careful attention needs to be paid to the performance of the sticky-wage hypothesis in the time-series dimension—by using the higher-frequency data that are available for some countries, for example. It would also be of interest to look again at industry-level wage and output data, which are available for a number of countries.

Second, and more fundamentally, research is needed on the underlying reasons for slow wage adjustment in an environment which, as was discussed in the Introduction, would not seem conducive to wage stickiness. Coordination failure, as suggested by Cooper [1990] and Eichengreen [1992], represents one interesting direction. Politicization of wage- and price-setting, arising from the desire of various groups to protect their income shares, is another possible source of stickiness (Bernanke [1995] discusses this point in a bit more detail). It would also be interesting to perform a comparative study of interwar wage-setting institutions and regulations among some of the countries in this sample.

Finally, future work might consider the interactions of wage stickiness and other proposed solutions to the aggregate supply puzzle, such as the financial crisis hypothesis of Bernanke and James [1991]. For example, in the spirit of the financial crisis story, it may be that "high" nominal wages had their depressing effect on output primarily by increasing financial (i.e., cash-flow) pressures on firms, rather than through the conventional labor cost channel.[25] (In the former scenario, the average worker's wage is the key variable determining output and employment. In the latter, conventional scenario, the key variable is the wage of the marginal worker.) In principle, the two channels of effect could be distinguished by comparing the effects of changing wages on employment in cash-rich and cash-poor firms.

References

Arellano, Manuel, and Stephen Bond, "Some Tests of Specification for Panel Data: Monte Carlo Evidence and an Application to Employment Equations," *Review of Economic Studies*, LVIII (1991), 277–97.

Beney, M. Ada, *Wages, Hours, and Employment in the United States, 1914–1936* (New York: National Industrial Conference Board, 1936).

Bernanke, Ben, "The Macroeconomics of the Great Depression: A Comparative Approach," *Journal of Money, Credit and Banking*, XXVII (1995), 1–28.

Bernanke, Ben, and Harold James. "The Gold Standard, Deflation, and Financial Crisis in the Great Depression: An International Comparison," in R. G. Hubard,

---

[25] Mark Gertler and Bruce Greenwald separately suggested this point to us.

ed., *Financial Markets and Financial Crises* (Chicago and London: University of Chicago Press, 1991).

Choudhri, Ehsan, and Levis Kochin, "The Exchange Rate and the International Transmission of Business Cycle Disturbances: Some Evidence from the Great Depression," *Journal of Money, Credit and Banking*, XII (1980), 565–74.

Cooper, Russell, "Predetermined Wages and Prices and the Impact of Expansionary Government Policy," *Review of Economic Studies*, LVII (1990), 205–14.

Darby, Michael, "Three and a Half Million Workers Have Been Mislaid: Or an Explanation of Unemployment, 1934–41," *Journal of Political Economy*, LXXXIV (1976), 1–16.

Eichengreen, Barry, *Golden Fetters: The Gold Standard and the Great Depression, 1919–1939* (New York: Oxford University Press, 1992).

Eichengreen, Barry, and T. J. Hatton, "Interwar Unemployment in International Perspective: An Overview," in B. Eichengreen and T. J. Hatton, eds., *Interwar Unemployment in International Perspective* (Dordrecht, Germany, and Boston, MA: Martinus-Nijhoff, 1988).

Eichengreen, Barry, and Jeffrey Sachs, "Exchange Rates and Economic Recovery in the 1930s," *Journal of Economic History*, XLV (1985), 925–46.

Eichengreen, Barry, and Jeffrey Sachs, "Competitive Devaluation and the Great Depression: A Theoretical Reassessment," *Economics Letters*, XXII (1986), 67–71.

Friedman, Milton, and Anna Schwartz, *A Monetary History of the United States, 1867–1960* (Princeton NJ: Princeton University Press, for NBER, 1963).

Galenson, W., and A. Zellner, "International Comparison of Unemployment Rates," in *The Measurement and Behavior of Unemployment*, Universities-NBER Conference Series, No. 8 (Princeton, NJ: Princeton University Press for NBER, 1957).

Haberler, Gottfried, "The World Economy, Money, and the Great Depression," Washington, DC: American Enterprise Institute, 1976.

Hall, Robert E., "Employment Fluctuations and Wage Rigidity," *Brookings Papers on Economic Activity* (1980:1), 91–123.

Hamilton, James, "Monetary Factors in the Great Depression," *Journal of Monetary Economics*, XIX (1987), 145–69.

———, "The Role of the International Gold Standard in Propagating the Great Depression," *Contemporary Policy Issues*, VI (1988), 67–89.

League of Nations, *International Trade Statistics 1937* (Geneva, Switzerland: 1938).

League of Nations, *Statistical Yearbook*, various issues.

Lebergott, Stanley, *Manpower in Economic Growth* (New York: McGraw-Hill, 1964).

Newell, Andrew, and J. S. V. Symons, "The Macroeconomics of the Interwar Years: International Comparisons," in B. Eichengreen and T. J. Hatton, eds., *Interwar Unempolyment in International Perspective* (Dordrecht, Germany, and Boston, MA: Martinus-Nijhoff, 1988).

Solon, Gary, Warren Whatley, and Ann Huff Stevens, "Real Wage Cyclicality between the World Wars: Evidence from the Ford and Byers Companies," University of Michigan, October 1993.

Temin, Peter, *Lessons from the Great Depression* (Cambridge MA: MIT Press, 1989).

Thorp, Rosemary, ed., *Latin America in the 1930s: The Role of the Periphery in World Crisis* (New York: St. Martin's Press, 1984).

Warren, George, and F. A. Person, *Gold and Prices* (New York: 1935).

Index

Abel, Andrew, 57n26
aggregate demand. *See* demand, aggregate
aggregate output. *See* output, aggregate
aggregate supply. *See* supply, aggregate
Altonji, Joseph, 167, 206
American Banker, 55
American Bankers Association, 63–64
Argentina: banking crisis, 91, 93; gold standard, 17n9
Ashenfelter, Orley, 167, 206
Australia: deflation, 80–81, 83; gold standard, 74; wages and aggregation bias, 299; wages and the gold standard, 85
Austria: banking crisis, 65, 90–91, 94–96; deflation, 81, 83; failure of the Kreditanstalt, 11, 62, 89, 95–96; gold standard, 74; wages and the gold standard, 85

Baily, Martin Neil, 175, 206n
Ball, Robert, 226, 255
banking panics: crises described by country, 89–94; and deflation, 71–72, 103–5, 110–11; deflation and industrial production, 97–102; as dummy variable, 288–89, 291; factors explaining which countries suffered, 94–97; and increases in money demand, 132–33; and industrial production, 47–49; macroeconomic effects of, 26–28, 30; and the money multiplier, 126; sources of, 44–45; vulnerability of commercial banks, 80n9
Bank of England, 75, 152
Bank of France, 76–77, 111, 137–42
Bank of the United States, 61–62
bankruptcy: cost of credit intermediation, effect on, 53–55; lack of non-U.S. data, 97; rates of, 41, 46. *See also* debt
banks: bank holiday of 1933, 59, 62, 115; central, 10–12, 74–78, 111; confidence about soundness of, 11–12; credit intermediation and the banking crisis, 51–55; and debt deflation, 25–26; deflation and depression, 88; failures, 26, 41, 43–44, 59, 61 (*see also* banking panics); universal

banking systems, 25n15. *See also* financial system
Barro, Robert, 57, 61n29
Belgium: banking crisis, 91, 93–94, 96; deflation, 81, 83; determinants of the money supply, 12–15; gold standard, 74, 281; wages and output, 31; wages and the gold standard, 85
Beney, M. Ada, 243, 260
Bernanke, Ben: banking panics, 26n, 27n, 71, 290n17; debt deflation, 25n14, 32n26; earnings and workweek reduction, 252; exchange-rate regime and macroeconomic performance, 17, 280n6; financial crises and deflation, 278n2–3; financial crisis hypothesis, 26–27, 89, 288–89, 301; gold standard, 16–17, 147; industry data, 260; larger firms and capital needs, 266; macroeconomic performance and monetary policies, 115; real wages, 32n25, 86; sticky wages, 29–31
Berndt, Ernst, 166
Bernstein, Irving, 171
Bodkin, Ronald, 166n
Bohn, Henning, 235n23
Bordo, Michael, 72
Borenstein, Israel, 261
Bouvier, Jean, 100–101
Brechling, F. P. R., 165–66, 226, 255
Brown, E. Cary, 63n
Brüning, Heinrich, 111, 150
Brunner, Karl, 42n3
Bry, Gerhard, 232
Bureau of Labor Statistics, 169, 243, 260
Burns, Arthur, 163–64, 182
business cycles: cyclical labor market behavior and frequency domain analysis, 176–79, 182–85; cyclical labor market behavior and recessions, 195–97; cyclical labor market behavior and time do main analysis, 185–95; industry response to, 174–76; and labor markets, 163–64, 197–99; literature on labor compensation, 166–68; literature on labor utilization, 164–66;